AF607805

Cosmopolitanism in the Age of Globalization

Cosmopolitanism in the Age of Globalization

Citizens without States

Edited by Lee Trepanier and Khalil M. Habib

THE UNIVERSITY PRESS OF KENTUCKY

The editors would like to thank Stephen Wrinn and his staff for their support and assistance in this project. In addition, Lee wishes to thank MiJung, and Khalil would like to thank Cressida, Jordan, and John Owen, for their love and support.

Copyright © 2011 by The University Press of Kentucky

Scholarly publisher for the Commonwealth,
serving Bellarmine University, Berea College, Centre College of Kentucky, Eastern Kentucky University, The Filson Historical Society, Georgetown College, Kentucky Historical Society, Kentucky State University, Morehead State University, Murray State University, Northern Kentucky University, Transylvania University, University of Kentucky, University of Louisville, and Western Kentucky University.
All rights reserved.

Editorial and Sales Offices: The University Press of Kentucky
663 South Limestone Street, Lexington, Kentucky 40508-4008
www.kentuckypress.com

15 14 13 12 11   5 4 3 2 1

Cataloging-in-Publication Data is available from the Library of Congress.

ISBN 978-0-8131-3418-5 (cloth: alk. paper)
ISBN 978-0-8131-3470-3 (pbk.: alk. paper)

This book is printed on acid-free paper meeting the requirements of the American National Standard for Permanence in Paper for Printed Library Materials.

Manufactured in the United States of America.

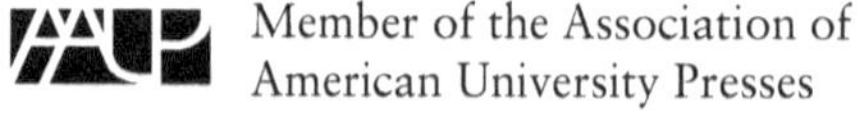

Contents

Lee Trepanier and Khalil M. Habib

Introduction

Since the end of the cold war and the advent of globalization, interest in cosmopolitanism, with its ideas of global justice and citizenship and the like, has been on the rise. Although cosmopolitanism is not new, it is easy to see why it has gripped the post-cold-war imagination. Cosmopolitan is a term often used to describe a citizen of the world: an enlightened individual who believes he or she belongs to a common humanity or world order rather than to a set of particular customs or traditions. Cosmopolitans consequently believe that peace among nation-states is possible only if they transcend their parochial identities and interests in the name of a global state or consciousness. To this extent cosmopolitanism appears democratic in spirit.

This inspiration for global community has its roots in classical antiquity, where politics was defined as being "based upon reason rather than patriotism or group sentiment."[1] The ideas of Zeno's "cosmopolis," Diogenes' "citizen of the world," and Cicero's "common right of humanity" influenced modern thinkers who sought to reconcile the idea of a universal community with a specific one.[2] For example, John Stuart Mill proposed *patriotism éclairé* as an alternative to nationality with the hope that, given the proper education, members of the human race would attain an ideal devotion not only to their countries but also to the world.[3] More recently, Kwame Anthony Appiah made an appeal for a "cosmopolitan patriotism" that recognizes the need of belonging to a particular community as a necessary condition to transform cosmopolitan ideas into a desirable political project.[4] Jürgen Habermas's "constitutional patriotism" and Ulrich Beck's "cosmopolitan nationalism" are other attempts to reconcile cosmopolitan values with national identity, whereas Will Kymlicka seeks a place and protection for minority rights in a cosmopolitan world.[5]

Kant is often cited as the founder of modern cosmopolitanism. At the end of the eighteenth century, Kant wrote of the "cosmopolitan condition" as a rational necessity to link nations together so that "a violation of rights in one part of the world" would be "felt everywhere."[6] This idea of the cosmopolitan condition influenced subsequent thinkers in their conceptions of cosmopolitanism. In the nineteenth century, Hegel proclaimed that "a human being counts as such because he is a human being, not because he is a Jew, Catholic, Protestant, German, Italian, etc." and that this view was of "infinite importance."[7] Later, Marx wrote of the predicted destruction of capitalism as a worldwide system, a destruction that would be the basis upon which a universal human emancipation and future association could be constructed. Durkheim, at the beginning of the twentieth century, looked forward to a "world patriotism" in which societies could "have their pride, not in being the greatest or the wealthiest," but in being the most just, the best organized, and in processing the best moral constitution. In the 1970s Aaron wrote that the technological fusion of the world would be the infrastructure upon which humans could achieve a global unity in which "the dialectic of universality" would be "the mainspring of the march of history."[8] More recently, Ulrich Beck wrote of "the cosmopolitanism of reality" that currently exists because humanity faces global risks that threaten its survival.[9]

For contemporary cosmopolitan theorists, a new methodology and theory are required to address these global risks. Because of globalization, where ideas, people, culture, institutions, and technologies have become global commodities in an integrated worldwide economy, new threats like terrorism, disease, and climate change pose a challenge not to just a few nation-states but to all people. Rather than approaching these problems from the perspective of the nation-state or from outdated forms of cosmopolitanism, contemporary cosmopolitan theorists call for a new methodology with universalism at its center.[10] Treating the human species as a single subject, with its differences recognized but ultimately discarded for conceptual consistency, universalism equates itself with globalization. It is only now, when globalization has reached every corner in the world, that we can treat humanity as a single object of study by adopting a universalistic framework to understand and to evaluate ourselves.

International relations and law are two disciplines where cosmopolitan theorists have made inroads with their new theory and methodology.

The realist paradigm and the idea of state sovereignty are replaced with cosmopolitan concepts. Traditionally both disciplines had seen the state as the ultimate legal and moral authority that reigns supreme both internally and externally. Cosmopolitan theorists look to international institutions and law to replace the sovereignty of the state, especially when it infringes upon its own citizens' rights and freedom.[11] They claim that the sovereignty of the state is a product of history rather than a permanent feature of the human condition: state sovereignty was the result of an international system that arose in the aftermath of the Treaty of Westphalia (1648) and not from some metaphysical reality.[12] Although the Westphalian model is still operative today, that does not mean it cannot be changed, especially as international relations and law are being reconstructed because of the pressures of globalization.

Cosmopolitan theorists have also contributed to political theory, philosophy, and the social sciences in the revival of Kant's ideas of a universal history and perpetual peace.[13] Maintaining key elements of Kant's thought, these theorists reconstruct his argument for our own times in the call for a citizenship based not on the state or nation but on the world.[14] Not surprisingly, nationalism, and the social sciences that are built upon it, is a particular target of cosmopolitan theorists.[15] The social sciences originally conceived of concepts like democracy, citizenship, and political community based on the nation-state. But in this globalized age, where "the ideals of citizenship clash with the sovereign nation-state in which they were first developed," these concepts appear to be outdated and consequently no longer useful to explain and evaluate this new globalized reality.[16] Unable to meet the pressures of globalization, concepts like democracy and citizenship must be transformed in order to have relevancy. Cosmopolitanism is the crucial step in transforming these concepts such that they will continue to possess importance.

This cosmopolitan vision—a universal and peaceful state that permits local attachments and tolerates minority rights—has dominated the discussion of global events and the conceptualization of ideas like democracy and citizenship. Although there have been critics of cosmopolitanism—Carl Schmitt, Jacques Ellul, Neil Postman, Wendell Berry, Mark Mitchell—these thinkers either call for a withdrawal from the world that is characterized by globalization or advocate a discredited ideology to replace it, such as fascism.[17] There are also critics of cosmopolitanism that focus on the United States' dominance of the global system and view the imposition of any Western values as a violation of non-Western cultures.[18] These critics may have valid objections to cosmopolitanism; however, they do not have a realistic and engaged response to the contemporary reality of globalization and cosmopolitanism. Whether or not one favors cosmopolitanism, the reality is that it exists and one must confront rather than withdraw from it.

What this subject still needs is an account of cosmopolitanism that is both critical and engaged. It needs to be comprehensive in terms of both its breadth and its depth. The subject is important and dynamic enough to warrant an examination of a range of perhaps sometimes uncomfortable debates. This volume addresses the topic from its beginnings to its contemporary manifestations, as cosmopolitanism has had a long and variegated history.

This new and unique volume aims to provide a thorough and in-depth understanding of cosmopolitanism by bringing together the work of political scientists, philosophers, historians, and economists. It seeks to examine the concept of cosmopolitanism in historical, theoretical, and comparative contexts. In addition to the range of interpretations on the idea of cosmopolitanism, this volume supplies readers with self-contained essays that focus on specific thinkers or topics related to their interest, while also providing a clearer overview of the history and the debates that characterize the field of cosmopolitanism than is usually offered in the rapidly growing body of literature on the subject. It therefore will be possible to build a rich and diverse framework for a thoughtful analysis of cosmopolitan's current claims and limits, which in turn will enable us to better identify and define it and develop a deeper understanding and appreciation of it.

The rationale behind this volume's publication rests on two fundamental premises. The first is the growing relevance of cosmopolitanism today and for the foreseeable future. The complex economic, social, and political developments in our age of globalization have only intensified the revival of cosmopolitanism as an alternative to nationalism and patriotism. The various ways in which cosmopolitanism as a political and moral principle can be applied to politics and organizations have brought cosmopolitanism to the forefront of international and domestic debates in unprecedented ways. Even a glance at international and national politics today shows cosmopolitanism assuming a growing importance in understanding and managing political and religious conflict. As many nations around the world attempt a liberal reordering of their politics, cosmopolitanism is assuming renewed importance more than it ever has.

The second premise of this volume is that any attempt to confine such an inherently complex concept as cosmopolitanism to a single school of thought or discipline is deeply problematic. A history of the idea of cosmopolitanism reveals that it is the kind of political and philosophical concept that eludes a single, absolute, and authoritative definition. Cosmopolitanism is therefore bound to frustrate any attempt to establish a grand and universal theoretical system or political manifesto, even as it invites theoretical reflection upon the most fundamental questions about human life and politics. Consequently, this volume does not attempt to propose or defend a specific view of cosmopolitanism. While there is overlap and theoretical agreement among some of the contributors, no specific conception of cosmopolitanism or approach to it is established or defended. Since this volume seeks to reflect the range of thought on the subject, the essay authors have explored the meaning of cosmopolitanism in the thought of a specific thinker or topic from within their own specialties. The result is a volume of unparalleled scope and depth that includes the expertise of many specialists from a range of disciplines examining a variety of perspectives on cosmopolitanism, from its ancient beginnings to its contemporary conceptions.

Finally, this volume seeks to reacquaint contemporary debates on cosmopolitanism with the vast, but often neglected, primary sources found in the history of political, religious, and moral philosophy. There are parts and essays examining thinkers and topics ranging from classical Western antiquity and Christian and Islamic medieval political theology and philosophy to early and late modern political theory, history, and economics, as well as American and European approaches to cosmopolitanism. These essays approach familiar and often sterile ground from a fresh perspective and aim to introduce many overlooked thinkers and topics into the current thinking on cosmopolitanism. As we hope to demonstrate, cosmopolitan studies are characterized by disparate and often ignored theoretical sources. By broadening and deepening the discussion, our aim is to complement our growing awareness of the concept of cosmopolitanism.

The book is organized chronologically, and it aims to clarify the debate over cosmopolitanism as it relates to the themes of citizenship and globalization. Whereas much attention has been so far given to the political, economic, cultural, and technological aspects of contemporary globalization, very little has been written on the philosophical consequences of cosmopolitanism as a type of global citizenship. Such a historical perspective and critical approach is simply lacking today.

Part 1 explores cosmopolitanism in the classical Greek and Roman, medieval Christian, and Islamic worlds. Mary P. Nichols challenges Nussbaum's contention that cosmopolitanism's origins are Socratic, while Thomas Pangle examines Cicero's and the Stoics' rational account of cosmopolitanism and its influence in international politics. John von Heyking explores the limitations of Aquinas's notion of natural law as a cosmopolitan concept and shows how Aquinas's objections to Averroes's philosophy are a continuation of the theme of cosmopolitanism. Khalil M. Habib turns to twelfth-century Islamic philosophy and provides a commentary on Ibn Tufayl's reflections on cosmopolitanism in the philosophical romance *Hayy Ibn Yaqzan*, which embraces cosmopolitanism in the individual soul but questions its possibility on the political level.

Part 2 focuses on the modern and contemporary accounts of cosmopolitanism. Mary P. Nichols looks at the dangers of embracing Kant's philosophy of progressive history as well as the difficulties in discovering alternatives to it. Richard Velkley shows how Hegel's philosophy, as influenced by Socrates' daimon, makes him neither a liberal nor a cosmopolitan, as many critics claim. Michael Palmer demonstrates how Heidegger's existential philosophy is radically committed to an anticosmopolitan politics, thereby indicting what is questionable about the cosmopolitan project. Gaelan Murphy focuses on the neglected aspects of aesthetic cultivation and economic arrangements in Kojève's philosophy of cosmopolitanism and empire. And Lee Trepanier explores Derrida's philosophy of deconstructionism as a way to negotiate the debate between cosmopolitan and democratic theorists on the question of citizenship, democracy, and political community.

Part 3 examines cosmopolitanism in the regime of the United States. Luigi Bradizza argues that James Madison rejected cosmopolitanism and instead promoted civic attachments through a common national political memory. Joseph R. Fornieri examines Lincoln's reflective patriotism as an alternative response to both nationalism and cosmopolitanism. L. Joseph Hebert Jr. deals with the United States and Tocqueville, who, as a follower of Cicero, shows the necessity of natural right for the American regime, distinguishing Tocqueville from contemporary cosmopolitan liberals.

Part 4, "Practical Cosmopolitanism," examines the political project of cosmopolitanism as it exists today. From the vantage point of Tocqueville, Paul Seaton discusses Manent's critique of the European Union as a cosmopolitan project and the problems inherent in it. In the final essay, Brian Domitrovic looks at Mundell's economic account of cosmopolitanism as a monetary policy that produces an ironic result, where larger countries believe themselves to be masters of their own economic destinies.

Any attempt to encapsulate an idea as broad and multifaceted as cosmopolitanism within the constraints placed even on a comprehensive volume of this nature confronts certain limitations. We simply cannot include every conceivable topic and thinker who has ever thought about or written on cosmopolitanism. If this volume encourages scholars and students to consult the specific thinkers and the works examined here and to reflect upon their findings, it will have fulfilled its purpose. By offering a close examination of many conceptions of cosmopolitanism from the past to the present, this volume strives to mirror, as much as possible, the complexity of the subject to which it is devoted.

Notes

We would like to thank Lew Lehrman and Kelly Hanlon for their support in this project.

1. Martha Nussbaum, "Kant and Cosmopolitanism," in *Perpetual Peace: Essays on Kant's Cosmopolitan Ideal,* ed. James Bohrman and Matthias Lutz-Bachmann (Cambridge, MA: MIT Press, 1997), 25–58; also refer to Martha Nussbaum, "Kant and Stoic Cosmopolitanism," *Journal of Political Philosophy* 1 (1991): 1–25.

2. David Hollinger, "Not Universalists, Not Pluralists: The New Cosmopolitans Find Their Own Way," *Constellations* 8, no. 2 (2001): 236–48. For more about cosmopolitanism in classical antiquity, refer to Daniel S. Richter, *Cosmopolis: Imaging Community in Late Classical Athens and the Early Roman Empire* (Oxford: Oxford Univ. Press, 2011). The specific references can be located in Cicero, *On Duties (De Officiis)* 3.6.27–32; and Diogenes Laertius, *Lives of Eminent Philosophers* 6.63, 6.1.

3. John Stuart Mill, *A System of Logic, Ratiocinative and Inductive* (Charleston, SC: BiblioBazaar, 2009).

4. Kwame Anthony Appiah, "Cosmopolitan Patriots," in *For Love of Country: Debating the Limits of Cosmopolitanism,* ed. Joshua Cohen (Boston: Beacon, 1996), 21–29.

5. Jürgen Habermas, *The Postnational Constellations: Political Essays,* ed. Max Pensky (Cambridge: Polity, 2001), 74–76; Ulrich Beck, *Cosmopolitan Vision* (Cambridge: Polity, 2006), 49; Will Kymlicka, *Multicultural Citizenship: A Liberal Theory of Minority Rights* (Oxford: Clarendon Press, 1995).

6. Immanuel Kant, *Kant: Political Writings,* ed. Hans Reiss (Cambridge: Cambridge Univ. Press, 1991), 107–8.

7. Georg Hegel, *Philosophy of Right,* ed. Allen Wood, trans. H.B. Nisbet (Cambridge: Cambridge Univ. Press, 1991), 209.

8. Emile Durkheim, *Professional Ethics and Civic Morals,* trans. Cornelia Brookfield (New York: Routledge, 1992), 74–75; Raymond Aaron, *Progress and Disillusion* (New York: Penguin, 1972), 4–5.

9. Ulrich Beck, "The Cosmopolitan Manifesto," *New Statesman* 20 (1998): 38–50, quoted phrase on 38; also refer to Ulrich Beck, "Towards a New Critical Theory with a Cosmopolitan Intent," *Constellations* 10, no. 4 (2003): 435–68; Beck, *Cosmopolitan Vision.*

10. For examples, refer to Daniele Archibugi, David Held, and Martin Köhler., eds., *Re-imaging in Political Community: Studies in Cosmopolitan Democracies* (Cambridge: Polity, 1998); David Held and Anthony McGrew, eds., *Governing Globalization* (Oxford: Polity, 2002); Carol Breckenridge and Sheldon Pollock, eds., *Cosmopolitanism* (Durham, NC: Duke Univ. Press, 2002); Steven Vertovec and Robin Cohen, *Conceiving Cosmopolitanism: Theory, Context, and Practice* (Oxford: Oxford Univ. Press, 2003); Daniele Archibugi, *Cosmopolitics* (London: Verso, 2004).

11. Lawrence Douglas, *The Memory of Judgment: Making Law and History in the Trials of the Holocaust* (New Haven, CT: Yale Univ. Press, 2001); Pavlos Eletheriadis, "Cosmopolitan Law," *European Law Journal* 9 (2003): 241–63; David Hirsch, "Cosmopolitan Law: Agency and Narrative," in *Law and Sociology,* ed. Michael Freeman (Oxford: Oxford Univ. Press, 2006); Geoffrey Robertson, *Crimes against Humanity: The Struggle for Global Justice* (New York: Penguin, 2006); Philippe Sands, *Lawless World: Making and Breaking Global Rules* (New York: Penguin, 2006).

12. Jens Bartelson, *The Critique of the State* (Cambridge: Cambridge Univ. Press, 2001); Chris Brown, "Kantian Cosmopolitan Law and the Idea of a Cosmopolitan Constitution," *History of Political Thought* 27, no. 4 (2006): 661–84; Andrew Linklater, *The Transformation of the Political Community: Ethical Foundations of the Post-Westphalian Era* (Oxford: Polity, 1998).

13. Martha Nussbaum, *For Love of Country* (Boston: Beacon Press, 1996); Pratap Bhanu Mehta, "Cosmopolitanism and the Circle of Reason," *Political Theory* 28, no. 5 (2000): 619–39; William E. Connolly, "Speed, Concentric Cultures, and Cosmopolitanism," *Political Theory* 28, no. 5 (2000): 596–618; Sharon Anderson-Gold, *Cosmopolitanism and Human Rights* (Cardiff: Univ. of Wales Press, 2001); Jacques Derrida, *On Cosmopolitanism and Forgiveness* (New York: Taylor and Francis, 2001); Catherine Lu, *The Political Theory of Global Citizenship* (New York: Routledge, 2001); Carol A. Breckenridge, Homi K. Bhabha, and Sheldon Pollock, eds., *Cosmopolitanism* (Durham, NC: Duke Univ. Press, 2002); Fred Dallmayr, "Cosmopolitanism: Moral and Political," *Political Theory* 31, no. 3 (2003): 421–42; Simon Learmount, Robin Cohen, and Steven Vertovec, eds., *Conceiving Cosmopolitanism: Theory, Context, and Practice* (Oxford: Oxford Univ. Press, 2003); Kok-Chor Tan, Russell Hardin, and Ian Shapiro, eds., *Justice without Borders: Cosmopolitanism, Nationalism, and Patriotism* (Cambridge: Cambridge Univ. Press, 2004); Arash Abizadeh,

"Does Collective Identity Presuppose an Other? On the Alleged Incoherence of Global Solidarity," *American Political Science Review* 99, no. 1 (2005): 46–60; Harry Brighouse, ed. *The Political Philosophy of Cosmopolitanism* (Cambridge: Cambridge Univ. Press, 2005); Jennifer Mitzen, "Reading Habermas in Anarchy: Multilateral Diplomacy and the Global Public Sphere," *American Political Science Review* 99, no. 3 (2005): 401–17; Seyla Benhabib and Robert Post, eds., *Another Cosmopolitanism: Hospitality, Sovereignty, and Democratic Iterations* (Oxford: Oxford Univ. Press, 2006); Jürgen Habermas, *The Divided West* (Hoboken, NJ: Wiley, 2006); Kwame Anthony Appiah, *Cosmopolitanism: Ethics in a World of Strangers* (New York: Norton, 2007); Costas Douzinas, *Human Rights and Empire: The Political Philosophy of Cosmopolitanism* (New York: Routledge, 2007); Robert Fine, *Cosmopolitanism* (Oxford: Taylor and Francis, 2007); Mica Nava, *Visceral Cosmopolitanism: Gender, Culture, and the Normalisation of Difference* (Gordonsville, VA: Berg, 2007); James D. Ingram, "What Is a 'Right to Have Rights'? Three Images of the Politics of Human Rights," *American Political Science Review* 102, no. 4 (2008): 401–16; David Harvey, *Cosmopolitanism and the Geographies of Freedom* (New York: Columbia Univ. Press, 2009); Robert J. Holton, *Cosmopolitanisms: New Thinking and New Directions* (Gordonsville, VA: Palgrave, 2009); Stan van Hooft, *Cosmopolitanism: A Philosophy for Global Ethics* (Montreal: McGill-Queens Univ. Press, 2009); Pnina Werbner, ed. *Anthropology and the New Cosmopolitanism: Rooted, Feminist, and Vernacular Perspectives* (Gordonsville, VA: Berg, 2009).

14. Jürgen Habermas, *Inclusion of the Other: Studies in Political Theory* (Cambridge: Polity, 1998); Habermas, *Postnational Constellations;* Immanuel Kant, *Political Essays,* ed. Hans Reiss (Cambridge: Cambridge Univ. Press, 1991); Robert Fine, *Political Investigations: Hegel, Marx, Arendt* (London: Routledge, 2001); Nussbaum, *For Love of Country;* Otfried Hoffe, *Kant's Cosmopolitan Theory of Law and Peace* (Cambridge: Cambridge Univ. Press, 2006).

15. Perhaps the most famous recent critique of nationalism from a cosmopolitan perspective can be found in the works of Ulrich Beck: Beck, "Cosmopolitan Manifesto"; Ulrich Beck, *Democracy without Enemies* (Cambridge: Polity, 1998); Ulrich Beck, "The Cosmopolitan Perspective: Sociology of the Second Age of Modernity," *British Journal of Sociology* 51, no. 1 (2000): 79–105; Ulrich Beck, *The Brave New World of Work* (Cambridge: Polity, 2000); Ulrich Beck, *What Is Globalization?* (Cambridge: Polity, 2000); Ulrich Beck, "The Cosmopolitan Society and Its Enemies," *Theory, Culture, and Society* 19, no. 1–2 (2002): 17–45; Beck, "Towards a New Critical Theory; Beck, *Cosmopolitan Vision.* However, this cosmopolitan critique of nationalism has its roots in Anthony Giddens, *The Class Structure of Advanced Societies* (London: Hutchinson, 1973); and Herminio Martins, "Time and Theory in Sociology," in *Approaches to Sociology,* ed. John Rex (London: Routledge and Kegan Paul, 1974), 194–246.

16. Beck, *Cosmopolitan Vision,* 49; Manuel Castells, *The Rise of the Network Society* (Oxford: Blackwell, 2000); Gerard Delanty, *Citizenship in a Global*

Age (Buckingham, UK: Open Univ. Press, 2000). This has prompted a debate between democratic and cosmopolitan theorists about what should be the basis of democracy. Refer to Nussbaum, *For Love of Country;* David Held, "The Transformation of the Political Community: Rethinking Democracy in the Context of Globalization," in *Democracy's Edges,* ed. I. Shapiro and C. Hacker-Cordón (Cambridge: Cambridge Univ. Press, 1998); A. McGrew, ed. *The Transformation of Democracy? Democratic Politics in the New World Order* (Cambridge: Polity, 1997); B. Yack, "Popular Sovereignty and Nationalism," *Political Theory* 29, no. 4 (2001): 517–36; Lu, *Political Theory of Global Citizenship;* Tan, Hardin, and Shapiro, *Justice without Borders;* Benhabib and Post, *Another Cosmopolitanism;* Appiah, *Cosmopolitanism;* Hooft, *Cosmopolitanism.*

17. Wendell Berry, *The Art of the Commonplace: The Agrarian Essays of Wendell Berry* (Berkeley, CA: Counterpoint, 2003); Jacques Ellul, *The Technology Society* (New York: Vintage, 1967); Neil Postman, *Technopoly: The Surrender of Culture to Technology* (New York: Knopf, 1997); Carl Schmitt, *Concept of the Political* (Chicago: Univ. of Chicago Press, 2007); *Political Theology* (Chicago: Univ. of Chicago Press, 2006). Also refer to the Web site www.frontporchrepublic as an example of the localist movement that sees cosmopolitanism as a threat to human flourishing.

18. Refer to Noam Chomsky, *The New Military Humanism: Lessons from Kosovo* (London: Pluto, 1999); Costas Douzinas, *The End of Human Rights: Critical Legal Thought at the End of the Century* (Oxford: Hart, 2000). The only article that provides a balanced account of cosmopolitanism is Joshua P. Hochschild, "Globalization: Ancient and Modern," *Intercollegiate Review* (2006): 40–48. A negative account of cosmopolitanism can be found in Lee Harris, "The Cosmopolitan Illusion" *Policy Review* (2003): 1–12.

Part 1

Classical Cosmopolitanism

Mary P. Nichols

Socratic Self-Examination

Cosmopolitanism, Imperialism, or Citizenship?

In contrast to traditional readings of classical political thought that focus on virtuous political communities and inegalitarian social orders, recent scholars have found in ancient thought philosophic resources for more open societies, liberal polities, democratic self-government, and even global perspectives. In a recent review essay, Patrick Deneen identifies a new democratic school of Platonic interpretation that holds that Plato "favored the open more dialogic possibilities of democracy" over any "closed systemization of either philosophy or politics."[1] Socrates, the ceaseless questioner or skeptic, takes a central place in this view. J. Peter Euben, for example, argues that Socrates appropriates for his "philosophical-political vocation" the democratic practices of Athens—such as "the tradition of democratic self-critique found in drama" and the Athenian practice of holding magistrates publicly accountable for their deeds while in office.[2] Similarly, Dana Villa emphasizes Socrates' service to his city as a gadfly, his "philosophical, dissident citizenship" that can serve as a model for liberal democracies.[3] Whereas Villa emphasizes the alienating and critical stance of the "Socratic citizen" as he questions his own traditions and beliefs,[4] Martha Nussbaum points out that it is precisely our own traditions that separate us from our fellow humanity. By "awakening each and every person to self-scrutiny," her democratic or egalitarian Socrates reveals what we have in common with others.[5] In place of the "absolute negativity" that for Villa accompanies Socratic questioning, she finds in Socratic self-examination the basis of "world citizenship."[6] For Nussbaum "cultivating humanity" requires "an ability to see [our]selves not simply as citizens of some local region or group, but also, and above all, as human beings bound to all other human beings by ties of recognition and concern."[7] When Nussbaum writes, "You can either package your humanity in your politics or your politics in your humanity," she suggests that one must make one or the other prior, and her advocacy of world citizenship makes clear what her priority is.[8]

Two years after Nussbaum published *Cultivating Humanity,* Thomas L. Pangle and Peter J. Ahrensdorf contributed a monumental volume on the history of international relations theory, from the classical idealism of the Greek philosophers to various twentieth-century schools of thought. In their discussion of classical idealism, they also recognize the "cosmopolitan" character of Socratic philosophizing, noting that "the philosophers' hearts leap across familial, national, cultural, and temporal boundaries," and quote Cicero's statement that "Socrates judged himself to be a native and citizen of the world."[9] Pangle and Ahrensdorf, to be sure, cannot be included in the democratic school of Platonic interpretation, since they insist that from the original Socratic perspective, "a truly cosmopolitan spirit" was "likely to flourish only among a few noble souls dispersed through the various cities and nations."[10] They nevertheless conclude that Socratic philosophers could "reasonably hope that those few may have some appreciable influence upon their respective cities, mitigating patriotic xenophobia, imperialism, cruelty, and punitive moral fanaticism." In other words, even though the emphasis is more on hope than on likelihood, those few might "cultivate humanity,"[11] making their political communities more cosmopolitan and hence like themselves.

My own reading accepts the critical character and openness of Socratic philosophy, but also its democratic thrust. If one understands the extent to which one does not know the truth about the whole, or one's knowledge of ignorance, as Socrates describes his human wisdom (*Apology* 23b), one must remain open to others and what they may contribute to one's pursuit of knowledge. Socrates is nevertheless better understood, I argue, contra Nussbaum as well as Pangle and Ahrensdorf, as a citizen-philosopher than as a world citizen.[12] Nor is Socrates' citizenship, in my view, merely that of a dissenting questioner. Plato's Socrates, after all, maintained his loyalty to Athens throughout his life. Unlike the sophists, who wandered from city to city in the Greek world, Socrates rarely left the confines of Athens, unless serving in the Athenian army (*Crito* 52b; see also *Phaedrus* 230c–d). Several times in the *Crito* Socrates has the Laws refer to Athens as his "fatherland," and he refers to the piety and respect he owes the Laws as he would a father (*Crito* 51a–c, 54c).

It is possible, of course, that Socrates' loyalty to Athens stemmed merely from his physical needs and his recognition of his dependence on his city for preservation and hence for his philosophizing. In this case, should historical development allow a more universal cosmopolitan order to provide for a philosopher's physical needs, nothing in Socratic philosophizing would prevent the philosopher's transferring his loyalties from his particular community to the world. So, too, if a greater tolerance of questioning in Athens compared to other Greek cities were the source of Socrates' allegiance—after all, Socrates was not prosecuted in Athens until he was seventy—he would owe even greater allegiance to a globalized world in which philosophy was tolerated along with every other way of life, and where he would not be prosecuted at all. And if that globalized world were characterized not simply by a toleration of difference, but by a recognition of humans' common humanity, there would be a greater harmony between the universal truth sought by the philosopher and the world in which he sought it, or even between the truth he attained and the world in which he attained it.

Hegel's discussion of Socrates provides support for such a position. Because Socrates' "Ideas," of the good, the noble, and the just, were abstract, indeterminate universals, as Hegel explains, they could not provide guidance to concrete life. Socratic philosophizing thus left a void, one filled by his "daimon," a sort of personal oracle, which guided him in the contingent affairs of his life. Only when the universal Idea became concrete in actual human life, according to Hegel, specifically, in the modern state, would human beings no longer need daimonic guidance of one sort or another concerning their particular lives.[13] According to Hegel, citizens of the modern state are Socratics without need of personal oracles like a daimonic voice. They are Socrates in fully developed form; as citizens of the modern state, they are world citizens in Nussbaum's sense.

Is there anything in Socratic philosophizing, then, that prevents a movement toward "world citizenship"? I address this question by examining Socrates' understanding of philosophy, as he presents it in the speech he gives about Love in Plato's *Symposium*. The *Symposium* presents a direct confrontation between Socrates and a host of Athenians whose encomia to Love offer more cosmopolitan perspectives than does Socrates' own. Socrates' view of Love and philosophy, in contrast to theirs, defends our attachment to particular communities. In-between ignorance and wisdom, and being both needy and resourceful, human beings (including philosophers) find access to the Idea of beauty only by loving particular human beings, institutions, laws, and studies, and then by giving birth and nurturing their own offspring as a result of love. The incomplete character of our search, our imperfect wisdom, thus connects us to generation, nurturing, and political life. Socratic philosophizing does not lead to world citizenship, then, not because Socrates recognizes the need for a political community merely for the sake of self-preservation,[14] but because for him humanity and politics, universal and particular, are inseparably linked. Tragedy lies not simply in the necessary connection between our potential for transcendence and our limitations; it occurs when our attempt to overcome the latter impedes the former. Socrates therefore packages neither his humanity in his politics, as Nussbaum criticizes, nor his politics in his humanity, as Nussbaum recommends. The Socratic "package" gives neither the one nor the other priority. When Socrates claims to the Athenian jury that if they made his ceasing to philosophize the condition of his acquittal, he would not be able to accept (*Apology* 29c–d), he was not prioritizing philosophy over his city but refusing to prioritize his city over philosophy. And, contra Hegel, something like Socrates' "daimonic" guidance will always be necessary for human beings.

A more "cosmopolitan" understanding of philosophy, I also argue, is one that Plato attributes to Alcibiades, an Athenian politician once associated with Socrates, one who became famous as a betrayer of his city. Appearing late in the evening in Plato's *Symposium,* and insisting that he will speak not about Love, as the other guests at the party have done, but about Socrates, Alcibiades describes Socrates as unconnected to time and place, a wise man whose wisdom frees him from connections to his city—and to any particular human beings, such as Alcibiades himself. While Alcibiades resents Socrates' distance from himself, I argue, he admires what he thinks is Socrates' freedom, self-sufficiency, and independence. If the questioning practiced by Socrates frees Alcibiades from the conventions and opinions of his city, his is a freedom that finds its fulfillment in a betrayal of his city and imperialism, rather than one conducive to world citizenship. Universal perspectives, paradoxically, are more political than philosophic. Plato therefore has two related objections, I argue, to world citizenship. In the first place, it impedes our fulfillment as human beings, as both philosophers and citizens, as illustrated by the lessons on Love, philosophy, and generation that Socrates recounts in the *Symposium.* In the second place, in its misunderstanding of the philosopher's allegiance to the truth as a transcendence of one's own, it nurtures the tyrannical ambitions of a man like Alcibiades.

Finally, I conclude with reflections on the poetic function of Plato's Socratic dialogues. Whereas Nussbaum understands the task of the narrative imagination as revealing our common humanity and thereby fostering world citizenship,[15] Plato understands his narratives of Socrates as preserving the different and the alien as well as the familiar. Seeing something strange in what is familiar and something familiar in what is strange keeps both philosophy and politics alive. For Plato, cultivating humanity requires cultivating our lives in our particular communities, including political ones.

The Intellectual Elite of Plato's *Symposium* and Their New World Orders

The occasion of Plato's *Symposium* is a party at the home of the young tragedian Agathon, who is celebrating the success of one of his tragic plays.[16] The pastime of the evening stems from an observation that one of the company, Phaedrus, made to his lover Eryximachus, also present, that although Love is a great god, "no poet has yet composed an encomium" for him as poets have for other gods (177a–b). Agathon and his guests, which include his own lover Pausanias, as well as the comic poet Aristophanes and Socrates himself, agree to correct the omission of the poets by offering in turn encomia to Love (177e). The poets, however, did sing of love, if not in simple praise. The chorus in Euripides' *Hippolytus,* for example, speaks of Love as a "tyrant over men," who leads them to disaster (*Hippolytus* 538–41). So, too, in Sophocles' *Antigone,* the chorus addresses Love, noting that "who has you within is mad" and "you twist the minds of the just" and destroy them (*Antigone* 790–93). The warnings of the chorus are borne out by the actions of those plays, both tragedies. The very enterprise of the evening aims not simply at supplying an omission on the part of such traditional poets by praising a neglected god, but at correcting their view of the prospects for human life. Phaedrus, from whom the proposal to praise Love originates and who delivers the first speech, sets the tone: Love causes the greatest goods for human beings (178c). The acme of his praise, however, goes not to one consumed by love for a beloved, but to one who can without such inspiration sacrifice himself because of his own self-sufficient virtue. It is a virtue to which even the gods must bow (180a). Phaedrus in his own way seeks transcendence.[17]

Agathon's lover Pausanias speaks next and might seem to take a more political perspective, since he argues for the superiority of Athens to other cities in its customs and laws about Love. But to do so, he engages in a subtle reinterpretation of those customs and laws, in order to justify his own pederasty. He is in fact free from what he regards as the prejudices of fathers against this custom, and his effort to present pederasty as a form of noble education would free others from censure as well. His speech is followed by that of the even more radical Eryximachus, a doctor by profession, who appeals to his scientific knowledge of the natural world and the power of arts such as medicine to exert control by instilling love and removing strife (186b–e). His knowledge situates him in the cosmos as a whole, and it is one without political boundaries. There is no reference to laws or to the city in his speech. His knowledge and skill enable him to serve all humanity. In Plato's *Protagoras,* set around fifteen years prior to the dramatic date of the party in the *Symposium,* we meet Eryximachus and his beloved Phaedrus listening to the discourses of the sophists, as well as Pausanias and his beloved Agathon. Plato thus suggests the influence of the sophists on these Athenians (see *Protagoras* 315c–e). They and those whom they influenced were cosmopolitans all, in one way or another. The sophists were itinerant teachers who claimed to be able to teach anyone, anywhere, the truth and skills they had to offer (see also *Euthydemus* 271c).

The only speaker at the Symposium absent from the gathering of sophists in the *Protagoras* is the comic poet Aristophanes, and his mockery of the sophistic hubris of the previous speakers recalls his mockery in the *Clouds* of what he saw as Socrates' intellectual pretensions, which he associates with the sophists (*Clouds* 331, 1111, 1309). Our earliest ancestors, the comic poet reports, assaulted the gods in the heavens, who forestalled their plot and punished them by cutting them in half—weakening them by giving them the human shape we know today. Love moves us to seek our lost half and to recover an original unity that no longer exists. We are saved only when the gods in their pity give us some relief through sex and allow us to get on with the ordinary deeds of life, including politics (190b–c; and 192a). Agreeing with cosmopolitans of today that politics is a distraction from the unity that would really fulfill us, Aristophanes warns of the impossibility of unity. But neither of the next speakers, Agathon and Socrates, finds his description of our needy and unhappy condition a satisfactory account of human life.

Agathon is only momentarily daunted when his turn to praise Love follows Aristophanes' turn. After all, his party celebrates the success of his tragedy on the Athenian stage, and he is the rising star of the day. Not surprisingly, his is the only speech that prompts the uproarious applause of all present when they hear the youth speak (198a). Agathon's work seems to have a universal appeal, meeting the enthusiastic approval both of the elite gathering at his home and also of the thirty thousand Greeks (not just Athenians) who have recently acclaimed his tragedy (175e, 194b). He delights the whole civilized world. Indeed, the ascendance of Love, as he proceeds to describe it, defies political boundaries and signals a new era for human beings, bringing "friendship and peace" in the place of force and necessity (195c). Plato thus appears to agree with Friedrich Nietzsche, who observed many centuries later that Agathon followed in the footsteps of a reformed tragedy, which reconstructed the art form on the basis of an optimistic worldview.[18] To be sure, the narrative imagination of Plato's Agathon encourages a transcendence of traditional virtues and traditional values, which have led to difference and enmity. What Eryximachus seeks to accomplish through knowledge and the art of medicine, Agathon seeks to accomplish through poetry (see 196d–e).

Agathon's account of Love's virtues demonstrates his reconstruction of poetry along the lines Nietzsche identifies. For example, Agathon says that Love is the most courageous of all, for he conquers even the god of war, Ares, who falls in love with Aphrodite (196c–d). Agathon thus alludes with approval to Homer's story of their adulterous affair (*Od* 8.265–368). And since all consent to the sway of Love, Agathon continues, he is perfectly just, for where there is consent there is justice (196b–c). And Love is moderate because moderation is the conquest of desire, and Love conquers all other desires. Ares and Aphrodite, like the other Olympian gods, were involved in supporting one side or the other in the Trojan War. But all such matters are forgotten at the door of Aphrodite's bedchamber. We are all alike. And we are like the gods if we are ruled by Love. Finally, Love's wisdom is clear, according to Agathon, inasmuch as he inspires poets with wisdom, for what one does not have one cannot give to another (197a). The god Love and the inspired poet, such as Agathon himself, are also one. He does not need any further unity such as that to which Aristophanes' maimed human beings aspire. He is whole. Not surprisingly, Agathon does not allude to his lover Pausanias at any point in the dialogue.

Nietzsche not only claimed that Agathon's perspective represented the decline of tragedy, and hence of Greece; he also attributed that decline to the influence of Socratic dialectic on the poets.[19] Plato, however, shows Socrates objecting to Agathon's optimistic view that love is beautiful and good, by practicing that very dialectic on Agathon himself. "Is Love of something or of nothing?" Socrates asks Agathon (199b–d). For Agathon, Love is, in a way, of nothing, as it is not directed to an object outside itself. The inspired poet is one with the god, and creates out of his own self-sufficiency. Like Love who possesses him, he is beautiful and good. When Socrates asks whether Love is of something, he calls attention to the hubris in Agathon's speech and tries to correct it by reminding him of love's dependence. Socrates illustrates how something might be understood only in relation to something other than itself by appealing to family relations: a father is a father of someone, and a mother is a mother of someone, of a son or a daughter. Socrates' examples call attention to mutual dependence, in particular in the relationship between parents and their offspring (199d–e). What one generates is both one's own and also other. Agathon's speech about poetic creation leaves no room for what is other or separate from himself. His poetry comes simply from himself—and of course the god within him.

Following the pattern of Socrates' examples, Agathon concedes that Love is "of something," of that which it desires or loves, of what it does not have and of which it is in need. If Love is love of beauty, Love lacks and is in need of beautiful things, as well as good ones, inasmuch as the good are beautiful. Love, then, is neither beautiful nor good (200a–201b). We do not know whether Socrates' questioning will be more effective in distancing Agathon from his optimistic vision of a world order of peace and love than Aristophanes' narrative of needy and unfulfilled beings was. In any case, Socrates does not rely only on questioning but proceeds to give a narrative of his own, about his own encounter as a young man with a priestess, Diotima, who teaches him about love. While preserving the conclusion of his dialectic engagement with Agathon—that love is directed to what it needs or lacks—his lessons teach that lovers do have access to the beautiful and the good through love. At the same time that Socrates corrects Agathon's optimistic view of the world, Socrates does not leave lovers in such a sad state as Aristophanes recounts. His correction of Agathon is thus also a correction of Aristophanes. His is an understanding of love that differs from any thus far expressed in the *Symposium*.

Socrates' Defense of Politics

When he was a young man, Socrates explains, he held Agathon's view of love's beauty and goodness, and he was similarly questioned by a priestess from Mantinea named Diotima. Her argument was this: That Love is not itself beautiful and good does not mean that it is ugly and bad. Rather, it is between god and mortal, and a great daimon, for the daimonic, which includes all divination and prophecy, serves as a link between the mortals and gods, carrying messages and prayers in both directions, because "god does not mix with human" (201–203a). Contra Agathon, lovers strive for something higher, outside themselves. While Socrates' account does not sever our connection to the divine—since Love links human and divine—it is much less immediate than Agathon's conception of the inspired poet suggests.

It is also more problematic, at least in one sense. If god and human do not mix, what is Love itself? Can it be a mixed being, and if it is not, how can it link divine and human? The same difficulty emerges when Socrates asks Diotima, "Who are Love's father and mother?"[20] Since god and mortal do not mix—indeed, that is why there must be some third to join them (203a)—Love's parents must both be one or the other to mate. But if they are one or the other, how could they generate an in-between?[21] Diotima responds to Socrates' question with a myth about Love's birth. As we might expect, if god and mortal do not mate, Love's mother, Poverty, and his father, Resource, are more alike than their names at first suggest. Poverty, in the myth, is very resourceful. And Resource himself is in need of her to bring forth his offspring; a resource is a resource not in itself, but only for the sake of some purpose. The common translation of the Greek word for "resource" as "means," or "way" indicates that it must be understood in terms of a relation, just as, to use Socrates' earlier illustration, a mother or a father is a parent of someone. But if Poverty and Resource are mixed beings, who are *their* parents? Diotima's myth simply reflects the question: how can one account for something between mortal and divine?

When Socrates inquires about Love's parents, he questions the intelligibility of an intermediate, which could exist as a link between human and divine only if it were not needed as a link, only if human and divine could mix. Socrates' question thus demonstrates that he knows that he does not understand, and in fact that he understands the problem. It is therefore Socrates himself who provides the model for an intermediate: in seeking wisdom, as Diotima explains, the philosopher is not yet wise, nor is he so ignorant that he doesn't know that he doesn't know (204a–b; see also *Apology* 22dff.).[22]

Just as ignorance alone cannot explain philosophizing, lack alone cannot explain love of the beautiful. If Love is neither beautiful nor ugly, and desires what it lacks, it would desire the ugly as much as the beautiful. The offspring of Poverty and Resource appears to favor Resource. Moreover, human complexity is manifest not only in our seeking knowledge, in Diotima's account, but in our generating or giving birth. As resourceful and needy beings, lovers give birth, the former attribute making generation possible, the latter making it necessary. Simple emptiness could not give birth, for it would have nothing to give. Nor would anything sufficient unto itself require generation for its fulfillment. It is when the (needy) lover meets someone with a beautiful soul, Diotima says, that he is "resourceful" (*euporei*) in speaking to him about virtue, and about what a good man should be and pursue (209b–c). Need finds resources within itself, and resources generate speeches about what is good. Therefore, Diotima's further revelations about Love as creative, generative, poetic, and even about lovers as pregnant build on her earlier statements about Love as in-between.

Diotima reaches the generative character of Love in response to another of Socrates' questions, "Of what use is Love to humans?" Socrates is unable to say what the lover of the beautiful derives from beautiful things. Only when Diotima substitutes good things for beautiful ones, does Socrates understand that Love is useful, because when we love good things and possess them, we are happy (204c–205a). But since everyone desires to be happy, and hence to possess good things, everyone is a lover. Socrates wonders at this result. Diotima attempts to explain through an analogy between lover and poet, whose literal meaning in Greek is "maker." We give one sort of maker, the poet, the name of poet, whereas the term should apply to artisans of all kinds, just as we apply the term lover to only one sort of lover (205b–c). But even if our way of speaking obscures the similarities between things, it is also based on a perception of their differences. We single out poets from other craftsmen and lovers from other human beings for good reason.[23] The beautiful cannot be reduced to the good.

To love the good—which is to love that the good be ours and that we thereby be happy—is to love ourselves. But this does not exhaust the experience of Love, as indicated by Socrates' question about Love's use. If Love merely led us to our good, its use would be unquestionable. Earlier in the evening, Phaedrus had given examples of lovers who gave their lives for those whom they loved (179b–c). Whereas to love the good is to love ourselves, to love the beautiful brings us outside of ourselves. Without a love of the beautiful, love of the good merges into love of one's own. Diotima therefore does not explain Love simply in terms of the good, as opposed to the beautiful. Although she demonstrates the use of Love by reference to the good, she reintroduces the beautiful, arguing that the lover desires to give birth in the presence of the beautiful. Lovers are pregnant, she claims,[24] and only the beautiful can act as midwife, providing relief from the pains of labor. By generation, by leaving behind something new in the place of the old, mortal beings partake of immortality. Even the beautiful itself may seem useful in Diotima's account, but the generation that it makes possible leads us beyond ourselves. Parents are willing to do anything to preserve and nurture their young, "to fight to the finish . . . for the sake of those they have generated, and to die on their behalf; and they are willingly racked by starvation and stop at nothing to nourish their offspring" (207a–b). Diotima does not stop Socrates from wondering, but gives him more cause to wonder (205a, 206b, 207d, and 208b–c). Our love cannot be reduced to our love of ourselves and of our own good.

It is fitting that Socrates should invent a woman to answer some of the previous speakers, whose downplaying of generation, offspring, and children is consistent with their homosexuality (178b, 179c, 180d, 186e). Of the previous speakers, Aristophanes alone describes the generation of offspring by men and women, and in his story generation arises not from a need or a desire of the parents, but merely as a by-product of their longing for a lost unity (191c).[25] And although Agathon focuses on the poet's productions (196e–197a), they come solely from the inspired poet. No other human being inspires or contributes to his creations in any way. His love of what he generates is only self-love. Unlike the love of parents for their offspring that Diotima describes, it could evoke no wonder by summoning sacrifice. Agathon does not even raise the question of Love's parents, unlike Socrates and some of the other symposiasts (cf. 195b with 178b, 180d, and, of course, 203a). Socrates invents someone other to address these men—a prophetess, whose inspiration distinguishes her from other human beings; a foreigner, who is a stranger in Athens; and a woman who points dramatically to what is missing from the previous speeches by presenting all human beings, men as well as women, as pregnant.

Diotima moves from the generation of children to the ways in which the desire for immortality is satisfied through fame. The "immortal memory" that Alcestis and Achilles sought for themselves, Diotima explains, is one "that we *now* hold" (208d, emphasis mine). They are dependent on future generations, even on poets. Diotima's examples include a legendary king of Athens, who dies "on behalf of the kingdom of his children" (208d). Diotima's emphasis on generation and offspring also allows for noble deeds for the sake of one's city. Diotima next refers to the virtue of prudence as an offspring of the love for immortality, as well as a range of activities that sustain and flourish in political communities.

The offspring most worthy of memory, "prudence and the rest of virtue" (209a), includes the productions of poets, craftsmen, and statesmen. An image of Plato's Socrates appears again, when Diotima refers to those pregnant in soul who seek someone beautiful and attempt to educate him by speaking to him about virtue and what his pursuits should be (209b–c).[26] Just as nurturing completes generation, so does teaching complete Love. The element of nurturing remains for Diotima even at the highest level, when she describes the ascent of the lover from a beautiful beloved, to beauty in souls, practices, and laws, then to knowledge of beauty itself, permanent and unchanging, unmixed with anything ugly—"the perfect end" of the lover's labors. The lover then gives birth to and nurtures, she says, not phantoms of virtue but true virtue. Only then, Diotima concludes, does he become "dear to the gods and immortal, if it is possible for any human being" (212a).

When Socrates responds to Agathon that Love lacks what it desires, or desires beyond itself, he reminds him of human insufficiency, dependence, and relationship. And when he presents Diotima's teaching that Love generates, and that generation—and nurturing—is a mortal's way to immortality, he reminds Agathon of death in a way that links mortals to their offspring, to future generations, and to their communities more generally. His emphasis on limitation, in contrast to Agathon's on self-sufficiency, places human beings in political communities. Because our political communities, like the children born to their parents, are our own, we are able to give ourselves to the task of nurturing them; and because they are not simply our own but have a life beyond ourselves, just as do the children of parents, our care involves some sacrifice or risk of ourselves. And because we love our own only insofar as it is good (205e), Socrates makes room for a politics that strives to ensure that one's own is good, a politics that goes beyond mere necessity or preservation as human beings seek to lead good and noble or beautiful lives. Insofar as the beautiful cannot be reduced to the good, self-interested political action might be mediated by the beautiful. To Agathon, Socrates insists that Resource is wedded to Poverty, while to Aristophanes he insists that Poverty is wedded to Resource. It is Socrates' intermediate position between lack and possession, and not that of either of these poets, that leaves open this possibility.

The lovers whom Diotima describes generate and nurture not only children, but also inventions of arts or crafts, poetic productions, laws of political communities, speeches about virtue, and even virtue itself in the souls of others (208e–212a). Lovers begin with a particular beloved in their ascent to the beautiful and end in generating and nurturing particular offspring that are shared with others. They may at first seem like the philosopher in Plato's *Republic* who ascends to the beings outside the cave of political life and is forced to return to pay his debts (*Republic* 519c–520c). This philosopher's priority is clear, but he does what is necessary. But the lover described here does not have to be forced to return to human and political life, because he never really leaves it. His attaining a vision of beauty coincides with his generating true virtue. Philosophic life so understood contributes to political life and serves as a model for it. That is, the state between poverty and resource that accounts for the pursuit of wisdom and its self-generation through questioning others also accounts for the ongoing human activities that keep political communities alive and flourishing.

Socrates'—or Diotima's—words that link mortal human beings to others are supported by his deeds. In concluding his speech in the *Symposium,* Socrates claims that he is persuaded by Diotima and that he tries to persuade others (212b). Of the speeches delivered at the *Symposium,* Socrates' alone culminates in an attempt to perpetuate itself in this manner (cf. 193a–b). And Socrates well knew the risk he ran by speaking to others, even if he did not engage in politics in the ordinary sense (see *Gorgias* 486a–b and 511a–b). After Socrates stops speaking, Aristophanes objects to an allusion in Socrates' speech to his own speech about love (212c). At his trial, years later, Socrates again alludes to Aristophanes and his portrayal of Socrates in the *Clouds* when he refers to a comic poet as one of the sources of long-standing prejudices against him (*Apology* 22b–e). For now, it looks as if there will be further conversation, this time a dialogue between Socrates and the comic poet himself. Once again, Socrates' speech alone of those delivered that evening provokes such an outcome. It is a brewing conversation interrupted, however, by the flamboyant entrance of

Alcibiades, who has come to honor Agathon for the success of his tragedy on the Greek stage (212d–e).

Alcibiades' Cosmopolitan Vision

The intoxicated Alcibiades bursts into the gathering supported by a flute girl and others of his company. He is crowned with a wreath of ivy and violets and thus resembles the god Dionysus (e.g., Euripides, *Bacchae* 81–82).[27] As a youth, he was pursued by Socrates, who claimed to be his lover, as Alcibiades will soon recount, and he was familiar with Socrates' questioning of himself and others (see *Alcibiades I* and *Protagoras*). Along with his freedom from received opinion and conventional behavior came his tyrannical ambitions (Thucydides 6.53 and 60–61). Indeed, in Plato's *Alcibiades I,* the young man confesses his desire to acquire power over the whole world (*Alcibiades I* 105a–e). Only one year after Agathon's party, Alcibiades led the disastrous Sicilian invasion and soon thereafter betrayed Athens and advised Sparta in its war against his city, and then he intrigued against both Greek cities with the king of Persia (Thucydides 6.88.9–6.93.2; 8.46.1–47.1). Dashing, daring, and unscrupulous, this talented Athenian contributed to his city's final defeat in the Peloponnesian War and its subsequent decline.

Xenophon recounts that when Socrates was accused of impiety and of corrupting the young, Alcibiades was one of the names most frequently mentioned (*Memorabilia* I.ii.12). Scholars as well speculate about the connection between Socratic dialectic and Alcibiades' freedom from the conventions and laws of his city. Allan Bloom, for example, suggests that Socrates' questions "liberate[d] Alcibiades from loyalty to his own city," and Lutz questions whether Socrates undermined Alcibiades' law-abidingness (see also *Republic* 538d–539a).[28] The freedom from accepted opinions and the conventions of the day produced by philosophic questioning might liberate an individual from political restraints. Alcibiades' lack of good citizenship, from this perspective, is a reflection of Socrates' independence from the city. Moreover, one might connect Alcibiades' "universal ambitions" with the universal ambitions of philosophy in its pursuit of the truth. Not simply the liberating character of philosophy but its goals and aspirations might find tyrannical expression in a politics of empire. Bloom points us to this possibility as well in his interpretation of the *Symposium*. In contrast to the more typical interpretations that contrast the purity of Socrates' love of the Ideas with Alcibiades' passion for the world, Bloom writes that the "Alcibiadean vision of politics seems like a political version" of the "vision of the Ideas and the beautiful."[29] This argument attributes to both a universality of outlook, whether it be the imperialistic drive that finds no impediment in the laws and customs of particular peoples or the love of the truth that leads a philosopher beyond the opinions of his time and place. Although Alcibiades was able to imagine new possibilities for himself beyond Athens, he was hardly a good citizen of the world in Nussbaum's sense. Transcending the political has political implications, as Nussbaum argues, but Plato's portrayal of Alcibiades suggests that, if one understands philosophy as "cosmopolitanism," nothing prevents imperialism.[30]

As I have argued, however, a cosmopolitan vision is more characteristic of Agathon than of Socrates, whose response to Agathon that love is in-between human and divine and completed by generation and nurturing understands human life as necessarily political. What is essential to Socratic philosophizing is therefore missed both by those who warn against applying Socrates' transcendent philosophic vision to politics, as Bloom does in his interpretation of Alcibiades,[31] and those who, like Nussbaum, urge that we do this on a world scale in the interest of our common humanity. Plato alerts us to all such partial interpretations of Socrates when he contrasts his portrayal of Socrates with that of Alcibiades.

When Alcibiades arrives at the symposium, he changes the terms of the agreed-upon entertainment and insists on praising Socrates rather than Love (214b–d). He first compares Socrates to the statues of Silenus, an old man in Greek myth with the ears of a horse. Both Socrates and Silenus have ugly exteriors. And when the statues of Silenus are "split open into two," there are images of gods within. So too does Socrates, Alcibiades says, hide within himself images "divine and golden, altogether beautiful and wondrous" (216d–217a; 222a). Although Socrates disguises himself as a lover of beautiful young men, he is really "full of moderation" within and contemns all the things most people pursue (216d–e). And when Socrates claims he is "ignorant and knows nothing" (221d–e; 216d), he conceals his wisdom, for when opened like the Silenus statues, his speeches are intelligent and contain "everything proper to examine for one who would be noble and good" (222a). Socrates' irony is only deception (218d). Alcibiades understands nothing in-between emptiness and fullness, ignorance and wisdom (see *Alcibiades II* 139a–b).

Alcibiades compares Socrates as well to the satyr Marsyas, who charms and possesses human beings by means of his flute. So too, Alcibiades confesses, does Socrates ravish those who hear him by means of his speeches. Indeed, when he hears Socrates, his "heart leaps and tears pour out." Alcibiades even insists that, like Marsyas's tunes, Socrates' speeches can be reproduced by anyone with the same effect, "even if he be a poor speaker," and regardless of "whether the hearer be a woman, man, or lad." All are "struck out [of their minds] and possessed" (215b–e). He assumes that Socrates' conversations can be simply conveyed from one speaker to another, as if the individual whom Socrates addresses makes no contribution of his own to the dialogue. He misses the dialogic character of Socrates' conversations, which address particular individuals, who therefore have a part to play (see *Phaedrus* 271b and 275e). It is therefore not surprising that he fears that engaging Socrates means a life of idleness or passivity, "sitting beside him until he grows old." He consequently "stops his ears as if from Sirens and runs away" (215b–216b).

Alcibiades' Socrates resembles Aristophanes' Socrates from the *Clouds* in his self-sufficiency—his asceticism and disdain for ordinary human life (cf. 220a–b with *Clouds* 415–17, 439–42, and 737, and cf. 219c and 221b with *Clouds* 223). When Alcibiades describes Socrates' virtues, he thus emphasizes his endurance and indifference to anything outside himself (wearing the same clothes in summer and winter, for example, or unaffected by drink). He captures Socrates' philosophic life with a story from the time they served in the Athenian army together. Having "gotten a thought, Socrates stood on the same spot from dawn on, considering it, and making no progress would not let up," not moving until the following dawn (220c). Although Socrates is on a military expedition, he is oblivious of his fellow soldiers, who, Alcibiades recounts, after they finish their dinner, bring out their bedding—for it was summer—and sleep outside to find out if Socrates will stand all night. Socrates is as oblivious of the military and political concerns of his city, at least in Alcibiades' story, as were the disciples of Aristophanes' Socrates in the *Clouds* who made maps unaware that Athens and Sparta were at war (*Clouds* 206–14). His philosophizing, as Alcibiades presents it, separates him from his city—even when he is serving in its army. His thinking could occur anywhere. He converses with no one, as Alcibiades tells the tale, and no one knows what he is thinking. Alcibiades' image of Socrates rivals Aristophanes' image of him as suspended in a basket investigating the heavens (*Clouds* 218–32). Although Alcibiades' mockery is mixed with some admiration, his blame with praise (222a), he seems to be among those who view Socrates through the lens of Aristophanes' momentous play (see *Apology* 22b–e).[32] Socrates' lessons about Love respond not merely to the two poets in the *Symposium,* the one who thinks that self-sufficiency is possible, the other who mocks its pretensions, but also to the latter's portrayal of the philosopher himself in the *Clouds.*

When Alcibiades proposed to yield sexual favors to Socrates in return for his wisdom (217a), he recounts, Socrates showed no interest in sex and denied that he had any such wisdom as Alcibiades supposed. When Socrates offers him a different sort of relationship—that they "will in the future, after deliberating, do whatever seems best to us two about these and other things" (219a–b), Alcibiades hears only a rejection. Just as he sees nothing in-between ignorance and wisdom, he understands love in terms of ruling and being ruled, referring to Socrates' "wondrous power" and his own "abject slavery" to Socrates (215e, 216c, and 219e). When he begins to pursue Socrates, he imagines that the roles of beloved and lover have been merely reversed (217a–219c, 222b, and 213c; *Alcibiades* I 135d); he has no conception of the reciprocal relation Socrates proposed.[33] If there is no middle between emptiness and fullness, love can be only domination and subjection. There is no space for reciprocity. Only in-betweens can both love and be loved (see *Lysis* 40d–e). When Socrates proposes that he and Alcibiades deliberate together about what is best for the two of them, he is offering Alcibiades a part in a conversation. But just as the dialogic character of Socratic speech eludes him, so too does Socrates' care for him. Moreover, he is not satisfied by any mere part (see, e.g., 213e and 214c–d; *Alcibiades I* 104e–105c). After proposing the exchange of Socrates' wisdom for his sexual favors, Alcibiades asked Socrates to consider what was best for the two of them, but Alcibiades' proposition indicated that he himself had already decided for them (cf. 219a and 218c). When Socrates responded that after deliberating they would do whatever looked best to them both (219b), he was not only offering a part to Alcibiades but claiming one for himself.

Throughout his "praise" of Socrates, then, Alcibiades presents Socrates as if he were self-sufficient, without particular needs and cares or attachment to ordinary human life. His wisdom renders him godlike and powerful, as indicated by his comparison of him to the Silenus statues and of his speeches to those of Marsyas's flute music, while his eroticism and knowledge of ignorance are only part of his exoteric presentation. Although Alcibiades disdains what he sees as the idleness of the philosophic life, he admires Socrates' freedom from and transcendence of ordinary human concerns. Socrates did not succeed in conveying to Alcibiades any alternative understanding of philosophy, or of Socrates himself. Of course, in terms of the dramatic action of this dialogue, Alcibiades arrives too late to hear Socrates' account of the lessons he learned from Diotima about Love and philosophy—its state between ignorance and wisdom, the connection between poverty and resource, and both to generation, and how this understanding of love supported philosophy and politics. By timing Alcibiades' arrival after Socrates' speech, Plato suggests more generally that Alcibiades did not hear what Socrates had to say about philosophy (216a–c). Indeed, he seems to have learned more about Socrates from the *Clouds* than from Socrates himself. Like Agathon, whom he honors for his poetic success, and whose view of the world leaves no room for Resource's mate, he understands only the resourceful side of Socrates. He imitates the poets by his recourse to "images" or "likenesses" in order to describe Socrates. Of course, the most famous images of Socrates are those left to us by Plato's dialogues. Whereas Socrates competes in the *Symposium* with poets, Alcibiades competes with Plato himself. Plato does not present him as an authority on Socratic philosophy, but rather as evidence of the dangers of misunderstanding it.

Plato's Narrative Imagination

In the *Republic,* Socrates criticizes poetry as unphilosophic. For example, poetry such as Greek epic or tragedy depicts the precariousness of human existence and the terror of death, as in its tales of the fall of heroes and of the various sufferings of human beings and of those whom they love. Far from making us sympathetic with others or leading us to deliberation or to a larger view of things, poetry from this perspective strengthens our attachments to what is peculiarly our own (e.g., *Republic* 387d–388e; and 605cff.). There have, of course, been many defenses of poetry against Socrates' critique, beginning with Aristotle's *Poetics,* in his argument that poetry is more philosophic than history. While the latter narrates particulars, events that have happened, poetry narrates events that might happen, revealing their underlying causes or truths and thus making universal truths or principles manifest in the particular actions and lives it portrays (*Poetics* 1451b3–10). Consistent with Aristotle's observation, Euben and Monoson implicitly defend poetry against the critique that it fosters an unreflective attachment to one's own when they point to the critical aspects of Athenian drama itself. Just as Euben refers to the "self-critique" found in Athenian drama, Monoson argues that the "strong and discerning mind" of the active spectator of the Athenian drama was a useful image for Plato in representing philosophy.[34]

Also consistent with Aristotle's distinction between poetry and history, Nussbaum contends that the narrative imagination can make us aware of our common humanity underlying different political orders and cultures. This is why she associates the "narrative imagination" with Socratic self-examination as essential components for cultivating humanity. While Socratic self-examination frees us from the opinions of our own time and place, it is by identifying with those alien or different from ourselves, as poetry helps us to do, that we come to understand the other "not as forbiddingly alien and other, but as sharing many problems and possibilities with us."[35] It is not primarily a toleration of difference that the narrative imagination makes possible, but a transcendence of difference. Far from strengthening our attachment to our own, as Socrates contends in the *Republic,* poetry for Nussbaum frees us from that very attachment.

I agree about the philosophic potential of poetry, and I would not contest the affinities between poetic narrative and the self-critical aspects of Socratic philosophizing as Plato presents it. After all, as Aristotle himself pointed out, the dialogues of Plato are themselves forms of poetry (*Poetics* 447b12). Plato gave an implicit defense of poetry when he chose to depict Socratic philosophizing in dramatic dialogues rather than to give a systematic account of it. But while Plato's narratives of Socrates are not as narrowly parochial and limiting as Socrates depicts poetry in the *Republic,* I argue, they defend both the familiar and the alien or different in a way that questions the human benefit of cosmopolitanism. My case turns on Plato's presentation of the relation of philosophy to wonder.

For Plato, philosophy begins in and is sustained by wonder (*Theaetetus* 155d). If the familiar were never unfamiliar, we would not question; we would see nothing beyond what we already know or think we know. We would rest self-satisfied with received opinion. In the *Theaetetus,* where Socrates traces philosophy to wonder, he asks the young mathematician *Theaetetus* to define knowledge. Nothing would be more familiar to the young man, who can demonstrate all he knows about mathematics to others (*Theaetetus* 147c–148b), but it turns out that he cannot say what knowledge itself is. If he has knowledge but does not know what knowing is, he does not know himself. There seems to be a discrepancy between what he knows and self-knowledge. Similarly, Socrates recounts in the *Phaedo* that when he was a young man, he sought in the work of natural philosophy ways of explaining the problems that puzzled him, but natural philosophy could not explain himself or his relation to Athens (*Phaedo* 97b–c and 98e). Natural philosophy, like mathematics, yields knowledge but not self-knowledge. And when Diotima describes philosophers as neither ignorant nor wise, her description is so puzzling to Socrates that he must ask who these could be (*Symposium* 204a–b). He cannot recognize himself in her account. He must invent a character quite different from himself, a foreigner and a woman, in order to have her explain philosophy to him. She in turn invents the mythical characters Poverty and Resource to answer his question about the generation of Love (203bff.). Philosophy is so strange even to the philosopher that it requires a series of projections or images, and then as a result it becomes even stranger. Who, after all, are Love's parents, and how could they generate someone between human and divine? Through Diotima's questioning Socrates about why human beings love, she makes Socrates strange to himself, as Socrates later makes Theaetetus when he questions him about knowledge. As teachers, both Diotima and Socrates keep questioning alive by showing what is strange and inexplicable in what is most familiar.

If the unfamiliar were in no way familiar, however, would we ever become aware of it? And if somehow we did, what hope would we have of answering our questions about it? We would have no cause to trust that we could ever come to know what we do not. And questioning would cease just as surely as if questions had not been raised in the first place. Meno, in the dialogue bearing his name, questions whether we can ever come to know what we do not know, inasmuch as not knowing it we would not know what to seek, nor would we know it when and if we discovered it (*Meno* 80d). Meno puts forward a "pugnacious proposition," Socrates says, that would end inquiry, for we would inquire neither about what we knew—since we knew it—nor about what we did not know—since we could not know it (*Meno* 80e). Therefore he will "trust" the stories told of old about how "all nature is akin" and how all things were known to us before birth so that by recollecting (or learning) one thing we can recollect (or learn) others (*Meno* 81c–d). The unfamiliar that we seek is connected to the familiar that we know, and it can be recollected because we once knew it. And so Socrates appeals to what Theaetetus knows about math for him to understand what he is trying to understand about knowledge (*Theaetetus*

185c–e and 195e–196c). Theaetetus must see the familiar in the unfamiliar in order to make progress.

The strange and the familiar are therefore both necessary for philosophy. If the former collapsed into the latter, there would be no questioning; we would be puzzled by nothing because everything would be familiar. If the latter collapsed into the former, there could be no basis for answering questions, Meno's pugnacious proposition would hold, and we would, as Socrates says, be idle (*Meno* 81d). Platonic dialogues are narrative imaginations that attempt to preserve both the familiar and the unfamiliar, in order to keep philosophy alive. Socrates' recourse to a stranger as his teacher about Love (201e, 204c, 211d) is not simply for the sake of his fellow symposiasts, but for his own as well.

Although Plato's Socrates may have become a household word, easily associated, as we have seen, with world citizenship, Plato made it difficult for his readers to view Socrates as just like everyone else. Although his dialogues attempt to make Socrates familiar, even beyond the confines of Athens, as a model of the philosophic life (see *Phaedo* 57aff.), they also preserve his strangeness. Plato's presentation of Socrates has this in common with Socrates' description of Diotima. One important way, but not the only way,[36] in which Plato highlights Socrates' strangeness is by attributing to him "a daimonic voice," which Socrates claimed came to him in childhood, always preventing him from doing something he should not do. His "voice" did not provide him with reasons for its negative commands, nor was it heard by anyone but Socrates himself. As Plato presents it, it was a puzzle even to Socrates. But its commands did not make Socrates a completely private man. Because it did not oppose his coming to court to face trial, Socrates says (*Apology* 40a–b), it indirectly supported the judicial processes of the city. And while it kept Socrates from engaging directly in politics, it did not prevent him from conversing with others, even about his daimonic voice itself (*Apology* 31c–d; see also *Phaedrus* 242b–c; and *Euthydemus* 272e). In his portrayal of Socrates, Plato makes the strange familiar while keeping its strangeness before us.

When Nussbaum recommends the study of other cultures, she too warns against making the strange too familiar and the familiar too strange. She exemplifies the first with "descriptive chauvinism," the second with "descriptive romanticism." The first "recreat[es] the other in the image of oneself, reading the strange as exactly like what is familiar."[37] Blind to the unfamiliar and strange, the descriptive chauvinist would not undergo the "expansion of sympathies" that characterizes Nussbaum's world citizen. He sees nothing strange or unfamiliar when he looks at cultures other than his own, but only his own ways of acting and thinking. Far from transcending received opinion, the chauvinist imposes his self-understanding on his views of others. Descriptive romanticism, on the other hand, "view[s] another culture as excessively alien and virtually incomparable with one's own, ignoring elements of similarity and highlighting elements that seem mysterious and odd." It is driven "by a romantic longing for exotic experiences that our own familiar lives seem to deny us."[38] We do not see what is familiar in the strange. This "vice" too is incompatible with world citizenship from Nussbaum's perspective, for romanticizing otherness will make it inaccessible to us.

Whereas Socrates would correct descriptive chauvinism by insisting on what is strange in what is familiar (Theaetetus's mathematical knowledge is not enough to explain knowledge) and descriptive romanticism by insisting on what is familiar in what we are trying to understand (the meaning of knowledge cannot exclude Theaetetus's knowledge), Nussbaum would correct both by "cultivating humanity." Familiar and strange both yield to what is common or universal. World citizens identify with others, neither imposing themselves upon them (descriptive chauvinism) nor celebrating their character as alien (descriptive romanticism). Understanding that different individuals and cultures all face common problems, albeit in different ways, will help us to recognize our "shared humanity."[39] It is the task of the narrative imagination, as Nussbaum conceives it, to support such an endeavor. It succeeds in educating us when it shows what is universal both in our own and in the other or foreign. In this light, differences become less important than what is shared, less threatening and less dangerous. They also become less defensible. The world citizen ends up with nothing that is simply his own, and at the same time he does not allow others to maintain the dignity of distance. Indeed, he resembles Alcibiades. No allegiance to his own city prevented him from betraying it, and his love of the world was so great that he seemed eager to possess it (see Thucydides 6.92.4).

Plato's narratives, in contrast, seek to give us enough distance from the familiar that we may question it and enough familiarity with the elusive so that we trust our pursuit of it. But although the familiar becomes questionable in Platonic dialogues, it remains our own, while the strange remains too elusive to become so. However much philosophy comes into conflict with traditional politics, then, the former does not ultimately undermine the latter, because it preserves the distinction between citizen and stranger. By doing so, it supports the citizen's defense of his own, while moderating tyrannical impulses that find no limits in what is strange or foreign. Philosophy and politics flourish or wane together. Nussbaum's world citizen, freed from his own through questioning and open to all things human through poetry, neither defends the familiar nor finds anything strange or wondrous in what is foreign.[40] Even if he travels the wide world, he is less a world citizen than Socrates the Athenian, who can appreciate the foreign because he knows he cannot assimilate it to his own. After all, he is only a philosopher, a lover of wisdom. Wise is a name we can give only to the gods (*Phaedrus* 278d).

Notes

1. Patrick Deneen, "Chasing Plato," *Political Theory* (June 2000): 424. In this school he includes Josiah Ober and Arlene Saxonhouse, as well as the three scholars whose books he reviews—J. Peter Euben, Gerald M. Mara, and Christopher Rocco. One might also include in this democratic school of Platonic interpretation S. Sara Monoson, who, like Euben, tracks the affinities between the democratic practices of Plato's Athens and Plato's understanding of philosophical activity (*Plato's Democratic Entanglements* [Princeton, NJ: Princeton Univ. Press, 2000]) and John R. Wallach, who finds in Plato's concept of leadership a political art for channeling democratic energies in virtuous directions and therefore one that can be redeployed in our own contemporary postliberal democracy (*The Platonic Political Art: A Study of Critical Reason and Democracy* [University Park: Pennsylvania State Univ. Press, 2001]). Deneen offers a perceptive and fair-minded account of the strengths and weaknesses of this school of interpretation as illustrated by the work of the authors he reviews.

2. J. Peter Euben, *Corrupting Youth: Political Education, Democratic Culture, and Political Theory* (Princeton, NJ: Princeton Univ. Press, 1997), 208.

3. Dana Villa, *Socratic Citizenship* (Princeton, NJ: Princeton Univ. Press, 2001), for example, 3 and 28.

4. Villa, *Socratic Citizenship,* 3 and 15.

5. Martha Nussbaum, *Cultivating Humanity: A Classical Defense of Reform in Liberal Education* (Cambridge: Cambridge Univ. Press, 1997), 26. Here Nussbaum distinguishes the democratic outlook of Socrates from Plato, who "was certainly an elitist about reason, and openly hostile to democracy" (25–26). Thus the "tradition" of Socratic questioning to which she appeals stems from "the historical Socrates," not Plato, even though in some of his works, she says, Plato "represents Socrates as he was" rather than as a mouthpiece for his own views (26). Earlier, in her monumental work on Greek thought, *The Fragility of Goodness,* Nussbaum did side with Plato against Socrates, even arguing that

it was Plato, in contrast to Socrates, who was able to understand the unique individuality of the human person. *The Fragility of Goodness: Luck and Ethics in Greek Tragedy and Philosophy* (Cambridge: Cambridge Univ. Press, 1986), 166–67, 173–74, 197, 199, and 218. Thus it might seem that it would be Plato who is the more promising source for "cultivating humanity." But here, because Socrates is commonly associated with a tradition of questioning beliefs, a democratic Socrates better serves her purposes.

6. Nussbaum claims to draw not only from Socrates' concept of "the examined life," but on "Aristotle's notions of self-reflective citizenship and above all on Greek and Roman Stoic notions of an education that is 'liberal' in that it liberates the mind from the bondage of habit and custom, producing people who can function with sensitivity and alertness as citizens of the whole world." Nussbaum traces the term *world citizen* to Diogenes the Cynic, who pronounced, "I am a citizen of the world." *Cultivating Humanity,* 8 and 50. See also Nussbaum, "Patriotism and Cosmopolitanism," in *For Love of Country?* by Nussbaum et al., ed. Joseph Cohen (Boston: Beacon Press, 1996). In addition to Nussbaum's essay "Patriotism and Cosmopolitanism," this book contains the responses of numerous critics.

7. Nussbaum, *Cultivating Humanity,* 10, emphasis mine.

8. Ibid., 4. Nussbaum distinguishes between a "sterner, more exigent version" of the world citizen, whose *primary* loyalty is to all human beings, and "a more relaxed version." The latter leaves open "how we order our various loyalties" but requires us to "recognize the worth of human life wherever it occurs and see ourselves as bound by common human abilities and problems to people who lie at a great distance from us." She claims that it is the more relaxed version "that will concern me here." Her rhetoric throughout, however, veers back toward the first, with which she admits at the outset she sympathizes. Ibid., 9. Thus, in her essay "Patriotism and Cosmopolitan," she insists that the Stoic view of world citizenship she proposes does not require that we "give up local identifications, which can be a source of great richness in life." But "our first allegiance" should be to "the moral community made up of all human beings" (7–9). And her description of the "loneliness" of the world citizen, who lives in exile "from comfort in local truths, from the warm, nestling feeling of patriotism, from the absorbing pride in oneself and one's own" (15) throws into doubt the "great richness" from local connections that she allows the world citizen.

9. Thomas L. Pangle and Peter J. Ahrensdorf, *Justice among Nations: On the Moral Basis of Power and Peace* (Lawrence: Univ. Press of Kansas, 1999), 47. Cicero's statement can be found in *Tusculan Disputations* 5.108.

10. As they say, the teaching of Socratic philosophers, in which group they include Aristotle and Xenophon as well as Plato, "is intended for the liberation of select wise, or potentially wise, individuals." Pangle and Ahrensdorf, *Justice among Nations,* 50.

11. Ibid.

12. For a different criticism of Nussbaum's view of Socrates and of Nussbaum's position on world citizenship more generally, but one I believe compatible with my own, see Michael Beaty and Anne-Marie Bowery, "Cultivating Christian Citizenship: Martha Nussbaum's Socrates, Augustine's Confessions, and the Modern University," *Christian Scholar* 33, no. 1 (Fall 2003): 23–34.

13. See Richard L. Velkley, "On Possessed Individualism: Hegel, Socrates' Daimon, and the Modern State," *Review of Metaphysics* 59, no. 3 (March 2006): 279–301 (reprinted in this volume). For Hegel's discussion of the connection between the Ideas and freedom, see Georg Wilhelm Hegel, *Lectures on the History of Philosophy,* trans. E.S. Haldane and Francis H. Simson (London: Routledge and Kegan Paul, 1982), 1:385–88, 406–7.

14. Nor, of course, because Socrates was a parochial Greek, subject to the prejudices or limitations of his time and place even when he attempted to transcend them.

15. Nussbaum, *Cultivating Humanity,* for example, 85. See chapter 3, "The Narrative Imagination," 85–112.

16. My analysis of Socrates' defense of politics in the *Symposium* is adapted from my "Socrates' Contest with the Poets in Plato's *Symposium,*" *Political Theory* 32, no. 2 (April 2004): 186–206. Translations from the Greek are my own, although for the *Symposium* I have relied on Seth Benardete's translation in *Plato's "Symposium,"* trans. Seth Benardete and with commentaries by Allan Bloom and Seth Benardete (Chicago: Univ. of Chicago Press, 2001). Citations of Greek texts in parentheses, unless otherwise noted, are to the *Symposium.*

17. It is not surprising that when Plato dramatizes a later encounter between Socrates and Phaedrus, in a dialogue named for the latter, Phaedrus leads Socrates outside the walls of the city into the countryside, in order to hear a speech. This is the only time dramatized by Plato when Socrates leaves Athens, although there is reference to his service in the army during the war. Socrates, in contrast to Phaedrus, is ready to return to the city, even before the dialogue is over and even when the noonday heat presses (Phaedrus 242a).

18. Friedrich Nietzsche, *The Birth of Tragedy, in The Birth of Tragedy and The Case of Wagner,* trans. and with commentary by Walter Kaufmann (New York: Random House, 1976), 81.

19. Ibid., 92.

20. There existed various accounts of Love's parents, none authoritative, given their variety. See R.G. Bury, *The Symposium of Plato* (Cambridge: W. Heffner, 1969), 22, note on 178b.

21. This difficulty explains why one might assume that Poverty is mortal and Resource divine, as scholars, not surprisingly, tend to do. See Bury, *The Symposium of Plato,* xl. And see Mark J. Lutz, *Socrates' Education to Virtue: Learning the Love of the Noble* (Albany: State Univ. of New York Press, 1998), 87.

22. As has often been noted, Diotima's description recalls Socrates in many of its details. As the offspring of Poverty and Resource, Love is, like his mother,

"always poor" and, like his father, "a plotter after the beautiful and the good" (203d–e).

23. As Allan Bloom observes, by pointing out that only certain individuals are called poets, Diotima "alerts us to the mysterious fact that poetry is privileged because it caters to the longing for the beautiful." "The Ladder of Love," in *Plato's "Symposium,"* 136.

24. Diotima's striking statement does not merge male and female roles in reproduction, begetting (*gennaō*) and giving birth (*tiktō*), but acknowledges the complexity necessary for generation. In other words, Love has a father and a mother.

25. Lutz, *Socrates' Education to Virtue,* 69; Waller R. Newell, *Ruling Passion: The Erotics of Statecraft in Platonic Political Philosophy* (Lanham, MD: Rowman and Littlefield, 2000), 74; and Bloom, "The Ladder of Love," 142.

26. Although Socrates claims in the *Theaetetus* that as midwife he does not generate but questions others, he also admits that he is in part the "cause" when those whom he questions "give birth to many beautiful things" (150 c–d). As to Socrates' practice of midwifery in that very dialogue, at the end Theaetetus declares that in his conversation with Socrates, "I for one have said even more on account of you than all I used to have in myself" (210b). For a different interpretation of this issue, and its relevance to the *Symposium,* see Harry Neumann, "Diotima's Concept of Love," *American Journal of Philology* 86 (1965): 57.

27. For a more developed account of Alcibiades' role in the *Symposium,* see my "Philosophy and Empire: On Socrates and Alcibiades in Plato's *Symposium,*" *Polity* 39, no. 4 (October 2007): 502–21.

28. Bloom, "The Ladder of Love," 166; and Lutz, *Socrates' Education to Virtue,* 127. Seth Benardete speculates that had Alcibiades not exposed Athens to disaster in Sicily, which ultimately led to the city's defeat in the war with Sparta, Socrates might not have been brought to trial, found guilty, and executed. "On Plato's *Symposium,*" in *Plato's "Symposium,"* 192.

29. Bloom, "The Ladder of Love," 166.

30. While Alcibiades' tyrannical and imperialistic ambitions seem antithetical to Nussbaum's cosmopolitanism, her world citizen is superior to most human beings, whom she recognizes will not so easily place "reason and the love of humanity" above their local attachments. This is why she finds world citizenship "a lonely business." "Patriotism and Cosmopolitanism," 15. Several of Nussbaum's critics have expressed reservations along this line. Michael W. McConell observes that the "moralistic cosmopolitan" is "not one who everywhere feels comfortable but who everywhere feels superior." "Don't Neglect the Little Platoons," in Nussbaum et al., *For Love of Country?* 82. And Sissela Bok observes, "Children deprived of a culturally rooted education too often find it difficult to experience any allegiances whatsoever, whether to the world or their community and family," and in their "exile" experience "responsibilities to none save themselves." "From Part to Whole," in Nussbaum et al., *For Love of Country?* 43.

See also J. Peter Euben's criticism of Nussbaum in *Platonic Noise* (Princeton, NJ: Princeton Univ. Press, 2003), 128–31.

31. See also Pangle and Ahrensdorf, *Justice among Nations,* 33–50.

32. Not surprisingly, Alcibiades quotes a line from the *Clouds* to illustrate Socrates' hubris (228; *Clouds* 362). The only other time Plato quotes from the play is when he has Socrates in the *Apology* use a line from the *Clouds* to show the sort of mockery he was subjected to by his old accusers (*Apology* 19c; *Clouds* 225 and 1503).

33. See Gary Alan Scott's excellent analysis in *Plato's Socrates as Educator* (Albany: State Univ. of New York Press, 2000), 121–34.

34. Euben, *Corrupting Youth,* 208. Monoson argues that Plato conceptualizes the philosopher as modeled on the *theatēs*—the audience member at the theater—whose experience watching plays "develops valuable mental and moral sensibilities, even sharpens [his] awareness that things are not always as they seem." *Plato's Democratic Entanglements,* 209–10.

35. Nussbaum, *Cultivating Humanity,* 9–11 and 85.

36. Other characters, for example, often call attention to how "odd" (*atopos*) they find Socrates (see, e.g., *Symposium* 175b; *Phaedrus* 230c; *Gorgias* 473a, 480e, and 481e; and *Euthydemus* 305a).

37. Nussbaum, *Cultivating Humanity,* 118.

38. Ibid., 124.

39. Ibid., 138.

40. See Nussbaum's slightly different formulation, "Reply," in Nussbaum et al., *For Love of Country?* 140.

Thomas L. Pangle

Roman Cosmopolitanism

The Stoics and Cicero

The Roman Platonist Marcus Tullius Cicero (106–43 B.C.), the last great republican statesman of antiquity, has left us in his philosophical writings the fullest doctrinal elaboration of Socratic political theory in its implications for international affairs. Through his modification of Stoicism, Cicero erected the basic conceptual framework of the "law of nations," within which, or against which, all subsequent international law and normative international relations theory has defined itself.

By Cicero's time, the need for a universal natural theology and an international code of political and military ethics had become pressing. The Roman conquest had largely extinguished independent civic life and had sapped the vitality of civil religion, melting the cities into a polyglot empire whose elite was suffused with the popularized philosophy or theology of a wide variety of Greek sects (Epicureans, Stoics, Skeptics, Peripatetics, Old and New Academics, and so forth). Could Socratic political philosophy provide some qualified legitimation of Roman imperialism, thereby placing some moral limits on that imperialism? Could Socratic political philosophy shed light on perhaps the most baffling feature of the new imperial political universe—the obscuring of the distinction between domestic and foreign policy? How were Romans to understand their moral relations to the vast and diverse nonslave populations that they ruled? These subjects were not fellow citizens in the strong or traditional sense, sharing in the common good of the "city"; yet neither were they simply foreigners or the conquered anymore. Decent Romans were serious in their wish not to treat their subject peoples like the downtrodden slaves of despotism (see, e.g., *Republic* 3.41). Cicero confronted a challenge that statesmen and theorists were to face time and again down through the ages: the possibility of genuine Socratic philosophy has to be kept alive, and the norms discovered and promulgated by Plato and Aristotle have to be applied, in conditions that are unmistakably decadent (*On Duties* 3.69, 3.74)—in circumstances for which the Greek philosophers' writings provide insufficient direct guidance. Rising to the occasion, Cicero laid down some of the most influential, and surely the most oft-quoted, pronouncements ever made on the moral limits of war, on the duties of civil societies toward one another, and on the obligations of citizens toward noncitizens.

If we are properly to understand exactly what Cicero intended to convey by these momentous asseverations, we must bear in mind not only the general historical context but also Cicero's own personal political situation, to which he emphatically draws our attention. He stresses that he is writing primarily not as a political philosopher or theorist but as a former victorious commander of Roman legions, as a former leading metropolitan statesman and successful provincial governor, and as the greatest orator Rome has ever known, who is living in enforced retirement after having gone down to defeat attempting to preserve the senile Roman Republic against Caesarism.[1] Cicero cannot rule out the possibility of a republican revival in some form, and he may hope that the emerging despotism can be tempered by respect for the republican past. He therefore tries to nurture an inspiring and applicable version of the Roman republican tradition (which included, of course, republican imperialism) while at the same time formulating a universal moral code that may preserve some dignity for political life under the Caesars and may limit and render more responsible the new universal despotism. At the heart of this complex and highly nuanced rhetorical project is an appeal to certain transnational rules of conduct embodied in the Stoic notion of "natural law" and the kindred conception of the "law of nations" *(ius gentium)*.[2]

Stoic Cosmopolitanism

The original leading Stoics who lived prior to Cicero we know only through fragmentary quotations, doxographical paraphrases, and second- or third-hand reports, often polemical, penned centuries after their death. But these original Stoics evidently promulgated the first widely influential cosmopolitan ethical ideal.[3] The founder of Stoicism, Zeno of Citium (c. 333–261 B.C.), was apparently much influenced by the Cynics, a loose philosophical sect probably stemming from a famous companion of Socrates named Antisthenes (c. 446–366 B.C.), whose obtuse and gracelessly moralistic asceticism is mordantly limned in Xenophon's *Symposium*. Antisthenes seems to have become the supposed source of a version of Socratism that made the image of Socrates famous as a kind of moral superman, in some contrast to the image of the Xenophontic Socrates. Zeno and his Stoics, following in the wake of the Cynics, seem to have meant by "natural law" a codification of what they understood to be the austere and radically unconventional ethic of obedience to rational law, practiced by the Socratic philosopher, an ethic they presented in a rather dogmatic, moralistic, and even censorious version.[4]

Philosophic physics and metaphysics, they apparently contended, reveal to the wise a knowledge of the cosmic order as ruled by a divinity who promulgates, administers, and enforces severe laws of behavior. Obedience to those laws rests on acknowledgment of the purportedly demonstrable thesis that the moral virtues, practiced strictly for their own sake, together with moral friendship, constitute the sole true good in life, the necessary and sufficient condition of true happiness, and the fulfillment of human nature. The virtues are of course exercised in the pursuit (or avoidance) of other things—such as preservation, health, independence, freedom from pain and poverty, the welfare of one's children, and so on—which, while fundamentally "indifferent" in relation to true happiness, are nonetheless of a mediocre relative value. The wise man at times concerns himself with these "mediocre" matters, not merely or chiefly as occasions for the exercise of his virtue; at such times he will perform what may be called "imperfect" or "median" duties. It is these median duties that constitute the benighted and impure moral life of the vast majority of unwise or unphilosophical men. In contrast, the life of the wise, because it is a life centered on devotion to moral virtue as an end in itself, is a life spent chiefly in performance of the "perfect duties." By thus living in obedience to the law of nature or reason, the wise man becomes the true friend of the gods and their only true priest, the knower of the proper sacrifices, to whom the gods communicate divinations of the future through dreams and scientific auguries, and whose soul they may preserve after death, at least until the next cosmic conflagration. The wise philosopher becomes a citizen in a cosmic city or world-state ruled by the gods; he thereby transcends in an important measure the tawdry demimonde of the many parochial cities with their ethnic divisions and prejudices, wars, slavery, traditional families, and conventional private property. From this transnational, sublime, spiritual height the wise man looks down in contempt, though he sees it his duty to participate in politics and family life in his own pure and sententious manner. He may accommodate himself to circumstances, but he will not cease to admire, and may well take as his exemplars, the Cynics, the most famous of whom was Diogenes (404–323 B.C.), who is reputed to have lived in a barrel, who is said to have been the first to use (applying it to himself) the term "citizen of the world" or "cosmopolite, cosmopolitan," and who was purportedly characterized by Plato as "a Socrates gone mad."[5]

The original version of Stoic natural law thus issued in what the Stoics proudly called "paradoxes": the wise man is the only true king, magistrate, juryman, citizen, and orator; the wise man alone is free, and "all the unwise are foreigners, exiles, slaves, and madmen" (Cicero *Lucullus* 136); the wise man alone is capable of friendship; he alone is beautiful and worthy of love affairs; all property by natural right belongs to him and his fellows, with whom he may share wife and children in a radical and incestuous communism; the wise man makes no moral mistakes and does no harm—but he is severe in insisting on the pitiless retributive punishment of the base and foolish unwise.[6]

Cicero's More Generous Stoicism

Given the exiguous state of our sources, it is impossible to be certain whether all the older Stoics were in earnest[7] when they advanced these rebarbative if high-minded teachings—teachings that isolate, and then reflect as in a distorting mirror, certain prominent aspects and paradoxical teachings of the Platonic and Xenophontic Socrates. But it is not surprising to find that the politic Cicero stays at some distance from this original version of cosmopolitan Stoicism: "In truth the principle of the Cynics is to be completely rejected" (*On Duties* 1.148). In the place of the Cynic principle, Cicero welcomes, promotes—and indeed contributes substantially to—a more plastic and humane version of Stoic natural law that seems to have emerged subsequently to, and certainly came to coexist alongside, the original harsh or strict version. This more pragmatic Stoicism, especially in the hands of Cicero, follows Aristotle in elevating the status of the "imperfect" or "median" duties that are in the reach of all decent human beings and simultaneously allows a broadening of the definition of "the wise" to include not only the truly philosophical but also those whom Aristotle called the "serious" men of "moral virtue."[8] The basic and, for most practical purposes, the most important level of the "law of nature" is thereby understood to be more readily accessible to all or most mature human beings. The natural law can be assimilated to the "law of *nations,*" a term that first appears in Cicero and that certainly received its greatest influence through him.[9] This notion of a more universally applicable natural law harmonizes with and may even be said to spring from a common opinion noted approvingly by Aristotle in his treatise on rhetoric.[10] Most prominently, Cicero attacks in public oratory the indignant and retributive punitiveness of the older Stoic outlook articulated by the Roman hero Cato the Younger (95–46 B.C).[11]

In his dialogue *On the Ends of the Good and Bad Things* (3.64), Cicero presents the same Cato the Younger, in a somewhat softened character, defending a more civic version of Stoic cosmopolitanism. The Stoics whom he follows, Cicero's character Cato says, "hold that the world is ruled by the spirit of the gods, and that it is, as it were, a common city and state of human beings and gods, and that each of us is a part of this world; from which it follows as a natural consequence that we prefer the common utility to our own. . . . And the nature of mankind, it is said, is such that there exists between each individual and the human race a quasi-civil right, and he who maintains it is just, while he who departs from it is unjust." Similarly the Stoic Balbus, in the dialogue *On the Nature of the Gods* (2.154; see also 2.78–79): "The world is as it were the common home of the gods and humans, the city that belongs to both." Cicero himself comes close to these views when he appears as a character in his dialogue *Laws* and delivers an admittedly subphilosophical or rhetorical legislative preamble.[12]

But the Stoic vision is given its most unqualified political articulation, and in this version is employed to legitimate the Roman Republic's imperialist foreign policy, in the famous words Cicero puts in the mouth of the statesman Gaius Laelius (Cicero's advocate of natural law in the *Republic,* speaking at 3.33–35):

> Nor will there be one law for Rome, a different for Athens, or different laws at one time and then another; but for all nations and for all time one sempiternal and immutable law, and one common as it were magistrate and ruler over all—that is, god, who is of this law the founder, the judge, and the promulgator; he who disobeys, flees from himself, denies human nature, and in so doing suffers the worst penalties, even if he avoids the other sufferings that are supposed to be punishments.

> . . . No war is ever undertaken by the best city except for honor or safety; . . . those wars are unjust, that are undertaken without cause. Now no war can be justly waged except for the cause of punishing or repelling enemies. . . . Our people, however, now holds sway over the whole earth through defending its allies. . . . Do we not observe that dominion has been given, by nature herself, to what is best—with the greatest consequent benefit to those who are weaker?

Cicero's Critique of Stoic Cosmopolitanism

There is, however, striking evidence in the *Republic* itself that Cicero does not find even this more relaxed Stoic doctrine philosophically adequate. Scipio Africanus the Younger, Cicero's quasi-philosophical spokesman in this dialogue, does applaud Laelius's speech—but as a high point of the criminal defense lawyer's rhetorical art (3.42). In Scipio's own previous and more extensive account of the history of the Roman Republic—which he presents as the model "best regime," a rival to the regime portrayed by Plato in his *Republic*—he repeatedly indicates the exploitative force and fraud that were essential to the founding of Rome, to its acquisition of sufficient territory and inhabitants, to its achievement of security, and to its ascent to grandeur.[13] The morally dubious actions carried out at the founding of Rome and in its early period cannot be explained away by reference to the ignorance or primitive character of the times. "We know," explains Scipio, that Romulus lived at a time when "letters and education were well established and all those ancient errors due to the uncultivated life of men had been overcome" (2.18; see also 2.19–20). What is more, the actions of Romulus and his successors were carried out in accordance with scrupulous conventional piety and constant obedience to the divine will as discovered through official divination; Romulus himself is to be deemed divine. Scipio surely mentions no divine punishment for any of the injustices perpetrated by the Romans on neighboring peoples, even for the rape of the noble Sabine women, a rape that involved the fraudulent exploitation of a religious holiday.[14]

To all this Laelius responds by acknowledging that Scipio's account is not intended as history but as a theoretical elaboration of the best regime, valid in and for all times and places: "You are attributing to others your own discoveries, rather than, as Socrates did in Plato, making a city yourself . . . ; you attribute to rational principle what was done by Romulus on account of chance or necessity" (2.21–22; cf. 2.52). It is not clear, however, to what extent Laelius agrees with or is even capable of facing the disenchanting "rational principle" that underlies Scipio's account of the best possible regime and its foreign policy. We do learn from the opening drama of Cicero's *Republic* that Laelius is distrustful of philosophy inasmuch as its contemplation of the heavens detaches one from defense of and service or devotion to one's fatherland and clients or allies (1.19 and 1.30–31). Any suspicions Laelius may have had about Scipio in this regard would seem to be at least partially confirmed by the conclusion to the whole work (6.9–end). There Scipio discloses that throughout the dialogue he has been speaking under the influence of a dream that has revealed to him the true beauty of nature and the true satisfaction of contemplation, in the light of which transpolitical vision he has become convinced of the pettiness of Rome and indeed of all political action.

The dream (which Scipio pointedly does not regard as divinely revealed [6.10]) intimates the true philosophical foundation or reason for Cicero's promulgation of the modified Stoic moral restraints on political ambition. The dream teaches that it is not ruling, but only thinking, and understanding achieved through thinking, that satisfies the sovereign part of the human soul. This is the reason why peace and leisure, or freedom from business of all kinds, are preferable to war and conquest and action. This understanding of things is what allowed Scipio to confront squarely the fact that even the best regime is too tarnished by its need to serve its own material and physical interests to be a tenable object of devotion or to satisfy the most important human spiritual needs. Still, as Scipio's and Cicero's whole lives so vividly indicate, the life of thinking is for humans a life that includes sharing or generosity, and above all the generosity of awakening the gifted young and promoting the virtuous and leisured political conditions most conducive to their preservation. The theoretical life cannot then be divorced from the life of civic action. Support for republican freedom receives a high justification, in the final analysis, insofar but only insofar as it makes possible or conduces to the promotion of the theoretical life.

Yet the dream of Scipio also indicates why it is so difficult for humans to arrive at and to accept this insight. In their primary manifestations, political ambition and devotion to the city, and the imperial expansion to which such ambition and devotion naturally lead, are fueled by hopes that are strong but that lack an adequate or coherent basis. Those hopes attain a firm basis, and political ambition discovers its necessary limits, only inasmuch as the hopes may be chastened and transformed, through severely self-critical reflection, and thus redirected toward the contemplative life. Scipio points the reader to the right critical questions by reporting the dream as having revealed that the life of public service is justified because through it one wins for oneself a great reward: a heavenly afterlife in the company of the immortal gods, who are absorbed in the contemplation and scientific study of nature. The dream teaches that the sooner the gods allow one to flee from this political life to that other contemplative life, the better. (As Cicero proves through arguments delivered in his own name in the Prologue to the *Republic,* it is not possible to flee political life and its responsibilities so long as one dwells on this earth; but "those of the highest authority and glory among the learned" perform their public service not necessarily "through engaging in public affairs but through investigating and writing about many political matters" [1.12]).

The dream thus presents the superiority of the contemplative life to the active life in a curiously complicated manner. Even while stating the superiority of contemplation, the dream holds up before us, as in a mirror, the strongest reason why we are unable or unwilling to accept the subordination of the active to the contemplative life. The dream appears to teach that one ought to sacrifice, to curtail in some substantial measure, the good of contemplation in this life—one ought to devote oneself to the prisonlike duty of politics in this life—because thereby one will become deserving of the promised reward of eternal contemplation in the next life (6.15–16). In this roundabout way, politics comes to be worthy of devotion. But the dream also notes in passing that some "learned men employ their outstanding minds on divine studies in their human lives" (6.18–19). The account thus provokes the question, Why not bend one's political efforts to maximizing the greatest good, the contemplative life, for oneself as well as others here on earth? Why is one commanded to sacrifice or to diminish for oneself the greatest good? Or is it only a temporary good that one is commanded to curtail, in order to achieve an enduring good? But then how is the curtailing of a lesser good in order to achieve a greater good a sacrifice? Why does it make one deserving of a reward? The dream in this way directs the reader's attention to the question of the rational basis for the hopeful belief in the divine providence that promises an afterlife. At the same time, the dream alerts us to the importance, in the psychology of the political man, of the concerns for the afterlife and for providence in one form or another. The dream thus helps us to see the great role played by providence in the moral beliefs that place some effective restraint on the imperialist leanings or longings natural to political men. Yet Cicero's wish to promote such restraint is modified by his wish to help others move toward an understanding of the true providence.

Cicero's agreement with his philosophical spokesman Scipio, as opposed to his Stoic spokesman Laelius, is indicated by Cicero's repeated declarations that he can accept only those portions of Stoic ethics that are consistent with and already implicit in the political philosophy of Plato and Aristotle, who, Cicero insists (following his Scipio [cf. *Republic* 2.22]), are in complete agreement in substance and differ only in their terminology. Yet Cicero seems to go beyond his character Scipio inasmuch as Cicero identifies himself as a "Platonic Skeptic" and contends that a cautious and responsible skepticism is the true heart of the Socratism shared by Plato and Aristotle and their authentic students. Cicero observes that the original Platonists and Aristotelians, in sharp contrast to the Stoics, made the theory and practice of rhetoric, as well as the careful and critical study of laws and of regimes, central to their political philosophy. Highlighting the absence of these studies, especially that of rhetoric, from Stoicism, Cicero raises the doubt whether the Stoics in fact have any political philosophy worthy of the name. Certainly he argues that it is only the Socratic study of rhetoric that equips one to present in a constructive fashion the paradoxes uncovered by the Socratic philosopher and to derive from those paradoxes maxims and precepts useful in actual political life. In undertaking this complex task, the flexible rhetorical skill of the true Socratic can make excellent use of the Stoic natural law terminology.[15] According to Cicero, the true Socratic writes in such a way that he need not declare his own views but may leave his teaching at a politically responsible provocation to the reader to think for himself: "Socrates' many-faceted principle of dialectic, and the variety of his subjects and the greatness of his genius, the memory of which has been made sacred in Plato's writings, have produced many kinds of warring philosophers, among which we follow as much as possible those whom we judge closest to the way of Socrates, concealing our own views while relieving others of error and in every dispute seeking what has the greatest similarity to truth."[16]

As he elaborates his refurbished version of Stoic natural law, Cicero never allows his reader to lose sight of the Socratic thesis that virtue is knowledge, or depends decisively on knowledge, and hence that genuine or perfect virtue is available only to the tiny minority who are truly wise and philosophical—a minority from which are excluded, Cicero sternly observes, many of those who claim or appear to be philosophical.[17] In particular, Cicero makes it plain that he thinks the Stoics as well as the Cynics have misrepresented the elastic and skeptical spirit of authentic Socratic wisdom. The deepest ground of Cicero's disagreement with all the Stoics comes to sight in the course of his questioning of their doctrine of divine providence:[18] this doubt has profound and far-reaching consequences for every level of Cicero's practical as well as his theoretical teaching. Among other things, it renders problematic the Stoic notion of a world government, and it puts a question mark after the Stoic claims of divine enforcement of the natural law, particularly in international relations and times of war.

Cicero presents his sustained criticism of the Stoic doctrine of providence not in his own name but through the mouth of a character named Gaius Cotta in the dialogue *On the Nature of the Gods*. Cicero, speaking as a character in this dialogue, evinces an anxious awareness of the potentially dangerous consequences of a discussion of providence. After all, as he reminds his interlocutors, he holds the office of high priest of the ancestral Roman religion. In Cicero's presence, Cotta responds to a presentation of the Stoic teaching on providence given by the Stoic Balbus (whose words I have quoted previously). Like Cicero himself, Cotta is a Platonic Skeptic who also happens to hold the office of high priest; mindful of his sacerdotal responsibilities, Cotta proclaims that he "always has and always will defend the opinions we accept from our ancestors together with the sacred ceremonies and rites." At the same time, he remarks, the ancestral creed is a matter of belief or faith, not philosophical demonstration, and therefore nothing in the divine law requires him to accept the theology of the Stoics (cf. *On Divination* 2.28). The Stoic Balbus, for his part, laments the fact that his friend Cotta and the Platonic Skeptics in general, whose integrity and gifts he admires, have "shifting and unsettled views of the immortal gods, and not, as our school, stable and certain views." As Vattel was later to stress, Cotta certainly eschews atheism, as does Cicero in his own name in the prologue to the drama.[19] In concluding his refutation of the Stoic doctrine of providence, Cotta insists that he has presented the case against Stoic providence only in order to be himself refuted; his last words declare his certainty that in the next round of the dialogue Balbus will easily vindicate the Stoic teaching. Cicero, however, never wrote this dialogue of vindication, and in this crucial sense the dialogue on the nature of the gods is "unfinished."[20] Instead, Cicero wrote his dialogue *On Divi-*

nation, an explicit sequel, in which Cicero in his own name questions the Stoic doctrine of divination, which he characterizes as "the very citadel of the Stoics."[21] Nevertheless, Cicero does himself conclude *On the Nature of the Gods* (3.93–95) by saying that while the Epicurean character, Vellius, found "Cotta's argument truer," to Cicero himself, "that of Balbus seemed to be closer to an image of the truth."[22]

Cotta is not satisfied to show the incoherence of attributing moral and civic virtues to gods understood as perfect beings, for he admits that this proves only that the gods as perfect beings and their providence are unintelligible, not that they do not exist (*On the Nature of the Gods* 3.38–39). Nor does Cotta leave his challenge at the level of an argument from the observable facts—the difficulties in explaining why the gods gave reason to humans in such a way as to allow most to abuse it and why they manifestly fail to punish the wicked, to compensate the heroic, or to protect the decent weak (3.66–85). (Balbus does not anticipate or resolve these difficulties by reference to an afterlife, perhaps because he has been penetrated by the implications of the Stoic contention that devotion to virtue as the sole highest good compels one to hold that immortality would add nothing to happiness [2.153].) Cotta seems to make his most telling point dialectically, when he responds to what he knows will be the Stoic rebuttal of the argument from the observable facts: the Stoics say that the gods are not concerned with the minor things but only with the major. To this Cotta observes that what "all mortals" hope for from the gods are the external goods of fortune and not the virtues that are for the Stoics supposedly the only true goods; "And this with good reason, because it is on account of virtue that we are justly praised and it is in our virtue that we rightly glorify ourselves, which would not be possible if we received virtue as a gift of god and did not attain it by ourselves."[23] With these reflections Cotta prompts his listeners to wonder why the Stoics care so much about providence and whether this care or hope, which is obviously not unrelated to their care for praise and glory, is not at some tension with that unqualified devotion to virtue as the end in itself that alone can make them deserving of providential support and whose absence can make others, when they lack such devotion, deserving of providential punishment.

The implicit question as to the coherence of the self-understanding underlying Stoic virtue reminds one of the major question Cicero addresses to the Stoics in his own name (in a very different context) in the dialogue *On the Ends of the Good and Bad Things.* Cicero suggests to Cato, the exemplar of Roman and Stoic virtue, that the Stoics have failed in self-knowledge inasmuch as they deny the Aristotelian thought that happiness depends on more than moral virtue, since happiness depends on the satisfaction of our natural needs, as the Stoics cannot deny except by verbal quibbles. Cicero then suggests that if or insofar as the strong-souled Stoic becomes fully honest with himself, he will return to the older wisdom of Plato and Aristotle. (Yet in this conversation with the noble Cato, Cicero cautiously refrains from presenting Platonism as a form of skepticism and makes little reference to the theoretical life.)

Cicero's suggestion, to the effect that self-critical reflection on the incoherence of Stoicism will lead a strong soul back to Platonism, may provide a clue for understanding the most obvious dramatic and substantive weakness in Cotta's challenge to the belief in providence in the dialogue *On the Nature of the Gods.* For Cotta really offers nothing but counter-assertion and gentle ridicule as his reply to that specific sort of evidence Balbus adduces when he appeals to immediate revelations from the gods, revelations experienced in visions, dreams, and prophecies.[24] Cotta and his creator Cicero thus cause one to wonder whether they think it possible to refute directly such evidence. But perhaps Cicero tacitly indicates that the religious experiences, or the memory and interpretation of them, take on a transformed character for one who has had the strength of soul fully to digest and to assimilate the Ciceronian critique of the incoherence at the heart of the Stoic concern for the good. Certainly the dream of Cicero's quasi-philosophical spokesman Scipio (*Republic* 6.9–end) is of a very different character, in substance and in provenance and therefore in the self-reflection that it provokes, from any of the dreams or revelations to which the Stoic Balbus refers.

In the dialogue *On Divination,* an emphatically private conversation between Cicero and his brother, we learn from the brother the momentous fact that Cicero himself has been vouchsafed divine revelation (in addition to the sense of divine inspiration he may manifest when delivering a moving oration [1.81]). While fleeing into exile, Cicero experienced a dream-vision in which a god appeared to him and comforted him with a somewhat enigmatic promise that he would find salvation (*salutem*) through that god or that god's temple. Yet Cicero's brother, in reminding Cicero of this impressive event, also reports that Cicero did not declare the dream to be an authentic revelation until the prophecy was in fact validated by the subsequent events; the revelation or the experience of revelation was not, then, self-validating. It was only after Cicero saw for himself that the god had fulfilled the promise of salvation in an intelligible way that Cicero declared, with somewhat odd phrasing, "It is not possible for anything to be more divine than that dream" (1.58–59). Cicero is apparently convinced, on the basis of his own experience as well as reasoning, that it is not possible to maintain consistently and seriously that the gods play with men, or, in other words, he implies that no experience can be sustained as revelatory in the strict sense if it does not implicate an intelligible good. What is more, this conviction is shared by Cicero's brother—the defender, if not of the Stoics, then at any rate of prophetic revelation through dreams and visions (2.100), who is convinced that he has also experienced personal revelation through dreams (1.58). The brother contends, appealing to the authority of Plato's *Republic* 571c–572b, that vivid dreams in which one encounters gods may be false if they do not conform to reason; such "false" dreams, even when they involve the apparition of a god, may be ascribed to poor digestion. This far-reaching concession sets the stage for book 2 of the dialogue on divination, in which Cicero discloses to his brother for the first time (after both have moved indoors and are seated together alone in a room) that on reflection he has become convinced that the apparently revelatory dream he had was nothing more than a dream, with a perfectly natural explanation.[25]

The Ciceronian Moral Code of International Relations

Cicero's reluctance to accept the Stoic teaching on providence helps us to understand not only the differences between the political theory of Scipio and the sermon of Laelius but also the reasons for the ambiguities that characterize Cicero's account, in his own name, of the natural law limits on international relations and warfare. Cicero makes his most important pronouncements on this subject in his treatise *On Duties (De Officiis)*. This is a work whose style and form can be characterized by saying that it represents what would today be called "an open letter to my son." As a self-consciously public paternal sermon, *On Duties* appears intended primarily as a manual for young Romans who are about to begin their careers as administrators and policemen of the imperial system (see esp. 3.6), in which the principal task is no longer the sharing in the republican rule of citizens over one another but rather the rule of a few so-called citizens over countless thousands of strangers. It is not surprising, then, to find that in this book Cicero conspicuously declares himself to be following Stoic ethics as much as possible, and not only when they coincide with Platonic and Aristotelian ethics.[26]

The treatise is divided into three parts or books: the first shows how the duties come to sight when we focus on moral virtue (the *honestum*) as our supreme end; the second part shows how duties manifest themselves when we focus on our natural pursuit of the expedient (*utile*), that is, the secondary, external goods of the body, of prosperity, and of honor; the third part teaches how to judge conflicts between the apparently moral and the apparently expedient. Near the beginning of the third part (3.12–17), Cicero discloses more starkly than he has previously that his entire treatise does not in fact have as its theme true virtue, or the virtue known to and practiced only by the wise, but instead treats a "second rank" of virtue that makes its possessors and practitioners "resemble"—especially in the eyes of "the multitude" or the "vulgar" (*volgus*)—the truly moral or virtuous men. (Thus for example, Cicero says, the multitude or the vulgar mistakenly suppose that men like Marcus Cato and Gaius Laelius were wise.) If the treatise *On Duties* had dealt with true virtue, Cicero concedes, it would have been arguably improper to introduce a comparison between the virtuous and the expedient, or the third part would have been superfluous, since—as we know on the authority of Socrates, Cicero reminds us (3.11)—the knowers of true virtue see clearly that the greatest good by far is the practice of that virtue that fulfills their souls; and serious conflict between such a great, intrinsic good and external, secondary goods would be ruled out. But since the virtues Cicero has been teaching in this treatise do not in fact truly constitute the fulfillment of the soul, since the greatest good they can bring is that they may help us to "progress" toward that distant true virtue, and since, moreover, those to whom he is addressing this teaching lack wisdom, it becomes an important task to try to dispel for them the spurious charms that tempt them to abandon their secondary virtue for the sake of apparently great external goods. For this purpose especially, says Cicero, it is well to follow the Stoics rather than the Platonists and the Aristotelians (3.19–20).

It is with this introduction that Cicero presents his most explicit teaching on the law of nature or the "law of nations." He begins with a stern declaration: "Therefore, for any party to take something from another, and for a man to enhance his well being by another man's loss, is more contrary to nature than is death, poverty, pain, or any other ill that can befall the body or external things" (3.21). To establish this principle, Cicero brings to bear an amazingly disparate series of arguments. First, he contends, "the human race" is naturally united in a "society" comparable to that of the parts of the body, and in such an organic community, the whole and all the parts will obviously die if the parts cease to consider their own welfare as merged into that of the whole (3.21–22). Second, not only is there a "law of nations" that upholds this principle, but the principle is also sanctioned with penalties of death, exile, imprisonment, and fine by the positive laws of the distinct and various peoples (3.23). But in the third place, however, Cicero hastens to add, the principle follows "much more" from the "reason which belongs to nature, and which is the divine as well as human law." This appears to be the case when one considers that "excellence and greatness of soul, along with comity, justice, and generosity, are much more according to nature than are pleasure, life, and riches" and that it "belongs to a great and excellent soul to contemn and hold as naught the latter goods in comparison with the common good" (3.23–24). Indeed, Cicero continues, "It is more according to nature to undergo the greatest labors and troubles in order to help and save all nations, if possible, in the manner of the heroic Hercules, whom human fame has assigned for the memory of his beneficial actions a place in the council of heaven, than it is to live in solitude not only free from troubles but reveling in the greatest pleasures and abounding in riches and excelling in beauty and strength" (3.25). Fourth and finally, to act against nature and her justice is to betray ignorance of the fact that in so doing one is injuring one's own soul, or inflicting a harm on oneself that outweighs any advantage one can possibly procure (3.26). Having lined up this imposing array of widely differing arguments, Cicero combines them in an imprecise but rhetorically powerful summation:

> If nature has prescribed this, that a human being should want to take care of another human being, whoever he may be, simply for the reason that he is a human being, then according to the same nature it is necessary that the interest of each is a common interest. If this is so, we are all embraced by one and the same law of nature; and if this is so, we are certainly prohibited by the law of nature from doing wrong to another. . . . Moreover, those who say that citizens must be respected, but not outsiders, sunder the common association of the human race; once this is gone, kindness, generosity, goodness, and justice are utterly destroyed; and those who destroy this must be judged impious even toward the immortal gods. The association set

> up by the latter among human beings is what they uproot; and the closest link in this association is the judgment that it is more against nature for a human being to take something, for the sake of his own welfare, from another human being than it is to suffer any loss to his external goods, body, or even his soul, so long as he retains justice. (3.27–28)

It is the invocation of the gods, it would seem, that clinches the case. Nonetheless, Cicero maintains his reserve in regard to divine providence.

After later raising—as a purely hypothetical question, to be sure—the possibility that the gods do not see all our actions (3.37 and 3.39), he explains the sanction for an oath by the gods: the one who swears such an oath "ought to remember that he has god as the witness, that is, as I judge, his own mind, than which god himself has given nothing more divine to men."[27]

Cicero does entertain an objection: "If a wise man were starving to death, might he not take the food of another useless human?" "No," Cicero replies; "My life is not more useful to me than is the temper of soul that prevents me from hurting another for my welfare." But what if "a good man were freezing to death; could he not rob the clothing from a cruel and inhuman tyrant?" To this Cicero replies that in all such cases, one must consider whether such an act were simply for one's own benefit or were to enable one to continue to do acts of public benefit: "The law of nature itself, which continues and preserves the good of mankind, dictates that the belongings of an idle and useless person should be transferred to a wise, good, and strong man in order that he may have the necessities of life without which there would be a great loss to the common good" (3.29–31). And as for the tyrant, "We have no society with a tyrant," and "it is not contrary to nature to rob someone whom, if one can, it is a moral duty to kill," just as "limbs are amputated" when "they jeopardize the other parts of the body" (3.32).

It thus becomes evident that in judging what is meant by the harm or injury done to another person or nation, one must always look not just to the welfare of the particular individuals or nations involved but to how their lives and well-being affect the overall balance of the good of humanity at large. Now the greatest good of humanity by far is served by the promotion of virtue or excellence as the supreme end; and to grasp that supreme end more precisely, so as to be able to reason properly in cases of serious moral conflicts, we must consider Cicero's treatment of the virtues in book 1 of his treatise.

The starting point of the teaching on duties that Cicero offers his son is an emphatic affirmation of the primacy by nature of the theoretical virtues, which conduce to "a happy life" and "greatness of soul and a contempt for the human things." We ascend to the "inquiry and investigation into the truth" when "we are free from business" or "lack-of-leisure." It is, however, "against duty to be led by such study away from the things that need doing"; for "the whole glory of virtue is found in action." "As Plato admirably wrote [Ninth Letter 358a], we are not born solely for ourselves, but our fatherland claims a share of us, as do our friends, and, in addition, as the Stoics hold, everything the earth holds was created for the use of humanity, and men moreover were generated for the sake of men."[28]

Within this framework Cicero treats the virtue of justice, and, in the context of his discussion of punitive justice, sets down his famous formulation of the "laws of war" (*iura belli*). Indeed, as much as a quarter of Cicero's thematic treatment of justice is taken up by the discussion of justice in war. To begin with, Cicero (in good Socratic fashion) drastically downgrades retributive justice in the name of deterrence and rehabilitation: "There are, moreover, certain duties to be observed even toward those by whom you have been done an injustice. In fact there is a proper way to exact retribution and to punish; I know that it suffices if that party, who has committed wrong, should repent the wrongdoing, in order that he should not do it again and others be deterred from injustice" (1.33; see also 1.88–89, 3.32). Cicero then writes these well-known lines: "In a republic the laws of war are to be maintained to the highest degree. For as there are two ways of deciding an issue, one through discussion, the other through force, the former appropriate for human beings, the latter for beasts, if one is not permitted to use the superior method recourse must be had to the inferior. Wherefore wars must be undertaken for this cause: that life may go on in peace without injustice" (1.34–35). This passage certainly implies that war is just when it is undertaken as a last resort in order to maintain the peace by punishing, and thereby deterring, serious and deliberate or at least uncompensated injuries carried out by a guilty state against an innocent state. It is easy to assume that Cicero also means that war is just *only* when it is undertaken as such punishment. But, as we shall see presently, this impression turns out to be very misleading.

Cicero continues: "When, however, victory has been procured, those who were not cruel or monstrous in the war must be given their lives." To exemplify the generosity appropriate to the victor who acts according to these principles, and who thus promotes peace and fellowship even among former enemies, Cicero adduces Roman republican behavior. But his list of examples cannot avoid becoming dubious, not to say ugly; and Cicero is compelled to add, "It is my opinion that a peace must always be concluded that is an honest peace; and had my opinion on this matter been the rule, we would now have, if not the best republic, at least a republic—which we now lack utterly."[29] Are there then natural sanctions, of a kind, for violations of this law defining just war? Is the death of the Roman Republic not an illustration of such sanctions? Did not the failure of the Roman Republic to seek always an honest peace contribute decisively to its decline and fall?

Much later, in book 2 of the treatise on duty, where Cicero turns from the consideration of duty insofar as it is dictated by the morally right to a second consideration of it insofar as it is dictated by the expedient, he answers these questions strongly in the affirmative:

> The truth is that as long as the empire of the Roman people was maintained through acts of beneficence rather than injustices, wars were waged either on behalf of allies or for the empire, wars were terminated with clemency or only the necessary harshness, our senate was a refuge for kings, populaces, and nations, our magistrates and rulers strove to win glory only from the equitable and faithful defense of provinces and allies; and thus our rule could more truly be called a paternal protectorate of the entire earth rather than an empire.[30] This policy and discipline declined gradually, and in truth after Sulla's victory we abandoned it. . . . By Justice, then, are we being punished. If we had not allowed the crimes of many to go unpunished, such license would never have come to center on one man. . . . And thus while the house walls of the city stand and remain—though even they now fear the worst crimes—the true republic we have completely lost. (2.26–29)

The history of republican Rome illustrates the natural sanctions against unjust empire inasmuch as the growth of the Roman Republic's collective practice of exploiting its neighbors, leading finally to open tyranny over them, eventually (and naturally) induced in leading individual Romans the same practice and the same attitude toward their fellow citizens.

Let us note in passing that Cicero's praise of the beneficence that marked the old republic's just wars implies that the prosecutor of a just war may be not only the injured party but a greater nation that generously takes up the cause of vindicating the injured.

Returning to Cicero's discussion of the laws of war in the context of the treatment of duty inasmuch as duty is dictated simply by what is right (1.35), we next learn that the laws of war and their underlying principle—the promotion of peace without injustice—not only define the just causes of war but also place limits on the conduct of war: "And since peace is to be concluded with those whom we have conquered by force, it is also the case that we must welcome those who lay down their arms and seek refuge in the word of our commanders, even if their walls have been hammered." In this respect at any rate, Cicero asserts, Rome has obeyed the laws of war. Moreover, the code of the Roman people teaches that "no war is just unless satisfaction has first been demanded or a denunciation as well as a declaration has been issued"; further, Roman republican practice shows that "it is not lawful for one who is not formally enrolled as a soldier to fight against the enemy."[31]

Much later and in a different context, Cicero adds that since "there is moreover a law also in war," "faith and the laws of swearing are often to be kept with enemies." He explains the qualification "often" by contrasting war waged against a "common enemy of all mankind" (a pirate, for example), in dealing with whom we are free to break our word or oath, with war waged against a "just and legitimate enemy, with regard to whom there holds the Roman code as well as many common laws."[32] Even an enemy whose aggression threatens the existence of our own nation does not necessarily become by virtue of that criminality an enemy of all mankind, and such an aggressor ought therefore to continue to enjoy respect and the consequent rights dictated by the laws of war. For with such an enemy we may hope one day to resume peaceful relations that require the continuation of trust. It is only an enemy who has, in effect, declared war on all nations, or on humanity as such, with whom we lose all such hope and who therefore loses the claim to such respect and to those rights.

Yet we must observe that this discussion of the exceptions to the law dictating the upholding of promises to enemies comes in the course of a general discussion of exceptions permitting deceit and infidelity, in cases where agreements have not "been secured through force or fraud." In other words, Cicero denies that promises, even when freely given and entered into with respectable parties, ought always to be kept. Further, he goes on to deny that there is any single rule of honor or justice that ought to be maintained in every circumstance. Near the outset of his treatise *On Duties,* and just before his discussion of the laws of war, Cicero lays down this far-reaching Socratic principle:

> Occasions often arise when those things, that seem most worthy of a just man, and of the man we call "the good man," are changed into their contrary—as for example, returning a deposit or fulfilling a promise; and what pertains to truth and fidelity sometimes changes, and it becomes just not to maintain them. It is necessary to refer to that which I laid down at the outset as the foundation of justice: first, that no harm be done to anyone, and second that the common utility be served. When the latter changes with time, duty changes and does not always remain the same. . . . Promises are not to be kept therefore, which are of no utility to the persons to whom one promised; nor, if the keeping does greater harm to you than it does good to the one to whom you promised, is it against duty to prefer the greater good to the lesser. (1.31–32)

Duty, it would seem, requires us to follow that line of conduct that will maximize the welfare of all the members of the relevant community to which we belong and of whose general welfare we partake, but for the sake of which we and other members may be called upon to make great and even ultimate sacrifices of our own welfare. It is not entirely clear how the common good can then claim to be the good also of those who sacrifice or are sacrificed for it, unless perhaps one were to say that the sacrifice is merely apparent, since it represents the act of virtue that is the supreme good of the soul. In that case, however, it is unclear why one should not maximize the apparent sacrifice of the whole community rather than its welfare. What is clear is that Cicero's speaking of a "law" of nature, or of reason, or of the god of reason—or indeed his equation of reason and law—must be understood very loosely. Reason's dictates cannot be expressed as law in any strict sense because every law must be reevaluated and modified in light of each new set of circumstances. Without such looseness or far-reaching qualification, the rule of law becomes the cause of harm: the rule of law becomes the rule of stupidity and thus a violation of both nature and reason.

We recall that according to Laelius's formulation in the *Republic* (3.34), natural "law" legitimates not only wars undertaken for defense but also those undertaken for honor.[33] In *On Duties,* Cicero makes it clear that the principles I have just cited may render war legitimate between two powers each of whom believes the other is challenging its own deserved exercise and extension of rule and of reputation. He would seem to hold that the common good of the community of nations is advanced in these cases by virtue of the fact that such wars—if they are limited, both in the scope of empire they seek and in the means they employ—represent a natural expression or extension of healthy republican ambition to rule (and thus also of healthy ambition to care for the whole community of mankind [see Dante *On Monarchy* 2.5, 2.10]). In such wars, fought for glorious supremacy and only incidentally or secondarily for defense, specific principles come into play, grounded in man's shared political nature and the respect due that nature. "When it is truly the case that war is fought for supremacy, and glory is what is sought, the causes must nonetheless in every way conform to what I said a little before about the just causes of war. But these wars, in which the glory of rule is the end, must be waged with less bitterness—just as even with a fellow citizen we contend in one way if he is an enemy, in another if he is a rival (with the one we contend for honor and dignity, with the other for our heads and reputations)." Thus, for example, prisoners taken in such a war ought to be freed without ransom. The just cause legitimating this kind of war renders it doubtful whether either party can be said to have committed an injustice in initiating hostilities. Expansion, within certain vague limits, and hence bloody if invigorating collision with other robust and growing republics, would seem to be an inevitable concomitant of healthy republican life. Cicero cannot exhort his son to be a good Roman without reminding him of the dedication to expansion that was an essential aspect of the noblest era of Roman republicanism: "Those who would guard the republic should . . . by whatever means they can, either in war or at home, augment the republic by empire, farmlands, and revenues. These are the things that belong to great men, these are the things that were performed over and over again in our forefather's time, and those who pursue these kinds of duties will attain, along with the supreme advantage of the republic, both gratitude and a great glory."[34]

When he turns from the virtue of justice to that of generosity, Cicero treats what is owed to strangers in peacetime. The general principle of generosity is that "to the degree to which persons are conjoined, in the same proportion they should be shown kindness" (1.50). To clarify the proper ranking of the degrees of social conjunction and therefore of obligation, we must consider what are "the natural principles of human community and society." The "first principle, which is found in the society of the whole race of human beings," is "reason and speech, which through teaching, learning, communicating, discussing, and judging bring humans together." "In no other respect are we farther removed from the nature of the beasts." From these principles it would seem to follow that we are the more closely bound and obliged to our fellows, of whatever nation, in proportion to the degree to which we share with them an active life of rational intercourse. Yet this turns out to be only qualifiedly true. Closer than our bond to the species is that to our fellows with whom we share "people, nation, and language"; closer still is the bond with our fellow citizens; still closer is the family bond, which is the "first principle of the city and as it were the seminary of public life." The principle determining this ranking is the following: "The desire to procreate is the nature common to animals." "Still," Cicero adds, "of all social relations, none is more excellent, none firmer, than when good men of similar character are joined"; "nothing is more conducive to love and union than the similarity of good character." The kinship of the soul is found in the friend, not in the family. There is a manifest split or strain in Cicero's list of the degrees of attachment and obligation, between what is owed to family and what is owed to virtuous friends outside the family (friends who may not even be of the same city or ethnic group).[35] The tension is apparently overcome by the assertion that no social bond is more serious or more dear than patriotism, since the civic association incorporates all the others. More specifically, Cicero concludes, "We owe the necessary material things most" to fatherland and parents and then, in the second place, to the rest of our family; and we owe "the community of living, giving counsel, speeches, exhortations, consolation, and sometimes even reproof, most to friends." These richly ambiguous, not to say contradictory, reflections (1.50–58; cf. 1.160) form the basis for Cicero's famous pronouncement on general obligations to strangers:

> The community in all things that nature brings forth for the common use of human beings is to be maintained so that the goods distributed

> by the laws and civil right may be held as those laws dictate, while all other goods should be used in compliance with the proverb of the Greeks, "all the things of friends are in common." These common possessions of all men seem to be, however, things of the kind set down by Ennius, and what he declares as regards one type of good may be applied to many types: "A man who, to one astray, graciously points out the way does it as one lights a torch from his own torch. No less light does it shed for him when he has lit the other's." From this one example the general lesson is clear enough: let whatever can be given away without detriment be bestowed, even on a stranger. From which we derive those common principles: do not check flowing water, allow the lighting of his fire at your fire, if someone asks, give him trustworthy counsel in his deliberations; give whatever is useful to those who receive but not hurtful to the giver. These principles should be followed, and we should always be contributing something to the common utility. But since the resources of individuals are meager, and the needy are infinite in number, ordinary generosity must be reckoned within the limits prescribed by Ennius: "No less light does it shed for him," so that we may have the means to be generous to our own. (1.51–52)

From this it follows, as Cicero subsequently remarks, that "they do wrong who keep strangers from the use of their cities and exclude them; . . . to prohibit strangers from the use of one's city is inhuman" (3.47).

Yet precisely in these pronouncements Cicero implicitly reaffirms the fundamental classical contention about the principle of natural right that ought to guide political life: the strongest natural human attachment, and therefore obligation, is to one's city and to one's true kin. From this it follows that whatever we owe to all other human beings, simply on account of our common humanity, is dwarfed in significance and substance by what we owe to our fellow citizens and true kin, given the richer common good and hence far closer ties that bind us to them.

Notes

This essay was originally published as "Classical Cosmopolitanism: The Stoics and Cicero," in *Justice among Nations: On the Moral Basis of Power and Peace*, by Thomas L. Pangle and Peter J. Ahrensdorf (Lawrence: Univ. Press of Kansas, 1999), 51–72.

1. Cicero *On Duties* 1.1–3, 2.2–6, 2.23, 2.29, 2.65, 2.67, 2.75–76, 3.1–4; *On the Nature of the Gods* 1.7; *Republic* 1.6–7; *On Divination* 1.2; 2.6–7.

2. See, e.g., *On Duties* 3.23, 3.69. For Cicero, and generally thereafter until Francisco Suàrez, *De Legibus Ac Deo Legislatore: In Decem Libros Distributus* (Conimbricae: Apud Didacum Gomez de Lourevro, 1612; see 2.19.8; see also Isidore of Seville *Of Etymologies or Origins* 5.4–7), the "law of nations" was a term referring not simply or primarily to international law, regulating relations among nations and alien individuals, but more broadly to that law or body of legal principles that seems to be commonly held by all civilized peoples; for example, the principle that theft is a punishable offense. International law—for example, the sanctity of ambassadors and "laws of war"—would be a major subdivision of the "law of nations" so understood (see, for example, Livy 2.4, 5.27, 5.36, 5.51, 6.1). See Ernest Nys, *Le droit de la guerre et les précurseurs de Grotius* (Brussels: A. Castaigne, 1910), 9–13; and Coleman Phillipson, *International Law and Custom of Ancient Greece and Rome* (London: Macmillan, 1911), 1:57–58, 70–85, 89–97. Cf. Aristotle *Rhetoric* 1368b7–9, on the "common law" as compromising "whatever unwritten matters seem to be agreed on by everyone."

3. Plutarch, in what is probably a deliberate rhetorical exaggeration, goes so far as to suggest that there is a link between Zeno of Citium's *Republic* and Alexander the Great's cosmopolitan imperial vision (*On the Fortune or Virtue of Alexander the Great* 329a–b. And Philo Judaeus (*On the Creation of the World* 3 and 142–43) contends that the biblical account of creation in Genesis is meant to teach the Stoic notion of cosmopolitan natural law and world citizenship (in other words, the principles of Stoicism are in fact the principles of the biblical God).

4. Xenophon *Symposium* 2.9–13, 3.4–12, 4.1–6, 4.34–45, 4.61–64, 6.5, 8.3–7. Diogenes Laertius *Lives of the Eminent Philosophers* bk.7 (on Zeno and other Stoics), secs. 1–3, 19 with bk. 6 (on the Cynics), secs. 1–2, 14, 19, 85, 104; Sextus Empiricus *Outlines of Pyrrhonism* 3.200 and context; for the best collection of the fragments and testimonials of Antisthenes, the Cynics generally, and other Socratic precursors of Stoicism, see Giannantoni, ed., *Socratis et Socraticorum Reliquiae,* 2.139–509, 523–89, 648–52; for the scholarly debate over the reliability of the philosophical genealogy offered by Diogenes Laertius, and over the precise relationship of Antisthenes to Cynicism, see Giannantoni's discussion at 3.223–33 and 3.512–27.

5. Diogenes Laertius *Lives of the Eminent Philosophers* bk. 6, secs. 5, 29, 37, 42, 54, 63–64, 69–74; bk. 7, secs. 25–26, 52, 86–89, 91, 99–109, 119–25, 128–31 134–39, 142–43, 147–49, 151, 160, 165; Dio Chrysostom *Discourses* 1.42, 14.16, 15.31, 36.17–38, 59.4; Sextus Empiricus *Against the Dogmatists 5 (Against the Ethicists)* 22–27, 59–67, 73–78, 180–81, 190–94, 200–201; Plutarch *On Stoic Self-Contradictions; Of Common Conceptions, Against the Stoics;* Von Arnim, ed., *Stoicorum Veterum Fragmenta,* vol. 1, frags. 190, 192,

195; vol. 2, frags. 528, 1195; vol. 3, frags. of Chrysippus, etc., 16, 314, 323, 324, 327, 330, 354, 366, 548, 567, 604–5, 611, 632, 638, 650, 654, 656, 690, 694, 729, 746, 750, 764, and frag. 117 of Philodemus, 241–42; Cicero *On the Ends of the Good and Bad Things* bk. 3, esp. secs. 11–14, 21–39, 41–73, and bk. 4, secs. 14–15, 20, 26–43, 45–60, 68–73; *Academica* 1.35–39; *On the Nature of the Gods* 1.16, 1.36–41, 2.1–167; *On Divination* bk. 1, secs. 6, 37, 39, 56–57, 72, 82–84, 118, 125–31; bk. 2, secs. 35–36, 88, 90, 100–102, 130; and Seneca *Of Leisure* 4, 6, 8. The ethical teachings of Epictetus seem to have been close to those of the original Stoics; for the persistent admiration of Cynicism, see Arrian's *Discourses of Epictetus,* esp. 3.22, "On the Cynic Calling."

6. Diogenes Laertius *Lives of the Eminent Philosophers* bk. 6, secs. 11, 29, 37, 72, 74; bk. 7, secs. 33–34, 100, 121–25, 131, 188–89; *Stoicorum Veterum Fragmenta,* vol. 1, frags. 216, 228; vol. 3, frags. 54, 332, 544, 560, 563, 587, 589, 598–603, 613–19, 623, 625–26, 640, 658, 660–69, 677; Cicero *Oration in Defense of L. Murena* 61; *On the Ends of the Good and Bad Things* 3.48, 3.68, 3.75–76, 4.7, 4.21–23, 4.55–56, 4.74; *Laws* 3.14; *Lucullus* (or *Academica* bk. 2) 136–37; *On Duties* 1.128, 1.148; *Tusculan Disputations* 4.54. For an instructive discussion of the sources and an intelligent critique of the recent scholarship, see Paul A. Vander Waerdt, "Zeno's *Republic* and the Origins of Natural Law," in *The Socratic Movement,* ed. Paul A. Vander Waerdt (Ithaca, NY: Cornell Univ. Press, 1994), 272–308.

7. Consider, for example, Plutarch's remark in *On Tranquillity of Mind* 472a ("Some think the Stoics speak in jest, when they hear them assert that the wise man is not only prudent and just and courageous, but also is the orator and poet and general and rich man and king") and what Plutarch reports, with apparent censure, of the bewildering contradictions that characterize Chrysippus's writings: "He has, not occasionally but frequently, confirmed arguments that are contrary to his doctrines, and so stoutly, and so earnestly and with such love of honor, that it is not easy to discover what he prefers" (*On Stoic Self-Contradictions* 1036b). In particular, Plutarch stresses Chrysippus's arrant contradictions in regard to punitive divine providence and concludes, "Is it possible that anyone can more plainly confess his speaking things contrary to himself than this man does?" (1042a; at 1055e–56a Plutarch quotes Chrysippus as saying, "Often indeed do the wise employ lies against the vulgar"; see similarly *Stoicorum Veterum Fragmenta,* vol. 3, frags. 554–55). Note the distinction Cicero draws between the teachings of Zeno and the teachings of his successors regarding divination (*On Divination* 1.6 [cf. 2.119]). See also Sextus Empiricus *Against the Dogmatists* 5.195–96. Yet on the other hand, the Stoics are reported to have condemned irony as unworthy of the wise man, despite their admiration for Socrates (*Stoicorum Veterum Fragmenta,* vol. 3, frag. 630). In his investigation of the right to lie, Grotius remarks that "if we may trust Plutarch and Quintilian, the Stoics include among the endowments of the wise man the ability to lie in the proper place and manner" (*On the Law of War and Peace,* 3.1.9.3).

8. See esp. *On Duties* 1.7–8 and 13–14, 2.35, 3.14–17.

9. See esp. *On Duties* 3.23 ("*natura, id est iure gentium*"). On the origins of the term *ius gentium,* see Phillipson, *International Law and Custom of Ancient Greece and Rome,* 1:70–83; and, more authoritatively, Schulz, *A History of Roman Legal Science,* 73 and 137.

10. *Rhetoric* 1373b4–18, 1375a27ff.; see also 1368b7–9. For prominent examples of references to unwritten laws common among all men, see Xenophon *Memorabilia* 4.4.19–21; Herodotus *Histories* 7.136; Demosthenes *Against Aristocrates* 61; cf. Phillipson, *International Law and Custom of Ancient Greece and Rome,* 1:53–54 and 57–58.

11. *Oration and Defense of L. Murena* 61–64 (cf. *Stoicorum Veterum Fragmenta,* vol. 3, frag. 640):

> There was once a man of high genius, named Zeno, the followers of whose teachings are called "Stoics." His dogmas and precepts are as follows: that a wise man is never moved by interest, and never overlooks the fault of anyone; that he who is moved by pity is nothing but a fool and a trifler; that a real man is not to be moved by entreaty or placated; that only the wise, even when deformed, are beautiful; even when impoverished, are rich; even when legally slaves, are kings; but we who are not wise are runaway slaves, exiles, enemies, and even lunatics—they say; that all sins are equal; that every offense is nefarious crime; that he is no less criminal who kills a cock, when he wasn't supposed to, than he who strangles his father; that the wise man never merely opines about anything, never repents of anything, never makes a mistake, and never alters his views. Now this most acute man, M. Cato, having been induced by most learned authors, has adopted all this—not as a matter of discussion, as is the case with most others, but in order to live accordingly. But *our* philosophers—I will admit, Cato, that I too in my youth, distrusting my own genius, turned to teachings—our philosophers, I say, those who derive from Plato and Aristotle, moderate men and temperate, hold that interest does have some weight for the wise man; that good men are compassionate; that there are grades of offense and of different punishments; that a man of constancy has room to overlook offenses; that even the wise man often has to opine about what he does not know; that he is sometimes angry; that he can be moved by entreaty and placated; that he sometimes alters a view he has expressed, if another is more correct; and that all his virtues are tempered by a certain moderation. If fortune had led you, Cato, endowed with your nature, to these teachers, . . . you would have been a little more inclined to leniency.

12. *Laws* 1.23 and 1.32:

> What is more divine than reason, I will not say among humans only, but in the whole heaven and earth?—Which, when it is matured and perfected,

is rightly called wisdom. Therefore, since nothing is better than reason, and it exists in humans and in god, it follows that there is in the first place a rational society common to humans and god. But among whom there is reason, there is right reason in common; and since this latter is law, we are to believe that humans and god are associated under law. Further, among whom there is a common law, there is also a common justice; but those who share in a community in these things are to be held to belong to the same city. If in truth they are subject to the same ruler and authority, this is much more the case; but they are subject to this celestial system and divine mind and powerful deity; hence this universe must be regarded as one common city of gods and humans. The entire human race is to be understood as bound in society together.

13. *Republic* 2.4–5, 2.12–13, 2.14, 2.15, 2.22, 2.26, 2.33, 2.44, 3.24; cf. 2.10, 2.25, 2.27, 2.31, 2.38, 3.16, 3.28; cf. *On Duties* 3.41.

14. *Republic* 2.5, 2.16–17, 2.26–27 (on piety and obedience to the gods); 2.4, 2.10, 2.17, 2.20 (on the divinity of Romulus); 2.12; cf. 2.45, 3.26 (on the absence of divine punishments).

15. *On the Nature of the Gods* 1.6–7, 1.10–11, 1.13; *On the Ends of the Good and Bad Things* bk. 3.10–14, and bk. 4 in its entirety; *Laws* 1.18–39; *Academica* 1.7, 1.13–18, 1.22, 1.46; *On Duties* 2.7–8, 3.20; *Tusculan Disputations* 2.4; perhaps Cicero's most extreme statement against Stoicism and in praise of the skepticism inspired by Socrates comes at the end of the dialogue *On Divination* (2.150).

16. *Tusculan Disputations* 5.11; cf. *On the Nature of the Gods* 1.10. Grotious observes in his discussion of the right to lie that "among the philosophers, Socrates and his pupils Plato and Xenophon and at times Cicero stand openly on the side of those who hold that it is not wrong to lie" (*On the Law of War and Peace,* 3.1.9.3). St. Augustine (*The City of God* 5.9) and Edward Gibbon (*The History of the Decline and Fall of the Roman Empire* [New York: F. De Fau, 1906–1907], vol. 1, chap. 2, sec. "Of Philosophers") present radical interpretations of Cicero as an esoteric writer that go beyond anything that can be indubitably established from the texts. But it is fair to say that Cicero recognized and grasped more profoundly the moral consequences of the grave problem a leading contemporary has stated as follows: "Inquiry has its own morality, and is necessarily subversive of political institutions and movements of all kinds, good as well as bad" (Hedley Bull, *The Anarchical Society: A Study of Order in World Politics* [New York: Columbia Univ. Press, 1977], xv). For the best account of the natural right teaching of Cicero in its relation to that of the Stoics and Plato and Aristotle, see the marshaling and interpretation of the texts in Leo Strauss, *Natural Right and History* (Chicago: Univ. of Chicago Press, 1953), 126–56; see also Leo Strauss, "On Natural Law," in his *Studies in Platonic Political Philosophy* (Chicago: Univ. of Chicago Press, 1983), 137–46.

17. See above all *On Duties* 3.13–17; see also 1.7–8, 1.13–14, 1.69–71, 1.148, 3.45, 3.69; *Tusculan Disputations* 2.11–13; *Republic* 1.3, 1.11, 1.26–29 (contrast 1.30), 1.54–55 and 62–69; *Laws* 1.18–19, 1.23, 1.34, 2.11–12; *On the Ends of the Good and Bad Things* 4.15, 4.37, 5.69.

18. The fundamental importance of providence in the Stoic teaching on international justice is underlined by Grotius, in his appeal to or revival of that teaching—especially because he makes a somewhat half-hearted and not very successful attempt to show how the Stoic principles retain their force even apart from dependence on providence (*On the Law of War and Peace,* Proleg., 12, 20, 26 n. 2, 45, 50).

19. Emmerich de Vattel, *The Law of Nations or the Principles of Natural Law* (Philadelphia: T. and J.W. Johnson, 1853), 1:114; see also Cicero *On Divination* 2.41, 2.148–50.

20. *On the Nature of the Gods* 1.2, 1.14, 1.60, 2.2, 2.168, 3.4–5, 3.85.

21. *On Divination* 1.8–10; cf. *Stoicorum Veterum Fragmenta,* vol. 3, frag. 654. Cicero goes so far as to characterize the Stoics as "those superstitious and nigh fanatic philosophers" (*On Divination* 2.118); but contrast *On Divination* 2.51–62—Cato did indeed mock the soothsayers, just as Chrysippus ridiculed portents (2.61–62) and Zeno doubted divination through dreams (2.119).

22. Commenting on these passages, Peter Brown remarks that Cicero "was far too much of a Roman to attack the established religion of his ancestors" (*Augustine of Hippo: A Biography* [Berkeley: Univ. of California Press, 1967], 80).

23. Cf. Plutarch *On Stoic Self-Contradictions* 1048b–c, 1049f–52b; *On Common Conceptions, Against the Stoics* 1075e–76a.

24. Compare *On the Nature of the Gods* 2.6–8, 2.166 with 3.11–17 and with *On Divination* 1.4.

25. *On Divination* 1.8–11, 2.8, 1.58–62 (cf. 2.127–28), 2.140–42 (cf. 2.150).

26. *On Duties* 1.6ff., 3.7ff., 3.20.

27. Cf. 3.102 and 104; as I will explain more fully, Grotius takes to task Cicero's teaching on oaths for its failure to take seriously what is implied in the invocation of the divinity (*On the Law of War and Peace,* 2.13.15.1).

28. *On Duties* 1.13, 18–19, 22; cf. *Republic* 1.26–29. As we have seen by now, it is characteristic of Cicero to provoke the reader's thought by combining the exhortation to virtue as the greatest happiness with the insistence that virtue requires self-forgetting devotion to others, together with devotion to virtue for its own sake—devotion that wins for its possessor the greatest glory and in addition the support of the gods, who visit condign punishment on the wicked. Compare, for example, *On the Ends of the Good and Bad Things* 2.45 with 2.64–65; or *Laws* 1.37, 1.41, 1.43, 1.48 with 1.58–60; or *Republic* 3.11 with 6.29; see above all *On Duties* 1.28 in the light of 1.19, 1.22, 1.70–71, 1.92, 1.153, 3.25, 3.29–31, 3.35, 3.101.

29. *On Duties* 1.33–35; cf. 3.46; contrast Dante *On Monarchy* 2.5.

30. This rather flattering judgment on the concern for morality in the war

policy of the Roman Republic is seconded by Grotius, at least regarding the Roman attention to the need for a just cause for initiating war. In *On the Law of War and Peace,* 2.1.1.1–2, Grotius says of the Romans: "Hardly any race has remained for so long a time scrupulous in examining into the causes of war." On the other hand, Grotius later admits the force in Mithridates' accusation of moral hypocrisy directed against Roman punitive war policy (2.20.43.3). See the authorities Grotius collects and cites, as well as Vitoria, *Vitoria's Political Writings* (Cambridge: Cambridge Univ. Press, 1992), 289–90. Rousseau goes still further than Cicero or Grotius, arguing that conquest was in fact "incompatible" with the basic republican principles of the Roman regime. "The Romans," Rousseau contends, were conquerors "by necessity and, so to speak, in spite of themselves." They became, he says, "masters of the world in the course of defending themselves" (*Considerations on the Government of Poland,* in *Oeuvres complètes* [Paris: Editions du Seuil, 1967], 3:1013). Polybius is more ironic in his praise of the Roman Republic's concern for a just cause of war. On entering into hostilities with Demetrius, the Romans, remarks Polybius, "sought a suitable opportunity and an excuse that would look good to outsiders; for the Romans gave thought to this part of policy, and in doing so thought nobly" (*Histories* 36.2, but see also 18.37, on Roman generosity to defeated enemies, and in particular to Hannibal and the Carthaginians).

31. *On Duties* 1.35–37; see also *Republic* 2.31.

32. *On Duties* 3.107–8; Grotius offers the following "refutation" of this teaching of Cicero (whom he otherwise regularly invokes as an authority): "Not only the person to whom the oath is given is taken into consideration, but also God, by whom one swears, and the reference to God is sufficient to create an obligation. Therefore we must thrust Cicero aside when he says [this]. . . . Elsewhere he said the same thing about a tyrant. . . . Again, that is not true which Cicero assumes, that there is no common ground of right with a robber" (*On the Law of War and Peace,* 2.13.15). See also 3.19.2: pirates "as human beings have a common share in the law of nature." Grotius cites as authorities against Cicero the deeds of Lucullus and Augustus, and then argues (3.19.3–4) that a promise to a pirate or a thief is made with him as such and therefore is not invalidated by the punishment or loss of rights the criminal deserves. But at the end of his discussion, Grotius makes an enormous concession: contradicting his previous apparent appeal to Roman authority, he admits that the position Cicero takes is in fact the law of nations (3.19.5).

33. This teaching is supplemented by the greatest modern disciple of Cicero, Edmund Burke (*First Letter on a Regicide Peace,* in *Works of Edmund Burke* [London: F. and C. Rivington, 1803], 5:158): "The rules and definitions of prudence can rarely be exact; never universal. I do not deny, that, in small, truckling states, a timely compromise with power has often been the means, and the only means, of drawing out their puny existence: but a great state is too much envied, too much dreaded, to find safety in humiliation. To be secure, it

must be respected." Softening Cicero's teaching, Burke does add some pages later that a sound just war policy ought to "satisfy the nation, that though they were to be animated by a desire of glory, glory was not their ultimate object; but that everything dear to them, in religion, in law, in liberty" was "at stake" (203). Even the most modernized version of Ciceronian principles does not cease to recognize the importance of national honor:

> It is of great advantage to a nation and is one of its most important duties to itself to make itself renowned. True renown consists in the good opinion which wise and enlightened men have of us. . . . Since a nation's renown is a real advantage, it has the right to defend that renown as it would any other possession. . . . We cannot, therefore, condemn the measures sometimes taken by sovereigns to uphold or avenge the honor of their crown. They are both just and necessary, and to attribute them to mere pride, except when too lofty pretensions are made, is to be grossly ignorant of the art of ruling, and to undervalue one of the strongest bulwarks of the greatness and safety of the state. (Vattel, *Law of Nations,* 1:191)

Hegel returns to, and indeed radicalizes or goes far beyond, the classical allowance for war justified by proudly agonistic patriotic honor (see Georg Wilhelm Friedrich Hegel, *Philosophy of Right* [Cambridge: Cambridge Univ. Press, 1991], sec. 334).

34. *On Duties* 1.38 and 2.85; see also 1.26; and Dante *On Monarchy* 2.5, 2.10–11; as well as *Paradiso,* cantos 6, 19, and 20; David Hume, in "On the Balance of Power," in *Essays: Moral, Political, Literary* (New York: Cosimo Classics, 2010), 316–33, observes:

> The Grecian wars are regarded by historians as wars of emulation rather than of politics; and each state seems to have had more in view the honour of leading the rest, than any well-grounded hopes of authority and dominion. If we consider, indeed, the small number of inhabitants in any one republic, compared to the whole, the great difficulty of forming sieges in those times, and the extraordinary bravery and discipline of every freeman among that noble people; we shall conclude, that the balance of power was, of itself, sufficiently secured in Greece, and needed not to have been guarded with that caution which may be requisite in other ages. (334)

Proceeding to criticize his own country, Hume adds: "We seem to have been more possessed with the ancient Greek spirit of jealous emulation, than actuated by the prudent views of modern politics" (339).

35. Compare *On Duties* 3.43: "The greatest perplexity with respect to duty arises with regard to friendship."

John von Heyking

Aquinas's Mediated Cosmopolitanism and the Impasse of Ancient Political Philosophy

While Saint Thomas Aquinas roots his political thinking in the natural law whose community is cosmopolis, with God as its ruler, he provides the basis for affirming the justice of, and citizen attachment to, particular regimes. All human relationships, with one another and with God, are mediated through a dense network of civic, social, and ecclesial ties. Aquinas would agree with the slogan that we should "think global, act local," though he would further qualify this that in thinking globally we are also thinking locally.

Aquinas's cosmopolitanism arises out of an impasse he saw in Aristotle's reflections on the best regime and whether a good citizen can be a good human being. That identity can only occur in the best regime, and, even by Aristotle's own lights of natural reason, that best regime can only be identified with the Christian city of God, because it is only in that regime where the natural human inclination to live in political society is fulfilled and perfected. Cosmopolis is therefore a symbol that arises out of Aquinas's thinking through of the natural basis and purpose of politics.[1] Aquinas's Christianity enabled him to see this natural completion. However, while the mystical city of God is said to complete humanity's natural inclination to live in political society, the city of God is apolitical, because it is not of this world. Even though Aquinas compares the Mosaic regime under the Old Law with Aristotle's understanding of the best regime, Aquinas provides only an incomplete picture of what the best regime would look like in the time of the New Law, of Christianity. This incomplete picture of a best regime under a Christian dispensation gives special weight to cosmopolitanism as a political ideal within Christianity (symbolized as the *sacrum imperium* during the Middle Ages). Even so, Aquinas's cosmopolitanism, unlike other cosmopolitanisms, both medieval and modern, provides a way of affirming both cosmopolitanism and attachments to particular regimes.

Must a "Perfect Community" Be a World State? A Clarification

Pope Benedict XVI surprised some in his encyclical *Caritas in Veritate* by calling for international organization to serve as a common political authority for all nations.[2] In doing so, though, he seems to have been following a line of reasoning in twentieth-century Catholic political thought that lends support to international governmental institutions. Previous examples include Jacques Maritain's work on the International Declaration of Human Rights and the support Pope Pius XI lent to the League of Nations. Pius argued that Roman Catholic support of international organizations is based on the Christian view of human equality before God, and that whatever our obligations to our individual political community, our obligation to God is paramount. Pius appealed to Aquinas to support this view: "It is therefore to be hoped that the doctrines of Aquinas, concerning the ruling of peoples and the laws which establish their relations with one another, may be better known, since they contain the true foundations of that which is termed the 'League of Nations.'"[3]

In his 1949 St. Thomas Aquinas Lecture, former University of Chicago president Robert M. Hutchins took up Pius's appeal and set forth numerous texts by Aquinas, purporting a basis in his thought for a "world state." He argues that Aquinas's apparent argument for a world state derived from his Aristotelianism, whose logic could be fulfilled only by Christianity. Writing in the wake of World War II, Hutchins drew from Aquinas's apparent argument, from *De Regimine Principum,* whose authorship has more recently been called into question, that a world state is necessary because the very existence of a plurality of states causes war, which therefore makes peace impossible. War is not only possible, but it is likely, because states, in Hutchins's view, "are specialized, each in a certain way."[4] In other words, each state takes itself as the carrier of absolute truth. Put in biblical terms, the state is an idol, which makes it warlike in its very nature. A world state, conversely, would solve this problem because it would negate the possibility of war. Aquinas's political teaching surpasses and fulfills that of Aristotle, whose best regime still has to prepare for war and thus cannot achieve perfection, a condition that must include peace. Hutchins does not explicitly address whether a world state would be itself idolatrous, but he seems to reject this view by identifying the world state with the Roman Catholic church. He does not consider how the Church would wield political authority. However, he cites Aquinas's apparent argument, in *De Regimine Principum,* that kingship is the perfect community. He sees Aquinas extending Aristotle's argument for the self-sufficiency of the polis to kingdoms, which encompass *poleis.* Hutchins attributes to Aquinas a form of Averroism found in Dante's argument for a universal monarchy. Dante sought a new emperor precisely because the universalism of the Christian church is not up to the task of wielding political authority.[5]

Since Hutchins's lecture, scholars, including James Blythe, J.P. Torrell, and Mary Keys, have called into question the authorship of his main source text, *De Regimine Principum.* The best that can be claimed is that Aquinas authored part 1 (of four) and for a specific political purpose, for the King of Cyprus. Blythe points to a fundamental difference between this treatise, whose primary author was in fact Ptolemy of Lucca, and Aquinas's more systematic political writings in the *Summa Theologiæ,* which is that the argument for the superiority of absolute kingship in *De Regimine Principum* contradicts the argument he makes in the *Summa* for kingship restrained by law.[6] The efforts of these scholars have made it possible to reconsider the question of Aquinas's qualified cosmopolitanism in light of his more systematic discussion of ethics and politics in the *Summa Theologiæ* and to treat *De Regimine Principium* as either spurious or, at best, an unreliable and incomplete guide to Aquinas's systematic political teaching.

Aquinas signals his cosmopolitanism directly in the very first article of his discussion of law in the *Summa* by claiming that "a law is nothing else but a dictate of practical reason emanating from the ruler who governs a perfect community. Now it is evident, granted that the world is ruled by Divine Providence . . . that the whole community of the universe is governed by Divine Reason."[7] Following this, human laws are "particular determinations" of the first principles of practical reason that are available to all and universal.[8] Aquinas's characterization of human law, which would specify a particular regime, as derived from universal first principles of practical reason, point to the transpolitical or cosmopolitan dimension of his teaching. Instead of looking to a universal empire as the instantiation of cosmopolis, as Hutchins and Dante before him do, Aquinas argues that the Church "completes" what politics has begun:

> Wherefore there are several authorities directed to one purpose, there must needs be one universal authority over the particular authorities, because in all virtues and acts the order is according to the order of their ends (*Ethics* I.1, 2). Now the common good is more God-like than the particular good. Wherefore above the governing power which aims at a particular good there must be a universal governing power in respect of the common good, otherwise there would be no cohesion toward the one object. Hence since the whole Church is one body, it behooves, if this oneness is to be preserved, that there be a governing power in respect of the whole Church, above the episcopal power whereby each particular Church is governed, and this is the power of the Pope. . . . Thus the community of a province includes the community of a city, and the community of a kingdom includes the community of one province, and the community of the whole world includes the community of one kingdom.[9]

Hutchins was correct to see in Aquinas that the perfection of a society requires unity at its head, though not necessarily in the form of a monarch. He was incorrect to see Aquinas making the case for a universal emperor, because Aquinas does not see the perfection of the city "perfected" in the political domain, nor even in the ecclesiastical domain, but in the city of God, which the ecclesia, not the empire, instantiates. As we shall argue, however, Aquinas leaves hanging what might be called the nature of the nature of politics, because he does not elaborate what the natural perfection of the city (or kingdom) consists of. His is therefore a mystical and ecclesiastical cosmopolitanism that leaves it possible to regard political cosmopolitanism as a default possibility on account of the incompleteness of his political teaching.

Cosmopolitanism and Particular Regimes

Scholars have noticed the incompleteness of Aquinas's political teaching and the role it plays in triggering his cosmopolitanism. However, they have not been able precisely to identify the nature of that incompleteness, which is the purpose of this essay. Our discussion of the scholarship, therefore, is meant not only to provide an overview of commentary on Aquinas, but also to delineate the contours of Aquinas's incomplete teaching.

Some, like Leo Strauss, regard Aquinas's view as a departure from Aristotle and ultimately corrosive to the notion of politics: "Thomas . . . virtually contend[s] that, according to natural reason, the natural end of man is insufficient, or points beyond itself or, more precisely, that the end of man cannot consist in philosophic investigation, to say nothing of political activity."[10] E.L. Fortin elaborates this insight:

> Through knowledge of the natural law man accedes directly to the common order of reason over and above the political order to which he belongs as a citizen of a particular society. By sharing in that law he finds himself, along with all other intelligent beings, a member of a universal community or cosmopolis ruled by divine providence and whose justice is vastly superior to that of any human regime and the perfect social order is further accentuated by the Christian and Thomistic teaching according to which the entire natural order is in turn subject to the order of grace or divine law. Hence, the simply best regime is not, as it was for Aristotle, the work of man or of practical reason guided by philosophy. It is synonymous with the kingdom of God and is actual or attainable at all times through God's saving grace.[11]

While Fortin is more reticent than Strauss to regard Aquinas's cosmopolitanism as politically corrosive, both wonder whether the addition of Christian revelation to Aristotelian political philosophy corrodes our ability to regard particular regimes as worthy of allegiance. Fortin points specifically to the problem of best regime, which has now been subsumed in Aquinas's theology. The city of God replaces the best regime, to which "one can pray," that Aristotle discusses in books 7 and 8 of the *Politics*. If this is lost, then how can one have a proper understanding of the natural good of which politics consists?

While more willing to see continuity between Aristotelian political science and Christian differentiation in Aquinas's great achievement, Eric Voegelin expresses similar reservations about his political thought when he questions his characterization of *civitas* as a perfect community: "From the sky, he drops the quotation from Aristotle that the *civitas* is the perfect community because it leads to felicity."[12] Aquinas's great achievement was in reconciling the noetic philosophy of Aristotle with the pneumatic religion of Christianity. His effort shows cracks in his political program, however, because he was unable to reconcile the order of the polis, which is rooted in the soul of Aristotle's "bios theoretikos" with the Christian vision of the gifts of grace. This problem is hardly unique to Aquinas. Indeed, the central medieval symbol of political order was *sacrum imperium,* whereby "universal empire as a power organization and the universal spiritual community tended toward each other and finally met, but they did not amalgamate."[13] The *sacrum imperium* ideal of the Middle Ages, which Aquinas attempts to evoke with his cosmopolitanism, could not form a stable concrete political community, because the authenticity of faith (the basis of the universal spiritual community) was mortgaged to political forces (the basis of the universal empire as power organization). Even so, *sacrum imperium* was a crucial symbol of medieval order. One might say it was its constitutive myth of political order. We shall return below to the problem of constitutive myth and its problematic place in Aquinas's political thought.

Those who think Aquinas's Christian cosmopolitanism undermines his political thought point to the uncertain status of the best regime, and thus the naturalness of the city, as the trigger that leads Aquinas away from a full consideration of particular regimes. Even so, John Finnis speaks for those who, for this same reason, regard Aquinas's cosmopolitanism as liberating from the strictures of particular regimes: "Aquinas will consider the *civitas* rather as if it were, and were to be, the only political community in the world and its people the only people. All issues of *extension*—of origins, membership, and boundaries, of amalgamations and dissolutions—are thereby set aside. The issues will all be, so to speak, intensional: the proper functions and modes and limits of government, authoritative direction, and obligatory compliance in a community whose 'completeness' is presupposed."[14] Finnis does not claim that there is only one *civitas,* because he explains that Aquinas's cosmopolitanism gets expressed, on the political level (as opposed to the universal Christian church or the mystical city of God), as a plurality of political societies, which in alliance, collectively promote the common good of humanity under God. Finnis cites Aquinas's *Commentary on the* Nicomachean Ethics: "For: it belongs to the love which should exist between human persons that one should seek and preserve the good of even one single human being; but how much better and more godlike that this should be shown for a whole people and *for a plurality* of *civitates.* Or: it is lovable that this be shown for one single *civitas,* but much more godlike that it be shown for the whole people embracing many *civitates.* ('More godlike' because more in the likeness of God, who is the universal cause of all goods.)"[15] The cosmopolitan goal of happiness for "a plurality of civitates" is sufficiently vague, because Aquinas, as Finnis shows, regards concrete questions of political form ("all issues of *extension*") as secondary. Aquinas considers them secondary because political life is given; political life is natural and therefore needs no elaboration. For Strauss, Voegelin, and Fortin, this explanation for the gap in Aquinas's political thinking that triggers his move away from the *civitas* and its accompaniment, his claim for the perfection of the *civitas,* is problematic, while Finnis regards his cosmopolitanism salutary.

Cosmopolitanism and the Completion of Nature

None of these commentators adequately clarify the reason for this gap in Aquinas's political thought that simultaneously holds politics to be natural (in particular regimes) and that its nature is completed only in cosmopolis. The main reason Aquinas holds to his cosmopolitanism, while taking for granted the perfection of the *civitas* and not feeling compelled to discuss "issues of *extension,*" is that in taking the naturalness of politics as given, politics provides the conditions in which we practice and reflect about it. We cannot step outside politics because politics constitutes part of the order of being. Aquinas's cosmopolitanism, therefore, enumerates the boundaries of politics without actually stepping outside of politics. To draw on Alasdair MacIntyre's insight concerning Aquinas's ethics, politics is a practice best known from within; its goods are internal to itself.[16] We can see him reflecting on politics from within the horizon of politics in the quotation above regarding the "plurality of civitates" as well as in his conception of the universal community as the city of God and the problems this poses for political authority. Neither the city of God nor the ecclesia is political, but the city of God is situated in the given political realm, which people in the Middle Ages referred to as the *sacrum imperium.* This is why, for instance, the city of God is a *city.*[17]

Aquinas points to this paradox of understanding politics from within the perspective of politics in his *Commentary on Aristotle's* Politics: "We say that the nature of each thing is what belongs to it when its coming-to-be is complete. For example, the nature of human beings is the nature that they possess after they have completely come to be. . . . But the disposition that something has when it has completely come to be is the end of all the things that precede its coming to be. Therefore, the end of the natural sources from which something comes to be is the thing's nature. And so the political community, since it comes to be from the aforementioned associations, which are natural, is itself natural."[18] This is a dense passage, as one might expect from its subject matter. The context of this passage is Aquinas's commentary on Aristotle's discussion of how the polis exists when its constituent parts (i.e., households, villages) come to be. A thing cannot "be" until it has reached its perfection or fulfillment. Thus, the fulfillment of the household is to be a constituent part of the polis. Aquinas applies the same logic when he claims that things fulfill their nature when "they have completely come to be." But this is problematic, and for the same reason it is problematic to speak of the nature of the human being as having been achieved when "its coming-to-be is complete." When has a human being completely come to be? At adulthood? When he has achieved perfect wisdom and is no longer a mere lover of wisdom? But would that in fact make him a god? At approximately age thirty (the age our body takes at Resurrection, according to Augustine)? For Aristotle, this paradox takes the form of his raising the question of when a human being can be said to have lived a happy life (the purpose of virtue, after all).[19] If happiness, the goal of our nature, can only be viewed in retrospect at the conclusion of a life lived toward virtue and happiness, then can we be said to be happy only upon death? For Aquinas, the question of the nature of man found in his coming-to-be can only be taken up in light of man's supernatural end.[20]

The same is true of the nature of the polis. Its nature can only be discerned from what stands beyond it.[21] This is where the problem of Aquinas's cosmopolitanism arises. The ecclesia and then the city of God stand beyond the polis. However, neither is political or "natural" in the common-sense understanding of politics, so their adequacy to stand as standards for the *political* common good or for statesmanship is problematic. I shall argue below that the closest Aquinas gets to filling in this gap is the telling example of his treatment of Mosaic Law as an example of Aristotle's practical regime. He problematically uses an example of a best practical regime that Christianity makes obsolete, except in certain of its practices and political obligations, which shows the deep problem for thinking politically in a Christian dispensation and explains the tendency toward cosmopolitanism as the highest fulfillment for politics after the crucifixion of Christ.

If these are the plausible reasons for Aquinas's cosmopolitanism, Mary

Keys provides compelling details that allow us to see why precisely the question of the natural perfection points to cosmopolis. Keys argues that, for Aquinas, Christian revelation adds to the Aristotelian understanding of the naturalness of politics, but Keys argues that, instead of distorting it, Aquinas brings out its implications. She demonstrates this by pointing to the impasse that Aquinas sees in Aristotle's thinking regarding regimes, and Aquinas's own "third political philosophical foundation." Keys shows how Aquinas regards Aristotle's account of the relationship between human virtue and civic virtue as deficient. Aristotle questions whether the good human being can ever be simply a good citizen.

Aristotle runs aground when, in attempting to clarify this relationship, he only considers particular regimes, such as oligarchy and democracy: "[Aquinas] finds cracks in Aristotle's foundations, fissures that come from not taking the common good of justice and its transpolitical reach quite seriously enough, or from forsaking foundational work too quickly in favor of focusing on regime particularities and preservation."[22] "There is no human virtue, or ethical virtue simply, if one's interest and action are oriented toward ruling or wholeheartedly supporting an imperfect regime; and yet there is likewise no full human virtue if one does not care and work for the welfare of one's political society, which cannot exist as such without a particular regime."[23] The particularity of regimes makes it impossible to unearth either the nature of politics or full human virtue. The good human being can only be a good citizen in the perfectly good regime, which Aquinas thought only exists as the city of God.[24] As a result, Aquinas must have recourse to a universalistic virtue theory to account for both: "Where the political dialectic of regimes leads Aristotle to a thorough inquiry concerning the best regime (or to his third political-philosophic foundation) in *Politics* 7 and 8, for Aquinas it prompts a return to the source, to the common and even universal moral dimensions of social and civic life, relating to virtue, law, and the common good."[25]

Aquinas ceases his *Commentary on Aristotle's* Politics at book 3 because Aristotle reaches an impasse in his thinking about civic virtue and full human virtue. In order to find full human virtue, Aristotle must look outside the polis for a transpolitical virtue, but his own philosophical anthropology forbids or at least hinders this, so he is left sifting through particular regimes, or finding the regime "one prays for" elucidated in books 7 and 8 in the *Politics*.

Particular Attachments as Mediations of the Good

Instead of following up on the regime for which "one prays" in Aristotle, Aquinas prayed, of course, for the city of God. Thus, his focus is the perfect and universal community ruled by God. God is the final good of human action, and the universal community would be the regime in which our actions were directed. Even so, one of the source texts Keys uses to demonstrate his cosmopolitanism also shows how Aquinas requires intermediate or proximate causes to carry the universal goal of our intentions. It shows that his cosmopolitanism was mediated in principle by particular attachments. Particular attachments, including one's particular regime or even particular friends, are not mere placeholders for universal qualities, which would make one indifferent to the individuality or particularity of one's attachments.

In *ST* I–II.19, "Of the Goodness and Malice of the Interior Act of the Will," which Keys describes as an "apparently apolitical section of the *ST* with surprising political-theoretical import," Aquinas describes how the will must intend "the good of the whole universe . . . apprehended by God, Who is Maker and Governor of all things."[26] Aquinas raises the problem that as mortals who necessarily have particular attachments and perspectives, we necessarily will particular things. He cites the example of the wife of a thief who wishes that her husband not be executed. It is perhaps reasonable for the wife as a wife to wish this. Aquinas argues that it is unreasonable for the wife as a citizen or a human being who intends the common good to wish this. Instead of regarding particular attachments as things to be wished away or as regrettable, Aquinas affirms the creaturely nature of human beings who wish particular things. Even so, this still produces conflict between particular and universal goods. Is there a way of willing a particular good with a right will?[27]

A way out of this conflicted choice is Aquinas's next move. He argues that for a human being to "will some particular good with a right will, he must will that particular good materially, and the Divine and universal good formally." Keys distinguishes what is "willed materially" as that which is willed or desired immediately from what is "willed formally" as the "overarching cause of that thing's being desired." She uses the example of swimming at the end of a long day's work. She wants to swim, and it so happens that this conduces to health, which is an integral component of the good life: "in willing swimming materially, I am evincing and rendering concrete my formal desire for the good."[28] The divine good is intended immediately, but it is instantiated proximately and in a particular mode. Aquinas's distinction does not get us out of the necessity of making tragic choices, because those particular modes can overlap and conflict. If we refer this insight to the question of why Aquinas chooses not to follow up and consider the best political regime for which one should pray, we might hypothesize that he did not consider this because even that regime, which would be the best one in nature, would conflict with the city of God. Even the best practical regime is an idol. In the deepest part of his political thought, then, Aquinas would appear to be more Augustinian than Aristotelian.[29]

Charity's Reconciliation with Friendship: Cosmopolitan Implications

Another source text that follows this line of reasoning and that can be used to see how we ought to will materially things in proximity is Aquinas's entire discussion of charity, which consists of an attempt to reconcile charity with Aristotle's understanding of friendship.[30] While Aquinas goes a long way toward synthesizing charity, which is universal, with friendship, which is preferential and particular, his treatment of this synthesis provides a philosophical (or theological) anthropology showing the necessity of cosmopolitanism arising from the very nature of those particular attachments.

Citing both Aristotle's discussion of friendship in *Nicomachean Ethics* VIII and John 15:15, Aquinas argues that charity is friendship and that "we ought to love one neighbor more than another. The reason is that, since the principle of love is God, and the person who loves, it must needs be that the affection of love increases in proportion to the nearness to one or the other of those principles. For as we stated above (a. 1), wherever we find a principle, order depends on relation to that principle."[31] Our proximate neighbor is our friend, and our distant neighbor is loved, though not directly, at least as a friend. Aquinas, like Aristotle, gives weight to the importance of physical proximity in friendship. Also like Aristotle, he does not feel the need to speculate on the optimum number of friends to sustain the good life, because, friendship being a moral practice understood from within, such numbers cannot be formulated in advance, as if friendship were an object whose meanings can be discerned externally to it.[32]

Similarly, we do not love God absolutely, but proximately in the love of neighbor.[33] This is Aquinas's answer to those who think loving God, the final good, makes us neglect our neighbor whom we love on account of God. This criticism asks why not simply eliminate the middleman and love God directly? Aquinas's answer would appeal to the heart of any lover of the sacred space provided by Gothic cathedrals:

> For every act of the one species belongs to the same habit. Now since the species of an act is derived from its object, considered under its formal aspect, it follows of necessity that it is specifically the same act that tends to an aspect of that object, and that tends to the object under that aspect: thus it is specifically the same visual act whereby we see the light, and whereby we see the color under the aspect of light. Now the aspect under which our neighbor is to be loved, is God, since what we ought to love in our neighbor is that he may be in God. Hence it is clear that it is specifically the same act whereby we love God, and whereby we love our neighbor.[34]

Aquinas appeals to our experience of viewing sunlight through stained-glass windows as a way of understanding how our love of God and love of neighbor are the same act. We do not see light as light except under its aspect of color. The natural world replicates this phenomenon. We view the sun, the greatest manifestation of light in our lives, as giving off a range of colors, from Homer's "rosy-fingered dawn" to whitish yellow at midday to deep red at sunset. We do not see light simply. So, too, love of God and love of neighbor are the same act, because love of God is manifest through our actions toward our neighbor. Borrowing the language from above of the four causes, we love our neighbor materially, but God formally.

Before drawing out how Aquinas's point concerning proximate aspects qualifies his cosmopolitanism, it is worth noticing that Aquinas's discussion of friendship, which seeks to reconcile Aristotle with Jesus Christ, also, by appealing to the teaching of Jesus, enables Aquinas to show the coming-to-be of friendship. Aquinas argues that "mutual indwelling" (*mutua inhaesio*) is one of the effects of love.[35] This is a significant discussion, because it shows Aquinas grappling with one of the central problems in any discussion of love and friendship, and therefore of politics, which is what and who is it that we love when we love another? What is a self? What is a soul? How is it that souls know and love one another? Can one speak, as Bertrand Russell does, of a "central fire" that friends adhere to in one another, and can one speak, as Aristotle does, of joint perception (*sunaisthesis*) of friends with one another?[36] Without clarity of this inner experience of mutual indwelling, all discussion of civic obligation and cosmopolitanism will be further confused.

In his discussion of mutual indwelling, Aquinas refers as frequently to the book of John and to Dionysius the Areopagite's *Divine Names* as he does to Aristotle. This signals that even though he regards caritas as consistent with friendship, the scriptural tradition provides an equal and even a more complete account of its effects. One can see in Aquinas's treatment a greater attention to interiority than that found in Aristotle's discussion of friendship, where such questions are subsumed under his observation that a friend is another self. The interiority that Aquinas explores, though, deepens friendship with another instead of signifying a withdrawal of the self from the other. Turning inward means also turning outward at a deeper level.

Mutual indwelling involves the lover's "penetrating" into the heart of the beloved, and vice versa. It is the act of the lover touching the soul of the beloved. Union, ecstasy, zeal, and "wounding" are the other effects of love discussed in this question of the *Summa*. In his answer, Aquinas says something somewhat startling that clarifies how cosmopolitanism is implicit in the nature of things. He reasonably claims that "the lover is said to be in the beloved, according to apprehension, inasmuch as the lover is not satisfied with a superficial apprehension of the beloved, but strives to gain an intimate knowledge of everything pertaining to the beloved, so as to penetrate into his very soul."[37] Aquinas here describes the soul's act in knowing and loving the other. One can find an equivalent statement by Aristotle near the conclusion of his discussion of friendship: "But one's being is choiceworthy on account of the awareness of oneself as being good, and such an awareness is pleasant in itself. Therefore one also ought to share in a friend's awareness that he *is* (or share his friend's consciousness of his existence [*sunaisthanesthai hoti estin*]), and this would come through living together and sharing conversation and thinking; for this would seem to be what living together means in the case of human beings."[38] For Aristotle, knowledge and love of our friend comes through a lifetime of "living together and conversation." The *ēthos* of our friend gets revealed to us through his speeches and his actions, which we must observe over the course of a life.

Aristotle's action-based account of friendship explains why the number of our good friends is necessarily few and the optimal number of fellow citizens in a self-sufficient polis is also few. Citizens of large societies commit daily injustice against their fellow citizens simply in not knowing them while expecting to live together at some level. Aquinas's greater focus on the interiority of love, with its discussion of mystical ecstasy between friends, does not lead him to forget Aristotle's point about the knowledge and love of our friend as a practice. He agrees with Aristotle that friendship is a form of "communication" (*communicatio*), a term rich in meaning but one that signifies the activity of living and conversing together as is appropriate for rational beings.[39]

This point is crucial to understand Aquinas's "action-based" notion of the common good that qualifies his cosmopolitanism. Aquinas seems to indicate that, despite his argument about friends' being neighbors in closer proximity, the nature of love itself is universal. Even though he claims we love God by loving neighbor, he also indicates we love all our neighbors when we love our friend. In the quotation on mutual indwelling, Aquinas notes that the lover, not satisfied with superficial apprehension of the beloved, seeks to gain intimate knowledge of the beloved by gaining "knowledge of everything pertaining to the beloved." In seeking intimate knowledge, we seek to know everything about the beloved. Aquinas does not seem as troubled as Kant was by this prospect. One reason for Aquinas's apparent lack of restraint is that, strictly speaking, the *communicatio* conducted by friends is related toward a third party, God, and is not about themselves. To be fair to Kant, however, friendship is situated within the moral law that structures their friendship. For his part, Kant thought respect needed to balance love and prevent friends from revealing too much of themselves "for the sake of decency, lest humanity be outraged. Even to our best friend we must not reveal ourselves, in our natural state as we know it ourselves. To do so would be loathsome."[40] Aquinas, who had as good a sense of our "natural," sinful state as Kant, does not have his sense of reticence when it comes to self-disclosure in friendship. Aquinas's insistence on this degree of "knowledge of everything pertaining to the beloved" raises the obvious problem of whether such a level could ever be achieved in a lifetime. Aquinas can comfortably answer in the negative and yet maintain the coherence of friendship, because the lover's deepest yearning for such knowledge can only be achieved in the city of God.

This is where Aquinas's understanding of friendship points to its completion in caritas for all. In loving our particular friend, we thereby seek to know all of him. However, one of the key ways of knowing all of him is to know those whom he loves and who love him, including family, friends, business colleagues, fellow citizens, and perhaps teachers above all. Aquinas would have agreed, in a deep sense, that the friend of my friend is my friend as well. By extension of this logic, to know one's friend is to know all human beings.[41] Only in the city of God do we find friendship completed, for the same reason that only in the city of God do we find the city completed. This would be another example of our formal end being God and our material end being the friend immediately before us. As with his argument that loving God and neighbor is the same act, Aquinas, in distinguishing formal and material ends, is pointing to the unity of the individual human agent.[42]

Customs as a People's Expression of Their Particular Good

Our look at Aquinas's understanding of friendship, which is a moral practice whose formal end is universal and divine but whose material end is immediate and proximate, clarifies why we need to regard his cosmopolitanism as qualified. The formal end of politics is universal, and its material good is immediate and proximate. Keys shows this in her demonstration of Aquinas's understanding of common good as an "action-based, associational theory."[43] Politics and political science are about action, and so there is a sense in which the common good is made and not predetermined: "Aristotle's and Aquinas's version of constitutive community is constituted not by a shared *identity,* but rather by a conversation and a sharing in actions and in the goods they instantiate and seek: every human association (*communicatio*) is based on certain acts, and 'human beings naturally communicate with one another in reference to [the useful and the harmful, the just and the unjust, and other such things]. But communication in reference to these things is what makes a household and city.'"[44]

As we have seen, there are limits to the scope of this activity that can be worked out only from within the practice itself. Finnis is partially correct when he points to Aquinas's cosmopolitanism for the reason he feels no need to consider questions regarding the extension of the city. The deeper reason is that the extension of the city, as with the number of friends one has, is discovered only in its practice. One cannot measure just how deeply one has mutually indwelt with one's beloved; rather, one can perceive this depth only in the reaching out of one's soul in a lifetime of "living together and conversing." Similarly, the city cannot fully know the limit of its extension except by reflecting upon how well it is governed and the quality of life for its citizens. Moreover, the city knows this extension because its citizens are already practiced in friendship. Citizenship without prior experience of mutual indwelling will lead to a deformed form of citizenship that is either overly nationalistic and parochial or superficially cosmopolitan. Without a solid basis in friendship, a citizenry, whether national or cosmopolitan, will be little more than a mob.

There are a number of activities that, in Aquinas's "action-based" account of the common good, citizens can perform with their rulers. Keys mentions communication of the just and the unjust, which is part of Aristotle's formulation of the object of citizens' deliberations and expressive of the human inclination to live politically (based on our capacity to speak of the just and the unjust and of the praiseworthy and the blameworthy). While in some way intimated, the ends for which citizens deliberate (and deliberation is about means) are not always obvious or pregiven, but neither do citizens "create" them out of thin air (otherwise, citizenship would give way to faction). A moral practice implies that its goods are uncovered from within the practice itself, and therefore it exhibits a degree of discovery of what exactly those goods are and in what particular mode they are to be sought. As noted above, human law determines the natural law in its particular, but, as Robert Miner has noted of Aquinas, the end is discovered in the practice of deliberation: "The acquisition of true knowledge about particulars is not anterior to the process of law-making, but is acquired through the very performance of the activity."[45] In deliberating and judging, citizens form customs. Customs are the accumulated determinations of the natural law in the form of human law, and they have authority over legislation because the actions of the ruler must finally receive consent by the community of free citizens: "Custom has the force of law, abolishes law, and is the interpreter of law."[46] Customs thus express the historical life of a self-governing community's common good.

Key to self-government is equality in the sense that all citizens take part in its activity, which is again one of the reasons Aquinas ceased his commentary on the *Politics*. Aquinas does not accept Aristotle's distinction between ruler and ruled and his acceptance of masters and slaves. Here again is an example of Aquinas's cosmopolitanism showing how the nature of politics gets completed. However, this case differs from others we have seen. Our previous examples of this, such as the implicit love of all contained within preferential friendship, have shown how Christian revelation completes the logic of our understanding of nature. In this case, equality seems asserted or to follow exclusively from the irruption of grace, which reveals that the distance between man and God is greater than the distance between a man and other men. In his more systematic *Summa,* Aquinas insists that "if they are free, and able to make their own laws, the consent of the whole people expressed by a custom counts far more in favor of a particular observance, than does the authority of the sovereign, who has not the power to frame laws, except as representing the people. Wherefore although each individual cannot make laws, yet the whole people can."[47]

Mosaic Law as the Best Regime That Points to Cosmopolis

Aquinas specifies the role the people take in self-government in his discussion of the Mosaic Law, whose mixing of regime elements he equates with Aristotle's best practical regime: "For this is the best form of polity, being partly kingdom, since there is one at the head of all; partly aristocracy, in so far as a number of persons are set in authority; partly democracy, i.e., government by the people, in so far as the rulers can be chosen from the people, and the people have the right to choose their rulers."[48] The best practical regime, in this case the Mosaic one, is the epitome of civic friendship, where the laws accustom citizens "to give of their own to others readily."[49] Aquinas cites the example of vineyard owners who are obliged to feed the poor to the extent that the poor eat their fill but do not take any away. Aquinas assumes the poor are genuinely needy (and not free-riding) and that, because the poor leave enough for others (including enough for the vineyard's owner to make a living) and return to their own residences, the regime enables citizens to judge who is needy and to ensure responsibility. This is not a large welfare state with abstract and overly rough determinations of poverty that are based not on the ethos of rich and poor, but on statistics, "for among well behaved people, the taking of a little does not disturb the peace; in fact it rather strengthens friendship and accustoms men to give things to one another."[50] "It is the essence of a nation that the mutual relations of citizens be ordered by just laws."[51] Yet, as we have seen, the number of friends, and of citizens, is something that is determined internal to the practice of friendship and citizenship.

Aquinas does not consider extension of this regime, but, in the next article, he does provide a principle for determining the difference between those who are one's fellow citizens in this regime of friendship and those who are not. Aquinas's discussion "Whether the Judicial Precepts regarding

Foreigners Were Framed in a Suitable Manner" explains that this regime is based on virtue and an understanding of the specific common good of this regime, which are prerequisites to membership. Citing Exodus 12:48, Aquinas explains that the Law sets down the principle that a society may never "exclude the men of no nation from the worship of God and from things pertaining to the welfare of the soul."[52] Moreover, one may be admitted to citizenship on account of "some act of virtue," such as Ruth and Achior.[53] Citizenship in the best practical regime is, in principle, open to all. This is a cosmopolitan principle for immigration, insofar as citizenship is not based on ethnicity, race, wealth, or some other principle frequently used today to restrict immigration.

Even so, would-be immigrants must also subscribe to and understand the worship of God in this regime in particular, because otherwise "many dangers might occur, since the foreigners not yet having the common good firmly at heart might attempt something hurtful to the people."[54] For this reason, nations with the best relations with the Israelites could obtain citizenship after the third generation. Aquinas, following the Old Law, thinks of the common good as a tradition handed down from one generation to the next, and not something a single individual can adhere to in isolation of a dense network of familial, religious, and civil obligations that extend across generations. Given the difficulties that many contemporary immigrants, especially children, have in North America and Europe in negotiating old ways with new ways, the Old Law's rule of the third generation makes a certain sense.[55] Even so, Aquinas's action-based notion of the common good necessitates a lengthy time period of acculturation and education into the customs of the best practical regime.

The status of the Old Law in Aquinas's thinking gets to the problematic root of the status of best regime in his thought, and therefore the trigger that points to his cosmopolitanism. The Old Law is part of the divine law, and of course the Old Law foreshadows the New Law, which is Christ. While the moral precepts of the Old Law can be known naturally, the root of the Mosaic regime is divine. Thus, while the Mosaic regime and the best practical regime of Aristotle are comparable at a certain external level, their inner substance is quite different. While it is true that the two are very similar in the ways that the laws order the relations of citizens, and this order expresses the essence of the regimes,[56] there is a deeper level where they part ways: "It must be observed that the end of human law is different from the end of Divine law. For the end of human law is the temporal tranquility of the state, which end law effects by directing external actions, as regards those evils which might disturb the peaceful condition of the state. On the other hand, the end of the Divine law is to bring man to that end which is everlasting happiness; which end is hindered by any sin, not only of eternal, but also of internal action."[57] Theorizing about the Mosaic regime as equivalent to Aristotle's best practical regime faces the thorny problem that the Old Law has been replaced by the New Law, and one of the ways the New Law advances from the Old is that it regulates internal action, whereas both the Old Law and the laws of Aristotle's best practical regime regulate external action. Moreover, the very notion of "law" in Christian revelation is problematic and can only be spoken of in approximation. This makes speaking of political analogues further problematic.[58]

Regardless of these complications at the heart of any attempt to consider the question of best practical regime under the Christian dispensation, it is important to note a complication it produces in Aquinas's thinking of the common good of any particular political regime. In *Politics* books 7 and 8, Aristotle considers the mythic or cultic aspects of the best regime. Its focus is on education, but on the type of education that makes citizens amenable to the highest form of leisure, philosophizing. In educating citizens in music and poetry, Aristotle prepares citizens in a form of liturgical contemplation that mimics philosophical contemplation. Today we might consider major sporting events as serving an equivalent function.[59] Thus, he devotes considerable effort to explaining how education in music, for example, is meant to produce citizens well-versed not so much in playing instruments as in judging players of instruments. Aristotle has in mind the kind of education in taste required by a citizenry that expresses its citizenship by being spectators at the tragic festivals. Music expresses not just harmonies, but also the songs that reflect the regime. For this same reason, the Athenian Stranger of Plato's *Laws* argues that poets in the Magnesian colony are, on the whole, unwelcome because they are redundant. He advises citizens to tell poets that "our whole political regime is constructed as the imitation of the most beautiful and best way of life, which we at least assert to be really the truest tragedy. Now you are poets, and we too are poets of the same things; we are your rivals as artists and performers of the most beautiful drama, which true law alone can by nature bring to perfection."[60] The regime of the *Laws*, as well as the best regime of Aristotle, is a religious poem, which is a point reinforced by recollecting that *nomoi*, in addition to meaning "laws" and "customs," also means "songs." The city understands itself as a city not only by regulating economic commerce and communication concerning the just and the unjust, but also when it experiences itself as a unity. The city as festivity is the city acting in itself, and it expresses its essential particularity in this manner. In festivity, the city observes its founding myth. As F.W.J. Schelling observed, "Nations do not make myths. Myths make nations."[61] Thus, the laws always return to their author, the myth.

Aquinas's political thought rarely reaches this depth of analysis, either by design or by negligence. Aquinas's decision to cease his *Commentary on Aristotle's* Politics seems to be intentional, and the "religious" aspect of politics might be one reason for this. If so, then this would be the point where Aquinas saw politics, understood under the exclusive light of reason, to be idolatrous. This is where Aquinas's Aristotelianism gives way to his Augustinianism. On the other hand, Aquinas still faced the problem of explaining how a particular regime expresses its inner substance. If "it is the essence of a nation that the mutual relations of citizens be ordered by just laws,"[62] then it would be strange for Aquinas not to recognize that the spirit of those just laws must be expressed in the myth that unites the people. The common good must be more than a set of external laws regulating debates concerning the just and the unjust, because such an arrangement serves only to mitigate faction, not to express what those factions have in common. As a Christian, Aquinas of course does not subscribe to the myth of nature, as the citizens of Plato's Magnesia and of Aristotle's best regime do, but he subscribes to the myth of the Incarnation of Christ. His understanding of human law, which touches externals only, prevents him from identifying Christian faith with the human law; Christianity does not serve as a civil religion for Aquinas.[63] This is one of the reasons the *sacrum imperium* could be nothing more than an ideal. This is also one reason why medieval political thinkers had to cope with the crack-up of this ideal with the rise of national churches, and eventually with the Reformation.[64] Thus, Christianity puts into question the status of the myth that sustains particular regimes. By leaving this status in question, there is always the potential for Christian cosmopolitanism to serve as the "civil religion" by default, at least at the level of the myth that legitimates the regime. Complicating matters further is the status even of Christian cosmopolitanism that has been in question since the Enlightenment (proclamations of Pope Pius XI and Pope Benedict XVI notwithstanding). The Augustinian myth of the two cities is one competitor in a competitive field of cosmopolitanisms. Kantian cosmopolitanism, based on international law and history's progressing toward a single state, is one competitor. The Islamicist ideal of the universal caliphate is another competitor.[65]

Conclusion

Aquinas held a modified version of political cosmopolitanism that is instructive for considering cosmopolitanism today. He shows us the role Christian revelation plays in raising up transpolitical virtues that can liberate from insular particular attachments. Even so, he reminds us that transpolitical virtues are always mediated by one's particular regime. One cannot be simply a cosmopolitan, any more than one can love God without loving God in the practice of neighborly love. Aquinas would likely insist that there are no cosmopolitans simply, but rather French, American, Canadian, or Ugandan cosmopolitans. While salutary, there is something unresolved about this state of things, because the essence of these particular attachments is less than fully articulate.

The difficulty with incomplete articulations of particular attachments is that it leaves the field open to attributing particular attachments to qualities less wholesome than virtue. If the cosmopolitan ideal is the only legitimate substance for a regime, then race and xenophobic ethnicity become the default ways of expressing the particular substance of a regime. Moreover, if the cosmopolitan ideal is held up as the ideal of the particular regime, there is the danger of its being imposed upon from above, as the example of Aquinas's own thoughts on coercion suggest. One might also consider the plight of nations under the rule of European bureaucrats as an example. Conversely, the quasi-sacral terms in which the American regime gets expressed might serve as an instructive way of giving civic piety its due without its becoming essentially idolatrous. Viewing oneself as an "almost chosen people" is a suggestive way of giving due weight to both cosmopolitan and particular attachments.[66] Keeping this balance without its distorting into excessive cosmopolitanism that disregards one's own regime, or excessive nationalism that exaggerates its claim to justice, requires an extraordinary degree of statesmanship and humility. Keeping this balance depends in large part on abiding by Aquinas's observation that we love the universal in the particular (i.e., loving God in loving one's neighbor and in loving one's neighbor who is most nearby) and on recollecting his insight that the common good, of friends and of citizens, is action-based, which reminds us that we judge our actions by what we see before us in face-to-face interactions with other persons. Aquinas reminds us that loving God and neighbor is to love persons. Our cosmopolitanism and our political obligations suffer when we forget persons.

Notes

1. Historically, the symbol *cosmopolis* comes down from the Stoics. For Aquinas, however, this symbol arises meditatively out of the impasse he saw in ancient thinking regarding the nature of politics and of human happiness.

2. Pope Benedict XVI, *Caritas in Veritate,* www.vatican.va/holy_father/benedict_xvi/encyclicals/documents/hf_ben-xvi_enc_20090629_caritas-in-veritate_en.html. According to James Schall, "The proposal about a better world international institution goes back to Robert Maynard Hutchins and Jacques Maritain, to the Hague Conventions, to the League of Nations, and even the Holy Roman Empire. The pope defines the need for authority at a higher level, but with sufficient restrictions to prevent it from being either a world government or a tyranny." "*Caritas in Veritate:* A Symposium," *Catholic Thing,* July 8, 2009, www.thecatholicthing.org/content/view/1871/2/.

3. Pope Pius XI, *Studiorum Ducem,* June 29, 1923, as quoted and translated by Robert M. Hutchins, *Aquinas and the World State* (Milwaukee: Marquette Univ. Press, 1949), epigraph.

4. Hutchins, *Aquinas and the World State,* 15.

5. See Dante, "On Monarchy," trans. Philip H. Wicksteed, in *Medieval Political Philosophy,* ed. Ralph Lerner and Muhsin Mahdi (Ithaca, NY: Cornell Univ. Press, 1963), I.ii–xi.

6. James M. Blythe, introduction to *On the Government of Rulers: De Regimine Principum by Ptolemy of Lucca with portions attributed to Thomas Aquinas,* trans. James M. Blythe (Philadelphia: Univ. of Pennsylvania Press, 1997), 5–7. See also Jean-Pierre Torrell, O. P., *St. Thomas Aquinas: Spiritual Master,* trans. Robert Royal (Washington, DC: Catholic Univ. of America Press, 2003), 2:303; Mary M. Keys, *Aquinas, Aristotle, and the Promise of the Common Good* (Cambridge: Cambridge Univ. Press, 2006), 64.

7. St. Thomas Aquinas, *Summa Theologiæ,* 5 vols., trans. Fathers of the English Dominican Province (1948, reprint, Westminster, MD: Christian Classics, 1981), I–II.91.1 (hereafter abbreviated as *ST*). See also *ST* I–II.21.4.

8. *ST* I–II.91.3; 94.2.

9. *ST* Supplement, 40.6. I thank David Goldman for alerting me to this passage. For a contemporary reflection on its political import, see Spengler [pseud.], "Why Do Nations Exist?" *Asia Times,* July 29, 2008, www.atimes.com/atimes/Front_Page/JG29Aa02.html.

10. Leo Strauss, *Natural Right and History* (Chicago: Univ. of Chicago Press, 1953), 164. See also 157–59 and 163.

11. E.L. Fortin, "The Political Thought of St. Thomas Aquinas," in *Classi-*

cal Christianity and the Political Order: Reflections on the Theologico-Political Problem: Collected Essays, ed. J. Brian Benestad (Lanham, MD: Rowman and Littlefield, 1996), 2:160–61.

12. Eric Voegelin, *The Middle Ages to Aquinas: History of Political Ideas II: The Collected Works of Eric Voegelin,* ed. Peter von Sivers (Columbia: Univ. of Missouri Press, 1997), 20:219.

13. Ibid., 20:66. For a summary of Voegelin's treatment of *sacrum imperium,* see my "Post-9/11 Evocations of Empire in Light of Eric Voegelin's Political Science," in *Enduring Empire: Ancient Lessons for Global Politics,* ed. David Edward Tabachnick and Toivo Koivukoski (Toronto: Univ. of Toronto Press, 2009), 192–97.

14. John Finnis, *Aquinas* (Oxford: Oxford Univ. Press, 1998), 221.

15. Aquinas, *Commentary on* Nicomachean Ethics, I.2, cited and translated by Finnis, *Aquinas,* 115, emphasis added by Finnis.

16. Alasdair MacIntyre, *After Virtue* (Notre Dame, IN: Univ. of Notre Dame Press, 1981); MacIntyre, *Whose Justice? Which Rationality?* (Notre Dame, IN: Univ. of Notre Dame Press, 1988).

17. See also Torrell, *St. Thomas Aquinas,* 2:292–93. For another example of the kind of argument made here on how politics provides the conditions for its understanding, with reference to Kant, see David Walsh, *The Modern Philosophical Revolution: The Luminosity of Existence* (Cambridge: Cambridge Univ. Press, 2009), 62–63.

18. St. Thomas Aquinas, *Commentary on Aristotle's* Politics, trans., Richard J. Regan (Indianapolis: Hackett, 2007), I.18.

19. Aristotle, *Nicomachean Ethics* 1100a10–20.

20. This is not the place to take up the perennial debate over "faith versus reason" in Aquinas. A good place to start, though, and one that suggests that "faith versus reason" is a false dichotomy because there is no such thing as "unassisted reason," is his statement that "every truth by whomsoever spoken is from the Holy Ghost as bestowing the natural light, and moving us to understand and speak the truth, but not as dwelling in us by sanctifying grace, or as bestowing any habitual gift superadded to nature." *ST* I–II.109.1.1.

21. See James Schall's discussion of this paradox with special reference to friendship. *At the Limits of Political Philosophy: From "Brilliant Errors" to Things of Uncommon Importance* (Washington, DC: Catholic Univ. of America Press, 1996), chap. 12.

22. Keys, *Aquinas, Aristotle, and the Promise of the Common Good,* 88.

23. Ibid., 91.

24. In pointing to the wise legislator or statesman as the epitome of political virtue, ancient political thought (as well as Judaism and Islam) appear to confirm Aquinas's criticism. The wise legislator or statesman, if he is to be understood as the perfection of his regime, would be alone in that perfection, which means he has no regime. For details, see Rémi Brague, *The Law of God: The Philosophical*

History of an Idea, trans. Lydia G. Cochrane (Chicago: Univ. of Chicago Press, 2007).

25. Keys, *Aquinas, Aristotle, and the Promise of the Common Good,* 88. Keys goes on to demonstrate how Aquinas's argument concerning the first principles of practical reason are his own innovation in virtue theory, because he found Aristotle's arguments on the teachability of virtue deficient. His argument is part of his larger argument that Aquinas thought Aristotle did not go far enough in seeing the social nature of human beings.

26. *ST* I–II.19.10; Keys, *Aquinas, Aristotle, and the Promise of the Common Good,* 119–20.

27. Aquinas's argument for the civic justice of execution for theft is unconvincing, as the thief's wife could also appeal to the injustice of execution to seek clemency for her husband. We twenty-first-century cosmopolitans might find his medieval sense of justice barbaric, but we would be incorrect to blame Aquinas's historical milieu. After all, Augustine opposed capital punishment. A better example of a particular good conflicting with a universal good might be a battalion commander trying to save his troops from the incompetence or injustice of the army's commanders in an otherwise just war.

28. Keys, *Aquinas, Aristotle, and the Promise of the Common Good,* 120n6.

29. Or is Augustine more Aristotelian than Thomistic? Augustine appears to affirm the naturalness of politics. See my *Augustine and Politics as Longing in the World* (Columbia: Univ. of Missouri Press, 2001), chaps. 5–6.

30. On this attempt, and its significance for politics, see Jeanne Heffernan Schindler, "A Companionship of Caritas: Friendship in St. Thomas Aquinas," in *Friendship and Politics: Essays in Political Thought,* ed. John von Heyking and Richard Avramenko (Notre Dame, IN: Univ. of Notre Dame Press, 2008), 139–62.

31. *ST* II–II.23.1 and 26.6.

32. One cannot expect the same level of circumspection from evolutionary anthropology. See Robin Dunbar, *How Many Friends Does One Person Need?* (New York: Faber and Faber, 2010).

33. *ST* II–II.25.1.

34. Ibid.

35. *ST* I–II.28.2.

36. See my "'Sunaisthetic' Friendship and the Foundations of Political Anthropology," *International Political Anthropology* 1, no. 2 (November 2008): 179–93.

37. *ST* I–II.28.2.

38. Aristotle, *Nicomachean Ethics,* trans. Joe Sachs (Newburyport, MA: Focus, 2002), 1170b10–12.

39. *ST* II–II.23.1. See also *ST* I–II.97.3.

40. Immanuel Kant, "Lecture on Friendship," in *Other Selves: Philosophers on Friendship,* ed. Michael Pakaluk (Indianapolis: Hackett, 1991), 215.

41. When asked why he wrote a history of civilizations, Arnold Toynbee replied that he had originally intended to write a history of England. However, he quickly realized that a history of England can only be understood by knowing the history of the European continent, which, in turn, can only be understood by knowing the history of Asia, Africa, and so on. The same logic led Toynbee to abandon his history of civilizations and turn to a history of world religions, which he regarded as the intelligible units of history. Arnold Toynbee, *A Study of History,* 12 vols. (Oxford: Oxford Univ. Press, 1935–1961). Voegelin thought that even then Toynbee had not gone far enough and so regarded his own inquiry into universal humanity, which became an account of human consciousness. Voegelin, "Toynbee's History as a Search for Truth," in *Published Essays, 1953–1965: Collected Works of Eric Voegelin,* ed. Ellis Sandoz (Columbia: Univ. of Missouri Press, 2000), 11:100–112. It should be noted that Søren Kierkegaard, in the voice of Johannes Climacus, makes a variation of the phrase *unum noris, omnes* [if you know one, you know all] the centerpiece of his friendship thinking. Kierkegaard's thoughts on friendship and cosmopolitanism (of which he is very critical) are more paradoxical than those of Aquinas, but they at least are free of the confusions introduced by Aquinas's insistence on treating friendship and love with the language of the four causes. See my "Friendship in Light of the Modern Philosophical Revolution," *Fideles* 4 (2009): 37–76.

42. Aquinas insisted that the completion of human nature is found in the individual human being in community, and not in monopsychism, as argued by the Latin Averroists. In *On the Unity of the Intellect against the Averroists,* Aquinas agrees with the Averroists insofar as a single agent is needed to bring perfection to a plurality of individuals. This is the basis of Dante's vision of world empire. However, asserting that individual human beings lose their individuality, including their capacity to think, as the Averroists assert when they argue for a single intellect for all of humanity, "is clearly false, impossible, and repugnant to what is obvious: it destroys the whole of moral science and all those things that pertain to civil interchange, which is natural to man, as Aristotle says." St. Thomas Aquinas, *Against the Averroists: On There Being Only One Intellect,* trans. Ralph McInerny (West Lafayette, IN: Purdue Univ. Press, 1993), IV.89.

43. Keys, *Aquinas, Aristotle, and the Promise of the Common Good,* 77.

44. Ibid., 85, quoting Aquinas's *Commentary on Aristotle's* Politics I.1n37.

45. Robert Miner, *Truth in the Making: Creative Knowledge in Theology and Philosophy* (New York: Routledge, 2004), 10–11. Keys agrees with this characterization of the "determination" of natural law: "Natural law as informing legal justice is thus too general to serve as a comprehensive architectonic norm; it constitutes the indispensable foundation, but it cannot direct the entire building of our ethical and civic lives." Keys, *Aquinas, Aristotle, and the Promise of the Common Good,* 194. Both Miner and Keys restate, from different angles, the point made above that our understanding of the end of politics comes from within politics itself.

46. *ST* I–II.97.3. Aquinas lists the customs of a country to be "one of the conditions of law." *ST* I–II.97.3.2.

47. *ST* I–II.97.3.3.

48. *ST* I–II.105.1.

49. *ST* I–II.105.2.1.

50. Ibid.

51. *ST* I–II.105.2.

52. *ST* I–II.105.3.1.

53. Citing Ruth 3:11 and Judith 14:6.

54. *ST* I–II.105.

55. On the other hand, it can reasonably be argued that being granted full citizenship sooner makes it easier for immigrants to get acculturated. The migrant groups with the greatest difficulties are those on the fringes of their host society (e.g., Turkish guest-workers in Germany or Arabs in France).

56. *ST* I–II.105.2.

57. *ST* I–II.98.1.

58. The Incarnation of Christ replaces law as the standard of action with the person of Christ, even though he fulfils the law. Aquinas constantly struggled against those who took the Incarnation into antinomian directions. See my "God's Co-workers: Rémi Brague's Treatment of the Divine Law in Christianity," *Political Science Reviewer* 38 (Spring 2009): 76–104.

59. James Schall, "On the Seriousness of Sports: Watchers All," *Vital Speeches of the Day* 49 (February 15, 1983): 271–74. I have attempted to demonstrate that rodeo, where the athleticism of the cowboy is confounded by the wiliness and strength of the horse or bull, exemplifies the relationship of liberty and equality for citizens of liberal democracies, especially those who live in the western part of North America. "The Zen of Stampede," *Calgary Herald,* July 1, 2000, Canada Day Edition, OS8. The recent addition to the urban space of Calgary, Alberta, of a statue commemorating Outlaw, a champion rodeo bull, exemplifies this myth. "Statue of Legendary Bull Unveiled," *CBC News,* May 27, 2010, www.cbc.ca/canada/calgary/story/2010/05/27/calgary-stampede-bull-outlaw-sculpture-bronze.html.

60. Plato, *The* Laws *of Plato,* trans. Thomas L. Pangle (Chicago: Univ. of Chicago Press, 1980), 817b–c. See Eric Voegelin's comment that as a "religious poem," the regime of the Laws is the Platonic equivalent to the city of God. *Order and History,* vol. 3, *Plato and Aristotle* (Baton Rouge: Louisiana State Univ. Press, 1957), 217–28.

61. See F.W.J. Schelling, *Historical-Critical Introduction to the Philosophy of Mythology,* trans., Mason Richey and Markus Zisselsberger (Albany: State Univ. of New York Press, 2008), 49 and Lectures 4 to 6. I thank Steven McGuire for this reference.

62. *ST* I–II.105.2.

63. The glaring exception to or hole in this theory is Aquinas's acceptance

of the coercion of heretics. See E.A. Goerner and W.J. Thompson, "Politics and Coercion," *Political Theory* 24, no. 4 (November 1996): 620–52.

64. See Voegelin, *The Later Middle Ages: History of Political Ideas III: Collected Works of Eric Voegelin,* vol. 21, ed. David Walsh (Columbia: Univ. of Missouri Press, 1998). Nicholas of Cusa is an instructive example of a thinker grappling with the problem of how national churches can contribute to the universal Christian church (see my "Prophecy and Politics in Nicholas of Cusa," in *Propheten und Prophezeiungen—Prophets and Prophecies,* Eranos—Neue Folge 12, ed. Matthias Riedl and Tilo Schabert [Würzburg, Germany: Königshausen und Neumann, 2005], 143–60). Other than Giambattista Vico, F.W.J. Schelling, and Eric Voegelin, few thinkers have taken up the problem of political myth and Christian cosmopolitanism. See Voegelin, *Revolution and the New Science: History of Political Ideas VI: Collected Works of Eric Voegelin,* ed. Barry Cooper (Columbia: Univ. of Missouri Press, 1998), 24:82–148; and Voegelin, *The New Order and Last Orientation: History of Political Ideas VII: Collected Works of Eric Voegelin,* ed. Jürgen Gebhardt and Thomas A. Hollweck (Columbia: Univ. of Missouri Press, 1999), 25:193–242.

65. It is questionable whether any vision of cosmopolitanism, or empire (its frequent political instantiation), is viable today. See my "Post-9/11 Evocations of Empire."

66. There are numerous studies of America's "civil religion." Examples include essays in *Civil Religion in Political Thought: Its Perennial Questions and Enduring Relevance in North America,* ed. Ronald Weed and John von Heyking (Washington, DC: Catholic Univ. of America Press, 2010); Jürgen Gebhardt, *Americanism: Revolutionary Order and Societal Self-Interpretation in the American Republic,* trans. Ruth Hein (Baton Rouge: Louisiana State Univ. Press, 1991); Ellis Sandoz, *A Government of Laws: Political Theory, Religion, and the American Founding* (Columbia: Univ. of Missouri Press, 2002).

Khalil M. Habib

Ibn Tufayl's Critique of Cosmopolitanism in *Hayy Ibn Yaqzan*

Since the end of the cold war and the rise of globalization, many have begun to look hopefully to a cosmopolitan era governed by universal tolerance that transcends local ethnic or national boundaries. Ibn Tufayl, speaking to us from nine centuries ago, explores the possibility of cosmopolitanism and offers a thoughtful response to its hopes in his book *Hayy Ibn Yaqzan*. Although Ibn Tufayl's work has been unjustly neglected in our times,[1] the importance and necessity of the study of this work is more evident today than it has been for many decades. While Ibn Tufayl is engaged in a valiant attempt to free human brings from a state of ignorance, the enlightenment and tolerance reached by Ibn Tufayl's hero Hayy is not the model Ibn Tufayl thinks is possible for political society and politics in general.

Although Ibn Tufayl believes that a genuinely enlightened individual is "cosmopolitan," that is, free from parochial prejudices and in a sense at home in all cities, Ibn Tufayl is not of the opinion that a cosmopolitan society or a cosmopolitan world order can ever exist in practice. The story's hero attempts but fails to establish a society in which citizens belong to their common humanity, rather than to any particular city or tradition. The notions concerning "progress" and "improvement of society" and the belief that the majority of human ideas about the most fundamental questions of reality could be aligned with enlightened beliefs are, therefore, tempered by Ibn Tufayl's strong streak of pessimism and his sense of the dangers and challenges to the conventions that help to stabilize political life. Because of the weight that Ibn Tufayl assigns to sectarian religion and the general character and spirit of a nation, he suggests that there can be no universal model of an enlightened state or moderate government. He teaches the arts of prudence, moderation, and understanding of the irresolvable differences among nations and peoples, rather than cosmopolitanism. For the East, he refers to the role of religion in stabilizing society and guiding morality, and for the West he tempers the extremes of cosmopolitanism by revealing its limitations.

My aim in this essay is to present the main philosophical arguments of *Hayy Ibn Yaqzan* and to suggest that this Islamic medieval tale teaches that genuine progress and enlightenment exist but are possible only in rare individuals and not in groups or any political organizations. Although Ibn Tufayl's hero, Hayy, discovers happiness and enlightenment in a life in accord with nature, rather than a life regulated by revealed religion or social convention, his awareness is hardly practicable by the majority of human beings or even desirable for human societies. Any attempt to jettison a society's mores will likely lead that society into destruction and cause it more harm than its own traditions ever could, Tufayl warns.

This essay is divided into three main parts. The first attempts an explanation of the two conflicting accounts of Hayy's origins and offers an interpretation of how they might fit together. The second part traces Hayy's intellectual development, which is divided into several seven-year periods. Each stage is unique and represents the protagonist's progress toward enlightenment.[2] The purpose of tracing Hayy's intellectual development is to show how it is possible for a rare individual to discover the natural order of existence—and hence be at home in the world—without the aid of religious scripture or particular political traditions and conventions. Hayy's failure to align society with his wisdom constitutes a limitation on cosmopolitanism. Consequently, the third section examines Hayy's introduction to society, his failure to enlighten his fellows, the lesson he draws from his failure to educate others, and his reasons for returning to his desert island to resume his life of philosophy. The argument and action of this narrative implies that Ibn Tufayl embraces the possibility of a qualified cosmopolitanism, provided that society is protected from what he calls "newfangled" sophistic teachings, and that the genuine philosopher does not compromise his happiness and way of life in the futile attempt to enlighten others.[3]

The literal translation of the title *Hayy Ibn Yaqzan,* "The Living One, Son of the Wakeful," is significant. "The Living One" stands for human intellect and alludes to a verse in the Holy Koran in which it is said about God that "neither slumber nor sleep overtaketh Him" (2:255). M. Saeed Sheikh points out that *Hayy Ibn Yaqzan* "symbolically represents the theme that human intellect partakes of the divine intellect and hence has the capacity to know reality in its innermost truths, independent of prophetic revelations as recorded by scriptures"[4] (124). The book's subtitle, *Asar al-Hikmat al-Ishraqiyyah*, "Secrets of the Illuminative Philosophy," is borrowed from a work by Ibn Sina of the same name, as are the names of the main characters of Ibn Tufayl's novel—Hayy, Salaman, and Absal.

The story's hero, Hayy, is cast upon an uninhabited Indian island as an infant. He is nourished and raised by a doe, and he succeeds by the powers of his own reason to arrive at self-knowledge and an understanding of God and nature, along with his own place within the cosmos. He is a prototype of the philosopher. The temperate climate of his desert island, "where human beings come into being without father or mother," underlies the extraordinary pattern of his paradigmatic life, his entirely "natural" development (103).

Ibn Tufayl offers two conflicting versions of his main character's origin as a castaway. The first account, an obvious metaphorical alternative to the Garden of Eden story in Genesis, tells us that Hayy was spontaneously generated, like Adam, without father or mother (103).[5] His fictitious island, described in terms reminiscent of Platonic symbolism, is situated under the sun, which Ibn Tufayl associates with God and knowledge. The splendor of the sun's natural light assists and supports human perfection, "setting afire all that it apprehends so that it alone remains, then it is like a mirror reflecting on itself, burning on itself" (107). According to this account, Hayy is born outside of any particular society or religious tradition and is under no divine commandments. He comes of age under the direct influence of the highest spirit that emanates continuously from God, which the narrator equates Platonically to the sun or the "good" (*Republic* 6.509). Here, the Highest Reality is responsible for, and is the source of, the growth and generation of all things, giving them their existence, beauty, truth, and understanding.[6]

For those who deny the plausibility of this account of Hayy's origin, however, Ibn Tufayl offers the following alternative account. Another island, "a large island, rich and spacious," was inhabited by people over whom "a proud and angry man, was king" (105). This unnamed king had a sister whom he "forbade to marry until he himself should find a fitting match." Moved by the powerful and spontaneous force of love, however, the sister secretly but lawfully married a kinsman named Aware and conceived a son by him—hence the title of the book, "The Living One, Son of the Wakeful." Fearing exposure of her secret and concerned about her family's safety for having gone against the will of her tyrannical brother, she cried out to God, trusting Him to protect her son as she placed him in a box and cast him out into sea. "The powerful current caught the box and brought it that very night to the coast of the other island," where it broke open, the baby cried, and a doe mistook the baby's cry for help from one of her own fawns. She nourished and eventually raised him, protecting him from harm (105–6).

Since both accounts are obviously metaphorical, one can read these two suggested beginnings as the two extremes of Hayy's existence. Ibn Tufayl teaches that every individual is a combination of nature and convention. On the one hand, each of us is born a member of the human species. On the other hand, each of us is also born in and conditioned by a particular regime with a unique tradition, speaking the common language of our ancestors; we are shaped by a shared history and formed by particular habits. Ibn Tufayl suggests here that the attachments acquired at birth are very powerful and difficult, if not impossible, for most of us to overcome. Thus birth plays an important role in defining individuals and nations. Parents claim authority over their children on the basis of birth, just as peoples claim rights to land or territory based on ancestral claims rooted in their origin. Local or tribal loyalties die hard, Ibn Tufayl implies. Hayy's mother's liberation from her brother's authority negates the family's or dynasty's ancestral claims. Only by separation from tradition and family can she claim freedom, just as John Locke proposed that birth does not confer rights.[7] On the other hand, her liberation from her brother's authority and family connection would spell the end of her authority over Hayy, for the source of her attachment to Hayy lies in family ties. According to the first account, however, Hayy is born to neither father nor mother. He is autonomous by nature. The first account is consistent with the general teaching that Hayy's perfection consists in his independence from others (133).

Combining the two accounts leads us to conclude tentatively that the progress of Hayy's education toward self-knowledge is due to his independence both from family and immediate relations and from the claims of revealed religion inherited along with family connection. Ibn Tufayl's book permits the reader to glimpse the shocking inference "that man may attain to supreme salvation by the inner light alone, without the aid of prophetic revelation"[8] or familial bonds to arrive at a life according to nature that answers the cryptic challenge of the oracle, "Know thyself!" As Lenn E. Goodman observes, "For Ibn Tufayl, as for the Platonist, to know oneself was to see in oneself affinities to the divine and to accept the obligation implied by such a recognition to develop these affinities—to become, in as much as was in human power, like God."[9]

Hayy's first seven-year stage of existence is childhood. He begins life dependent on his doe-mother but gradually grows into an autonomous being. Like a young fawn, Hayy follows the doe, observing and imitating her behavior as he learns to crack nuts with his first teeth. Her body provides him with warmth and her instinct to protect him shields him from harm. His dependence on her is rewarded by a protection more instinctual than loving.

His first cries for assistance are directed by his immediate needs and environment. Since his capacity to reason has yet to develop, he cannot make the logical connection between his tears and a future desire. His cries are immediate and natural reactions to need. At this stage he follows his "mother" everywhere, careful never to lose sight of her: "She stay[s] with him, leaving only when necessary to graze. The baby [grows] so fond of her he would cry if she were late, and then she would come rushing back" (109).

Eventually he learns to walk and, having grown teeth, he joins the doe on feeding expeditions. When he is cold, she warms him with her body. For several years he lives among the deer, "imitating their calls so well that . . . his voice and theirs could hardly be distinguished" (109). He discovers desires and aversions, memory and recollection, and the capacity to retain the idea of an object that he had previously encountered, "for their images were fixed in his mind" (110).

Slowly Hayy develops a more meaningful sense of the outside world and his place in it, as he becomes aware of how different he is from his animal companions. He discovers that fawns begin to grow horns but that he does not have natural weapons or tools. Consequently, the animals are able to wrestle food away from him, for he is considerably weaker and slower than they. He observes how they all have fur, hair, or feathers but that he is naked. Hayy's sense of shame and frustration marks this particular stage of his development: "The fact that the private parts of the animals were better concealed than his own disturbed him greatly and made him very unhappy" (110). It is important to note that, like Adam in the Garden of Eden, Hayy enjoys a protected existence where "there were no beasts" to threaten his life. Unlike Adam, however, Hayy lives under no commandments from God and gradually comes to knowledge and shame without being punished for it (137, 150). His God is not punitive, for His divine authority and existence do not depend on human adulation. Like the Platonic god in the *Republic,* the God Hayy discovers through his reason alone "in Himself, has no need of [humans] and is utterly independent of them" (133).

Hayy's second stage of development begins at age seven and ends at age fourteen. This stage ends the previous one of total dependence and helplessness. At the age of seven, he begins to engage in rational, human thought processes, sublimating his shame and frustration into a form of practical reason that allows him to think of material objects around him in terms of means to ends in order to help himself. He starts to compare and contrast himself to the animals in his natural environment, and having finally "lost hope of growing feathers or fur on his own," he resolves to "make up the deficiencies." Taking "some broad leaves from a tree [and putting] them on, front and back," he makes himself a belt. However, the leaves soon wither and dry, representing his first confrontation with death. He improves his "clothing" by using the skin of an eagle: "Boldly taking hold of the eagle, Hayy [cuts] off the wings and tail. . . . He stretch[es] off the remaining skin and split[s] it in half, trying it about his middle, hanging down, half in front and fasten[s] the wings to his arms" (110). He now "so terrifies the animals that not one of them would fight with him or get in his way." Only his inseparable "mother" doe remains with him until her death (111).

As she dies, their roles reverse—he has become the caretaker. He feels grief for the first time and tries to call out to her and to "discover the place where she was hurt so he [can] take away the hurt and allow her to recover" (111). He is not successful. One of the most important lessons that Hayy will learn is that of his own defenselessness against human mortality. Although he comes to understand his powerlessness, Hayy never rebels against death. Rather, he finds his freedom in understanding his mortal relationship to created beings. Because of his extreme separation from other humans, the attachments that usually stem from birth never take root in him. His liberation from the fear of death is remarkably easy.

Nevertheless, and entirely by himself, Hayy discovers the soul in his very human quest to search for the mysterious force in the body that failed in the doe. Thinking about her dying shifts his attention away from imitating others and the mundane practical concerns of daily existence to an in volvement with something deeper—the soul. His quest to discover the vital element ensconced in a living organism, giving life to its limbs, "leads him to learn about anatomy and biology and to use logic in order to solve the problem he is facing."[10] Hayy experiments, examines, compares, contrasts, and reasons until he learns that motion governs the natural world, that the soul and the body must be distinct, and that the soul is higher than, and the master over, the body. He ponders:

> What I'm looking for is [no longer in the body]. . . . I can see that [the body] is empty. I cannot believe it serves no purpose, since I have seen that every organ exists to carry out some specific function. How could this chamber, with its commanding position, have none? I can only believe that what I was searching for was here but left, leaving the chamber empty and the body without sensation or motion, completely unable to function.
>
> Realizing that whatever had lived in that chamber has left while its house was intact, before it has been ruined, Hayy saw that it was hardly likely to return. . . . The body now seemed something low and worthless compared to the being he was convinced had lived in it for a time and then departed. (114)

He has now separated himself from the animals around him. He has gained, entirely free from human social contact, an awareness of death and the mysterious power of the soul. He is repulsed by the decay and terrible stench of his "mother's" decaying body. His revulsion and contempt send him to bury the doe, and then he resumes his natural philosophizing (115).

As Hayy enters the third stage of his life, between the ages of fourteen and twenty-one, he makes the realization that each individual deer has the same form and figure as his mother and so must also share in that force that gave her motion and direction. Pursuing his spontaneous logic, Hayy generalizes this observation and concludes "that each animal, although many in respect of its parts, its various senses and types of motion, [is] nonetheless one in terms of that spirit which stems from a single fixed place and diffuses from there to all the organs. All parts of the body," he concludes, "are simply its servant or agents" (117). Drawing on his own relationship to his handmade tools, he reasons that "the spirit employ[s] the body much as he himself employ[s] the tools. . . . The same body handle[s] all these tools, using each appropriately for its own purpose" (117).

In the same way as Plato in the *Theatetus*, Hayy concludes that the soul uses the eyes as tools to see, the ears to hear, the nose to smell, the limbs to move, and the liver to digest. Each of these organs of the body is at the service of the "spirit and would be deprived of it functions were it not directed by the spirit through what we call the nerves" (117–18). These reflections lead him to conclude, entirely on his own, that understanding the mastery of the soul over the body leads to human happiness. Hayy's perfection lies in living a life according to nature, in which he orders his existence through reason (or the soul). His natural philosophy, spontaneous and honest, is free of any social, religious, or political authority. His own self-mastery is his version of cosmopolitanism, and his ultimate happiness will result in the "triumph over misery" gained by his awareness and contemplation of the divine order. He feels a natural proclivity to become like God, "for it is God alone" who "brought him his awareness of the Necessarily Existent being" (142–43), and not any social pressures or coercion. Whether Hayy's example serves as a practical model for a cosmopolitan society (as Attar suggests) or not, however, remains to be seen. He is, after all, still isolated in his existence.

Hayy reaches the age of twenty-one and enters the fourth stage of his development, which lasts until the age of twenty-eight. This period is marked by a consideration of all objects in the world, their generation and their decay. He remarks that "inasmuch as things differ they are many, but inasmuch as they correspond they are one" (119). At this stage in his development, Hayy broadens his reflections to include the universe and his own place within it. He concludes that the spirit within him is one, and it is this which is his real self; all physical organs are mere tools. Shifting his attention to animal species in general, he observes that each whole species—deer, horses, asses, etc.—is one in this respect: "The spirit present throughout the species must be a single entity, undifferentiated except through its division among all those [various, individual, physical parts]," just as water is one and may be divided into different bowls, cooler in some and warmer in others (120). Taking these thoughts to a spiritual level leads him to conclude that the whole plant and animal species, like water, "must too have a single substance in which all partake, and which makes them all one being" (120–21).

Some commentators, such as Attar, apply the same categories Hayy deduces from the animal world to the human species and conclude from this that the universalism Hayy observes in animal and plant species is the basis for his full-blown cosmopolitan outlook, since we are all members of the human species. Therefore, cosmopolitanism must be the necessary conclusion of any enlightened society. Although it is true that each human is a member of the human species, no such universal model of politics is possible in practice. Hayy's own rejection of society and his subsequent return to the solitary life of his desert island could never inform politics. In order to achieve his brand of universal cosmopolitanism, Hayy must remain outside society.

Observing plant and animal species, Hayy notices a hierarchy. Although plants and animals are alike in nutrition and growth, he concludes that "animals are higher than the plants in that they possess sense perception, locomotion, and sensation as well" (121). Much later, when Hayy moves on to spiritual development, he will conclude that God is identical with what Aristotle calls the Unmoved Mover, who is thought thinking itself (107) and the Being from whom all other beings emanate (130–35). However, in his young manhood, his thoughts are still limited to the physical. His enlightenment or discovery of metaphysics will come much later. Once Hayy reaches the highest level of philosophical reflection, his soul will be able, through conjunction with the active intellect, to rejoin God in a realm that transcends the material world, in which Hayy "becomes like Him . . . in self-knowledge" (147). At this stage of his development, however, the only beings he knows or believes to exist are physical (122).

Hayy's examination of the physical world forces him to conclude that by necessity all that comes into being changes and decays, and so must have a cause other than itself (127). He comes to the conclusion that the "proneness of a body to certain kinds of motion as opposed to others must be due to its disposition or form" (127). "Clearly the acts emerging from forms did not really arise in them, but all the actions attributed to them were brought about through them by another Being." At this point in the narrative, Ibn Tufayl interjects the following: "This idea to which he had now awakened is the meaning of the Prophet's words: 'I am the ears He hears by and the sight He sees by.' As it is written in the unshakeable Revelation: 'It was not you but God who killed them; and when you shot, it was not you who shot, but God'" (127). Hayy's rational insights appear to be in harmony with Revelation; in reality, Ibn Tufayl's point is that Hayy has discovered God, or the Mover of the universe, purely by his own reason without the assistance of scripture or established religious institutions: "He has no sacred text to subscribe to, no prophets to follow, no prayers to perform, no fasting, or pilgrimage to undertake, no strict rules to adhere to."[11] His contemplative life is supported in nature, rather than in political authority or religious scripture, and so can be carried out only in nature, in solitude, outside of society's distractions.

Having completed four stages of seven-year periods, Hayy reaches the fifth stage of his development, which begins at age twenty-eight and ends at age thirty-five. At the beginning of this stage, his attention turns to heavenly bodies (128). He studies the size of the sun and the moon and all the stars in the skies and examines their movement. His study of their motion leads him to conclude that, first of all, the firmament is spherical (129), and then that "all that is in [it] are . . . one organism whose parts are joined organically together" and that all bodies from his previous studies—earth, water, air, plants, and animals—are "enclosed within this being." He uses a simile to describe his observations: "The whole [is] like an animal. The light-giving stars [are] its senses. The spheres . . . [are] . . . its limbs. And the world of generation and decay within [is] like the juices and waste in the beast's belly, where smaller animals often breed, as in the macrocosm" (130). By now he has come to the profound realization that humans must be no more than a tiny insignificant organism within the vast space of the universe.

In this middle period of his life, Hayy turns his attention to the question of creation. Observing "the oneness of all bodies in the world of generation and decay," Hayy wonders whether the world was created out of nothing or nonbeing. He questions whether the world always existed (130). Perplexed, he examines these conflicting positions and thinks through their implications. After several years of hard rational work, he comes to the understanding of a divine creator:

> If he [assumes] that the universe had come to be in time, *ex nihilo,* then the necessary consequence would be that it could not have come into existence by itself, but must have had a Maker to give it being. This Maker could not be perceptible to the sense; for if it could be apprehended by sense perception, then it would be a material body, and thus part of the world, itself in time and in need of a cause. If this second cause were physical, it would need a third; a fourth, and so ad infinitum—which is absurd. Thus the world must have a noncorporeal Cause. (131)

Alternatively, if Hayy assumes that the world is eternal, and

> that it had always been as it is now, and [had] not emerged from non-being, this would imply that its motion too was eternal and had never begun, never started up from rest. Now every motion requires a mover. This mover can be either a force distributed through some body—self-moving or externally moved—or a force which is not distributable or diffusible in physical bodies. . . . Yet it has already been proved that every material body must be finite. So every force engaged in an infinite task, that force cannot belong to a physical thing. But we have found the motion of the heavens to be ceaseless and eternal, for *ex hypothesi* it has gone on forever and had no beginning. Ergo the force that moves them must be neither in their own physical structure nor in any external physical being. It can only belong to some Being independent of all material things and indescribable by any predicate applicable to them. (132)

His mind is now clear: "He was no longer troubled by the dilemmas of the creation versus eternity, for either way the existence of a non-corporeal Author of the universe remained unscathed, a Being neither in contact with matter nor cut off from it, neither within nor outside it—for all these terms, 'contact' and 'discontinuity,' 'inside' and 'outside' are merely predicates of the very physical things which He transcends" (133). Hayy concludes that "since matter in every [physical] body demands a form, as it exists through its form and can have no reality apart from it, and since forms can be brought into being only by this Creator, all being . . . is plainly dependent on Him for existence itself" (133). Hayy's Creator's power is infinite, perfect, and if He did not exist, nothing in the universe could exist (133). Knowing this will bestow happiness and allow mortals to contemplate the "Necessarily Existent" Being (143), a spiritual condition in which one's personal identity "dies" and only the awareness of the "everliving ONE" exists in a vision of total autonomy (150). In a conclusion critical to understanding Ibn Tufayl's cosmopolitanism, Hayy acknowledges: "But He, in Himself, has no need of [created beings] and is utterly independent of them" (133).

The same could be said, and needs to be said, of the enlightened philosopher's relationship to his fellows, for the philosopher's perfection consists in imitating God, or the Creator, as much as possible (147). Thus the supreme love for God enters Hayy's spiritual scheme: "Given room for . . . growth, reason might mature to wisdom," but "wisdom seeks more than knowledge; it seeks an active relationship of love . . . with God" (11). Hayy's cosmopolitanism lies in his independence from others, as Ibn Tufayl indicates by the protagonist's eventual abandonment of society in favor of a life devoted to contemplation. It is this understanding of the world and the human place within it that informs the cosmopolitanism that characterizes Hayy's enlightened life.

Indeed, at the age of thirty-five, and at the start of his sixth stage of development, his awareness has transcended his interest in created things, including his own particularly. "By now thought of this Subject [God, the Creator, is] so deeply rooted in his heart that he [can] think of nothing else" (134–35). He realizes that God cannot be apprehended through the senses, for the senses can apprehend only physical objects, but "by some non-physical means . . . which is neither inside nor outside, neither in contact with it nor disjoined from" the world (135). The awareness that brings him to understand this Being must be his soul, he guesses, by which he has come to know Him as "non-corporeal and not qualifiable by any physical predicates." Hayy's physical self, then, is not his true self; his true identity must be "that by which he had apprehended the Necessarily Existent" (136).[12]

Hayy concludes that his true essence, that nobler noncorporeal being within him that "allowed him to apprehend this Being, [is] unlike bodies and would not decay as they did" (137). Hayy weighs the implications of his awareness of the Creator against his own mortality and draws the following moral lesson:

> Leaving the body at death, anyone with an identity like his own, capable of awareness such as he [possesses], must undergo one of these three fates: If, while in command of the body, he has not known the Necessarily Existent, never confronted Him or heard of Him, then on leaving the body he will neither long for this Being nor mourn His loss. His bodily powers will go to ruin with the body, and thus make no more demands or miss the objects of their cravings now that they are gone. This is the fate of all dumb animals—even those of human form.
>
> If, while in charge of the body, he has encountered this Being and learned of His goodness but turned away to follow his own passions, until death [overtakes] him in the midst of such a life, depriving him

> of the experience he has learned to long for, he will endure prolonged agony and infinite pain, either escaping the torture at last, after an immense struggle, to witness once again what he [has] yearned for, or remaining forever in torment, depending on which direction he tended toward in his bodily life.
>
> If he knows the Necessarily Existent before departing the body, and turns to Him with his whole being, fastens his thoughts on His goodness, beauty, and majesty, never turning away until death overtakes him, [turns] towards Him in the midst of actual experience, then on leaving the body, he will live on in infinite joy, bliss, and delight, happiness unbroken because his experience of the Necessarily Existent will be unbroken and no longer marred by the demands of the bodily powers for sensory things—which alongside that ecstasy are encumbrances, irritants and evils. (137–38)

The first and second fates belong to various lives or types that Hayy will eventually encounter within society. The last fate is his, and the ascetic lessons he draws from it inform his decision later to return to his desert island, rather than to remain among his fellows. For Ibn Tufayl, solitude is the only path to understanding and enlightenment.

Hayy, in the spiritual quest that marks this sixth stage of his life, comes to realize that certain obligations follow from his awareness of Him: "Hayy [sees] that his nobler part, by which he knew the Necessarily Existent, [bears] some resemblance to Him . . . and the obligation . . . to endeavor, in whatever way possible, to attain His attributes, to imitate His ways, and remold his character to His, diligently execute His will, surrender all to Him . . . and rejoice in His rule" (142). Hayy eventually experiences a mystical annihilation, in which "the self vanishes; it is extinguished, obliterated—and so are all other subjectivities. All that remains is the One, True identity, the Necessarily Existent—glory, exaltation, and honor to Him" (143).

It is only in his fifties, at the end of the seventh stage of his development, that Hayy meets another human being for the first time. That person, Absal, introduces Hayy to society, at which point Hayy will also for the first time perceive that the universe consists of two different worlds—a natural one, the only world he has known up to now, and an artificial one inhabited by trivial, materialistic beings whose lives are described in the second fate mentioned above, unenlightened, uneducated, and incapable of genuine knowledge. They frustrate his attempts to teach them enlightened, universal cosmopolitanism. Their hopeless and limited materialism sends Hayy back into voluntary isolation.

Absal was a young man of ability and high principle who had grown up on a nearby island, where, according to the second account of Hayy's origins, Hayy was born. Absal teaches Hayy to speak his language. Once the two can communicate, Hayy shares with Absal his knowledge of the Creator. Upon hearing Hayy's description of a Being that transcends the physical world and is the uncaused cause of all things in the universe, "and the joys of those who reach Him and the agonies of those veiled from Him," Absal's "mind catches fire" and he concludes that "Reason and tradition were at one within [Hayy]" (160). Absal looks on Hayy "with newfound reverence" and resolves to become his disciple, following his example and direction, for he believes Hayy is a man of God, one of those who "know neither fear nor sorrow" (160).

Absal introduces Hayy to all the religious traditions connected to his culture: the divine world, Heaven and Hell, rebirth and resurrection, the humanly constructed laws and the notions of justice informing them. Absal describes to Hayy the acts of worship, prayer, poor tax, fasting, and pilgrimage, "and other such outward practices" (161). Hayy has two concerns about their religion: "First, why did [their] prophet rely . . . on symbols to portray the divine world, allowing mankind to fall into the grave error of conceiving the Truth corporeally and ascribing to Him things which He transcends and is totally free of (and similarly with reward and punishment) instead of simply revealing the truth?" Second, Hayy wonders, "Why did [their prophet] confine himself to these particular rituals and duties and allow the amassing of wealth and overindulgence in eating, leaving men idle to busy themselves with inane pastimes and neglect the Truth" (161). Hayy is dumbfounded that their revealed religion relies on reward and punishment to enforce the laws, rather than the inner motivation toward love, which he has experienced on his island. If the people genuinely understand the Truth as Hayy does, what need do they have of all these laws, "for which human beings might struggle and risk amputation" (162)? Hayy cannot understand why God, in His perfection and independence, would authorize or depend upon such a system of rewards and punishments to compel belief and obedience. His perplexity stems from his "naïve belief that all men [possess] outstanding character, brilliant minds and resolute spirits. He [has] no idea how stupid, inadequate, thoughtless, and weak willed they are, 'like sheep gone astray, only worse'" (162). Hayy's naïveté leads him to believe that he could enlighten the inhabitants of the island about the true nature of God and virtue, an experiment that will end in total failure. His failure to reform society, however, brings him closer to a genuine understanding of what Ibn Tufayl considers to be the human condition and the philosopher's relationship to politics and civic religion. Although Hayy is the prototype of the cosmopolitan individual, by the end of story he will understand the limits of enlightenment and societal "progress."

Pitying humans and hoping that he may save them from their ignorance, Hayy resolves to reach out and to teach them the truth so that they will no longer be governed by the incoherence of their particular laws, but by a universal reason and enlightenment. He seeks, like the modern proponents of world citizenship, to reform their society along cosmopolitan lines, free from parochial habits and opinion. Absal warns him how defective the inhabitants of the island are in character and how heedless of God's Word they are, but Hayy simply cannot accept his counsel. Absal eventually compromises, blinded by his own hope that through "Hayy God might give guidance to a body of aspiring acquaintances of his, who are somewhat closer to salvation than the rest" (162). This will be the test group: if Hayy fails to teach *them,* it would be impossible for him to teach the masses.

Hayy begins to teach his profound wisdom to Salaman, Absal's close friend and the ruler of the island, and Salaman's inner circle but meets only with frustration: "But the moment [Hayy rises] the slightest bit above the literal or [begins] to portray things against which they [are] prejudiced, they [recoil] in horror from his ideas and [close] their minds. Out of courtesy to the stranger and in deference to their friend Absal, they [make] a show of being pleased with Hayy, but in their hearts they [resent] him. . . . The more he [teaches], the more repugnant they [feel], despite the fact that these [are] men who [love] the good and sincerely [yearn] for the Truth" (163). Hayy eventually abandons his hope of enlightening Salaman and his inner circle and, in desperation, turns his attention to different classes and types of people. Again, he meets failure: "They . . . made their passions their god. . . . They [destroy] each other to collect the trash of this world, 'distracted by greed 'til they [go] down to their graves.' Preaching is no help; fine words have no effect on them. Arguing only makes them more pig-headed. Wisdom, they have no means of reaching; they were allotted no share of it. They are engulfed in ignorance. Their hearts are corroded by their possessions. God has sealed their hearts and shrouded their eyes and ears" (163).

This is the moment when Hayy begins to understand the human condition, his unique relationship to it—and the limits or impossibility of spreading enlightenment and establishing a cosmopolitan society. He realizes that any attempt to persuade through reason or convert others through force, as their prophet has tried to do, is bound to fail. Indeed, he recognizes the necessity for religion, rather than enlightenment or cosmopolitanism, to bring a simulacrum of order to society: "The sole benefit most people could derive from religion [is] for this world, in that it help[s] them lead decent lives without others encroaching on what belong[s] to them. . . . He [sees] that most men are no better than unreasoning animals, and realize[s] that all wisdom and guidance, all that could possibly help them [is] contained already in the words of the prophets and the religious," and that his own teaching would do more harm than good (164). These people, distracted by the social character of their lives, can never be motivated by a love of the universal, Hayy's true cosmopolitanism.

Upon observing the limits of people caught up in society and their need for rules and guidelines, rewards and punishments, Hayy employs irony in order to quit this society without creating social disarray: "He [tells] them that he [has] seen the light and realize[s] that they [are] right. He urge[s] them to hold fast to their observance of all the statutes regulating outward behavior and not delve into things that [do] not concern them, submissively to accept all the most problematical elements of the tradition and shun originality and innovation, follow in the footsteps of their righteous forbears and leave behind everything modern [presumably his lessons in cosmopolitanism]. He caution[s] them most emphatically not to neglect religion or pursue the world as the vast majority of people do" (164). The dangers of Absal's aspiring group's achieving wisdom present too great a risk to the smooth running of the community: "If ever they were to venture beyond their present level to the vantage point of insight, what they had would be shattered" (165).

The anticosmopolitan conclusion of this story could not be clearer. Hayy's maturity consists in understanding that the world is not, and can never become, rational. Any attempt to improve and elevate human life by displacing political and religious traditions by reasoned philosophy, as

Salaman had suggested, would result in utter degradation of human life and society. Although he is able to imagine the best possible human life for a solitary individual on the basis of his natural reason alone, he now understands how vital it is for communities to preserve the conditions, especially the moral and religious beliefs, they require to maintain political order. Since Hayy's perfection and happiness are founded on philosophy, and as his experience with Salaman makes clear, philosophy arouses political opposition. Ibn Tufayl seems to teach that either one must preserve culturally constructed norms to live in a society, or one must pursue perfection in isolation. Hence, Hayy voluntarily returns to his desert island with his friend Absal. There, away from the distractions of human institutions, the two will lead philosophical lives, free from prejudice and ignorance. By the end of the book, Ibn Tufayl makes absolutely clear his preference for the higher and ultimately greater satisfaction of the philosophical life over the social or communal, where religion is (and must remain) a moral and political tool for the guidance of ordinary mortals. Ibn Tufayl suggests a solution for those of us who do not possess a desert island of our own. This island-space can be imagined, he advises, where we philosophers can exercise prudence by practicing secrecy and irony. By doing so, his readers can live and even thrive as solitary philosophers while residing in imperfect cities (165).[13]

Hayy is cosmopolitan only insofar as he does not distort his awareness of the true order of things by futilely seeking to convert others to his way of life. Like the divine Being whom he seeks to imitate as much as possible, his full maturity is grounded in an understanding that his happiness does not depend on any created thing, be it his own biological parents, whom he never seeks to discover at any point in his life, or his fellow humans. He does not need to be a philosopher king in order to achieve his end. He is genuinely autonomous; his life of contemplation is an end in itself, requiring nothing more than a modest existence where the mundane practical concerns of his body are met. His story affirms the possibility of attaining true happiness and self-knowledge without the assistance of established religion and laws, but equally it affirms the impossibility of an enlightened society. Although Hayy is in spirit a "citizen of the world," Ibn Tufayl teaches that the majority of humans must be protected from newfangled theories by self-styled intellectuals and must necessarily belong to either a tribe or a nation, governed by laws and religious customs designed to help them lead decent lives (164). For Ibn Tufayl the awareness of human mortality is natural, and our knowledge of its relationship to the opinions that we hold about the true, the good, and the beautiful is the portal through which self-knowledge and the best life can become possible.

It is fitting to conclude, as does Ibn Tufayl, with his anticosmopolitan teaching:

> And this—may God give you spirit to strengthen you—is the story of Hayy Ibn Yaqzan, Absal and Salaman. It takes up a line of discourse not found in books or heard in the usual sort of speeches. It belongs to a hidden branch of study received only by those who are aware of God and openly I have broken the precedent of our righteous ancestors, who were sparing to the point of tightfistedness in speaking of it. What made it easy for me to strip off the veil of secrecy and divulge this mystery was the great number openly spread by the self-styled philosophers of today, so widely that they have covered the land and caused universal damage. Fearing that the weak-minded, who throw over the authority of prophets to ape the ways of fools, might mistake those notions for the esoteric doctrines which must be kept secret from those unfit to know them, and thus be all the more enticed to embrace them, I decided to afford them a fleeting glimpse of the mystery of mysteries to draw them to true understanding and turn them away from this other, false way. (165–66)

Notes

1. A notable exception is Samar Attar, *The Vital Roots of European Enlightenment: Ibn Tyfayl's Influence on Modern Western Thought* (Lanham, MD: Lexington Books, 2007), 50, 63.

2. Ibn Tufayl, *Hayy Ibn Yaqzan, a Philosophical Tale,* trans. with an introduction and notes by Lenn E. Goodman (Los Angeles: Gee Tee Bee, 2003), 7. All references to *Hayy Ibn Yaqzan* (most of them given parenthetically in the text) are to this edition.

3. Since very little has been written on *Hayy Ibn Yaqzan,* except for Samar Attar's excellent work, the reader must judge my essay on the basis of its own merits. Although I agree with the importance Attar places on Hayy's story, I do not agree with her conclusion that Ibn Tufayl teaches a cosmopolitan politics.

4. M. Saeed Sheikh, *Islamic Philosophy* (London: Octagon Press, 1982), 124.

5. See, for example, the reference to Genesis in *Hayy Ibn Yaqzan,* 107.

6. Compare Koran 2:255. For an excellent discussion of the relationship between the Platonic notion of generation and knowledge in Avicenna's meta-

physics, see Lenn E. Goodman, *Avicenna* (London: Routledge, 1992), 49–122, particularly 51–53.

7. See, for example, chapters 2–11 in the *First Treatise on Government* and the first chapter of the *Second Treatise,* in which Locke reinterprets man's relationship to God to argue that birth does not confer rights.

8. Sheikh, *Islamic Philosophy,* 129.

9. Lenn Evan Goodman, *Ibn Tyfayl's Hayy Ibn Yaqzan* (Los Angeles: Gee Tee Bee, 2003), 17.

10. Attar, *The Vital Roots of European Enlightenment,* 43.

11. Ibid., 47.

12. It is around this stage in his development that Hayy, inside a cave, begins to meditate on his inner awakening, reminding one of both Plato's allegory of the cave in the *Republic* and Muhammad, who is traditionally believed to have withdrawn to a cave on Mount Hira in which he received the divine inspiration for the Koran. Unlike Plato's cave, Hayy's cave is not a social womb in which ignorance impedes intellectual enlightenment, and unlike Muhammad's cave, Hayy's cave is a place of private enlightenment in which his discoveries cannot inform society, as Muhammad's clearly did. For an interesting comparison of these two examples, see Goodman, *Ibn Tyfayl's Hayy Ibn Yaqzan,* 218n.

13. For a similar treatment of the relationship between philosophy and politics in Farabi's reading of Plato, see Leo Strauss, "Farabi's Plato," in *Louis Ginzburg: Jubilee Volume,* ed. Saul Lieberman, Shalom Spiegel, Solomon Zeitlin, and Alexander Marx (New York: American Academy for Jewish Research, 1945), 359–83.

Part 2

Modern and Contemporary Cosmopolitanism

Mary P. Nichols

Kant's Teaching of Historical Progress and Its Cosmopolitan Goal

Immanuel Kant provides a philosophical justification for cosmopolitanism in education and for internationalism in foreign policy. Like today's internationalists, Kant asks teachers to promote universal perspectives in their students, educating them in "love toward others" and "feelings of cosmopolitanism." Children should be made acquainted with their interest in "the progress of the world," Kant concludes his work *On Education,* "so that it may give warmth to their hearts." And so they will "learn to rejoice at the world's progress, although it may not be to [their own] advantage or that of their country."[1] So too does Kant's political teaching provide "preliminary articles for perpetual peace among states" so that we "can hasten this happy time for our posterity."[2] Kant's recommendations for education and international organization are supported by his teaching of historical progress toward "a universal cosmopolitan condition" and "an international government for which there is no precedent in world history."[3] This historical progress is the argument of his "Idea for a Universal History from a Cosmopolitan Point of View." While Kant does not imply that there can be a complete coincidence between morality and politics, or that politicians who advance international goals do so for moral reasons, Kant argues that a good international order is necessary for the moral order of a people (IUH 21; see also PP 112–13). Kantian morality, of course, is not based on *feelings* of cosmopolitanism or love of humanity. Rather, it is based on "the idea of humanity." Human beings act morally when they guide their actions by maxims that they are able to will as a universal law binding all rational beings.[4] In abstracting from all "private ends" that distinguish them from other rational beings (MM 51), those who follow Kant's famous categorical imperative act morally, regardless of whether it is to their advantage or that of their country. In this sense they are cosmopolitans, something for which education according to Kant's recommendation prepares them.

In this essay, I explore Kant's teaching of historical progress by examining his "Conjectural Beginning of Human History." This work clearly suggests that history intends humanity's moral as well as political progress. Here Kant speaks not merely of "a perfect civil constitution," but also of humanity's "progressive cultivation of the disposition toward goodness."[5] Kant's description of this progress, I argue, suffers from difficulties that he himself recognizes. But even so, he presents his teaching on history as our best hope, given the two options he faces, early modern liberalism and what he regards as Rousseau's inadequate attempt to correct it. By studying Kant's teaching on history, we learn not only the dangers of embracing his cosmopolitanism but also the difficulty and desirability of finding a satisfying alternative to it.

Kant's Account of the Origin of History: Its Scope and Purpose

At first sight, "Conjectural Beginning" does not appear to be a weighty undertaking. Kant himself depreciates his work as "a mere pleasure trip," "at best only . . . a permissible exercise of the imagination guided by reason undertaken for the sake of relaxation and mental health" (CB 53). It is not "serious business," he implies, since it presents conjectures rather than records of actual occurrences (CB 53). Kant later claims that the recorded events of history, appearing to human beings as an endless panorama of pointless suffering and injustice, lead them to a despairing dissatisfaction with Providence (CB 68). It is this despair that his teaching about history—its progression toward a perfect condition—attempts to relieve. The "mental health" he is trying to effect is not merely his own, but that of humanity as a whole. His "conjectures," far from having less worth than the recorded events of history, will counter the baneful influence that those recorded events have on the human psyche. Under Kant's ironic self-depreciation lies the importance of "Conjectural Beginning."[6] As an account of the origin of the human race, "Conjectural Beginning" resembles both Genesis and Rousseau's *Second Discourse*. Indeed, it explicitly refers us to both works.

Kant claims at the outset that he will follow the biblical account and even take Scripture as his guide. He is in need of a guide, he says, since his goal, knowledge of human origins, cannot be as certain as knowledge of the recorded events of history. Our understanding of our origins must therefore be conjectural.[7] Kant asks his reader to "check at every point whether the road which philosophy takes with the help of concepts coincides with the story told in the Holy Writ" (CB 54). The reader will find, however, not only particular discrepancies between Kant's account and the Bible's, but also a different understanding of humanity's end or goal. Indeed, Kant is examining the beginnings of human history in order to show that they contain the seeds of a development leading to perpetual peace and perfect culture in this life.

Kant also refers to Rousseau's account of human origins, specifically to his presentation of "an inevitable conflict between culture and the human species" (CB 60).[8] In his *Second Discourse* Rousseau describes the natural state of humanity as one of simple peace and harmony. Human freedom or "perfectibility" makes possible historical development,[9] including the development of reason, speech, and morality, in contrast to the simple goodness of the natural state. Human development, however, is also the source of countless conflicts and evils (SD 114ff.). Human beings cannot be content, in Rousseau's view, ultimately because the simplicity of their natural state is in tension with their historical development, their "culture," and because both simplicity and reflection are essential features of our humanity. Although Kant admits that Rousseau tries to show in such works as the *Emile* and the *Social Contract* how the conflict between nature and culture might end, he claims that the conflict remains "altogether unresolved" (CB 61). The resolution, Kant says, awaits further historical development (CB 61–62). Kant's account of historical development will substitute a vision of historical progress for Rousseau's ambivalent view of history's benefits to humanity. History may be the source of humanity's ills, but it also leads to their correction. Kant's "Conjectural Beginning" is thus a reply to both the Bible and Rousseau, and it will attempt to show us a way toward the relief of suffering in this world that neither the Bible nor Rousseau provides.

Kant begins his account of "the development of freedom from its original predisposition in human nature" (CB 53) by assuming "the existence of man," who "could speak" and "even discourse," or "speak according to coherent concepts" and "hence to think"—"skills," Kant says, "he had to acquire for himself" (CB 54–55).[10] "The existence of man" must be his starting point because it is something that "human reason cannot derive from prior natural causes" (CB 54).[11] Although he will proceed to describe the power of reason—the four steps through which it frees humanity from nature—he first indicates a step that his own reason will not take. The power of reason is circumscribed. It is from a recognition of this limit that reason's power can become clear. Had humanity been derived from prior natural causes, reason's releasing human beings from "the womb of nature," its last step (CB 59), would become suspect, as humanity's origin in nature would make its release less plausible. Nor does Kant refer explicitly to God's creation of Adam and Eve, even though he intersperses his account with references to Genesis so that we might compare his account with the biblical one. The latter, of course, begins not with the existence of human beings, as does Kant, but with their divine cause.[12] Reason is as unable to derive humanity's origin from a superhuman source as from a subhuman one. Moreover, the last step of reason is the achievement of equality with all rational creatures, including God (CB 59). Had Kant tried to derive humanity's existence from God's creation, reason's elevation of human beings to the status of gods would have seemed to suffer from lack of self-understanding.[13] Reason's conscious self-limitation is in the service of its greatest self-assertion.

Kant does follow Genesis in beginning with a single adult pair rather than with many human beings. In this he differs from Rousseau, whose state of nature is inhabited by a number of isolated human beings, who form couples for no longer than it takes to satisfy their sexual desires. Because Kant attributes this greater degree of sociability to the natural state of human beings, it is easier for him than for Rousseau to foresee a resolution to the conflict between nature and society. Kant's argument for the harmony of the natural state, however, sheds doubt on that very harmony. He must begin with a single couple, he says, because, if there were more than one couple, war would begin at once, "what with men's being close to each other and yet strangers" (CB 54). Although Kant here disagrees with Hobbes's view that the state of nature is one of war, he makes a large concession to Hobbes's position when he concedes that, if human beings did live together in a state of nature, there would be war. He later admits that war, or the threat of war, dominates human history (CB 66). When he gives a second reason for beginning with a single adult pair, he assumes without argument that nature's highest end for humanity is sociability. There must then have been a single adult pair in the beginning, for "undoubtedly to that end the descent of all men from a single family was the best arrangement" (CB 54). Kant does not tell us how he knows that nature's end for human beings is sociability, an end in tension with their mutual hostility that his previous argument indicates.[14] His peculiar argument for human sociability, with its implications of mutual antagonism, throws a dubious light on the prospects for perpetual peace.

Kant's Account of the Development of Freedom

Kant describes four steps of reason as the basis for human freedom. In the beginning, instinct guides human beings toward some foods and away from others.[15] Human beings break away from instinct when they notice that there are foods other than those to which their instinct guides them. Reason, aided by the imagination, compares the unfamiliar food to the familiar and "create[s] artificial desires," which eventually "generate a whole host of unnecessary and indeed unnatural inclinations called luxuriousness" (CB 56). Like Rousseau (e.g., FD 36), Kant distinguishes between natural and artificial desires and observes that artificial desires are harmful to human beings. He mentions, for example, our coming to desire food that is not good for us (CB 56). Reason thus initially has harmful consequences. Kant nevertheless places this development of reason in a positive light by arguing that while individuals suffer from the development of reason, the species benefits (cf. Rousseau, SD 140). Through this first step of reason, a human being becomes "conscious of his reason as a power which can extend itself beyond the limits to which animals are confined" (CB 56). Eventually, reason's progress will enable us to achieve the status of moral beings (CB 58–59). And the knowledge we gain through science will prevent us from choosing objects that harm us. After the initial stirring of reason, Kant says, human beings do "not *yet* know the secret properties or the remote effects of anything" (CB 56, emphasis mine). Scientific knowledge will replace the immediate impulsion of instinct in helping human beings to desire what benefits them.

The deeper problem that results from reason's freeing human beings from instinct, however, is not so much the choice of what is harmful as the inability to choose. No longer guided by nature alone toward any of the objects they confront, human beings experience themselves as standing "at the brink of an abyss" (CB 56). And here science cannot help. Although it indicates the effects of choosing different objects, so that we avoid immediate physical harm, it does not reveal that any objects in the external world are intrinsically good or choiceworthy for their own sakes. Objects are good or bad only because they satisfy or thwart human desires. As Kant writes in his *Foundations of the Metaphysic of Morals,* "All objects of the inclinations have only a conditional worth, for if the inclinations and the needs founded on them did not exist, their object would be without worth" (MM 46). Kant thus accepts a modern view of nature, as maintained, for example, by Hobbes: the value of the objects we desire is in our desires rather than in the objects themselves.[16]

As a consequence of this view of nature, human beings are alienated from nature and unhappy. Although knowledge of nature, or science, can teach them how to control nature for their preservation and convenience, it does not bring them into any harmony with nature that truly contents them. Hobbes, for example, accepts what seems to be the inevitable result of this view of nature: human beings are condemned to the restless pursuit of one object after another. The world contains nothing that satisfies our desires (*Lev* 80ff.). Rousseau, on the other hand, while accepting the harsh fact that nothing is in itself lovable, denies that alienation is its concomitant. He teaches that we need not pursue one object after another without satisfaction, for our imaginations can endow objects with beauty and therefore make them lovable.[17] Kant's solution is more radical. Since nothing in the world can fully satisfy our desires, we should not depend either on the world or on our desires for satisfaction. The ultimate satisfaction Kant recommends—action grounded on a universal law applying to all rational beings—disengages human beings from the world and the objects they desire. The abyss caused by a world of objects without any intrinsic value is avoided only when an individual, thus freed, accepts his identity with all rational beings.[18] This identification with all rational beings is the final step of reason. Rather than restoring human beings to the initial harmony with nature that was theirs when they were guided by instinct alone, reason impels human beings "from the tutelage of nature to the state of freedom" (CB 59–60). This achievement comes from a progress that this first step of reason initiates.

As the first step of reason involves food, the second step involves sex. When animals experience sexual desire, they immediately seek satisfaction. As in the case of eating, desire ends with satisfaction, and new desires arise in time. Animal life is a sequence of desires and satisfactions. Human beings, however, can prolong and increase sexual desire by removing its object from their senses and holding it in their imagination. Inclination is thus rendered "more inward and constant" and transformed from sexual desire into love. Desire no longer merely arises and disappears with satisfaction but is prolonged over time. In this way human beings gain a constancy or identity that animals lack. The "refusal" or rejection of impulse that an individual shows when he removes what he desires from his senses manifests a mastery of impulse by reason. It is therefore an advance over the first step of reason, which "shows merely a power to choose the extent to which to serve impulse" (CB 57).

The distance between desire and its object that imagination produces makes possible a sense of decency—the "inclination to inspire others to respect by proper manners, that is, by concealing all that might arouse low esteem." Rather than simply desiring to possess his beloved, in an immediate sense, a human being begins to seek his beloved's esteem. From here, he soon seeks the esteem of others as well. In this concealment of whatever causes disrespect, Kant detects "a hint of the development of man as a moral creature." "Here," he says, "lies the true basis of sociability" (CB 57).

Rousseau is the precursor of Kant in tracing sociability to a transformation of sexual desire. In the *Emile,* Rousseau attempts to give an imaginary boy named Emile a natural education that prepares him to live in society (for example, E 327). Until adolescence, Emile's justice involves forming and keeping agreements with others in his own interest (E 98–100). But with adolescence comes sexual desire. Through arousing Emile's imagination, Rousseau transforms sexual desire into pity, which connects Emile to other sentient beings whose suffering he perceives, and into love, which connects Emile to a particular woman and, through her, to a particular country (E 219 and 324–44). According to Rousseau, sociability is therefore still rooted in the passions, although they are developed or channeled in certain directions. While Kant follows Rousseau in tracing sociability to a transformation of sexual desire, he maintains that this desire, like all others, must ultimately yield to reason, which becomes the cause of action—including social interaction. The desire to be recognized for something more than physical existence prepares humanity to act eventually from reason rather than desire. Sociability is most manifest in a community of rational beings (MM 50). The restraints growing out of human beings' recognition of one another as rational beings, Kant writes, "are far more essential for the establishment of civil society than [are] inclination and love" (CB 59).

Humanity goes even further beyond natural impulses in reason's third step, "the conscious expectation of the future." To some extent, the first two steps forced human beings to think about the future. The one who compares different foods does not eat immediately, but intends to eat in the future. So too the one who imagines a beloved no longer present to his senses and who works to obtain her esteem must think about future enjoyment. In the two initial steps, which necessitate restraint, reason "insinuate[s] itself into the first immediately felt needs"—those of food and sex (CB 57). Its third step is an advance, because it does not involve any particular need. This restraint of all immediate desires for the sake of future goods is made possible, presumably, by the restraint human beings acquire through the first two steps reason takes.

The second and third steps lead human beings to do what Rousseau calls "living outside themselves," as Rousseau describes the alienated and unhappy "social man" in the *Second Discourse.* Human beings lose the self-contained and independent life of the natural condition when as social beings they depend on the opinions of others for their view of themselves (SD 179). Moreover, Rousseau argues, human beings become alienated from themselves as they imagine that their happiness lies in some future condition. Instead of enjoying the present, they "live in the future," seeking a never-ending series of objects. They become the restless, discontented individual described by Hobbes (SD 179; E 82; *Lev* 80). In the natural condition, in contrast, natural man lives in the present: "His soul, agitated by nothing, is given over to the sole sentiment of its present existence without any idea of the future, however near it may be" (SD 107). Consequently, he has no fear of death. Absorbed by the present, those who live in the natural state finally die without its being perceived that they cease to be, and almost without perceiving it themselves (SD 109).[19]

In spite of the unhappiness that comes with society, Rousseau does not maintain that it is either possible or desirable for humanity to return to the natural state. Although he attributes simplicity and harmony to the natural state, Rousseau also speaks in the *Second Discourse* of the advantages of development. In the epoch of the first revolution, when the human race became differentiated into families, "the habit of living together gave rise to the sweetest sentiments known to man" (SD 146–47, also 115).[20] And Emile's education, as we have seen, is one that prepares him to live in society. In its last stages, he meets his future wife, Sophie, and at the end of the book, they look forward to the future, to the time when they will have a family (E 480). Because Rousseau educates human beings to live in families and political communities, their education involves them in the opinions of others and in thinking about events in the future. Thus, there is an unresolved tension in Rousseau's thought between the value of solitude and independence and the value of society, just as there is tension between natural simplicity, with its freedom from complexity and dependency, on the one hand, and perfectibility, on the other, which allows change into a more complex being who transcends mere animal existence.

Although Kant mentions no undesirable consequences of seeking the esteem of others, he does acknowledge the evils that Rousseau attributes to an awareness of the future. This step, Kant writes, is "the most inexhaustible source of cares and troubles, aroused by the uncertainty of [the] future." Kant mentions the man's foresight of the hardships of labor and the woman's of the pangs of childbirth, citing God's pronouncement of the punishment of Adam and Eve for their sin. Moreover, human beings foresee not only the miseries that may come to them while they live but also their inexorable deaths. Experiencing the unhappiness that reason brings, humans denounce its use as a crime because of its ill consequences, Kant says, citing God's denouncing the disobedience of Adam and Eve (CB 58). But if an action is determined to be a crime because of its consequences, more distant consequences could revise our understanding of the act. Kant's progressive account of reason's steps indicates the benefits for humanity that come from individual hardship. Whether the human race has won or lost by moving "from the tutelage of nature to the state of freedom" is not an open question "if one considers the destiny of his species" (CB 60). The miseries that history brings are justified by the end for which they are the indispensable means. And foresight of the future, which had been the source of humanity's ills, becomes necessary for overcoming the despair that arises from living in the present.[21] "This capacity for facing up to the very distant future, instead of being wholly absorbed in the present," Kant claims, "is the most decisive mark of a human's advantage." For it is this capacity that enables an individual "to prepare himself for distant aims according to his role as a human being" (CB 58).

In speaking of the miseries produced by reason's third step, Kant mentions the possibility that humans may derive comfort from the prospect of "living through [their] children who might enjoy a better fortune" (CB 58). Seeing oneself in one's children might be a helpful, if not necessary, transition to identifying oneself with the human species. For it is only by doing the latter that individuals can accept the miseries that history brings. Individuals suffer because of the conflicts of history, but humanity benefits. Insofar as one is "a member of a whole (a species)," Kant writes, "he must admire and praise the wisdom and purposiveness of the whole arrangement" (CB 60). Moreover, an individual's identifying himself with his species serves as preparation for reason's fourth and final step.

In this last step, a human being understands that he is the true end of nature and that other animals are "mere means and tools to whatever end he pleases." One may not treat other human beings as mere means to one's own ends without denying humanity's status as the end of nature (CB 58). Hobbes's citizen, by implication, has not taken this step, for in contracting with others for the sake of his own preservation he is treating them as means to his own ends. But with this final step of reason, human beings treat one another as "ends in themselves" and "enter into a relation of equality with all rational beings" (CB 59). One who progresses this far in freedom follows what Kant calls in other works "the categorical imperative" (for instance, MM 31). Those who follow this imperative act as purely rational beings with regard for any private interests or passions. They live as members of "a realm of ends," "a systematic union of different rational beings through common laws," where they "abstract from the personal differences" that separate them, "and thus from all content of their private ends" (MM 51). Acting only on maxims that can hold good as universal laws, they do nothing that other rational beings would not also do in the same circumstances (see also MM 38). Although Kant might seem to strengthen the individualism of early modern liberalism by grounding it in reason rather than in passion and self-interest, nothing distinguishes one whose acts conform to universal law from any other moral being. Individuals, insofar as they are distinct from others, do not belong to Kant's realm of ends.[22]

Kant's description of the rational being who acts according to the categorical imperative recalls Rousseau's description of the citizen in the *Social Contract* who wills the general will. The citizen overcomes his private interests and desires, and transcends attributes that belong to him as a particular being, in order to act simply as a citizen, willing the same common good any other citizen would also will.[23] In overcoming his private interests and passions, the citizen achieves a moral freedom, as opposed to the freedom experienced in the natural condition, where there are no passions or interests that need to be overcome (SC 56). The citizen is no more distinct from any other citizen than Kant's rational being is from other rational beings. Kant, of course, goes further than Rousseau, providing human beings not merely identity with fellow citizens in a small republic but identity with all rational beings.

In asking us to accept the end of reason's progress as good, Kant might seem to be rejecting one side of Rousseau's thought. He seems to choose perfectibility, sociability, moral freedom, and reason, while rejecting simplicity, independence, self-containment, and natural goodness. Kantian morality, however, offers some of the desirable characteristics of Rousseau's natural state. In acting only on the basis of universal humanity, the moral actor avoids the complexity that plagues Rousseau's civilized man, who is pulled in different directions by his nature and his social duties. Since he follows duty irrespective of any demands made upon him by others, he is independent of others. Since he "is subject only to his own, yet universal, legislation," and obeys no law that does not arise from his own will (MM 51), he is completely self-contained. Moreover, he does not suffer the miseries of society described by Rousseau, where individuals live outside themselves. The one who acts morally, for Kant, by definition does not seek the good opinions of others when he acts, for then he would lose his autonomy. Nor does he compare himself to others with pride and envy, for as rational beings humans do not differ. He does not live in the future, constantly desiring what is never present, for he acts not for the sake of a future object but because his action is that of a rational being (MM 44–45, 60–61). Far from living in constant fear of his own death, he gains a certain immortality through his identification with his species. Like Rousseau's "natural man," he would seem to die "almost without perceiving it" (SD 109; cf. IUH, 14). Total independence coincides with total community. A similar coincidence is found in the natural state Rousseau describes in the *Second Discourse*, where there is both asociality and homogeneity.

Kant thus suggests that we can attain the blessings of Rousseau's simple natural condition without having to give up civilization. Indeed, it is only through the final development of civilization that those blessings can be attained. Kant transforms Rousseau's idea of history into the idea of progress.

The Limits and Dangers of Kant's Cosmopolitanism

Kant's teaching of history's progress is intended to comfort his readers in the midst of their sufferings and to encourage them to advance the ends of their species. But there could be little comfort if progress appeared impossible or even improbable.[24] Kant gives a brief description of the human condition after history has begun (CB 63–65). The early division of human beings into farmers and herdsmen, whose interests were antagonistic, posed the constant threat of war. As long as rulers faced war, Kant observes, they depended on the people. Consequently, the worst despotisms did not develop. But eventually, and inevitably, the herdsmen were attracted to "the glittering misery of the cities." The threat of war then subsided, and "all liberty" came to an end. Humans suffered "a despotism of powerful tyrants and—culture having barely begun—not only an abominable state of slavery, but along with it soulless self-indulgence mixed with all the vices of an as yet uncivilized condition." Humanity was "irresistibly" diverted from "the progressive cultivation of its disposition to goodness" (CB 65). Kant seems to be referring here to a very early period in human history. But surprisingly, he does not describe any progress away from the abominable state of slavery and soulless self-indulgence. He allows us to wonder how much progress has actually occurred. This final description of humanity, as the title of this section of "Conjectural Beginning" says, is "The End of History." But progress has stopped in a "perpetual peace" of brutish pleasure and slavish servitude rather than in one of perfect culture. Since this situation is "irresistible," human beings appear to need a redeemer, a miracle. Although Kant cites the Old Testament to support his description of progress, "Conjectural Beginning" contains no reference to the New Testament. Human beings are as yet unredeemed.

The existence of the historical progress necessary to encourage us depends on the four steps of reason. While the first three steps indicate development away from mere animal existence, they do not in themselves constitute cause to rejoice at human progress. The third step, the conscious expectation of the future, is "the most inexhaustible source of cares and troubles" (CB 58). If human development went no further, history would not be clearly preferable to the merely natural state. As Kant writes, "Rousseau was not far wrong in preferring the state of savages, so long, that is, that the last stage to which the human race must climb is not attained" (IUH 21). It is only with the fourth step of reason that we achieve the freedom that constitutes human dignity.[25] "We are *civilized,*" Kant insists, but "to consider ourselves as having reached *morality*—for that, much is lacking" (IUH 21, emphasis Kant's). The "fourth step of reason," for example, is based on imperfect understanding. In taking it, the human being "came to understand, *however obscurely,* that he is the true end of nature" (CB 58, emphasis mine).[26] This crucial step requires, at the very least, Kant's clarification. But even if Kant does not completely persuade us of the necessity of history's progress, does his project for humanity nevertheless deserve our sympathetic understanding? Is the project possible and desirable?

Both the means and ends of Kant's project demand that human beings view themselves and act as members of their species rather than as individuals. They must sacrifice their private inclinations and interests in order to effect the destiny of humanity, for the beneficiary of the endeavor will be the human race, which shall attain its goal at the end of history, and future generations, who will live then (IUH 14). That goal, moreover, is moral as well as political—not merely a perfect civil constitution but the completion of culture, life as a moral species. Moral beings treat one another as ends and thereby act only on maxims that can serve as universal laws for all. Kant includes a note in "Conjectural Beginning" on the conflict "between man's striving toward the fulfillment of his moral destiny, on the one hand, and, on the other, his unalterable subjection to laws fit for the uncivilized and animal state" (CB 61). But if our subjection to these laws is unalterable, how can "art [become] strong and perfect enough to become a second nature—the ultimate moral end of the human species" (CB 63)? Perhaps Kant means that there are some needs so basic that art cannot transform them but that with the perfection of culture, these basic needs will no longer interfere with morality.[27] He gives three examples of the conflict between nature and culture.

Kant's first example involves a conflict between sexual desire and the demands of civilized life. Around the age of sixteen, youth are disturbed by sexual desire. Whereas in a simple state of nature, no harm comes from the immediate satisfaction of desire, in a complex society a sixteen-year old has not acquired the means, skills, or external circumstances necessary to discharge the responsibilities of adulthood and provide for a family. Culture therefore demands that he suppress natural desires. Surprisingly, Kant emphasizes that he is not condemning the natural desires, "for surely nature has not endowed living beings with instincts and capacities in order that they should fight and suppress them." Kant no longer mentions any transference of the desired object to the imagination nor any gain in inwardness through self-restraint. He appears to be conceding nature's power over humans. But although that power is unalterable, in the end it will not be distressing, for "a perfect civil constitution could end [this conflict], and such a constitution is the ultimate end at which all culture aims" (CB 61). Kant does not say how a perfect civil constitution would do this, but it seems clear that it would not require the young to restrain their desires until they are older, for such suppression would only accentuate the conflict rather than resolve it. What "fortunate external circumstances" would allow the young to marry early and still continue to learn the skills necessary to provide for their families and to contribute to culture's progress? Perhaps a technology that provided birth control, or a welfare state that supported families at least for a time, would free the young from the responsibilities that interfere with their education. Their satisfaction of desire would then no longer conflict with the demands of culture.

Kant's second example of the conflict between nature and culture is the brevity of the life of the talented individual. Just as Kant's first example takes a second look at reason's insinuation of itself into immediately felt needs, his second example looks again at the "inexorable death" of which our capacity to foresee the future makes us aware. Culture would profit from the continued life of the exceptional individual, Kant writes, for: "A single man of talent, who had reached mature judgment through long practice and acquisition of knowledge, could further the arts and sciences far more than whole generations of scholars if only he could live, mentally alert, for the length of their life-spans added together" [CB 62]. Because of the deaths of talented individuals, the progress of humanity toward "its destined goal appears to be subject to ceaseless interruptions." Nature takes the lives of exceptional individuals, however, for she has ends other than the advance of knowledge (CB 62). Kant does not say what end nature could have in depriving us of our greatest benefactors. Nor does he indicate any way in which the progress of history might resolve the conflict, as he did in the case of sexual desire. Indeed the natural mortality of exceptional individuals itself retards the progress of history. Kant seems to have a complaint against nature that he leaves unresolved.

Although Kant laments the death of talented individuals, he clearly subordinates their existence to the good of humanity. He describes them as those who can best serve the goals of humanity and further its progress toward its destined end. It is for this reason that their deaths are lamentable. The inequality among human beings, Kant clearly recognizes, loses significance in light of the good of the whole that superior individuals have a duty to promote. The lives of the unequal few are justified in light of the good of all. Indeed, Kant's final example of the conflict between nature and culture is that between the natural equality of all and the inequality imposed by social institutions. This conflict will be overcome, he says, when historical progress brings the recognition of universal human rights (CB 62).

Of these three examples of conflict between nature and culture, Kant leaves only the second without a solution of any kind. In the first case, culture will develop so as not to conflict with natural sexual desires; in the last, it will develop so as to fulfill nature's highest intention for humanity. Standing midway between nature's care for the human being "as an animal" and its care for him "as a moral species" (CB 61–62) is the death of talented individuals, the purpose of which Kant gives us no reason to understand. Near the end of "Conjectural Beginning," he returns to the brevity of life and the dissatisfaction it causes. Here he gives an argument justifying death, but the issue is the death of human beings in general rather than the death of exceptional ones. Kant reproaches those who want to live longer, for they "must be [poor judges] of [life's] value," for "its greater length would only prolong a game of unceasing war with troubles" (CB 67). Kant's argument, however, is hardly comforting, since it in effect urges acceptance of death because of life's miseries. But even if life were undesirable while culture remained imperfect, when it did become perfect, Kant's argument would not apply. For then the miseries of life that might make death acceptable would no longer exist. All the more would death be a source of discontent. By his perplexing treatment of death, Kant suggests that an individual's vision of his own death reminds him that he is not identical with his species, which will live on when he dies. Kant acknowledges an irreducible individuality that the universalism of his project ignores.

Even if Kant's project were possible, and human beings could identify with their species, would it be desirable for them to do so? What kind of life awaits them at the end of history when a perfect culture has assured perpetual peace? In "Idea for a Universal History," Kant acknowledges that "a cosmopolitan condition" does carry the "danger that the vitality of mankind [will] fall asleep," but he finds "a principle of balance among man's actions and counteractions" (IUH 20). Actions and counteractions, however, seem to indicate conflict. In the end, what conflict will there be? Kant questions whether a condition of perpetual peace is desirable near the end of "Conjectural Beginning" by criticizing the longing for an original state, "an age of simplicity and innocence," where there is to be "contentment with mere satisfaction of natural needs, universal human equality and perpetual peace" (CB 67). The original state Kant describes here surprisingly resembles the final condition that he is encouraging us to seek. For then also there will be perpetual peace, universal equality, and the satisfaction of natural needs. But Kant now disapproves of such a state as the "unalloyed enjoyment of a carefree life, dreamt away idly, or trifled away in childish play." It could not satisfy human beings, Kant says, for, if it could, they would have never left it. Kant asks us to overcome our desire for such idleness and "to give value to life by actions" (CB 67–68). These actions, paradoxically, are those that contribute to the goal of the human race (CB 68)—a state that uncomfortably resembles that which Kant is now deprecating as idleness and childish play.

The end of history therefore does not seem as good for humanity as the progress toward it—the actions by which human beings give value to their lives. Kant may not be asking that present generations sacrifice themselves for the sake of future ones who will enjoy perfect culture as it first appeared (see IUH 14); rather he may be sacrificing the good of future generations for the vitalization of present ones. Nature has willed that "[man] alone should have the credit and should have only himself to thank [for the advance from the lowest barbarity to the highest skill and mental perfection]—exactly as if she aimed more at his rational self-esteem than at his well-being" (IUH 14). Present generations will act to bring about perpetual peace and develop perfect culture. Future generations, however, will be the mere beneficiaries, who will have to honor their predecessors more than they esteem themselves.

But can the progress of history be of greater value to humanity than the end of history, if the progress is justified only by its end? Kant has been justifying the brutalities of history by arguing that they are necessary for progress toward the end. The inequalities of which Rousseau complained, for example, are inseparable from the development of culture (CB 62). War "is the greatest source of the evils which oppress civilized nations," but, without the perpetual fear of it, Kant questions whether "there would be the culture which in fact exists" (CB 66). And inasmuch as war is necessary for the further development of culture, "only in a state of perfect culture would perpetual peace be of benefit to us" (CB 67). In retelling the story of Cain and Abel, Kant talks merely about the farmer's "resorting to force in order to end the nuisance which [the herdsman] had created" (CB 63). But he is referring to Cain's murder of his brother. It is this ascendancy of the farmer and his way of life, according to Kant's account, that leads to human associations, the beginnings of art and culture, and finally civil authority. We might come to believe that the murder of others is justified if it promotes a distant future wherein we no longer treat one another as mere means to our own ends. As Pangle and Ahrensdorf ask, "Will not the Machiavellians in fact contribute more than the men of the categorical imperative to the achievement of perpetual peace . . . ?"[28] Indeed, the respect for others as rational beings that Kant encourages might be consistent with a contempt for human life insofar as it is immersed in particular passions and interests, especially if those interests are in conflict with human progress. Ironically, Kant's rationalism might eventuate not in the treatment of others as ends but in the brutal, even if selfless, action of fanatics.

This of course is the legacy of Kant only at its worst. His philosophy of history is understandable, if not justifiable, in light of the threat that human beings turn to a narrow hedonism as the goal of life or give way to an idle longing for an impossible past. This would, indeed, constitute "the end of history," but one consistent with "a despotism of powerful tyrants," "soulless self-indulgence," and "the end of all liberty" (CB 65). In the face of such possibilities, Kant spoke of dignity, action, and morality. It is a sign of both Kant's prescient understanding and care for humanity that he cautioned us about his project at the same time that he encouraged us toward noble and self-sacrificing actions aiming at the good of the human race.

Notes

An earlier version of this essay appeared in *Polity* 19, no. 2 (Winter 1986): 194–212.

1. Immanuel Kant, *Education* (Ann Arbor: Univ. of Michigan Press, 1960), 120–21.

2. Immanuel Kant, *Perpetual Peace,* trans. Lewis White Beck (cited as PP), 85ff.; and "Idea for a Universal History from a Cosmopolitan Point of View," trans. Lewis White Beck (cited as IUH), 22, both in *On History,* ed. Lewis White Beck (Indianapolis: Bobbs-Merrill, 1963).

3. For an excellent discussion of whether Kant's thought demands "a world-republic" rather than its surrogate, an ever-widening league of federated nations, see Thomas L. Pangle and Peter J. Ahrensdorf, *Justice among Nations: On the Moral Basis of Power and Peace* (Lawrence: Univ. of Kansas Press, 1999), 190–209, especially 202–3. "International government," in the passage quoted in the text, seems broad enough to allow for either possibility. In any case, Kant uses the expression "world citizenship" for this condition of perpetual peace to which human history is moving (see PP 102–3). For contemporary controversy over whether the use of "world citizen" is appropriate, see Martha Nussbaum et al., *For Love of Country?* ed. Joshua Cohen (Boston: Beacon Press, 1996).

This book includes Nussbaum's essay "Patriotism and Cosmopolitanism" and the responses of numerous critics.

4. Immanuel Kant, *Foundations of the Metaphysics of Morals,* trans. Lewis White Beck (Indianapolis: Liberal Arts Press, 1959) (cited as MM), 44ff.

5. Immanuel Kant, "Conjectural Beginning of Human History," trans. Emil L. Fackenheim (cited as CB), in *On History,* 61, 63, 65.

6. Emil L. Fackenheim points out that expositors of Kant find it difficult to take Kant's philosophy of history seriously. Fackenheim himself presents a persuasive case that it deserves serious attention for understanding Kant's philosophical system as a whole. Like the *Third Critique,* Fackenheim argues, Kant's philosophy of history "seeks to join together what the first two critiques have put asunder"—namely, nature and morality. Fackenheim's perceptive analysis explores the dilemmas underlying such a philosophy of history in terms of Kant's system as a whole and the reasons that Kant's philosophy of history ultimately fails. "Kant's Concept of History," *Kant-Studien* 48 (1956–1957): 381–98, especially 381, 387, 389, 397–98.

7. Commenting on this passage, William A. Galston points out that Scripture does not distinguish between the certainty of humanity's origins and that of its history. Both may be known equally well through revelation. Hence "the principle underlying Kant's procedure contains an implicit reservation against the Biblical account." *Kant and the Problem of History* (Chicago: Univ. of Chicago Press, 1975), 16.

8. Kant refers to both Rousseau's *On the Influence of the Sciences* and *On the Inequality of Man* for his presentation of the conflict (CB 60–61). In the former, Rousseau criticized what Kant refers to here as culture, the improvements of the sciences and arts, for corrupting the virtue of simple souls. See Jean-Jacques Rousseau, *The First and Second Discourses,* ed. Roger D. Masters, trans. Roger D. Masters and Judith R. Masters (New York: St. Martin's Press, 1964). Rousseau's *Discourse on the Sciences and the Arts,* known as the *First Discourse,* is cited as FD, and *Discourse on the Origin and Foundations of Inequality among Men,* known as the *Second Discourse,* is cited as SD. For an excellent discussion of the differences between Kant's "Conjectural Beginning" and Rousseau's *Second Discourse,* see Galston, *Kant and the Problem of History,* 93–102.

9. Although Rousseau writes that a human being's "being a free agent" distinguishes him from other animals and that "it is above all in the consciousness of this freedom that the spirituality of his soul is shown," Rousseau recognizes the difficulties in asserting that human beings are free from necessity, or the mechanical laws of physics (SD 114). Consequently, he soon replaces freedom with "the faculty of self-perfection" or "perfectibility" as the distinctive human trait (SD 114–15). Kant, as we shall see, in effect bridges this difference by attributing to human beings a predisposition to freedom. Kant's formulation, Galston points out, "stands somewhere between freedom and unfreedom." *Kant and the Problem of History,* 76 and 102. See also Susan Meld Shell, *The Rights*

of Reason: A Study of Kant's Philosophy and Politics (Toronto: Univ. of Toronto Press, 1980), 58–59.

10. Kant therefore does not accept the classical notion that human beings are rational by nature. As Fackenheim says, "The development of freedom and rationality must be self-development." Fackenheim refers to Kant's use of the term "animal rationable" rather than "animal rationale." He states the "paradox": "the act which actualizes the disposition to freedom and rationality already presupposes their actuality." "Kant's Concept of History," 388.

11. Rousseau might seem to locate the origin of humanity in prior natural causes when he substitutes "perfectibility" for freedom and traces the development of society, speech, and reason to "accidents," such as natural disasters that brought isolated human beings in the state of nature into greater physical proximity (SD 140). But for Rousseau to have recourse to "accidents" admits Kant's point: human reason cannot derive the existence of man from prior natural causes. Kant, after all, claims to be indebted to Rousseau.

12. The first reference that Kant gives is to the twentieth verse of the second chapter. When he cites God's command that Adam and Eve not eat the fruit of a certain tree, he refers us to Eve's telling the serpent what God said (3:2, 3) rather than to the words of God himself (2:16–17). Kant, in effect, eliminates God even from his citations to the Bible, since he replaces God with the woman's perception of God.

13. Kant cites Genesis 3:22, the passage in which God observes that "the man has become like one of us, knowing good and evil," to support his statement that, with the fourth step of reason, "man had entered into a relation of equality with all rational beings whatever their rank" (CB 59).

14. On the mutual antagonism of human beings throughout history, see also IUH 15. In "An Old Question Raised Again," Kant speaks of "a divinatory historical narrative of things imminent in future time" as known a priori rather than through experience. "But how is a history a priori possible?" he asks. "Answer: if the diviner himself creates and contrives the events which he announces in advance." Trans. Robert E. Anchor, in *On History,* 137.

15. According to Kant, this instinct is the command of God to which Genesis refers. Humanity's transcendence of instinctual guidance is his disobedience of God (CB 55).

16. Thomas Hobbes, *Leviathan,* ed. Michael Oakeshott (New York: Collier Books, 1975) (cited as *Lev*), 72–79.

17. Jean-Jacques Rousseau, *Emile or On Education,* trans. Allan Bloom (New York: Basic Books, 1979) (cited as E), 158, 168–69, 329, 391, 447.

18. "The inclinations themselves, being sources of want, are so far from having an absolute worth for which they should be desired that, on the contrary, it must be the universal wish of every rational being to be wholly free of them" (MM 46).

19. Rousseau writes that those in the state of nature fear only pain and

hunger. He refers to "pain and not death," he says, "because an animal will never know what it is to die; and knowledge of death and its terrors is one of the first acquisitions that [comes with] moving away from the animal condition" (SD 116).

20. In the *Social Contract,* Rousseau is more explicit. By forming a society based on the social contract, the human being "deprives himself of several advantages given him by nature," but "he gains such great ones, his faculties are exercised and developed, his ideas broadened, his feelings ennobled, and his whole soul elevated to such a point that if the abuses of this new condition did not often degrade him beneath the condition he left, he ought ceaselessly to bless the happy moment that tore him away from it forever, and that changed him from a stupid, limited animal into an intelligent being and a man." *On the Social Contract and Geneva Manuscript and Political Economy,* ed. Roger D. Masters, trans. Judith R. Masters (New York: St. Martin's Press, 1978) (cited as SC), 53–55.

21. See Galston's discussion of the ways in which "civil society is not as radically problematic for Kant as it is for Rousseau," *Kant and the Problem of History,* 97ff.

22. For a "communitarian" criticism of Kant's understanding of the individual, see Michael J. Sandel's *Liberalism and the Limits of Justice* (Cambridge: Cambridge Univ. Press, 1982).

23. Rousseau's description of the citizen applies equally well to Kant's moral action: "only, then, when the voice of duty replaces physical impulse and right replaces appetite, does man, who until that time only considered himself, find himself forced to act upon other principles and to consult his reason before heeding his appetites" (SC 55–56).

24. As Kant writes, "human nature is so constituted that we cannot be indifferent to the most remote epoch our race may come to, if only we may expect it with certainty. Such indifference is even less possible for us, since it seems that our own intelligent action may hasten this happy time for posterity" (IUH 22).

25. For further discussion of the gap between the first three steps of reason and the fourth (that is, between humanity as a natural and a moral species), see Fackenheim, "Kant's Concept of History," 388–89.

26. Kant also writes that a human being's idea of the animals as his tools "entails (*obscurely, to be sure*) the idea of contrast, that what he may say to an animal he may not say to a fellow human; that he must rather consider the latter as an equal participant in the gifts of nature" (CB 58, emphasis mine).

27. See Galston's discussion, *Kant and the Problem of History,* 83–84.

28. Pangle and Ahrensdorf correctly caution that "Kant resolutely resists any surrender to the notion that immoral means may deliberately be employed to or promoted to further just ends." *Justice among Nations,* 208.

Richard Velkley

Infinite Personality and Finite Custom

Hegel, Socrates' Daimon, and the Modern State

> Socrates could thus very well afford to be ignorant; he had a genius, on whose science he could rely, which he loved and feared as his god, whose peace was more important to him than all the reason of the Egyptians and Greeks.
> —J.G. Hamann, *Socratic Memorabilia* (1759)

Recent scholarship on Georg Wilhelm Friedrich Hegel's political philosophy has stressed its place in the modern tradition of reflection on autonomy and rights, thus rejecting negative assessments of Hegel as an authoritarian, post-Napoleonic "Prussian" opponent of liberalism (Karl Popper and others) as well as revising sympathetic readings of him as a "communitarian" critic of "atomistic" individualism (Charles Taylor and others). A group of eminent writers (one that includes Paul Franco, Frederick Neuhouser, Terry Pinkard, Robert Pippin, Steven B. Smith, and Allen Wood) argues that Hegel, deeply indebted to Rousseau and Kant as turning away from early modern "negative freedom," rethinks their accounts of "positive freedom" of self-determination based on the principles of the general will or moral law, and embeds those accounts in the customary and institutional framework of the modern constitutional-monarchical state. Hegel understands citizenship in this state as realizing the highest aspirations of modernity for universal recognition of the autonomous personality as secured by the rule of law, systems of impartial justice, suffrage rights (albeit limited), and freedoms of religion, publication, teaching, and so on—under the sovereignty of the patriotic (particularist but neither ethnocentric nor expansionist) state. Furthermore this scholarly approach to Hegel regards his conception of politically realized freedom as the heart of his whole philosophical endeavor and construes the dialectical (logical or metaphysical) arguments as providing chiefly the terms for explicating the rational will's or practical reason's inherent striving to actualize itself in ethically (*sittlich*), politically, and publicly "mediated" forms of recognition.

Undoubtedly such readings of Hegel as heir and reformer of modern liberalism are more accurate than readings of him as nostalgic for the unity and wholeness of the Greek city-state, not to mention those that would ally him with twentieth-century totalitarianism. In his discussions of Greek political life, Hegel, as early as the 1802 essay on natural law, underscores its limitations. What Hegel calls the unreflective natural morality of Greek ethical life, lacking the principle of free subjectivity, cannot be the basis for the modern state. Instead, the modern state in its most rational form realizes "subjectivity" in an ethical life (*Sittlichkeit*) of a peculiarly modern character, one that crucially includes a form of "civil society" unknown to antiquity (about which more later). Yet Hegel claims that a transformed (*aufgehoben*) version of the ancient unifying bond of custom, whose purest expression was the "pre-reflective" noble and beautiful morality of the Greek city, sustains an attenuated but all the same genuine existence in the modern state.

Having said this, one must also say that the recent interpretive approach has given not enough attention to Hegel's claim that the spirit of free subjectivity and "infinite personality" actually first emerged in Greek antiquity, not indeed as a common Greek possession but in those individuals who called themselves variously sophists and philosophers—and above all in the person of Socrates. Due regard for this claim can correct or supplement the current scholarly tendency by leading to the following conclusions:

(1) ***The focus on liberalism is too restrictive.*** One observes that Hegel's account of freedom is not adequately discussed if one limits the context of discussion to modern political philosophy, or to viewing Hegel as critic and reformer of the modern liberal tradition. More precisely, one sees the need to absorb Hegel's argument that the modern principle is the fulfillment of something first apparent among the Greeks, and hence not sufficiently described as an alternative or successor to Greek prephilosophic *Sittlichkeit*. Reflection on this Greek anticipation of the modern principle does not lead to abandonment of familiar Hegelian theses about the distinctiveness of modernity, but it does result in a deeper comprehension of these theses and

of Hegel's ultimate philosophic intention concerning the history of Spirit (*Geist*), the essence of modernity and of modernity's highest product, the modern state.

(2) ***The modern state has a philosophic origin and meaning.*** One grasps that Hegel's account of the history of political freedom is inseparable from his account of the emergence of philosophy as a possibility of the Spirit discovered by the Greeks. Accordingly, the significance of the modern state cannot be appreciated in narrowly political terms, or even solely in terms of a broader theoretical characterization of practical reason—its internal exigencies and their achievement of full satisfaction only under the conditions of modern political life—as much recent writing on Hegel favors. To express the main issue in a formula: Hegel regards the modern state—and only the modern state—as realizing what philosophy itself has been striving to attain, at least implicitly, since Socrates.

(3) ***Freedom has roots in philosophic reason.*** It then follows that what Hegel has in mind in his account of freedom is not expressible only in terms of modern doctrines of rights, although the philosophic core of freedom does not reach full maturity, in Hegel's thinking, until such doctrines emerge. The Socratic origination of free or "infinite" personality, as Hegel understands it, is not just an anticipation of modern moral-political freedom but the disclosure of philosophy's essence as freedom—and conversely, of freedom as in some crucial way philosophic.[1]

(4) ***Practical-political reason does not stand in a simple relation of priority to speculative logic.*** It also follows that if Hegel conceives the modern state as fulfilling the ends of philosophy, one must be suspicious of the tendency to read the speculative logic as only a theoretical structure erected to support a practical or political account of reason's character and goals (as in a theory of publicly mediated rationality). It seems one must say that for Hegel the political, the moral, and in general the practical are essential to fulfilling philosophy's striving. (Certainly this correction retains the intimate relation between philosophic ends and practical or political ends—and gives greater depth to that relation.)

(5) ***The problem resolved by the modern state concerns the relation of philosophy to practical life.*** To state now a bit more fully the formula on the modern state introduced in point 2 above: The radical freedom of philosophic thought, which first comes fully into view in Socrates, finds

itself in conflict with the realm of customary law and piety, and throughout its history philosophy strives to resolve or transcend that conflict—a goal that only the modern state adequately and finally attains.

Accordingly, the modern state's significance is philosophic insofar as it reconciles a conflict inherent in the life of reason as philosophic. If one then is to call Hegel's account of the modern state his "political theory" or "political philosophy," one would have to say that his account is not just his theoretical or philosophic treatment of political life (as the disciplinary classification might convey) but also his political or practical resolution of the central problem of the philosophic life.

(6) ***One must revisit historical categories commonly employed in the discussion of the modern state.*** Thus it is common to say that Hegel's account of the modern state's reconciliation of religion, politics, and philosophy addresses the fractured spiritual condition of the Enlightenment, just as it is common to say that its general actualization of freedom bears only a distant relation to Greek antiquity with its customary piety, institutions of slavery, and restriction of political freedom to the few. Instead, one must note that in Hegel's thinking both the problem and the promise of the Enlightenment are already present in the Socratic challenge to the Greek state. In Hegel's view, Greek antiquity is not as naive, and modernity's spiritual disorder not as unprecedented, as much writing on him pronounces.

In what follows I investigate Hegel's claim that Socrates is the turning point of world history—a claim that strikingly resonates with the judgment of another German thinker, one who sought the overthrow of the Socratic legacy.[2] And in this investigation I will discuss how Socrates' daimonic voice has a surprisingly central role in Hegel's account of his philosophic revolution.

My starting point is three passages on Socrates in the main text of the *Philosophy of Right* as published by Hegel in 1820.[3] These passages discuss, respectively, Socrates' moral subjectivism, his ironic mode of speaking, and his daimon.[4] Two more explicit comments on Socrates are in the expanded text (1833) produced by Hegel's student Eduard Gans, who worked with lecture notes of other pupils (Hotho and Griesheim).[5] Furthermore, "the problem of Socrates" arises implicitly in other passages, especially Hegel's preface. These passages supply a basis for moving to other discussions of Socrates: in the lectures on the philosophy of history and in the lectures on the history of philosophy, the second of which has Hegel's most expansive and probing statement on Socrates.

In 138R Socrates is put forward as an example of the spiritual stance of morality (*Moralitaet*) that Hegel familiarly distinguishes from ethical life (*Sittlichkeit*). Ethical life is the customary ways of a community, or (in premodern societies) the ancestral ways of one's family, city, country, or homeland. It covers prepolitical and political forms of the customary and is characterized by following tradition without feeling the need for the conscious articulation and justification of principles. According to Hegel, this way prevailed in Greece until the age of Athenian democracy, at which time it underwent irreversible decay. Morality, by contrast, seeks the grounds of duty and right solely in an internal and subjective source, in the power of judging that advances its own criteria for right. In the light of these criteria, the actual world of custom appears deficient, and indeed moral judgment "evaporates" (*verfluechtigt*) all determinate aspects of unreflective custom. Assuming a stance of self-determination, morality cannot abide the merely "given" and accepts as certain only what it can determine for itself to be true. It is "inwardly" directed, oriented toward "subjectivity." But the term "subjective" need not have the pejorative sense of merely personal whim; in morality the subjective mind seeks to ground itself in reason. But even in its highest manifestations, morality remains a narrow form of reason. Socratic morality is not merely skeptical, for it puts forward ideas of the good to replace discredited custom. It is, however, "uncompromising," in that it allows no qualifications or dilutions of the pure rational standard in relation to actual forms of life. It has little room for prudence. Hegel's Socrates belongs to the same tribe as the Stoics.[6]

Hegel introduces Socrates here not as a philosopher seeking knowledge of the whole of things natural, human, and divine, but as the initiator of a revolution in moral thinking. In this account there is nothing inherently otherworldly about the revolution; there is no reference to a supersensible realm of ideas. On the contrary, Socratic thought is directed toward an inward power, the power of the subject. As the teacher of a new inward-orientation, Socrates is given the title "inventor of morality" in the lectures on the philosophy of history.[7] All the same, Hegel says that the ground was prepared for Socrates by the decay of custom in Athens. The moral stance arises in epochs when what is recognized as right and good in actuality and custom is unable to satisfy the better will. When the existing world of freedom has become unfaithful to the better will, this will no longer finds itself in the duties recognized in this world and must seek to recover in ideal inwardness alone that harmony which it has lost in actuality.[8]

The same point is elaborated in an addition of Gans: "Only in ages when the actual world is a hollow, spiritless, and unsettled existence (*Existenz*) may the individual be permitted to flee from actuality and retreat into his inner vitality. Socrates made his appearance at the time when Athenian democracy had fallen into ruin. He evaporated the existing world and retreated into himself in search of the right and the good."[9] That the ethical life of custom has internal tensions leading to its decay is a theme much elaborated by Hegel in both the *Phenomenology of Spirit* and the *Philosophy of Right.* Tragic conflicts of family and city (*Antigone*) and within the family itself surely precede the appearance of Socrates. In bringing to light a fundamentally new level of conflict between individual and city, Socrates embodies the inner principle of the age as a hero of world history. He exposes the new principle and in so doing becomes the sacrificial victim of the dialectical conflict he uncovers. Socrates' destructive power is the completion of a destructive process under way, and certainly for Hegel the process has a positive aspect. But observe: Socrates can be such an agent of transformation only because his stance is essentially willful. The Socrates of Hegel's account is not a purely contemplative seeker of truth.

The affinity of Hegel's Socrates with Kant is unmistakable, and Hegel's criticism of Kant is the best-known locus of the contrast between *Sittlichkeit* and *Moralitaet.* Hegel ascribes "abstractness" to the moral stances of both Socrates and Kant, an abstractness arising in both cases from the same cause: the assertion of the supremacy of the subjective ground of right and duty, and disregard for the rationality inherent in existing custom, the rationality that custom is itself unable to see. Morality misses the point that the mutual dependence and recognition of humans in the social realm is the presupposition of the individual's effort to use reason independently. Separating itself from the social sphere that can give its rationality content, morality is only an abstract formalism that tries to give itself content, with arbitrariness as the result. The previously cited addition of Gans continues with a remark about the present age, which refers clearly to the influence of Kantian morality: "Even in our times it happens that reverence for the existing order is in varying degrees absent, and people seek to equate prevailing standards with their own will, with what they have recognized."[10] This modern consciousness is, however, not confined to its Kantian version. It is evident in other forms of "conscience" (*Gewissen*) as "the absolute entitlement of subjective self-consciousness" making universalist demands on the narrow basis of "infinite formal certainty of itself."[11] Having no regard for "objective content" and thus turning away from the "substance" of ethical life, this attitude is one that "the state cannot recognize."[12] Such morality is self-contradictory in that "its appeal solely *to itself* is directly opposed to what it seeks to be," that is, "the rule for a rational and universal mode of action which is valid in and for itself." There are overtones here of Hegel's critique of "the monstrous spectacle" of the French Revolution's overthrow of all existing conditions on the basis of the "abstractions" of pure thought alone, "for the first time in our knowledge of the human species."[13] The connection with Kant's "infinite autonomy" is evident. More immediately, this attitude is related to evil, the subject of the paragraph just following the first discussion of Socrates.[14] Evil is a condition in which the "pure inwardness of the will" consciously prefers "arbitrariness, its own particularity" over the universal. Conscience, as formal subjectivity, consists simply in the possibility of turning at any moment to *evil;* for both morality and evil have their common root in that self-certainty which has being for itself and knows and resolves for itself.[15] As already noted, Hegel says "Socrates is the inventor of morality." It would go too far to say that Socrates is also the inventor of evil, but as the inventor of morality he must be, in a special way, familiar with "the common root" of morality and evil.

Morality has as well a positive side for Hegel—just as evil does. This positive side lies precisely in the relation between the moral will and universal principle, and Kant is credited with offering the first full philosophical elaboration of it. Hegel writes, "Knowledge of the will first gained a firm foundation and point of departure in the philosophy of Kant, through the thought of its infinite autonomy."[16] And also, "The point of view of Kant's philosophy is sublime inasmuch as it asserts the conformity of duty with reason," although Hegel immediately adds, "This point of view is defective in that it lacks all articulation."[17] More generally, the inward turn of conscience is praised as "an exalted point of view, a point of view of the modern world," which by the "descent into the self" and the "deepest inner solitude within oneself" has moved beyond "more sensuous ages," which were satisfied by "the external and given, whether this be religion or right."[18] Hegel's comments on Socrates in this context make him the decisive precursor of modernity. Later in the *Philosophy of Right,* one reads,

"Socrates's principle of morality, of inwardness, was a necessary product of his age, but it took time for this to become universal self-consciousness."[19]

The most substantive comment on the positive side of the Socratic innovation in the *Philosophy of Right* occurs in the preface, although Socrates' name does not appear there. The reference occurs in later paragraphs of the preface, which are famous for their claim that "what is rational is actual; and what is actual is rational."[20] Here Hegel means not that all particulars existing at a given time can be rationally justified, but rather that the philosophic account of reason provides the basis for understanding and justifying the most essential features of a time, since the actual (*wirklich*) is that which reason itself tends to realize or "actualize." That reason tends toward actuality is for Hegel the truth of Aristotle's "concrete" account of the essence of reason.[21] However, the subject of discussion just before this maxim is Plato's *Republic*. Its central point is that Plato was moved to write his account of the "state" by the deeper tendency of his world, to which he failed all the same to perform justice. Hegel's charge against Plato is *not* that Plato put forward a merely utopian project, unrelated to actuality. Plato sought to give expression to the *ethos* of the Greeks, and especially to address "a deeper principle" that was emerging in it. The account of the "deeper principle" points clearly to Socrates, as discussed later in paragraph 138. The tendency first appeared as an "unsatisfied longing" and a "corrupting force"; the "deeper drive" behind it was "free infinite personality." Plato sought to counteract this longing "with the help of the very longing itself." Who but Socrates would represent the longing for "free infinite personality"? The "infinite formal certainty of itself" characterizing morality is, as already noted, attached to Socrates' "evaporation" of custom through his turning to "inward" criteria of right. That Plato sought a corrective to the longing "by means of the longing itself" suggests that he used the figure of Socrates to correct Socrates' own thinking. Thus the *Republic* presents Socrates as a (not wholly willing) teacher of ethical life, and his philosophical longing or *eros* is put in the service of forming laws and customs to counteract the acid effect of dialectic. The outcome, Hegel says, was a "particular *external* form of Greek ethics," by whose means Plato "imagined he could overcome the corrupting force."[22] With respect to Socrates, the most striking remark comes just before the famous maxim on reason and the actual: "But he [Plato] proved he is the great spirit (*der grosse Geist*) by the fact that the very principle on which the distinctive character of his Idea turns is the pivot on which the impending world revolution turned." Again the principle of "free infinite personality" is in question, and it is said here to be the pivot (*Angel*) for the world revolution of the Spirit. It is this principle, therefore, that reason seeks to actualize in the course of history, and which constitutes the inner rationality of the actual as it unfolds in history. Plato did not—and could not—fully achieve that actuality, and indeed he resisted the force striving to actualize itself even as he gave expression to it. However, in his greatness of spirit he tried to give it suitable political actualization. Insofar as Hegel sees the modern state—and the philosophic spirit of his own thought—as giving appropriate actuality in ethical life to the principle of infinite personality or morality, it is the successor to and true fulfillment of Plato's effort. Like Plato, Hegel—indeed all of history—is coming to terms with the Socratic revolution.

Hegel confirms this reading of the preface by an explicit linkage of Plato and the modern state in paragraph 185 of the *Philosophy of Right,* near the start of the discussion of civil society. (This is the subject of section 2, following section 1 on the family, in "Ethical Life," the third large part of the *Philosophy of Right.*) First one must note that Hegel gives the name "civil society" (*buergerliche Gesellschaft*) to the shape of spiritual life arising in the modern period based on "the system of needs," which are the ever-expanding bonds of mutual dependence forged by the efforts of individuals acting as individuals to satisfy desires that are inherently limitless. Hegel builds on insights of Rousseau, Kant, Smith, and Ricardo on this peculiar form of orderliness, which gives a lawlike character to human activities intending only personal satisfaction, such that raw passion is civilized and "universalized" insofar as it must accept the rational conditions (rules of exchange, property-holding, contract, and the like) for its satisfaction. The progress of commerce, industry, arts, and sciences tends to create new desires even as it promises satisfaction (this is the problem of limitless corruption decried by Rousseau), but nevertheless it also tends to distribute the benefits of progress and to encourage productive and responsible behavior on the part of citizens who increasingly have grounds for feeling gratitude and loyalty toward the whole system (the rejoinder to Rousseau from Kant, Smith, and the new economic science). In Hegel's view this system is an essential condition for the modern state's great achievement: the combination of maximum individual freedom with the "substantial unity" of a law-abiding citizenry that feels itself patriotically bound to the state. Modern citizens are prepared to make the highest sacrifices for the state, even as on a daily basis they pursue private aims and cherish constitutional limits on the state's ability to interfere with those pursuits. Perhaps the following statements offer the best summation:

> The principle of modern states has this enormous strength and depth, that it allows the principle of subjectivity to attain fulfillment in the *self-sufficient extreme* of personal particularity, while at the same time *bringing it back to substantial unity* and so preserving this unity in the principle of subjectivity itself.[23]

> In the states of classical antiquity, universality was indeed already present, but particularity had not yet been released and set at liberty and brought back to universality, i.e. to the universal end of the whole. The essence of the modern state is that the universal should be linked with the complete freedom of particularity and the well-being of individuals.[24]

Civil society, the modern system of needs, is the hidden mechanism that accomplishes the "releasing" of particularity and its return to "substantial unity," although the state and not civil society is the locus of the highest duties of the citizen, because the individual's will and the common will can fully actualize themselves only in the "objective spirit" of the state's laws and institutions.

Where are Plato and Socrates in all this? Hegel returns to Plato's defect in his account of the failures of ancient states in *EPR* 185. Those states experienced an "influx of ethical corruption," which was the "ultimate reason for their downfall." Their basis in "*original* natural intuition" of a patriarchal and religious principle "could not withstand the division of the same and the infinite reflection of self-consciousness in itself." Plato in his *Republic,* Hegel says, "presents the substantial ethical life in its ideal *beauty* and *truth;* but he cannot come to terms with the principle of self-sufficient particularity, which had suddenly overtaken Greek ethical life." Plato's only response is to exclude particularity completely from the state through the laws concerning private property and the family. Although there is "substantial truth" in Plato's opposition to the new spirit, his thought and the ancient world as a whole lacked "the truly infinite power which resides solely in that unity which allows the *opposition* within reason [*Vernunft*] *to develop to its full strength,* and has overcome it so as to preserve itself within it and *wholly contain it within itself*."[25] Infinite self-reflection first appeared among the Greeks, Hegel remarks, but its actualization was reserved for a later age: "The principle of the *self-sufficient and inherently infinite personality* of the individual [*des Einzelnen*], the principle of subjective freedom, which arose in an inward form in the *Christian* religion, and in an external form (which was therefore linked with abstract universality) in the *Roman* world, is denied its right in that merely substantial form of the actual spirit [in Plato's *Republic*]."[26] Here one should note Hegel's view that the infinite self-opposition of reason is a feature of the will, "for the theoretical is essentially contained in the practical; the idea that the two are separate must be rejected, for one cannot have a will without intelligence. On the contrary, the will contains the theoretical within itself."[27] The will has the power of remaining identical with itself while also positing itself as the negative of itself in the willing of any determinate object. As such, will is characterized (according to logic as speculative philosophy) by "infinity as self-referring negativity, this ultimate source of all activity, life, and consciousness."[28] Now one can say that Socrates, in bringing this infinity to light, first brought to light the character of the will as infinite negativity. Only the modern state achieves its successful incorporation into ethical life.

The *Philosophy of Right* also discusses two other features of Socrates, each of which links him to and separates him from modern subjectivity: his irony and his daimon. Socratic irony is different from the stance of the modern ironist, made famous by Friedrich Schlegel, in which "subjectivity regards itself as the ultimate instance" and distances itself from whatever could be regarded as objective. Modern Romantic subjectivity "knows itself as that which *wills* and *resolves in a particular way* but may *equally well* will and resolve otherwise."[29] It sees itself as beyond all law, "the master of both law and thing," and merely plays with things while enjoying itself: "This shape [of subjectivity] is not only the *emptiness* of all ethical *content* of rights, duties, laws . . . in addition, its form is that of *subjective* emptiness [*Eitelkeit*], in that it knows itself as this emptiness of all content and, in this knowledge, knows *itself* as the absolute."[30] Hegel observes that this is very different from "the method which Socrates employed in personal dialogue to defend the Idea of truth and justice against the presumption of the uneducated consciousness and that of the sophists." Socratic irony is only a "manner of speaking in relation to *people*," in which another's consciousness is treated ironically, but not the Idea itself. For Plato all dialectical irony is in the end submerged in the substantiality of the Idea. Elsewhere (in the lectures on the history of philosophy) Hegel relates this moderate irony to Socrates' knowledge of ignorance and the nonscientific or nonsystematic character of his philosophy.[31] But clearly the infinite negativity disclosed by Socrates is the precondition for Romantic irony as well as the nonironic reconciliation of subjectivity and ethical life in the modern state.

The Socratic daimon enters the argument of the *Philosophy of Right* in a context that, initially seeming odd, is quite telling.[32] The modern state is a whole whose powers of decision lie completely within its own limits, Hegel claims, for the actualization of freedom in the state entails that it is a self-organizing totality. Its organic structure requires a constitutionally limited monarch who gives the personality of the state a concrete embodiment in a personal will. But the monarch's will only expresses the rational whole, of which he is the symbolic apex. His will is the final will to be consulted when governmental deliberations have reached their end. In contrast, in the states of antiquity the highest decisions depended on consulting a sphere beyond human powers—in oracles, the entrails of animals, the flight of birds, and so forth.[33] Hegel expressly refers back to his account of Socrates as the great turning-inward of consciousness, and he now asserts: "In the *daimon* of *Socrates* (see par. 138 above) we can see the beginning of how the will which in the past had simply projected itself *beyond* itself turned to itself and recognized itself within itself—the beginning of *self-knowing* and hence truthful freedom." This suggests a parallel between Socrates' daimon and the constitutional monarch. In each case one has something like the voice of reason, or the rational will, embodied in a being that has a distinct existence and yet exists only for the sake of another: Socrates' philosophic life in the one case, the grand edifice of the state in the other. The daimon is thus the first step on the path toward the supremacy of the rational will in affairs of state, or so the analogy suggests. But the daimon is only a "beginning." How is the Socratic turn incomplete? Yet perhaps the better question is: how is the Socratic turn to "inwardly" based decision evident in the daimon at all? Is it not more evident in Socratic dialectic—or irony?[34] And—to raise a different sort of question that cannot be pursued here—does Hegel subtly intend by his association of the monarch with the daimon to cast some doubt on the former? Is constitutional monarchy perhaps not as rational as Hegel seems, on the surface, to claim it is? (After 1819 Hegel had ample grounds for discontent with the Prussian monarchy.)[35] But the primary intent of the comparison is plain: Socrates begins the movement of thought whereby the divine is brought down from beyond and realized in the world, a process completed in the modern state, for "the state is the divine will as present spirit, *unfolding* itself as the actual shape and *organization of a world*,"[36] and "the state consists in the march of God in the world."[37] The final paragraph of the *Philosophy of Right* presents a variant of Cicero's remark that Socrates brought philosophy down from the heavens and into the cities, but now "the state as the image and actuality of reason" replaces Socrates as the agency through which the spiritual comes earthward.[38]

This brief and thought-provoking acquaintance with the daimon in the *Philosophy of Right* suggests that the daimon is an important clue to the character of Socratic rationality as prefiguring the rationality of the modern state. More enlightenment on the subject is helpfully provided by two accounts in other lectures. In those on the philosophy of history, Socrates enters in the middle of the story of Athenian corruption and decline.[39] Here the accents are strikingly more negative. Socrates has clear kinship with the crowd of sophists, as is suggested in the *Philosophy of Right,* and again he represents the principle of "inwardness becoming free for itself." Again, out of the background of the unreflective, concrete unity of spirit in Greek ethical life—the ethos of the beautiful—"thought" arises as the principle of decay. The conflict of ethical life and thought occurs only in the European world, Hegel says, for in Asia the dominance of "abstraction" permits neither to exist. In Greece the sophistic maxim "man is the measure" becomes the excuse for individual caprice and opens the door to all passions. Now Socrates is called "the inventor of morality" who argues with the sophists, asserts the "absolute independence of thought" in determining the right and the good, insists on the universal character of thought, and stipulates that consciousness of virtue characterizes genuine virtue. Yet Socrates is like the sophists in setting citizens against custom and the state. Here his destructive force is given a different twist: Socrates introduces a new sort of oracle through his daimon. "Socrates said that he had a *daimon* in him, that advised him what he should do, and revealed to him what is useful to his friends." Socrates' personal daimon is an oracle that competes with the sacred oracles of the city. The positive sense given to the oracle in the *Philosophy of Right*—as the beginning of the immanentizing of the divine, and of the movement toward complete rational self-reliance—is not as evident here, although it can be glimpsed. Hegel's major theme is that the daimon introduces a disturbing and disruptive form of transcendence. The life grounded in "thought," which the daimon protects, is one estranged from the world. "Through the rising inner world of subjectivity the break with reality (*Wirklichkeit*) comes on the scene." Socrates is not at home in the state and its religion, only in the thought-world (*Gedankenwelt*), although he continues to fulfill civic duties. Plato carries forward this tendency, and in the wake of these philosophers "many citizens separate themselves from political life and the affairs of state in order to live in the ideal world." The Athenians tried to remove the destructive principle by condemning Socrates, but in fact they were only condemning themselves, for they had already fallen under the spell of thinking. And Hegel indicates that all was not lost: in a new way the Athenian spirit gained "satisfaction for itself" in sophisticated self-mockery, as is evident in the Athenian capacity for relishing Aristophanic satire.

The two accounts of Socrates and his daimon reveal an ambiguity. Although both show that the Socratic turn to thought has a destructive effect on ethical life, in *Philosophy of Right* the turn discloses an infinite power of self-reliant thinking pointing toward the ultimate self-sufficiency of the human world, and in the lectures on the philosophy of history it points more toward an estrangement from the world, a lingering in the "ideal" that does not seem to hold much promise for the future. The descriptions of the daimon are the locus of the ambiguity: is the daimonic voice "immanentizing" and earthly, or is it estranging and otherworldly? Admittedly, in both cases the voice has a disruptive effect, and the new principle promoted by the voice must be reconciled with the world of ethics and politics.

One acquires a better view of this duality and its meaning in what is by far Hegel's fullest treatment of Socrates, in the lectures on the history of philosophy, where the daimon has a central role.[40] The daimon reveals what is inherently problematic about the transference of the divine from external powers to infinite subjectivity, and it expresses the fundamental conflict between philosophy and the state that animates Western history since Socrates. Now it is clear that the problem is not solely the emancipation of "particularity" as destroying the unreflective unity of custom. The "negative power of thought" in Anaxagoras and the sophists is sharply distinguished from Socrates' turn to the "universal I" as the good. This "I" as transcending nature and the senses (Kantian overtones once again) provides a point of security and rest to thought, unlike the restless negativity of thought in Protagoras. Thought becomes more than the source of ideas about the good; it now *is* the good. With this insight Socrates is a turning point in the history of thought.[41] Socrates demands that the end of all action and indeed of the world be found in thought, so that "thought is now at home with itself," and not with anything outside itself. Of custom it can only be said that "no one knew whence it came" (Sophocles); lack of grounding in thought is custom's fatal flaw. The Socratic demand lives on after Socrates, and into the modern world.

The Socratic revolution is in a sense a revolution in the will, since it is the rational will's bid for self-grounding. Surely it has destructive consequences for the state and its religion, but it does not elevate mere particularity above custom. Socrates and Plato seek to raise thought above merely particular interests.[42] The true meaning of this achievement—wherein morality (*Moralitaet*) replaces the natural unreflective ethos (*Sittlichkeit*)—is the new exploration of the "depths of consciousness." Socrates is the highest representative of an "inwardness" arising at the time of the Peloponnesian War and inseparable from the dissolution of Athenian political life. After him, inwardness becomes the common feature of human life.[43] But Socrates as an individual has an extraordinary, even bizarre, character. His virtues have the quality of something self-wrought, as if he formed himself like a work of art.[44] Again, he embodies an extreme form of willfulness. In a sense this is characteristic of antiquity, Hegel claims, where higher virtues are the products of the heroic will of the individual. Virtue has not yet acquired the status of a universal expression of Spirit, as in the modern world, and is instead the individual's peculiar genius. In antiquity the contrast between the ordinary virtues of ethical life and the higher virtues of heroes is greater than in the modern world. The gulf between Socrates' unique character and the world in which he lived forms the basis of his irony, which Hegel calls "tragic."[45] To overcome that separation and to annul the tragedy of philosophy constitutes the destiny of Spirit. But Socrates' ironic distance should not be confused with mere delight in scoffing at the ordinary. There is a genuinely dialectical quality of his thought in his "midwifery," whereby he takes the individual soul from its concrete starting point and leads it to the universal. He thus anticipates the true sense of dialectic as the unfolding of the immanent logic of the concept, in which "consciousness creates out of itself the true."[46]

Does Hegel here give any support to his claim in the lectures on the philosophy of history that Socrates' turn to thought involves "estrangement" from the world? If thought becomes more at home with itself, why should it not be more at home with the world? The problem, Hegel now says, more helpfully, lies in the abstractness of the Socratic universal. As the end of the individual it lacks true development. It is indeed Socrates' great insight that consciousness contains the divine, but his account of thought in his "religion of the good" is narrowly moral. Although discovering that law arises from consciousness and that law's essence is not oppressive, Socrates gives no content to his account of consciousness as positing itself as the end.[47]

Everyone is encouraged to find the law in himself, and this renders everyone homeless in the laws of the state. At this juncture Hegel adduces Aristotle's criticism of Socrates for neglecting habituation and for requiring that virtue be a science, to support Hegel's own view that Socratic morality lacks "heart" and has no connection with "the real spirit of the people." The Aristotelian account of the basis of virtue in the "active understanding" of character, and not in perception alone, points to a defect in Socrates that Hegel, as one will see, believes to be evident in his daimon.[48] The Socratic perception of the good, or the Socratic universal, is indeterminate in that it exposes the weakness of all particularity, such as the particular laws of the Greeks, and offers no path toward a determinate end. Now Hegel puts forward the true dialectical account of determinacy. Only in relation to the whole does the universal lose its abstractness and one-sidedness and become determinate. In moral terms, the universal of the individual's inwardness must be shown wanting and must be superseded by the universal implicit in the life of a people. Universal moral claims typically come into conflict, but the coherence of the life of a people—qua people—resolves such conflict. The infinity of consciousness that Socrates uncovers remains, in his thought, only the possession of individuals.[49]

From these lectures one learns the root of the ambiguity mentioned above. The Socratic turn to the authority of inwardness or consciousness is surely not inherently otherworldly, and it marks the first great step toward "immanence." All the same it involves some homelessness or estrangement, which is not adequately described as just the decline of the authority of ancestral custom. Socrates does not dissolve the unity of ethical life into the chaos of self-seeking particularity, like the sophists. He stresses the supreme authority of the universal, but it is a universal lacking "determinate" relation to individuals. In Hegel's terms, it is not a "concrete universal."

The problematic abstractness of this universal lies not in some metaphysical characteristic, such as its belonging to a supersensible realm; instead this universal belongs to the turning-inward of consciousness.

Individuality or personality is liberated in the Socratic revolution, for the revolution consists in disclosing the infinite power of thought as immanent within the individual. Yet this universal discovered in "free infinite personality" also leaves something crucial in the life of the individual wholly indeterminate.

What is this unfulfilled aspect? Hegel approaches this by pointing to the limited effectiveness of Socratic teaching. He claims that Socrates' thought acquires its power through contingent, personal attributes of his mind, or the impressive force of his character. From that source also come Socrates' notable failures as a teacher—Hegel mentions Critias and Alcibiades—since force of character can have particular effects contrary to the philosophic and intellectual intent of the teacher. Hegel now states that "the characteristic form" of Socratic subjectivity, or the characteristic way that thought becomes the deciding factor in the life of Socrates, is the daimon, "the personal mind (*Geist*) that appears to him to be *his* mind"[50] The daimon expresses the revolution wherein thought turns to itself, away from external powers. But it also discloses how this turn, in the case of Socrates, is infected with arbitrariness. The daimon cares for that individual side of Socrates' consciousness not covered by insight into the universal, and accordingly it is related to somnambulism, magnetic states, and unconscious impulses. It is not the seat of opinions and convictions, but a new sort of oracle (internal rather than external) addressing contingent affairs demanding decisions. One can ask why an internal oracle is necessary, if reason grasps the authority of the universal and at the same time the contingency of all oracles? It is because the universal still lacks a certain effectiveness and leaves a void that must be filled by something radically particular and divorced from reason. One recalls that the collapse of the authority of custom, of publicly recognized common law, produces a void, and that the problem of the Socratic way of thought is its uncovering a gulf between the requirements of self-grounding reason and those of public, social, and political authority and law. The Socratic teaching of a higher universal morality cannot be effectively translated by Socrates himself into a new form of political authority. Such was Plato's critique of Socrates, in Hegel's account. But this still leaves unexplained why Socrates would have need of a daimonic voice. After all, this does not assist with making rational insight generally effective. The voice has no popular or public authority.

Although Socrates as compared to the public of his time is remarkably self-reliant in his thinking, his is not a wholly modern form of autonomy. He is a divided being, in Hegel's view, seeking the ground of life in thought and at the same time relying on a subjective oracle in his personal affairs, as the latter are not addressed by his thought.[51] The oracle mediates between Socrates' inwardness and his external affairs and is separate from his will although not separate from his being altogether. In a sense Socrates as a practical being—with personal interests—does not possess his own will, or his will is possessed by another will. For the ordinary Greek, such a personal oracle is an absurdity, for the divine addresses matters of state and public affairs, not trivial personal concerns. Socrates offends the public with proposing not just new gods but a personal alternative to the public oracles and gods.[52] How could a private citizen presume to have his own oracle, and therefore to be a kind of oracle? Yet, however offensive this may be to the ordinary citizen, Hegel says it is something that the ordinary citizen also intuits as having truth: Socrates brings to light the truth that every self-conscious being can replace the external powers of the public oracles. Indeed Socrates' reputation for wisdom has the sanction of the Pythian oracle itself. The Greeks themselves are moving beyond their old oracles toward new ones, toward the private insight of the individual as the ultimate instance. Again Hegel states that they justly accuse Socrates of undermining the state, but in accusing him they only accuse themselves.[53] This means that they are not yet capable of being responsible for themselves, and not yet disposed to accept the freedom of consciousness they are discovering. In this they show that their will is not their own will or that it is still possessed by external powers. Hence Socrates' daimon reflects the Athenian condition in exemplary fashion, and in discomfiting dialectical encounters with Socrates the Athenian citizen must face the psychic reality of *eros* without satisfaction. "Socrates had the formal effect of bringing about a discord in the individual."[54]

In other terms, the conflict between the subjective freedom of rational self-grounding and ethical life makes its first appearance as the conflict between Socrates and the state, but it also emerges as a conflict within Socrates himself. The conflict first appears in Socrates, and not in the sophists, since the sophists simply would abandon the gods and the oracles. Socrates' need for a daimon discloses his need for the divine, but his thinking allows for only a distorted and incomplete satisfaction of the need. The problem lies not in the project of rational self-grounding as such, but in the first form that this project assumes in the history of spirit—the Socratic form. In ethical life the divine is not simply the authority behind law, or the constraint on individual passion and whim. It addresses the problem of contingency or the human interest in providential order. The indeterminate universal found in reason's first efforts to find the truth in itself necessarily lacks the power to give meaning to the contingent, and hence Socrates' need for a personal supplement to reason, the daimonic voice that responds to contingency. Yet this might only trivialize the need for the divine, which in its highest and noblest form supports and sanctions the state. The real meaning of the conflict of Socrates and the state, therefore, concerns not whether there is a necessary place for the divine—Socrates readily admits this—but the nature and role of the divine. If the highest way of life is rational self-grounding, then perhaps the highest manifestation of the divine consists in its support of that life—as an individual's endeavor. But this would be the case only if rational self-grounding can achieve merely a limited kind of universality, one that lacks the power to comprehend and endow the contingent particulars of life with meaning, or with something like providential order. The universal in this indeterminate form is inherently "estranged" and "homeless." Hegel argues that Greek philosophy, and indeed all philosophy before its culmination in his thought and age, could have only a limited a view of the universal or reason in the decisive respect. It could not grasp that infinite inwardness has the *dynamis* to realize itself concretely insofar as reason's negative power of "releasing" the particular also necessarily "returns" the particular to the whole.

Hegel concludes that Socrates' life reveals the principle whose "development is the whole of subsequent history." This content, or the dialectical basis of history, is the truth that the principle of self-grounding thought, which at first must spell the ruin of the people and the state, will ultimately become the constitution or the "substance" of a people. The modern state fulfills this destiny.[55] Indeed the modern state discloses itself as the true meaning of the human concern with destiny or providence.[56] Hegel, perhaps with greater clarity and depth than recent interpreters and advocates—whether of liberal, communitarian, or postmodern persuasion—sees the problem inherent in the coexistence of the infinity of philosophic reason and the finitude of ethical and political life. Whether his account of the modern state provides the solution eluding Socrates' daimon is surely one of the most thought-worthy and engaging questions posed by Hegel's work.

Notes

An earlier version of this paper was delivered to the Philadelphia Area Political Theory Colloquium at the University of Pennsylvania, March 2004, and appeared in *Review of Metaphysics* 59, no. 3 (March 2006), under the title "On Possessed Individualism: Hegel, Socrates's Daimon, and the Modern State."

1. The universal or almost universal tendency of the Hegel scholarship has been to relate the emergence of infinite personality to Christianity, thereby obscuring its philosophic origin and missing Hegel's claim that the problem of freedom in the history of Spirit revolves around the relation of philosophic reason to political life. Christianity absorbed and transformed the philosophic discovery of infinite personality in a radical and effective universalization of it.

2. See F. Nietzsche, *The Birth of Tragedy out of the Spirit of Music,* section 15: "We cannot fail to see in Socrates the one turning point and vortex of world history."

3. *Grundlinien der Philosophie des Rechts oder Naturrecht und Staatswissenschaft im Grundrisse,* in Georg W.F. Hegel, *Werke in zwanzig Baenden* (hereafter *W*), ed. Eva Moldenhauer and Karl M. Michel (Frankfurt: Suhrkamp, 1969–1979), vol. 7. The English translation employed with occasional modifications is *Elements of the Philosophy of Right* (hereafter *EPR*), ed. Allen Wood, trans. H.B. Nisbet. In citations of the *Philosophy of Right,* "R" designates a remark appended by Hegel to the primary text of the numbered paragraph. "A" designates additional material provided by Eduard Gans from student lecture-notes. "P" designates the preface to the *Philosophy of Right* and is followed by the page number in the Wood edition.

4. *EPR* 138R, 140R, 279R.

5. *EPR* 138A, 274A.

6. *EPR* 138R.

7. *The Philosophy of History* (hereafter *PH*), trans. J. Sibree (New York: Dover, 1956), 269; *Vorlesungen ueber die Philosophie der Geschichte, W* 12:329: "Sokrates ist als moralischer Lehrer beruehmt; vielmehr aber ist er der *Erfinder* der Moral."

8. *EPR* 138R; *W* 7:259.

9. *EPR* 138A; *W* 7:260.

10. Ibid.

11. *EPR* 137, 137R; *W* 7:254–55.

12. *EPR* 137R; *W* 7:255.

13. *EPR* 258R; *W* 7:400–401. The same passage praises "the achievement of Rousseau to put forward the *will* as the principle of the state," wherein the will is "thinking itself," although in the imperfect form of a universal will arising out of the contractual union of individuals. Rousseau introduces the idea of the will

as having the universal form of willing (the general will) as its object, whereby "thinking" offers not merely the form or means of the will, but its content.

14. *EPR* 139.

15. *EPR* 139R; *W* 7:261.

16. *EPR* 135R; *W* 7:252.

17. *EPR* 135A; *W* 7:253. See also 133A.

18. *EPR* 136A; *W* 7:254.

19. *EPR* 274A; *W* 7:440.

20. *EPR* P, 20; *W* 7:24.

21. *Lectures on the Philosophy of History* (hereafter *LHP*), trans. E.S. Haldane (London: Kegan Paul, 1892), 1:20–21; *Vorlesungen ueber die Geschichte der Philosophie, W* 18:39–40. The *Werke* text of the lectures and the Haldane translation are based on Karl Ludwig Michelet's 1840 edition.

22. *EPR* P, 20; *W* 7:24.

23. *EPR* 260; *W* 7:407.

24. *EPR* 260A; *W* 7:407.

25. *EPR* 185R; *W* 7:342.

26. Ibid.

27. *EPR* 4A; *W* 7:47.

28. *EPR* 7R; *W* 7:55.

29. *EPR* 140R(f); *W* 7:277–80.

30. *EPR* 140R(f); *W* 7:279.

31. *LHP* 397–402; *W* 18:456–61.

32. *EPR* 279R.

33. *EPR* 356.

34. This is to say nothing about the fact that in the best-known account of it (Plato, *Apology* 40a–c) the daimon counsels Socrates against action, except in the case of Socrates' appearance at his trial and delivery of his self-defense, whereby, Socrates claims, it gives a sign that death is not evil. The daimon's negative function accords better with Hegel's criticism of it in the other lectures than with the point he makes in this context.

35. See Terry Pinkard, *Hegel: A Biography* (Cambridge: Cambridge Univ. Press, 2000), on "Hegel and the Prussian Reaction: 1819–1820," 435–50.

36. *EPR* 270R; *W* 7:417–18. This paragraph on the relation of the state to religion is the lengthiest in the *Philosophy of Right;* its length is reflective of its philosophical weight.

37. *EPR* 258A; *W* 7:403. See also 260A.

38. *EPR* 360; *W* 7:512. See also *LHP* 388–89; *W* 18:445–46.

39. *PH* 267–71; *W* 12:326–30. (I have modified the translation.)

40. *LHP* 384–448; *W* 18:441–516.

41. *LHP* 384–86; *W* 18:441–43.

42. *LHP* 387; *W* 18:444.

43. *LHP* 390–91; *W* 18:448–50.
44. *LHP* 392–94; *W* 18:450–53.
45. *LHP* 398–402; *W* 18:457–61.
46. *LHP* 407; *W* 18:468.
47. *LHP* 409; *W* 18:470.
48. *LHP* 410–14; *W* 18:471–76.
49. *LHP* 417–20; *W* 18:486–90.
50. *LHP* 421; *W* 18:490.
51. *LHP* 422–24; *W* 18:492–95.
52. *LHP* 431–35; *W* 18:498–503.
53. *LHP* 441–46; *W* 18:509–14.
54. *LHP* 449; *W* 18:519.
55. *LHP* 447–48; *W* 18:515–16.
56. *EPR* 360.

Michael Palmer

An Introduction to Martin Heidegger

"Radical-Committed" Anticosmopolitanism

The death of Martin Heidegger was front-page news in the *New York Times* on May 27, 1976: "Martin Heidegger, a Philosopher Who Affected Many Fields, Dies." An obituary of some two and a half thousand words followed. I note this not because the *New York Times* was the most noteworthy place where Heidegger's death was remarked, and his life's work remarked upon, but because these two and a half thousand words were probably the first that the overwhelming majority of the readership of the *Times* had ever read about Heidegger; fewer still, no doubt, had ever read many words by him. This was despite the fact that his thought was influential, and has since grown ever more so, in such wide-ranging fields as physics, psychology, sociology, linguistics, literary criticism, theology, and, of course, philosophy. To borrow a famous remark of Hannah Arendt: before World War II Martin Heidegger was "the secret king of thought" of the twentieth century; after the war, we could say, he became "the king." Among the Germans, of course, fascination with all things German, including Heidegger, has never been lacking; equal fascination with Heidegger later emerged among the French. But in North America, with some exceptions, such as Thomas Langan, *Heidegger,*[1] interest in Heidegger arose only after a virtual avalanche of Heidegger studies began in Europe.[2]

Why, then, was Heidegger's work so little read for so long in North America? Not for any good reasons. First, there is the notorious obscurity, certainly in English translation, of Heidegger's language. In the *New York Times* obituary, Bertrand Russell remarked of Heidegger's philosophy, "One cannot help suspecting that language is here running riot." Second, there is the fact that Heidegger, himself, elaborated no social or political philosophy and frequently denied that his ontological speculations had any moral-political intention.[3] Third, if distaste for ontology were not enough to deter most North Americans, another, more reasonable, species of distaste is relevant: Heidegger's sole significant foray into public life was to welcome the destruction of Weimar Germany and the advent of Hitler's Nazi revolution.[4]

None of these considerations, however, relieve contemporary political theorists of the task of confronting the thought of the most influential philosopher of the twentieth century. That the first should be thrown out of court goes without saying. The second and third are more troublesome. Karl Löwith identified, decades ago, the limitations of any "political" judgment.

> Political circumstances play such a role in the selection of, and attention to, contemporary literature and philosophy that the average American student knows more about Jean-Paul Sartre than about Karl Jaspers, and more about Jaspers than about Martin Heidegger of whom Sartre was a pupil. This sequence of familiarity is politically conditioned, for Sartre is a Frenchman who was engaged in the resistance movement, and Jaspers a German who for ten lonely years was barred from academic activity by the Nazis, while Heidegger, who supported National Socialism in 1933, neither resisted the regime subsequently nor was dismissed from his post during its period of domination.
>
> Whatever one may think about these matters, the sequence derived from political circumstances—Sartre, Jaspers, Heidegger—must be reversed with regard to philosophical priority and significance.[5]

David Farrell Krell (*Basic Writings*, 28n31), a prominent editor and translator of Heidegger, admits that it will not do "to close the eyes and stop up the ears to the dismal matter" of Heidegger's association with National Socialism, but he offers a quasi-apology: "It is of course convenient to decide that Heidegger's involvement in political despotism 'taints' his work: that is the fastest way to rid the shelves of all sorts of difficult authors from Plato to Nietzsche and to make righteous indignation even more satisfying than it normally is." Of course, the pertinent question is whether "indignation" at the philosophies of Plato and Nietzsche is not based on false interpretations of them, which their admirers maintain, whereas what "taints" the philosophy of Heidegger is based on a correct reading of him. Leo Strauss, one of the foremost political philosophers of the twentieth century, offers a less apologetic judgment than Krell on "the dismal matter": "We cannot help holding these facts against Heidegger. Moreover, one is bound to misunderstand Heidegger's thought radically if one does not see their intimate connection with the core of his philosophic thought." But Strauss does not in the least dismiss Heidegger's philosophical importance. Strauss rather echoes Löwith's point that Heidegger's thought is the "living kernel" of a "school" of philosophy that has been very influential, especially in Europe, but also in North America after World War II: existentialism. Strauss remarks, "Existentialism is a 'movement' which like all movements has a flabby periphery and a hard center. That center is the thought of Heidegger. To that thought *alone* existentialism owes its importance or intellectual respectability."[6] George Parkin Grant, Canada's leading twentieth-century social theorist, asks, "How could this amazing unfolder of the nature of modernity, this person who can illuminate the philosophic past, how could he opt for National Socialism at the political level?" and adds, "This is much more than an historical question about Europe in the 1930s. If one uses it as an oyster knife to open up his brilliance, the whole question of the destiny of modernity can be revealed."[7]

Clearly, whatever we may conclude about the connection, intimate or otherwise, between Heidegger's philosophy and his political stance toward Nazism, reason and all the evidence demand that we attend to his writings with the utmost seriousness. If we ourselves are thinking people, what in the world could be more worthy of our serious attention than the thought of Martin Heidegger? Even if it should turn out that the most influential philosopher of the twentieth century thought political philosophy to be impossible, this would of course be a problem of the greatest urgency for political theorists, if for no other reason than that it might be true.[8]

In this essay, I deal thematically with only one essay of Heidegger: *Was ist das—die Philosophie?* (*What Is That—Philosophy?*).[9] I shall also advert primarily to his "Memorial Address," a public lecture delivered in 1955 in celebration of the 175th birthday of Conradin Kreutzer, the only other famous person born in Heidegger's home town, delivered within two months of *Was ist das—die Philosophie?* The former is one of two parts of Heidegger's book *Discourse on Thinking.*[10] I also refer to other writings of Heidegger when I think they help to clarify what may be more obscure in the lecture under discussion. I propose to interpret this lecture in the spirit one would attempt, for example, in interpreting a single "minor" Platonic dialogue, fully aware that it cannot be supposed to reveal Heidegger's thought as a whole, but supposing it may be read as a coherent statement addressing a discrete and important theme. I believe *Was ist das—die Philosophie?* is an excellent introduction to Heidegger's thought for intimidated students and recalcitrant scholars alike. What could be a more important question for a philosopher to ask, after all, than "What is philosophy?" What follows is a modest attempt to explicate Heidegger's philosophical essay from within and to indicate the deep thread that ties Heidegger's thinking about what philosophy is to his radical anticosmopolitanism, which is, in turn, tied to his far more than flirtation with the Nazi revolution of 1933.[11] And there can be no doubt—and at long last in the Heidegger scholarship there is a consensus that there can be no doubt—about the intimate connections between Heidegger's "existential" thinking, even as early as *Being and Time*,[12] still his magnum opus, and the "existential" politics of the Nazi revolution: Heidegger, Joseph Goebbels, and Adolph Hitler were equally as contemptuous of "liberalism," "consumerism," "Bolshevik socialism," and such, all of which could be subsumed under the rubric of that disgusting thing against which Hitler was always raving: "rootless cosmopolitanism." This doubtlessly explains the interest in Heidegger in the early stage of the Third Reich: Heidegger's disgust was equally as strong, if more sophisticated and profound, as Hitler's.

As regards the title of this essay, one may ask two pertinent questions. First, what do I mean by "radical"? Second, what do I mean by "committed"? By "radical," I mean that all of Heidegger's thinking goes to the very root of things. By "committed," I refer to one of Heidegger's most famous *existentialia* (ways of existing) of "authentic" *Da-sein* (Being-there) in *Being and Time*. And there is, as we shall see, an intimate connection between the thinking of Martin Heidegger about what "philosophy" is in this lecture and his radical anticosmopolitanism. For example, one of his answers to the question posed by his lecture is that philosophy is in its essence Greek: "The word *philosophia* tells us that philosophy is something which, first of all, determines the existence of the Greek world. Not only that—*philosophia* also determines the innermost basic feature of our Western-European history" (29). The German for "innermost basic feature" in this passage is *Grundzug*. Steiner notes, "In German, and most notably in Heideggerian German, *Grund* portends intensely concrete but also numinous strains of rootedness, of earthly ancientness and provenance," the polar opposite of cosmopolitanism.[13] "Autochthony" figures prominently in the lecture, and it too may be said to be the polar opposite of cosmopolitanism. Both of these words also find their etymologies in Greek: "autochthony" is a combination of two Greek words, probably *autos* and *chthōn;* "cosmopolitan" is probably from *kosmos* and some form of *politeia.*

The title of Heidegger's essay (*Was ist das—die Philosophie?*) asks a Greek question in a Greek way (35); he does not transliterate his Greek (but I shall mine, throughout). Our first impression is that he appears to ask a traditional question in a traditional way. We soon discover that what he has to say about philosophy is not as traditional as the traditional manner in which he begins to say it. Certainly, philosophy has become questionable for Heidegger. Heidegger begins with a question, the theme of the discussion is a question, and he proceeds by questioning. Steiner remarks the "deliberately helpless and halting" phrasing of the German title,[14] and Brann (2n2) suggests that the way Heidegger poses the question introduces into it "a motion of pointing and distancing as in 'What have we here?'" In an essay of less than forty brief pages, Heidegger asks a question at least four dozen times, and he repeats the question of the title—*Was ist das—die Philosophie?*—at least a dozen times. As he famously remarks elsewhere, in the final sentence of his essay "The Question concerning Technology" (*Basic Writings,* 317), "questioning is the piety of thought."

Heidegger tells us almost immediately that "the aim of our question is to enter *into* philosophy, to tarry in it, to conduct ourselves in its manner, that is, to 'philosophize'" (21). He tells us immediately that with the question "What is philosophy?" we are touching on a widespread, indeterminate theme. "Widespread" comes from the first short sentence of the lecture, "indeterminate" from the second. Brann (3n3) notes that "indeterminate" translates *unbestimmt;* thus, "the first sentence introduces the principal wordplay of the lecture. *Bestimmen* ordinarily means 'to determine'; however, *stimmen,* transitively, means 'to tune' but also 'to put in a mood.' Hence *unbestimmt* might be read as 'untuned' or 'moodless.'" In *Being and Time,* Heidegger uses the word *Stimmung* for one of the *existentialia* of *Da-sein. Stimmung* is usually translated "mood." Our "being in a mood," as we colloquially say—being "attuned" to the world around us in a certain way, as Heidegger says—is a mode of being open to Being (*Sein*). (For the first thematic treatment of *Stimmung* in Heidegger, see *Being and Time,* sec. 31.) Our treatment runs the risk of lacking cohesion, even though we may always "hit upon something that is correct," unless we lead the discussion in a definite direction, onto a path. Heidegger emphasizes that we direct the discussion onto *a* path and that "it must, in fact, remain open whether the path which [he] should like to indicate in what follows is, in truth, a path which allows us to pose and answer the question" (21). We must philosophize: our path must be such that that of which philosophy treats may affect us, touch (or move) us "in our very nature (*Wesen,* essence)" (23).

But, Heidegger asks, "does not philosophy thereby become a matter of affection, emotions, and sentiments?" (23). He elaborates upon this hypothetical objection, borrowing what he calls the *mot* (French for "word," or "answer" in the case of a riddle) of André Gide—"It is with fine sentiments that bad literature is made"—and applying it a fortiori to philosophy. Is the posited objection sound? Yes—if sentiments are something irrational, and philosophy is "not only something rational but the actual guardian of reason" (23). But proceeding thus, Heidegger avers, we have answered our question before even properly posing it: "If what is considered to be reason was first established only by philosophy and within the course of history, then it is not good judgment to proclaim philosophy in advance as a matter of reason" (24). To begin by considering philosophy as rational or irrational is already to take for granted (unreasonably) what reason is. Such a path leads nowhere. On the other hand, if we consider that that of which philosophy treats may personally move us in our essential nature as human beings, we might discover that "this being-moved has nothing whatsoever to do with what is usually called feelings and emotions, in short, the irrational" (27). Henceforth, we must take greater caution in choosing the path of our discussion "so that we do not flounder around in either convenient or haphazard conceptions of philosophy," for example, the conception "everyone" considers "correct," that philosophy is a matter of reason. Indeed, our aim is precisely to move from correct statements about philosophy to an apprehension of the essence of philosophy.

The path Heidegger moves along is the path of the word "philosophy" speaking from its source, that is, "philosophy" speaking Greek, that is, φιλοσοφια (*philosophia*). That we have uttered the word "philosophy" in our discussion indicates, whether we are aware of it or not, that we are in fact already, however awkwardly, traveling on this path (29). By translating "way" instead of "path," Brann (7) can render the felicitous "*philosophia* is a way along which we are underway." How is a word a path? For Heidegger, a word is not a "sign" for a "thing," but an "event"; indeed, a word is a series of events; the word *philosophia* is not something static, but is itself a dynamic history. The question "*Was ist das—die Philosophie?*" is an inquiry into the meaning of a word. The essay is a testimony to what it means for Heidegger to think radically into the meaning of a word. Etymological excavations are fundamental to Heidegger's thinking and the source of much of the controversy concerning his thought. (Here, allegedly, is where language is "running riot.")

Greekless readers must tolerate my rendition of transliterated Greek words and phrases in this essay. They are necessary if we are to follow the etymological digging that is central to Heidegger's argument. (Heidegger's own Greek, as mentioned earlier, is never transliterated.) General readers may be comforted to know that Greek scholars have little advantage over the unschooled here, because Heidegger's etymologies are frequently so idiosyncratic that they are almost always contested by philologists, classicists, and philosophers. For that matter, Heidegger does the same thing with the German language, which is what permits Steiner, in *Heidegger,* frequently to distinguish German from *Heideggerian* German. Similarly, Brann, throughout the notes in her translation, distinguishes between Heidegger's meaning for a particular German word and the "dictionary word." Heidegger notoriously asserted everywhere in his writings that classical Greek and, of course, German, were especially powerful, spiritual languages through which—indeed, only through which—one could genuinely philosophize or think; one simply could not do so in English, assertions redolent with a spirit of disgust for cosmopolitanism.

Philosophy determines the history of the West (and now, the entire world). "In origin the nature of philosophy is such that it first appropriated the Greek world, and only it, in order to unfold" (31). It may be germane to note here that the Greek word *historia,* from which both English and German derive their word for "history," originally meant "to learn by inquiring or questioning." It is significant and characteristic of Heidegger that he should say philosophy appropriated the Greek world, not vice versa. To say philosophy is in essence Greek is not, of course, to deny that the originally Greek nature of philosophy has been mediated by Christianity and the thinking of the (so-called) Middle Ages. It is to say "nothing more than that the West and Europe and only these, are, in the innermost course of their history, originally 'philosophical.' This is attested by the rise and domination of the sciences" (31). Science is a fruit of the West, and the seed was first planted in the soil of nascent Greek philosophizing. Heidegger goes so far as to say that the oft-heard expression "Western-European philosophy" is in truth a tautology (31).[15] This rise to domination of the sciences is what has permitted the West "to put a specific imprint on the history of mankind upon the whole earth" (33); for example, this is what has brought into being our cosmopolitan world in which "nature becomes a gigantic gasoline station, an energy source for modern technology and industry," in which "farming and agriculture, for example, now have turned into a motorized food industry," to borrow two famous sentences from the "Memorial Address" (50, 54).

Heidegger bids us consider what it means that the present era in history is characterized as the "Atomic Age." It means that the atomic energy discovered and harnessed by modern science is viewed today as the force that will determine the future course of history. But this is either to forget or be ignorant of the fact that philosophy is the mother of the sciences and gave birth to them, that "there would never have been any sciences if philosophy had not preceded them and proceeded" (33). Heidegger, following Nietzsche, always emphasizes that "science" is subordinate to "philosophy." He makes the same point in his "Memorial Address" (50): "We remain as far as possible from a reflective insight into our own age. Why? Because we forget to ponder; because we forget to ask: What is the ground that enabled technology to discover and set free new energies in nature?" The context of the quotation is Heidegger's emphatic lamenting—although he would deny it is a "lament"; this would be too "ethical" a stance for him—of modern man's "homelessness," his utter lack of "rootedness" or "autochthony" in a "homeland." The translators note in this context (49n5) that "the German *Bodenständigkeit* (to-stand-on-a-ground) is translated *rootedness* or *autochthony* depending on a literal or a more figurative connotation." If the urgent necessity of being "autochthonous," in one's "homeland" is not the opposite of being a cosmopolitan, I cannot imagine what is! Furthermore, it is very difficult not to read these statements as "ethical" ones.

To avoid this error, we must ponder the Greek word *philosophia,* truly hear it, and reflect upon it and the historical tradition to which it binds us. We must "surrender" to this tradition. "Tradition does not surrender us to a constraint to what is past and/ irrevocable. Surrendering is a delivering into the freedom of discussion with what has been" (33/35; in the bilingual text, English appears only on the odd-numbered pages; I have indicated the page break in the English pages in my quotation). It is characteristic that Heidegger links "surrendering" and "freedom": what "freedom" means is unclear, but it certainly has nothing to do with willing; if anything, free dom is a consequence of "releasement" from willing. In any event, when we truly hear the word *philosophia,* and reflect upon it, we find it inscribed on the birth certificate of the contemporary world epoch, which is called the "Atomic Age," and we can ask our question "*Was ist das—die Philosophie?*" "only if we enter into a discussion with the thinking (*Denken*) of the Greek world" (35). Here Heidegger mentions "Thinking" (*Denken*) for the first time in the lecture. Not only what is in question, but how we question, even today, Heidegger insists, is Greek in origin (35).

The question "What is that?" in Greek is *ti estin.* The *ti estin* that asks such things as "What is the beautiful? What is knowledge? What is Nature? What is movement?" is a form of questioning developed by Socrates, Plato, and Aristotle (37). Heidegger calls our attention to the fact that in such questioning, which seeks more exact delimitation of what Nature, movement, or beauty are (changing the order, and dropping "knowledge"), "an interpretation is given of what the 'what' means, in what sense the *ti* [what] is to be understood" (37). The "whatness," the *quiddity* of the "what," has been understood differently in different periods of philosophizing. But throughout the history of philosophy, the question "What is that?" has remained an originally Greek question. In what appears to be a later addition to this lecture, Heidegger emphasizes that the question "What is philosophy?" is a historical, "fate-full" question: it is, in fact, "*the* historical question of our Western-European *Da-sein*" (41). As was remarked earlier, *Da-sein* literally means "Being there"; it is the term Heidegger coined in *Being and Time* for the way a human being is—with full emphasis on both the words "human" and "being"—and is intended as an ontological category, not an "ethical" one (but see my note 3).

The question is, What does it mean that our epoch in world history is characterized as the "Atomic Age?" Again we get help from the "Memorial Address" (50): We live in the age of "technology," in which "the world now appears as an object open to the attacks of calculative thought, attacks that nothing is believed able any longer to resist," in which "nature becomes a gigantic gasoline station." Technology threatens humanity with nuclear annihilation, certainly; but to become preoccupied with this problem, according to Heidegger, is to be dazzled by the superficial; more important is the danger of the loss of humanity's essential nature, the danger that "meditative" thinking, which is rooted in Being in a manner differently, more profoundly, than "calculative" thinking, will disappear. It is again difficult not to read this distinction as an "ethical" distinction. Calculative thinking has produced the deadly bombs, but, "precisely if the hydrogen bombs do *not* explode and human life on earth is preserved, an uncanny change in the world moves upon us" ("Memorial Address," 52).

This threat to our humanity from technology and calculative thinking did not arise contingently. The essence of technology emerged from rationalism, which is the fruit of Greek philosophy, when it adopted, or (better) was granted a particular understanding of Being, and thereby of Truth. This enabled the West to develop modern mastering science, with its determining power over every aspect of our lives, which in turn led to our modern cosmopolitan way of living on this earth, meaning on this planet—not the "ground on which one stands," or in which "authenticity" is "rooted." Heidegger's emphasis on "rootedness" is, I again stress, the key to understanding his radical anticosmopolitanism. We begin to understand what Heidegger means when he says, "That of which philosophy treats concerns us personally, affects us, and indeed touches (moves) us in our very nature" (23). Heidegger's fundamental concern in this essay is to indicate by means of pondering the question "*Was ist das—die Philosophie?*" how the present threat to our humanity, something that concerns each one of us, vitally, here and now in our present hour of history, is a destiny (or "fate") that unfolds from nascent Greek philosophy. Applying to Heidegger what another said of his own enterprise, it is not self-forgetting and pain-loving antiquarianism nor self-forgetting and intoxicating romanticism that induces Heidegger to turn with passionate interest, with unqualified willingness to learn, toward the thought of classical antiquity; he is compelled to do so by the crisis of our time, the crisis of the West, the crisis, for Heidegger, of authentic *Da-sein*. The question "*Was ist das—die Philosophie?*" is a path leading from the *Da-sein* of the Greek world down to us, and beyond us, and on which we are traveling, standing at some yet-to-be-determined point (41). We are questioning the nature of philosophy, which, Heidegger informs us, if our questioning is to be more than mere "chatter," must have become worthy of question. But philosophy can have become questionable for us only if we already know what philosophy is—a hermeneutical circle, a spiraling downward, deeper into the question, so characteristic of Heidegger; circles are never merely circular in Heidegger: they are, to change our metaphor slightly, centripetal. And to what we should attend in the circle, *philosophia* again indicates (43).

According to Heidegger, the Greek language, uniquely, is *Logos*. "In the Greek language what is said in it *is* at the same time in an excellent way what it is called" (45). In the *legein,* the speaking, or direct presentation of a Greek word, the thing itself is made to lie immediately before us. *Philosophia* goes back to the adjective *philosophos,* which was coined by Heraclitus, according to Heidegger, and allegedly expressed something quite different from the adjective "philosophical." It meant to love the *sophon. Philein* (to love) signifies for Heraclitus *homolegein,* that is, to speak in correspondence with the *Logos.* This correspondence with the *Logos* is in-accordance-with (*harmonia*) the *sophon.* In short, *harmonia,* "being-in-accordance-with," is the distinctive feature of *philein* (loving) for Heraclitus. The *aner* (man) *philosophos,* then, is whoever speaks in correspondence with the *Logos,* which correspondence is in accord with the *sophon* (47).

But what is the *sophon?* Brann (15n19) notes that Heidegger never translates the word *sophon,* but glosses it as "the beings in Being," and that its normal meaning is "the wise [thing]." The *sophon* is, according to Heidegger, that which says "All being is in Being," that is, "Being *is* in being," with "is" meaning "gathered together," "collected," so that "Being is being" means Being gathers together being(s); but "Being is the gathering together—*Logos*" (49). Note the air of anticosmopolitanism in these "collecting," "gathering-together"—we might say, today, "communitarian"—words in Heideggerian German. "Being is being" translates Heidegger's *Das Sein ist das Seiende.* In English, unfortunately, we must use one word, the participle "being," for German's two words, *das Sein* (verb) and *das Seiende* (noun). In Greek, the equivalent verb is *to einai,* and the noun is *to on;* in Latin, *esse* and *ens;* in French, *l'être* and *l'étant.* William Barrett tells us that Heidegger's own suggestion was that *das Sein* be rendered "Being," and *das Seiende,* "beings."[16] Elsewhere, Barrett renders "the Is of what-is" for *Das Sein des Seiendes.*[17] In what follows, I will render "Being" for *das Sein,* and "being(s)" for *das Seiende,* with a few exceptions in the service of clarity. In sum: the *aner philosophos,* who loves the *sophon,* is whoever speaks in correspondence with the *Logos,* which is in harmony with the gathering together of being(s) in Being; the *aner philosophos* is whoever is in harmony with Being.

Now, "All being is in Being" sounds trivial to us; but Heidegger maintains it is this fact, "that in the appearance (*Scheinen*) of Being being(s) appear, that first astonished the Greeks and first astonished them alone" (49). This observation prepares Heidegger's account of the birth of Greek philosophy. Sophist reasoning, he claims, was that "which always had ready for everything an answer that was comprehensible to everyone and which they put on the market" (51). The demands of the public realm and its suppliers are always the great threat to Thinking.[18] The rescue of astonishment at the most astonishing thing—being(s) in Being—from Sophist reasoning was the accomplishment of a few who strove for the *sophon,* but in the process, the original *harmonia* with the *sophon* that characterized the *aner philosophos* was lost, and replaced by a striving *toward* the *sophon. Philein* no longer meant *homolegein;* it became rather a yearning (*orexis*) determined by Eros—and *philosophia* was born (51). Brann (18n27), remarks that Heidegger's use of the definite article in *Den Eros* "invokes the god and his particular passion." We should emphasize that he is speaking of the pagan, Olympian, "ethnocentric" gods, not any universal (cosmopolitan) God.

In sum: "philosophy" supplanted "thinking" when the original harmony with the gathering of being(s) in Being, which thinkers such as Heraclitus and Parmenides possessed, became instead a matter of pursuing the question "What is a being (that which is) in so far as it is?" and the question "What is Being (the Is of what-is)?" was abandoned. This "step" (*Schritt*) permits Heidegger to avoid *Fortschritt,* which implies a "progress" (as Brann, 19n28, acutely observes). This step from asking after Being to asking after being(s), which was the direct consequence of the intrusion of the public realm into the realm of thinking, was accomplished by Socrates, Plato, and Aristotle (53). "Philosophy" asks what that which is (being) is insofar as it is. It asks about being(s) and forgets the question of Being. This "forgetfulness" is what is characteristic of our modern cosmopolitan world, which means that, for Heidegger, it is not really a "world" in which human beings can authentically "be."

Heidegger draws special attention to how Aristotle circumscribes philosophy in its nature when he says (*Metaphysics* A2, 982b9ff.) that philosophy is *epistēmē tōn prōtōn archōn kai aitiōn theōrētikē* (theoretical knowledge of governing first principles and causes) (55). Heidegger suggests that if we translate *epistēmē* and *theōrētikē* without modern misconceptions, Aristotle's statement means that philosophy is a kind of competence, a competence at "being on the lookout for something and of seizing and holding in its grasp what it is on the lookout for" (57). And what is philosophy on the lookout for? The *prōtai archai kai aitiai* (governing first principles and causes) of Being. It is these that constitute the Being of being(s) according to Aristotle. Heidegger asks, "*In what sense is Being conceived that such things as 'principle' and 'cause' are qualified to set their seal upon beings and take possession of them?* (59, original emphasis); and his answer, in plain terms, is "technologically." Heidegger asks this emphatic question (his only italicized sentence in this essay) in the very center of it: it is literally its core, and more than literally. The driving force of the history of the West, which culminates in the "Atomic Age," and therewith the dangers of the disappearance of humanity's essential nature, is the West's misconception of Being, the decisive event for which was the Greek pre-Socratic "step" from thinking to Socratic-Platonic-Aristotelian philosophy, from attending to the question of Being, to attending to the question of being(s), from what Heidegger also calls, though not simply synonymously, "meditative" thinking versus "calculative" thinking, throughout his "Memorial Address." Hans-Georg Gadamer, one of Heidegger's most important students, the greatest figure in twentieth-century hermeneutics, has widely pronounced that Heidegger's misreading of Plato is the great hole in his mentor's thinking.

May we not say that Aristotle's answer to the question "What is philosophy?" is only one among many? Philosophy's self-understanding has changed frequently in the course of history, has it not? Of course, says Heidegger, but "philosophy from Aristotle to Nietzsche, precisely because of these changes throughout their course, has remained the same; for the transformations are the warranty for the kinship in the same" (61). Yet, significantly, while Aristotle's circumscription of philosophy is certainly not applicable to the thinking of Heraclitus and Parmenides, it is just as certainly a "free consequence" of this earlier Greek thinking. Heidegger says "free consequence" because "in no way can it be seen that individual philosophies and epochs of philosophy have emerged from one another in the sense of the necessity of a dialectic process" (63). This is a clear, if implicit, rejection of Hegel, despite Heidegger's profound indebtedness to Hegel.[19] What does he mean?

There have been individual philosophies and different epochs of philosophy since Aristotle, but they share in common that they all let the question "What is Being?" in the sense of "What is the Is?" recede into the background, and all attend instead to the question "What is being?" or "What are the beings that are?" They forget about the whole and attempt instead an ordered articulation of the beings that inhabit it. Heraclitus and Parmenides stood outside of this, according to Heidegger, as original thinkers who were still open and attentive to the question of Being, of which the West has grown increasingly forgetful over time. In different historical epochs, Being reveals itself in different ways, but the successive epochs of philosophy do not therefore follow one another in a determined fashion. We can attend to the revelations of Being or ignore them, and whether we attend to or ignore them is not itself predetermined. We may close ourselves off from Being or we may open ourselves up to it. What is held in our grasp and what is let slip away, what is pondered and what is left unthought, is not determined by some dialectical process, but depends on us, neither the masters nor the slaves of Being (as man, in turn, depends on Being).

May we not answer our question *Was ist das—die Philosophie?* by reducing, through a comparative abstraction, the various definitions of philosophy that have appeared in the history of philosophy to one (63)? This, according to Heidegger, would be an empty formula; we would merely be "collecting by historical methodology" correct information about philosophy rather than entering into it (65). The authentic answer to our question must be "a philosophizing answer which, as response, philosophizes in itself" (65). We must talk through with the philosophers that of which they speak. "It is one thing to determine and describe the opinions of philosophers; it is an entirely different thing to talk through with them what they are saying, and that means, that of which they speak" (67). We hold a dialogue with the philosophers not, as we might suppose, by addressing ourselves to them, but by letting our discussion be addressed by what addresses the philosophers, and this is the Being of being(s). Our speaking must "co-respond" to the Being of being(s) if the answer to our question is to be a philosophizing one (69). One of Heidegger's foremost students, Hans-Georg Gadamer, expresses the conviction that "philosophy is a human experience that remains the same and that characterizes the human being as such. . . . There is no progress in it, but only participation."[20]

May we not then abandon the "history of philosophy"? No! Before we can set up a theory about the characteristic feature of the answer that corresponds to the Being of being(s), we must first attain "correspondence," and we attain correspondence only by "conversing with what has been handed down to us as the Being of being(s)" (71). Although "historical assertions about the definitions of philosophy" do not provide us with the answer to our question, we cannot simply repudiate this "history." Rather, we adopt and transform what has been handed down to us through tradition. Heidegger calls such an adoption and transformation a "*Destruktion*" and explicitly refers us to *Being and Time,* section 6 (71). *Destruktion* does not mean what our English word "destruction" means, but rather that "putting aside merely historical assertions about the history of philosophy," we must "open our ears, to make ourselves free for what speaks to us in tradition as the Being of being(s)" (73). It is significant that Heidegger changes the metaphor for philosophizing from "seeing" what is ultimately True to "listening" to it. Among other things, this anticipates his move away from philosophy and toward poetry.

Further reflection reveals that to be in correspondence with the Being of being(s) is the fundamental trait of our nature or essence (*Wesen,* 73): the Being of being(s) must always somehow let itself be for us to some degree; we are thus always somehow in correspondence with it. The relation of human being to Being is not one of subject to object (contra especially Descartes); there is a region within which all beings always are, and therefore are always in contact with one another, and the region itself is Being: "All being is in Being" (49). This means that human beings are always and everywhere in correspondence with, and hence able to be in accord with (in the sense of *harmonia*), the Being of being(s). Nevertheless, "we rarely pay attention to the/ appeal of Being" (73/75). "Philosophy," Heidegger now asserts, "is the correspondence to the Being of being(s), but not until, and only when, the correspondence is actually fulfilled and thereby unfolds itself and expands this unfoldment" (75).

Heidegger recurs to André Gide's *mot* about "fine sentiments." *Philosophia,* he reiterates, "is the expressly accomplished correspondence which/ speaks in so far as it attends to the spoken appeal of the Being of being(s). The correspondence listens to the voice (*Stimme*) of the spoken appeal" (75/77); Brann (29n44) claims that *Stimme* ("voice") is "the grandest of the *stimm*-words." "Correspondence" then means, in the translation of Brann (29), "being at-tuned (*be-stimmt sein*) (*être-disposé*) namely by the Being of beings." Being de-termined or dis-posed means being placed in a particular relationship with what is. "Correspondence" is an "attunement," and "only on the basis of the attunement (*disposition*) does the language of correspondence obtain its precision, its tuning (*Stimmung*)" (77).

Heidegger reassures us that by calling philosophy a "tuned correspondence" he is not surrendering thinking to the "sentiments." Rather, he is pointing out the fact that "every precision of language is grounded in disposition of correspondence . . . of heeding the appeal" of the Being of being(s) (79).[21] He claims to follow Plato and Aristotle in this. He quotes the former (*Theaetetus* 155d): "Very much is this especially the *pathos* [emotion or experience] of a philosopher, namely, to be astonished; for there is no other determining point of departure for philosophy than this" (79). We are to understand this to mean that the *pathos* of astonishment (*to thaumazein*) is the *archē* (beginning and governing first principle) of philosophy; that is, it pervades philosophy, and is not just a point of departure for it that is then left behind once we begin to busy ourselves with "doing philosophy." He quotes the latter (*Metaphysics* A2, 982b12ff.): "Through astonishment (*to thaumazein*) men have reached now, as well as at first, the determining path of philosophizing (that from which philosophizing emanates and that which altogether determines the course of philosophizing)" (81).

Heidegger's interpretation of these passages hinges on his translation of *pathos*. He notes that "*pathos* is connected with *paschein,* to suffer, endure, undergo, to be borne along by, be determined by." To protect us from conceiving *pathos* in a very modern, very un-Greek, psychological sense, he asserts that we should translate *pathos* as tuning (*Stimmung*), in his sense (83). We will then understand astonishment (*to thaumazein*) more exactly: to be astonished is to step back from what is while at the same time being forcibly drawn to and held fast by it. "Astonishment is disposition in which and for which the Being of being(s) unfolds: Astonishment is the tuning within which the Greek philosophers were granted the correspondence to the Being of being(s)" (85).

A very different tuning governs modern philosophy; Heidegger refers explicitly to Descartes's *Meditations* (85). For classical philosophy, the fundamental tuning is astonishment; for Descartes, it is doubt. With the *archē* (beginning and governing principle) of a different sort of tuning comes a different way of asking the question of what being(s) in Being are. Descartes's question is: what is that being that is a true being in the sense of *ens certum,* that is, being in certainty? Asking after being(s) in a new way, Descartes understands Truth in a new way. His *cogito ergo sum*—"I think therefore I am"—makes certainty the measure of truth; this certainty is that of a subject about an object, and "thus the nature of man for the first time enters the realm of subjectivity in the sense of the ego" (87). With modern philosophy, the question of Being, the question that asks after the "Is of what is," the question with which even the classical philosophers were no longer in harmony, falls into utter oblivion. "I am therefore I think" is more in accord than "I think therefore I am," the Cartesian "ego," with Heidegger's meditations on authentic *Da-sein*. Modern philosophy seeks what is present as an object completely divorced from the enveloping background within which what is present is enabled to be present. The enveloping presence that enables subject and object to be present for each other, and without which there could be no subjects and objects, is utterly lost. With modern philosophy, thought becomes groundless; we, ourselves, homeless. This is Heidegger's analysis of human "alienation," which is, at its profoundest level, our alienation from Being, the Is of what is, our embracing the contemporary world of cosmopolitanism, or what is today called "globalization."

We have seen what the *archē* of modern philosophy is. What, Heidegger asks, is its *telos*, its end or fulfillment? What is its tuning (*Stimmung*)? Where must we seek it? Heidegger mentions Hegel, Schelling, Marx, and Nietzsche as possibilities. Presumably one fundamental tuning prevails in contemporary thinking, but it apparently eludes us. "We are trying to listen to the voice (*Stimme*) [see Brann, 29n44] of Being. Into what kind of mood (*Stimmung*) does this voice put contemporary thinking?" (89). Even though what we come across today seems to be a variety of tunings: for example, Nihilism, "doubt and despair"; and Positivism, "blind obsession by untested principles" (91); we find fear and anxiety (*Angst*)—that which so excited the French existentialists—mixed with hope and confidence. We even find a calculating kind of reasoning that seems to be free of any kind of tuning (i.e., technical thinking); but this is illusory: even the coldness of calculative thinking, which dominates in this preset historical epoch called the "Atomic Age," is "attuned to confidence in the logically mathematical intelligence of its principles and rules" (91).

While Heidegger does not answer the question "What is the *telos* of modern philosophy?" he indicates a path. We have made acquaintance with what philosophy is and have learned how it is—"the manner of correspondence which is attuned to the voice of the Being of being(s)" (93). But this is only a beginning. For this co-respondence (this *Ent-sprechen*) is a speaking (*Sprechen*), which means it is in the service of language (*Sprache*), which is very difficult for us today to comprehend because of our instrumental view of language; in our time, we consider it more correct to say, "language is in the service of thinking, rather than that thinking, as co-respondence, is in the service of language" (93). This conception of language is at the opposite pole from the Greek experience of language, the nature of which is revealed for the Greeks as *logos*. We today are only beginning, according to Heidegger, to glimpse what *logos* and *legein* mean. Not that our task is to return to experiencing language as the Greeks did, for this is not possible. What we must do is "enter into a conversation with the Greek experience of language as *logos*" (95). Our task is to think language; our task is to think the meaning of the famous Heideggerian dictum "Language is the house of Being."

When we do make the attempt to think language, we are led to compare Thinking and Poetry, *Denken* and *Dichten,* because each of these, in its distinctive way, is in the service of language, and this being in the service of language is what constitutes the "secret kinship" of thinking and poetic creation. But alongside this "secret kinship" is an "abyss"; Heidegger quotes Hölderlin's poem "Patmos": "They dwell on the most widely separated mountains" (95). To the objection that the question concerning philosophy must be kept separate from the question concerning poetry, Heidegger responds: "This distinction would be possible and necessary only if in the discussion it should turn out that philosophy is not that which it is now interpreted to be—a co-respondence which discusses the appeal of the Being of being(s)" (97). Heidegger is a thinker, not a poet. He does not speak of poetry as one proposing the abandonment of rigorous thinking in favor of poetic creation. He thinks poetry; he questions poetry—just as he thinks and questions *philosophia*—for, as the famous last sentence of *The Question concerning Technology* tells us, "Questioning is the piety of thought."

Heidegger draws his reflections to a close. His task has been "to prepare all who are participating for a gathering in which what we call the Being of being(s) appeals to us" (97). Is this an arcane, "academic" (in the pejorative sense) concern? Not for Heidegger. He admits (indeed insists) that it is not his task to wind up a practical or philosophical program. But if the root of human alienation is our alienation from Being, if we in our time are homeless, our thought groundless, if we live in an oblivion of Being because we have closed ourselves off from Being, then the vital task of thinkers is to open their thinking to Being in the manifold revelations. If we are to listen to Being, astonishment (*to thaumazein*) must again be the tuning or mood (*pathos*) of philosophy, must again be the *arch* (governing first principle) of our thinking. It is in the service of this project—to revive the astonishment at the most astonishing thing—being(s) in Being—that Heidegger offers his lecture.

At the so-called everyday level, we seem fated to live in a "famished time," a "time of need," in which the highest human experiences are what

George Parkin Grant calls "intimations of deprival." "What is worth doing," Grant laments, "in the midst of this barren twilight is the incredibly difficult question."[22] Heidegger tells us in his "Memorial Address" (50) that our "day" is a dreadful "night" in which "an attack with technological means is being prepared upon the life and nature of man compared with which the explosion of the hydrogen bomb means little." In what we may call his last word on the subject, Heidegger enigmatically opines that from the darkness in which we now find ourselves, "Only a god can save us."

But this profound level of our alienation from Being has its political, and radically anticosmopolitan, counterpart: not groundless, homeless cosmopolitan man, but man genuinely experiencing "autochthony," "rootedness" in the "blood and soil" of the "homeland," the man of a "gathered community" with its own "fate-full" historical "destiny" to which that community is "committed," can live "authentically": National Socialism—a radical anticosmopolitan ideology if there ever was one—fits the bill perfectly, although it is only fair to say that Heidegger's philosophy does not necessarily lead to it. Heidegger did, however, remain either disingenuously evasive or belligerently silent about this, from his "Letter to the Rector of Freiburg University" in 1945 until his death in 1976. Steiner offers a judicious assessment of Heidegger's involvement with National Socialism; nevertheless, what especially disturbs Steiner is not so much Heidegger's speeches and deeds during 1933–1934, "nauseating as they are," but his "very near intolerable silence" on Hitler and the Holocaust after 1945.[23] Despite everything, none of the myriad details that have been unearthed since 1978 and exposed in the scores of volumes that have been written on the issue have altered in any fundamental way what one needs to know to assess Heidegger's philosophy, his political acts, and the relationship of the former to the latter. It is reported, however, by Wolin, "that one of Heidegger's only expressions of contrition over his ruthless behavior during the Nazi years comes in a letter to Jaspers of March 20, 1950. There he confides that he did not disdain visiting Jaspers because of the latter's Jewish wife, but instead, because he was 'simply ashamed.'"[24] We can only "wonder" (*thaumazein*) at what "mood" (*Stimmung* or *pathos*) Heidegger was experiencing (*pathos*), on what ground he was standing (*Bodenständigkeit*), what his "attunement" (*Bestimmtheit*) or his "co-respondence" (*Ent-sprechen*) to the Being of being(s) (*Das Sein des Seiendes*) must have been, what he was "thinking," when he wrote those words.

Notes

I wish to thank the editors of this volume, especially Khalil Habib and the anonymous referee, for suggestions that improved this essay considerably. I also wish to thank my wife, Rachel, for, among other things, valuable assistance in the writing of it, which is why I dedicate it to her.

1. Thomas Langan, *Heidegger* (New York: Columbia Univ. Press, 1959).

2. Among the most important articles for political philosophers are Fred R. Dallmayr, "Ontology of Freedom: Heidegger and Political Philosophy," *Political Theory* 12 (1984): 204–34; and W.R. Newell, "Heidegger on Freedom and Community: Some Political Implications of His Early Thought," *American Political Science Review* 78 (1984): 775–84. Newell is especially illuminating to readers concerned with Heidegger's anticosmopolitanism, but to anyone for its brilliant elucidation of the indebtedness of Heidegger's philosophy to the tradition of nineteenth-century German Idealism. On the latter topic, see especially Michael Allen Gillespie, *Hegel, Heidegger, and the Ground of History* (Chicago: Univ. of Chicago Press, 1984).

3. See the interview Heidegger gave to the German magazine *Der Spiegel* on September 23, 1966, published only after his death, as was his wish, available in English translation by Maria P. Alter and John D. Caputo, "Only a God Can Save Us," *Philosophy Today* 20 (Winter 1976): 267–85; reprinted in *The Heidegger Controversy*, ed. Richard Wolin (Cambridge, MA: MIT Press, 1993), 91–116. Nevertheless, Heidegger's protests to the contrary notwithstanding, it is very difficult to read Heidegger without thinking that concepts such as *Da-sein* (Being-there) and "commitment" do not carry ethical overtones, that to live an "authentic" existence is not superior to leading an "inauthentic" one. In *Being and Time*, sec. 51n12, the famous section "Being-towards-Death and the Everydayness of Da-sein," he himself refers the reader to Tolstoy's story "The Death of Ivan Ilyitch," as presenting the phenomenon in an exemplary way. For Tolstoy, this was certainly a story with a "moral." One wonders, if "Being" is not something like Heideggerian language for "God," as many interpreters take it to be, why Heidegger should concern himself about the fate of *Da-sein* at all.

4. For a brief account of Heidegger's activities at the advent of and during the Third Reich, see David Farrell Krell, "General Introduction" in Martin Heidegger, *Basic Writings* (New York: Harper and Row, 1977), 27–28 (hereafter cited as *Basic Writings*, followed by the page number in parentheses), including the sources there cited, the best known of which is Hannah Arendt, "Martin Heidegger at Eighty," available in *Heidegger and Modern Philosophy*, ed. M. Murray (New Haven, CT: Yale Univ. Press, 1978). George Steiner, *Heidegger* (London: Fontana Press, 1978), 111–21, evenhandedly reprises all the basic facts of Heidegger's involvement with National Socialism. Hundreds of articles and books on Heidegger and National Socialism have now been published, but the de-

bate really got rolling with, among the books available in English, Victor Farías, *Heidegger and Nazism,* ed. Joseph Margolis and Tom Rockmore (Philadelphia: Temple Univ. Press, 1989; original French edition, 1987); Günther Neske and Emil Kettering, eds., *Martin Heidegger and National Socialism: Questions and Answers* (New York: Paragon House, 1990; original German edition, 1988); Tom Rockmore, *On Heidegger's Nazism and Philosophy* (Berkeley: Univ. of California Press, 1992); Wolin, *Heidegger Controversy;* Berel Lang, *Heidegger's Silence* (Ithaca, NY: Cornell Univ. Press, 1996). The best place to begin is Wolin, *Heidegger Controversy,* which includes most of the documents concerning this contentious issue.

5. Karl Löwith, "Heidegger: Problem and Background of Existentialism," *Social Research* 15 (Winter 1948): 345–46. Elsewhere, Löwith left no doubt about what he himself thought about "these matters": see his "Les implications politiques de la philosophie de l'existence chez Heidegger," *Les Temps Modernes* 14 (1946–1947), now available in English in Wolin, *Heidegger Controversy,* 167–85. See also Karl Jaspers, "Letter to the Freiburg University Denazification Committee (December 22, 1945)," 147–51 in the same volume; both are translated by Wolin. In the half century since Löwith wrote the statement quoted, Jaspers's philosophical reputation did considerably decline in status, although there has been a recent resurgence of interest in him.

6. Leo Strauss, "Philosophy as Rigorous Science and Political Philosophy," *Interpretation* 2 (1971): 2. Thus, both Löwith, "Heidegger" and" Les implications politiques," and Strauss, "Philosophy as Rigorous Science," maintain that the Nazism of Heidegger is embedded in the core of his thinking. National Socialism's "philosophy," if one may call it philosophy, was radically anticosmopolitan. Dallmayr, "Ontology of Freedom," 204–6, cites the same Strauss passages, but he either misconstrues or misrepresents them.

7. Larry Schmidt, ed., *George Grant in Process: Essays and Conversations* (Toronto: House of Anansi Press, 1978), 66.

8. On this very question, see Mark Blitz, *Heidegger's* Being and Time *and the Possibility of Political Philosophy* (Ithaca, NY: Cornell Univ. Press, 1981). See also Catherine H. Zuckert, *Postmodern Platos: Nietzsche, Heidegger, Gadamer, Strauss, Derrida* (Chicago: Univ. of Chicago Press, 1996).

9. *Was ist das—die Philosophie?* (Pfullingen, Germany: Günther Neske Verlag, 1956) was a prefatory lecture delivered before a colloquium that was held in Normandy in August 1955. The edition I use in this essay is the German-English bilingual text published in 1958: Martin Heidegger, *What Is Philosophy?* The translation and the introduction are by Jean T. Wilde and William Kluback (New Haven, CT: College and Univ. Press, n.d.), originally published by Twayne in 1958. The importance of this lecture as an introduction to Heidegger's thinking may be implicit in the fact that no translation of *Being and Time* appeared in English before 1962. All quotations in my text, except where otherwise noted, are from the Wilde and Kluback edition and are cited (in parentheses) by

page number only; I make only minor revisions, the most frequent of which is "being(s)" for "being." I have also consulted this edition of the lecture: Martin Heidegger, *What Is That—Philosophy?* trans. and annotated by Eva T.H. Brann (Annapolis, MD: St. John's College Press, 1991), hereafter cited simply as Brann, followed by page numbers in parentheses. Brann also usually translates "beings" for Wilde and Kluback's "being."

10. Martin Heidegger, "Memorial Address," in *Discourse on Thinking,* trans. John M. Anderson and E. Hans Freund (New York: Harper and Row, 1966), hereafter cited as "Memorial Address," followed by page numbers in parentheses. The "Memorial Address" was originally published as Martin Heidegger, *Gelassenheit* (Pfullingen: Günther Neske Verlag, 1959). *Gelassenheit* (Releasement or Letting Be) is a key term in Heidegger after the war.

11. Heidegger's published writings in English, not to mention those in German, are now voluminous; the secondary literature is a veritable industry. Walter Biemel, *Martin Heidegger: An Illustrated Study,* trans. J.L. Mehta (New York: Harcourt, Brace, Jovanovich, 1976), 187–206 (original German publication, 1973), provided a useful bibliography; he noted that one thousand titles had to be added by 1972 to a Heidegger bibliography published in 1968. Imagine the situation four decades later! For this reason among others, I cite only a small fraction of the literature on Heidegger, only what is readily available in English, and only what I have found especially helpful.

12. I use Martin Heidegger, *Being and Time: A Translation of* Sein und Zeit, by Joan Stambaugh (Albany: State Univ. of New York Press, 1996), hereafter cited in the text as *Being and Time,* with Heidegger's own section numbers. The text first appeared in the *Jahrbuch für Phänomenologie und phänomenologische Forschung* 8 (1927) and was published simultaneously as a separate volume.

13. Steiner, *Heidegger,* 27.

14. Ibid., 25.

15. Heidegger is probably more responsible than anyone else in the twentieth century (Nietzsche having died at the end of the nineteenth) for "Western" interest in things "Eastern"; but whatever oriental thinking or meditating may be, it is not philosophy, at least not according to him.

16. William Barrett, *Irrational Man: A Study in Existential Philosophy* (Garden City, NY: Doubleday, 1958), 211–12.

17. William Barrett, *What Is Existentialism?* (New York: Grove Press, 1964), 137; see also William Barrett, *The Illusion of Technique* (Garden City, NY: Doubleday, 1978).

18. Compare the remarks about the deplorable "dictatorship of the public realm," again a reflection of contempt for any kind of cosmopolitanism, in Heidegger, "Letter on Humanism," *Basic Writings,* 197.

19. See Gillespie, *The Ground of History* (Chicago: Univ. of Chicago Press, 1984); and Newell, "Heidegger on Freedom and Community."

20. See Hans-Georg Gadamer, *The Idea of the Good in Platonic-Aristotelian*

Philosophy, trans. P. Christopher Smith (New Haven, CT: Yale Univ. Press, 1986), 6.

21. In his various writings, Heidegger speaks of the "call" of Being, of the "appeal" of Being, of the "voice" of Being; sometimes all three appear in the same writing. What is essential is not to confuse any of these expressions with the "call of conscience" in *Being and Time,* secs. 55–57.

22. George Grant, *Technology and Empire: Perspectives on North America* (Toronto: House of Anansi, 1969), 178. The writings of Grant, though he is not, himself, a Heideggerian, are yet very much informed by Heidegger's insights, which are utilized in such as way as to facilitate access to Heidegger's thinking by English speakers. For the most recent of a growing number of discussions of Grant's political and social thought, see Hugh Donald Forbes, *George Grant: A Guide to His Thought* (Toronto: Univ. of Toronto Press, 2007). For a long time, most of Grant's work had been published only in his native Canada.

23. Steiner, *Heidegger,* 108–21, quotations on 118.

24. Wolin, *Heidegger Controversy,* 146.

Gaelan Murphy

Alexandre Kojève

Cosmopolitanism at the End of History

> It is part of education, of *thinking* as consciousness of the individual in the form of universality, that I am apprehended as a *universal* person, in which [respect] *all* are identical. A *human being counts as such because he is a human being,* not because he is a Jew, Catholic, Protestant, German, Italian, etc. This consciousness, which is the aim of *thought,* is of infinite importance, and it is inadequate only if it adopts a fixed position, for example, as *cosmopolitanism*—in opposition to the concrete life of the State.
> —G.W.F. Hegel, *The Philosophy of Right.*

> The Era where all *humanity* together will be a political reality still remains in the distant future. The period of *national* political realities is over. This is the epoch of Empires, which is to say of *transnational* political unities but formed by affiliated *nations.*
> —Alexandre Kojève, *Outline of a Doctrine of French Foreign Policy,* August 27, 1945

The tension between the aspirations of rational cosmopolitanism and the inability to make that abstraction fit with concrete life on the ground is at the core of the German Idealist understanding of politics. Kant's conception of politics substitutes the authority of the rational justice of the *Rechtstaat* for the mediated self-interest of the contractual State. The result is a constitutional State in which the autonomous human being could live according to the rational a priori morality of the categorical imperative. Kantian freedom is the freedom to obey the law out of respect for its reasonableness. If we are autonomous but not rational, then obedience without compulsion is impossible. However if we are rational and hence able to recognize a priori laws, then these rational laws will be followed "even by a nation of devils."[1]

The problem with this attempt, as Hegel points out, is that the conception of a priori reason upon which it is based is "abstract." So long as there is a gap between reason and experience within transcendental idealism, we will know that we have experience, and we will know we are thinking about experience, and therefore there must be a priori categories, yet we won't know anything about these categories.[2] The moral law of Kant's categorical imperative does not succeed in supplying the formalism of transcendental idealism with determinate content, because the criterion of Kant's reason remains the formal requirement of noncontradiction. Thus, lying is forbidden by the categorical imperative because it implies a "contradiction in conceivability."[3] This leaves unasked, and hence unjustified, why a "contradiction in conceivability" is an appropriate standard for a moral law. The implication of the categorical imperative is that there is not a sharp distinction between the authority of reasons and the act of reasoning, since the source of the authority of reasons is that they have been produced by an act of reasoning and were not simply given to us. Under this schema what counts as reason is what is recognized as reasonable by the individual subject. Viewed in this light, Kantian autonomy comes at the price of political objectivity. While it may be true that only a cosmopolitan political order is rational, once reason is emptied of particular content, we are left with the shell guideline of consistency that cannot guide concrete political life.

It is for this reason that, for Hegel, the justice of a rational State can't be understood in terms of the application of an abstract, or a priori, political program. The unity of the *noumena* and the *phenomena* must exist not only in the hypothetical, as it does in Kant, but as part of concrete reality that is itself prior to thought. The rational State comes into existence at a specific historical moment as a part of the concrete here and now, in which free individuals are prepared to accept its existence and the reciprocity of rights and responsibilities it represents as the condition for their own freedom. Recognition of the reason of the law happens in accordance with the particular language and customs from which it is derived and in which terms freedom is conceived. It must be this way, because otherwise those who will be ruled will not know their duties as duties, their freedom as freedom, and hence will not recognize the State for what it is supposed to be—the concrete manifestation of freedom.[4]

The German Idealist tradition highlighted by Kant and Hegel produces three critical ideas. First, modern politics must be universal and applicable to everyone. What counts is that you are a human being, not "a Jew, Catholic, Protestant, or German." Second, the order of this cosmopolitan politics is based upon the authority of reason. Third, the constitution of modern States cannot be given, they must be made. The rational cosmopolitan order must be consistent with local traditions, customs, and mores. The result is a seemingly impossible tension between Kantian rationalism and Hegelian historicism.

In this essay I outline Alexandre Kojève's reconciliation of these two positions through the formation of what he calls the Universal and Homogeneous State (UHS). Despite the promise of a priori reason, rational individuals still have their own ideas concerning the nature of justice. So long as rational people can disagree, Kantian reason ends in subjectivity. Kojève addresses this problem in his *Outline of a Phenomenology of Right* by bracketing our rational disagreements through a purely "behavioral" account of justice.[5] This phenomenological account examines justice as it appears, without introducing subjective ideas that exist only in our heads. However, phenomenology presents its own problem; it is historicist. By grounding his account in positive experience, Kojève appears to be relativizing justice.[6] He addresses this by reintroducing the rational element through an a posteriori interpretation of the phenomenon of justice.[7] He attempts to demonstrate how the historical phenomenon of law is necessarily derived from an idea of justice, which in turn arises from the anthropogenic act of the struggle for recognition. Thus, while there is no reason to prefer one rational account of justice over another or one historical practice of justice to another; it is possible to identify what justice is phenomenologically, how the various ideas of justice originate in the anthropogenic act, and how these differences evolve dialectically into the final justice of the end of history. In so doing, he provides an account that is both rational and concrete.

However, Kojève is also aware of the Janus face of political cosmopolitanism. Cosmopolitanism read in light of the philosophical anthropology necessary to justify its realization does not result in the just State. Rather, the global, cosmopolitan State that exists at the end of history gives way to a "reanimalized" existence. Life really is a tragedy—the satisfaction of the human desire for justice ends in animal contentment and nihilism, in which we no longer care about justice. In this vein Kojève's defense of cosmopolitanism should be read, as Michael Roth points out, as part of his larger effort "to establish a Hegelian self-consciousness for our times," which in turn "must be read *against* his nihilistic description of the animalization of man." Into the liberal conception of cosmopolitanism must be introduced a notion of "aristocratic equality," which would allow the preservation of "aristocratic sweetness of living" and the "humanization of free time,"[8] through the formation of a Latin union as the nonspatial model of cosmopolitanism.

The Phenomenology of Right

For Kojève, the phenomenological essence of Right "is realized and revealed (or is manifested) in and by: The interaction between two human beings, A and B, which necessarily provokes the intervention of an impartial and disinterested third, C, whose intervention annuls the reaction of B opposed to the action of A" (42). On the basis of the observation of the behavior of the participants, it is only the intervention of a third party that allows the distinction between a situation in which one has the right to something from one in which one does not. For example, in the absence of the intervention of a third, the situation in which A takes what is owed to him and the situation in which A steals from another appear the same. "One must say, therefore, that Right cannot be revealed to man without him noticing or postulating a disinterested intervention of a third. In other words, this intervention is a necessary or 'essential' constitutive element of the phenomenon of 'Right.' And it is thanks to this element that this phenomenon can be described or defined by a 'behaviorist' method" (39). This is to say that there is a properly juridical situation only where there is an independent judge. "This is obvious and has always been accepted: one cannot be judge and party at the same time" (72).[9]

The intervention of an independent judge is composed of three elements: the act itself, the will, and the intention (70). First, there must be an act that alters the environment by objectively affecting the world. Otherwise it would not appear as an objective phenomenon (74–75). Second, the act must be generated by a voluntary will, conscious and free. It is free in the sense that it has its own cause and is not mechanically generated by the interaction. It is conscious in the sense that "the 'intervention' is conditioned (without being determined) by the interaction to which it is related" (76). It must be this way because otherwise the third is not a judge but rather is just another force (of nature, of God, etc.), and the intervention will appear as destiny and not justice. Third, the intention of the act makes the action properly juridical by introducing impartiality and disinterestedness. While normally impartiality and disinterestedness are introspective terms, they can be defined phenomenologically by restricting consideration solely to the phenomenon. Under these circumstances, the intervention is impartial if the intervention "will not and could not be altered by the sole fact of interchanging A and B" (79). The existence of a disinterested judge will be observed phenomenologically if the intervention alters the interaction of A and B without objectively altering C and thereby affecting his material interest. This latter provision creates a problem, since the intervention is by definition an act that changes the world; in addition, because C both lives in the world and has an interest in it, there is no such thing as a disinterested judge (81). If it is impossible for a judge to be disinterested in fact, then there is an authentic juridical phenomenon only if the judge abstracts from his person and acts *as if* he were not a person, which is observed only if the judge could be "anyone at all," such that the intervention "remains the same when a given C is replaced by any other C . . . if C′ and C″, while being different, intervene in the same manner in a given case" (82).

However, if, from a phenomenological point of view, disinterested means that the same judgment would be made by anyone at all, in practice the person of C is always relative to a certain social group as it is found in a specific place at a specific time, and C is therefore not "anyone at all" (85). "Anyone at all" can only mean "anyone at all" from among those that are alive and available at that time. Thus, "if one wants to define real Right, i.e., a given real or 'positive' Right, one must say: 'disinterested, i.e., supposed to be able to be anyone at all *inside a given Society at a given moment of its historical existence*'" (88). Which is to say that it appears that there is no universal justice; the best that can be done is to realize our justice.[10] But if what we are realizing is solely our justice, then there is no cosmopolitan justice. For our justice is both partial and interested in relation to us; hence there has never been the intervention of an impartial and disinterested third from a cosmopolitan perspective.

What salvages the phenomenon of justice and makes it autonomous from politics is that the authentic judge does not have a material or political interest in the specific interaction he is judging. Without a material interest, there is no apparent reason for the judge to intervene. If the judge nonetheless does intervene, it is because he is motivated by a theoretical interest, even when this interest cannot be observed directly. This theoretical interest is the idea of justice that motivates the judge. Thus, while the phenomenon of Right is bound by time and hence historically contingent, the intention of the judge that creates the phenomenon is oriented outside of time. The true judge is interested only in justice, not politics. Phenomenologically, this interest is observed in the following case: if "a given interaction does or does not provoke a specific intervention, this intervention will recur or be lacking *every time* that an *identical* interaction to the given interaction occurs" (96–97). Hence, for there to be an observable case of Right, not only must C be "anyone at all," but C must act the same each time the situation occurs. "In other words, C must be 'anyone at all' not only in relation to space but also in relation to time" (97). While every authentic judge attempts to realize an ideal that exists outside of time, that ideal can be achieved phenomenologically only in the cosmopolitan state at the end of history, because it is only then that "anyone at all" is "anyone at all" in relation to both space and time.

This leads us to the cusp of Kojève's neo-Hegelian theory of cosmopolitan politics. What transforms the intervention of the third from an act of fate (contingent and mysterious) or an act of God (dependent upon grace) is that it is an act that is knowable (in space) and predictable (in time). This act can be truly knowable and predictable only if it occurs within a society that involves all of humanity (it is universal) and has no private interests or exclusive groups (it is homogeneous) in which the intervening judge, at any given moment, is truly anyone at all (91). Even if Right as a phenomenon exists only in time and by this very fact necessarily changes, without an idea of justice that points outside of time, there can be no Right, even historically contingent Right. If the UHS were to exist, there would be no reason for this idea of justice to change, because it would have no opposition from within or without. In this way historically contingent Right would be transformed into the Right of the End State. In that case the Right of the End State would no longer be relative to history and would be the final Right, the realization, or perhaps the fulfillment of natural Right.

> "At the limit," positive Right coincides with natural Right; for the Right *realized* in and by the universal and homogenous State is just as much one, just as *universally* and *eternally* (i.e., "necessarily")

valid, as the would-be "natural Right." We can say, therefore, that the "positive" Right of the universal and homogenous State realizes "natural" Right, which is nothing other than *the* Right as such—that is, the "essence" of Right. In the universal and homogenous State, therefore, the "rationalist" theory of Right coincides with the "historical or sociological" theory.

That is the very core [*le fond*] of Hegelianism, or, if one prefers, of the dialectical understanding of history.

. . . All this is not a beginning but a *result,* not a being but a *becoming,* and a becoming properly so-called—that is, a becoming *in time,* in history. Thus, "absolute Right" does not exist from the beginning [and] it does not *yet* exist. But it does not follow that all Right will *always* be "relative." The Right of the universal and homogenous State will not be so: it will be "absolute" since it will be the only one and will not change. But it will be so only at the end of history, when the State in question will be a reality.[11] (91–92)

The Dialectic of History: Aristocratic and Bourgeois Justice

The phenomenological analysis of Right demonstrates two things. First, what makes the juridical situation an authentic phenomenon distinct from other phenomena (political, religious, etc.) is the intention to realize an idea of justice that exists outside of time and independent of political considerations. Second, except for the limit case of the End State, the phenomenon of Right is always incomplete. The idea of justice that provokes the intervention of an authentic judge and the specific interactions to which it is applied remain relative to history. However, because both the rational ideas that govern justice and the concrete cases that make up real Right change dialectically, it is possible to identify the origin and progress of these changes.

For Kojève, the dialectic is a rational account of knowledge meant to describe the world as it really is. For knowledge to be knowledge, it must correspond to the thing as it exists "without adding anything to it, without taking anything away from it, without modifying it in any way whatsoever."[12] Therefore, a dialectical philosophy of history is appropriate only because history itself is dialectical. The dialectic is both a procedure of rational thought and an account that can be tested empirically by comparing the results with historical experience.[13] In this way Kojève's dialectical realism is both rational and concrete. Both empirical history and the philosophy of history that describes that history operate according to the threefold structure of Identity (the given that is eternally identical to itself, governed by abstract reason—the thing is this), Negativity (that which is not the given, governed by the negative reasoning of contradiction—the thing is not this), and Totality (the totality of the constituent elements of Identity and Negativity, governed by positive rationality).[14]

What this means is that both human experience and the rational account of that experience begin with the given condition of our existence. This condition is fixed and identical to itself (A = A). However, we live in time, people act, and things change. People seek to change the existing conditions of their existence by opposing the given A with a non-A. This in turn stimulates its own negative reaction. Other people act in order to negate the non-A, thereby creating a non-non-A. The result of this negation of a negation is not a return to the beginning, because in historical reality, $-(-A) = C$ and not A. As Kojève states, "All new Right is an optional negation of a given Right. And as soon as this negation has taken place, one can no longer come back to the negated Right; for to negate the new Right is to negate the negation of the old. And in dialectical or historical reality, the not-not-A is not A but C [which], being the synthesis of the thesis A and the antithesis not-A (= B), is other than A and not A" (158n).[15] The result is an account of history that ends in neither traditionalism nor the "fury of destruction" of radicalism, because the moment of negation, while constitutive, remains a moment. The characteristically human element is found not in the negation but in the preservation of the given reality in the present in the form of historical memory, which preserves (*aufhebung*) that which must be preserved and allows human beings to remain themselves even while they change.[16]

Kojève's account of the evolution of Right applies this understanding of the dialectic and his account of the anthropogenic struggle for recognition to the phenomenon of Right. Because historical change is dialectical, the evolution of Right is likewise dialectical. What gives justice its absolute character is that while all concrete cases of Right are historically contingent, and hence relative, the Idea of Justice is inherent in the anthropogenic act that creates the human being—the "I" opposed to a "non-I" as a subject opposed to an object. This "I" is born when the oneness of the natural world is broken up into "I" and "non-I" by "anthropogenic desire," the desire for another desire.[17] Anthropogenic desire is the desire to be recognized as an autonomous value: the desire to have subjective certainty recognized by another subjective certainty, transforming it into objective reality. The encounter of two beings motivated by anthropogenic desire results in a fight for recognition, because so long as neither is for the other what it is for itself, they cannot reconcile their subjective certainties in the objective world.[18] In this fight each consciousness is forced to choose between its human desire for recognition and its animal desire for life. One chooses its animal life, submits, and becomes the slave, while the other chooses recognition and becomes the master.[19]

Kojève takes this idea and applies it to the problem of Right. Inherent in the struggle for recognition is the opposition between man as man, who wants to be recognized, and man as animal, who wants to live. This gives rise to the opposition between what is and what ought to be. "The animal *is* and it wants to remain in existence. But according to man, he *ought* not to do so and he *ought* not to be if he only wants to be what he is—an animal which refuses the risk. As for man, he still *is* not. But if he opposes himself to the animal which is, this is because he *ought* to be and attain existence. In short, human reality creates itself by the anthropogenic act not only as *reality*, and reality conscious of itself or 'reflective,' but also as a positive *value* or as a *duty* to be and do. Man not only risks his life; he also knows that he ought to" (217).

This ought that originates in the struggle for recognition is determined by it. Inherent in the struggle is the mutuality of risk and recognition. The value of recognition is equal for both combatants, because each combatant values recognition only insofar as the other values it. The risk is equal, because it depends upon the mutual value placed upon recognition. It is only because the value and the risk of the struggle are equal for both parties that they consent to the struggle instead of running away. They mutually risk their lives for recognition, and hence the anthropogenic justice that originates in the struggle for recognition is the justice of equality, reciprocity, and consent.

In practice, however, the equality of the struggle for recognition ends in the inequality of slavery based upon unilateral recognition. In this way the struggle for recognition gives rise to two historical conceptions of justice: aristocratic and bourgeois justice. Aristocratic justice is justice as equality of status. It is the justice of brothers in arms, defined by the strict equality of the struggle and the competition to be primus inter pares. The system of law of a society of masters is that of the subjective right to do as you please within your own objective domain (landed property), provided this does not infringe upon the subjective rights of other masters (landed gentry) (244). By contrast, bourgeois justice is the justice of equivalence. For the slave the equality of the struggle has become the inequality of slavery. The slave's choice to submit demonstrates that in his eyes the advantage of security is equivalent to the benefits of mastery (223). The slave justifies his inequality with the master by saying that their positions are equivalent, for "in his eyes the troubles of the Struggle are *equivalent* to those of Servitude, because the benefits of security *compensate* for the burdens of Servitude" (252). This substitution of equivalence for equality shifts the loci of verification from the objective world to the subjective measurement of the individual. In the world of masters, subjective right is measured in terms of objective status, hence the significance of land and title. In the bourgeois world, by contrast, objective right is measured by the individual subject, since it is only the individual who can decide whether two things that are different are nonetheless equivalent. When two things are different (i.e., unequal) whether they are nonetheless equivalent can only be determined by the individual for whom they are supposed to be equivalent. The authority of status based upon the land is replaced with the authority of the individual. In this way, the fundamental principle of bourgeois Right is the equivalence of rights and duties. If, according to aristocratic Right, the Lord can do as he pleases because of his status as a Lord; in the mind of the slave, the Lord has the right to do as he pleases because he has the duty to fight to protect the slave, and the slave has the duty to work because he has the right to security.[20]

Kojève dramatizes the essence of these two conceptions of justice through the example of dinner, which I quote at length.

> If it is a matter of sharing food for dinner between two persons, one of whom had lunch and the other not, we [bourgeois] will say that the share will be just if the latter receives more. And we will say that it is just to give a child a slice of cake that is larger than the slices of the adults. It is also just that the weak carry less than the strong, and it is from an ideal of Justice that the practice of the handicap was born. From all of this, one need only go one step further in order to assert that it would be just to give a thing to the one who desires it the most. And one commonly says that it is just to give it to the one who needs it the most (cf. the principle of "communist" Society: to each according

> to his needs). Or once again, one will say that it is just to give the thing to the one who has made the most effort to have it (cf. the principle of "socialist" Society: to each according to his merits)—and so on.
>
> In all these cases, a master would be struck by the injustice of inequality from the start. Thus, a poor but proud man will hide the fact that he has not had lunch in order to see the Justice of equality alone applied. And a weak person may through pride or amour-propre (the Bourgeois will say vanity) carry the same weight as the strong. Likewise, a child may be upset by a bigger share for himself if he wants to be treated "like an adult" first and foremost. And there are athletes who prefer to forfeit a match when the Justice of equivalence requires that others be handicapped. In short, the master can require equality without taking account of equivalence, of the compensation of his inequality with others. By contrast, the Bourgeois or the Slave will be satisfied by the equivalence of conditions, without taking account of their inequalities. When the Master will say that the share is unjust because it is unequal, the Bourgeois will consider it just because it is equivalent. (254–55)

What drives the historical evolution of Right is the dialectical relationship between aristocratic and bourgeois Right. Aristocratic Right cannot change while remaining aristocratic. Every master is recognized in his universality, and each master is strictly equal to each other. Thus, even in the passing of generations there is no change. One person does not replace another, for, insofar as they enjoy the status of the Lord, they are the same. They are defined by their role and not their individual person. If an aristocrat does change, he does so by ceasing to be an aristocrat. For instance, an aristocrat who engages in commerce, that is, in the exchange of equivalent goods, introduces a form of bourgeois Right into his conception on the basis of his commercial experience. Similarly, if a society of aristocrats expands the subjects of Right, by including women and children, for example, it does so by recognizing their equality without the necessity of violent struggle. The system of law that governs the expansion of equality, therefore, is no longer aristocratic Right based upon equality of risk.

The bourgeois, on the other hand, must change in order for its idea of justice to be realized in the world. The slave must achieve political power, and since the slave can only achieve power by risking his life, he incorporates aristocratic equality of risk into his conception of justice. Thus, real aristocratic Right is always somewhat bourgeois, and real bourgeois Right is always somewhat aristocratic. They both are always in a state of coexistence, and all real Right is the still-not-resolved Right of the citizen, the synthesis of equality and equivalence. The task of philosophy is to resolve this synthesis by rationalizing our historical ideas of justice based upon either aristocratic or bourgeois conceptions by removing the inequalities in bourgeois Right and the nonequivalences in aristocratic Right. The interplay between aristocratic and bourgeois Right eventually ends in the UHS, in which universal equality (racelessness) coincides with objective equivalence (classlessness), and hence no further juridical evolution is necessary (268).

Kojève dramatizes this synthesis by returning to the example of dinner.

> Let us take up again the example of sharing food for dinner. The principle of equality will require a share of equal portions between those having right, and it will no longer be concerned about anything else. But the principle of equivalence will ask if the equal portions are truly equivalent. If one observes that some are more hungry than others, one will see [to it] that this is not so. One will then share the food differently, making the portions proportional to the hunger of each one. The principle thus being satisfied, one will leave matters there. But the other principle will be offended by the inequality of shares, and it will try to eliminate it. However, in order not to offend the principle of equivalence, it will be necessary to eliminate the inequality of the participants. One will therefore ask why some are more hungry than others. And if one observes that this difference results from the fact that some have had lunch and others not, one will see to it such that from now on all might have lunch. The principle of equivalence will therefore have incited that of equality to realize itself more perfectly. And by becoming perfect, equality coincides with equivalence; for if those having right are truly equal, the equality of their parts no longer differs from their equivalence; their equivalence is nothing but their equality. (269)

This still-unresolved synthesis is manifest in the modern world in the tension between the bourgeois Right of market relations, based upon the exchange of equivalent yet unequal goods and services, with the aristocratic Right of socialist equality. Thus economic inequality is justified by bourgeois equivalence. As Kojève notes, "the salary of a factory manager is supposed to be equivalent (although very unequal) to the salary of a worker, either because it requires more effort (intellectual or moral effort being understood—[i.e.,] 'responsibility') or because it has a greater return (from the point of view of the owner's benefits)" (255). However, if contemporary politics appears governed by the conflict between competing visions of equality, the dialectical evolution of the division of labor and the attendant political emancipation of women and subjugated classes under the aegis of the Modern State indicate an emerging synthesis of equality and equivalence. As he explains:

> Let us assume that at a given moment a being acting in a certain way is considered a human being: a warrior for example, idle in time of peace. By relying on the principle of equality, one will consider human all the beings who act in the same way, and them only. But by relying on the principle of equivalence, one could observe that an action different from the action in question can be equivalent to it, and that there will then be good reason to consider human the being who carries it out. Thus, for example, the fact of working for Society can be equivalent, from the social and political point of view, to the fact of defending Society with weapons in hand, and the act of providing children to Society, i.e. future citizens, can be equivalent to the act of working or waging war. One will therefore recognize workers and women as human beings in the same way as warriors. But by taking into account the difference of their actions, one will assign different "statuses" to them. But placed in the midst of recognized human beings, one will, in accepting the principle of equality, try to equalize them—that is, to equalize their actions. One will require, for example, that warriors work in time of peace and that workers take part in wars. (269–70)

International Right: Union of Federated Republics

The problem Kojève is confronting is to determine how definitive juridical standards are possible in the face of historicism. Kojève's argument is that the UHS, the legalistic, cosmopolitan, rational State, driven by the principle of reciprocity of rights and duties, embodies the coincidence of equality and equivalence and is complete, universal, nonrelative, perfect. Moreover, it is supposed to be complete not only rationally but, because that rationality is dialectical, as part of empirical reality.

At the same time, it is quite clear that this State does not exist. Not only is there no World State, but insofar as International Right exists, it has never been in the form of actual, enforceable laws (315). We are left with the same problem that confronted Kant. Despite the identification of the rational principles of the civil constitution, the perpetual peace of Federated Republics does not have empirical existence. The difference, however, is Kojève's substitution of a posteriori dialectical reasoning for Kant's a priori reason. The problem of international law is not simply a problem of reason but rather a problem inherent in the phenomenon of Right—the lack of an impartial and disinterested third that is able to definitively enforce the synthesis of equality and equivalence in the judicial equity of the citizen. This cosmopolitan judge cannot come from politics, because politics is defined by material interests. If there is to be an impartial and disinterested third, it can come only from a politically neutral party, which does not exist in international relations.[21] So long as international relations are the political relations of sovereign States, the political considerations of friends and enemies will prevail over considerations of justice. If there is to be international Right, it can come only from an apolitical society that somehow has political power without itself being politicized (319).

In Kojève's view this becomes possible when States share a "common" society that crosses their political boundaries. So long as the Right of this society is not the Right of the individual States, then this Right will be only a theoretical Right. However, if this society succeeds in getting the territorial States to adopt their Right as the system of law, then a juridical union between those States will be possible. For instance, if State A has to resolve a controversy between citizen A and citizen B (of State B), and it does so while applying its own domestic law, citizen B will not be able to turn to his own State for recourse so long as the States share the same domestic Right (derived from Society C, of which they are all members). Similarly, if States A and B share the same domestic law (again derived from society C), then society C can act as an impartial and disinterested third in their interactions, and they will have no juridical reason for objecting. This would involve a sacrificing of each State's sovereignty, for they would no longer be sovereign in relation to C. However they would not have to sacrifice their autonomy in the role of the administration of justice, and the State that resulted would necessarily be a Federation (325).[22]

At first this federal State will not be universal and will have to maintain a political element. As a political State, it will have to act politically toward those States that exist outside the Federation of Right. However, "as a juridical entity, the State limits itself to imposing abroad its domestic Right. In other words, it tends to create a *Federation* of States or a federal State by becoming itself one of the federated States, the Federation having for a base and for a result the existence of a unique Right, common to all the federated States, and implying—in its 'public Right' aspect—an element of 'federal Right,' regulating the relations of the federated States among themselves, [and] in particular the federal organization of justice" (327). In terms of the relationship between States and other levels of governance, the fundamental principle of the State will be the federal administration of the existing Idea of justice, implying the local administration of the domestic law of the State. The principle of this shared domestic law is the bringing together of equality and equivalence, represented formally in terms of a reciprocity of rights and duties and made real by the principle of redistributive justice. The result is a fairly accurate description of the modern redistributive State, in terms both of its underlying principle and of the movement from individual, and inadequate, nation-States to larger "Federations" or "Empires" such as NAFTA or the European Union.[23]

Cosmopolitanism and the Humanization of Free Time

In a seemingly contrarian addendum in the *Introduction to the Reading of Hegel,* Kojève suggests that historical events since 1806, including both world wars, have been simply the "extension in space of the universal revolutionary force of Robespierre-Napoleon." Everything since then has "had only the effect of bringing the backward civilizations of the peripheral provinces into line with the most advanced (real or virtual) European historical positions." This process of elimination of historical anachronisms is more advanced in North America than in Europe, such that "one can even say, from a certain point of view, the United States has already attained the final stage of Marxist 'communism,' seeing that, practically, all the members of a 'classless society' can from now on appropriate for themselves everything that seems good to them, without thereby working any more than their heart dictates." At bottom, if "Americans give the impression of rich Sino-Soviets, it is because the Russians and the Chinese are only Americans who are still poor but are rapidly proceeding to get richer."[24]

This idiosyncratic notion of Marxist capitalism is a recurring theme for Kojève. In a 1957 lecture given in Dusseldorf, he argued that Marx was fundamentally correct; the long-term combination of the unleashing of the productive forces of capitalism with the appropriation of surplus value by the owners of production is untenable.[25] What Marx was unable to see, however, was that the answer to this problem would come from within capitalism. The true prophet of Marx is Henry Ford, who, by paying his workers enough that they could afford the products they produced, solved the internal contradiction of capitalism. This "Fordite capitalism" is a shift from the nineteenth-century model of paying workers as little as possible to the twentieth-century model of paying them as much as possible, and it is in this sense that the United States represents the Marxist goal of a classless society.[26] He argued that twentieth-century colonialism followed the model of nineteenth-century capitalism. What is necessary under these conditions is to "Fordize" the global economy by extending "the universal revolutionary force of Henry Ford" in space, transforming colonialism from a "taking" to a "giving" mode. Viewed in the larger context of Kojève's thought, this movement from a taking to a giving colonialism is part of the process by which the UHS expands throughout the globe. The future of global politics is the progressive integration of national economies, succeeded by their political integration. As he predicted in a 1950 letter to Leo Strauss (written, not incidentally, on Secrétariat d'Etat aux Affaires Economiques letterhead): "If the Westerners remain capitalist (that is to say, also nationalist) they will be defeated by Russia and *that* is how the End-State will come about. If, however, they 'integrate' their economies and policies (they are on the way to doing so), then *they* can defeat Russia. And *that* is how the End-State will be reached (the *same* universal and homogeneous State). But in the first case it will be spoken about in 'Russian' (with Lysenko, etc.), and in the second case—in 'European.'"[27]

This prediction of economic and political integration provides a template for understanding contemporary global politics. The ongoing global economic crisis has been caused by the "internal contradictions" of a global economy driven by manufacturing overcapacity, financial speculation, and unsustainable debt loads. The integration of "Western" economies has reached a limit in the expansion of markets and as a result is suffering from structural overcapacity. These economies have managed to maintain economic growth through the development of "innovative" banking schemes, without any direct connection to the production and sale of real goods, for which there is no demand. This shell game is in the process of dissolving. The core of the problem is the overcapacity of manufacturing, which is in turn driven by a lack of markets for products. In this regard the auto industry is once again emblematic of the process.[28] The North American auto industry is restructuring under the twin weights of large benefit packages for its workers (Ford's solution) and a decreasing demand for its products (overcapacity). The Fordite solution to the problem of capitalism, to pay the workers as much as possible, has become the problem. This solution worked by filtering the surplus value of production through the workers and then back into economic production in the form of increased sales. It no longer works, because the workers (and all others) already have all the cars they need; hence, the surplus pay is no longer funneled back into the company. As a result the long-term trend in all advanced capitalist economies is that the engine of growth has moved from manufacturing to the financial sector, on the one hand, and government spending, on the other.

The answer to this problem cannot be a return to the previous model of paying workers as little as possible, combined with protectionist measures designed to insulate the national from the global economy. The problem is overcapacity, the associated reduction in trade, and the unproductive use of capital. A reduction in the income of "workers," combined with protectionist measures that insulate national economies, will reduce demand, thereby compounding the problem. The short-term answer of increasing capital through government spending will work only if the resulting debt burden is offset by economic development. This can occur only if the capital is transformed into real economic development and there is a market for the goods that are then produced. Hence, global Fordite capitalism; a market of billions exists—they just need the surplus value to purchase cars. What is unfolding is the global integration of economies, designed to enable "Fordite capitalism," followed by the political and juridical consolidation of State power necessary to regulate it juridically.[29]

Phrased in this manner, these might appear to be salutary developments for Kojève. However, the inevitability of the Universal and Homogeneous State is spoken with an ironic voice. For Kojève, a human being is always a discursive being, a subject opposed to an object, an "I" opposed to a "non-I." As human beings, we speak, and because words are not things, a human world is a conceptual world of discourse that exists in opposition to the inanimate world of things.[30] If the human is rooted in the struggle for recognition, and the idea of justice results from the struggle for recognition, then justice is a quintessentially human phenomenon that exists in opposition to nature (225). The problem is that if what justifies justice is the human preference of the ought over the is, the cost of realizing rational, cosmopolitan equality is that there would no longer be a preference for the ought over the is, for the ought would be realized and therefore become identical with the is. As a consequence, the realization of the End State is also the end of our humanity, and life in the UHS is a return to nature, or a "reanimalized existence." At the end of history, we return to our beginnings. Life really is a tragedy—the satisfaction of the human desire for justice ends in animal contentment, in which we no longer care about justice.

What disappears at the end of history is not the animal, Homo sapiens, but rather the historical human being, the person who thinks about the world and acts in order to realize his dreams of it; and the history that ends is not cosmic or biological time, but rather historical time—the progressive realization of meaningful action. In order for cosmopolitan justice to be true, it must be realized. Once realized, it will no longer have reason to change. If the world no longer changes, then the thought that describes that world will no longer change. If thought no longer changes, then thought/words (*logos*) will no longer be dialectical (that is discursive); it will instead resemble "the singing of bees" or maybe the "silence" of mathematical algorithms, but in any event, nothing human. History ends with the rule of the Last Man. As Kojève rather famously put it in the same 1962 footnote concerning the American Marxist utopia, the cosmopolitan beings of the end of history, living amid abundance and security,

> would construct their edifices and works of art as birds build their nests and spiders spin their webs, would perform musical concerts after the fashion of frogs and cicadas, would play like young animals, and would indulge in love like adult beasts. But one cannot then say that all this "makes Man *happy*." One would have to say that post-historical animals of the species *Homo sapiens* (which will live amidst abundance and complete security) will be *content* as a result of their artistic, erotic and playful behavior, inasmuch as, by definition, they will be contented with it. But there is more. "The *definitive annihilation* of Man *properly so-called*" also means the definitive disappearance of human discourse (*Logos*) in the strict sense. Animals of the species *Homo sapiens* would react by conditioned reflexes to vocal signals or sign "language," and thus their so-called "discourses"

> would be like what is supposed to be the "language" of bees. What would disappear then is not only Philosophy or the search for discursive Wisdom, but also that Wisdom itself. For in these post-historical animals, there would no longer be any "[discursive] *understanding* of the World and of self."[31]

This places us in a quandary. It is necessary to Fordize the global economy in order to extend in space the synthetic justice of the citizen, in order to realize the Universal and Homogeneous State. The problem is that the successful resolution of this would result in an end of philosophy—and hence of the justification of the End State. Since history is contingent and free, we are left with a choice. We could refuse the UHS and instead promote "historical" or "national" interests, in full awareness of the pointlessness of such a gesture. Or we could support the UHS and promote global economic equality and the "interests" of humanity, in full awareness of the animality, and hence nonjustice, of that humanity. It is in the face of this choice that Kojève's oeuvre must be understood. Hegelian self-consciousness must be read against the triumph of the Last Man.

In the same note he gives a nascent view of what this "reading against" might look like. In 1959 Kojève went to Japan and there observed "a Society that is one of a kind, because it alone has for almost three centuries experienced life at the 'end of history'—that is, in the absence of all civil or external war." Under the Tokugawa Shogunate, the existence of the Japanese nobles, "who ceased to risk their lives (even in duel) and yet did not for that begin to work, was anything but animal." Instead, "*snobbery* in its pure form created disciplines negating the 'natural' or 'animal' given which in effectiveness far surpassed those that arose, in Japan or elsewhere, from 'historical' Action—that is, from warlike and revolutionary Fights or from forced Work." In the twentieth century, this snobbery has been democratized, for despite "persistent economic and political inequalities, all Japanese without exception are currently in a position to live according to totally *formalized* values—that is, values completely empty of all 'human' content in the 'historical' sense." Every "Japanese is in principle capable of committing, from pure snobbery, a perfectly 'gratuitous' *suicide* (the classical épeé of the samurai can be replaced by an airplane or a torpedo), which has nothing to do with the *risk* of life in a Fight waged for the sake of 'historical' values that have social or political content."[32] This ideal of "japanization" works as an alternative to reanimalization, because "no animal can be a snob," and thus, "every 'Japanized' post-historical period would be specifically human." In philosophical terms this means that "to remain human, Man must remain a 'Subject *opposed* to the Object,' even if 'Action negating the given and Error' disappears. While henceforth speaking in an *adequate* fashion of everything that is given to him, post-historical Man must continue to *detach* 'form' from 'content,' doing so no longer in order actively to transform the latter, but so that he may *oppose* himself as a pure 'form' to himself and to others taken as 'content' of any sort."[33]

This notion of japanized snobbery is part of a coherent vision of how aristocratic sensibilities might balance the rule of the masses through the consolidation of State power. In 1945, Kojève wrote a foreign policy memo for Charles De Gaulle designed to plot out France's foreign policy for the postwar era.[34] He outlines a "Latin" or "Catholic" Empire that would provide a home for Latin civilization as a mediating bulwark between the Anglo-Saxon-Protestant Empire and the Soviet-Orthodox Empire, in order to preserve and protect the values of the "humanization of free time" and introduce "aristocratic sweetness of living" into bourgeois well-being.[35] The alternative to the barbaric Statism of Stalinism and the invidious self-interest of capitalism is found in the unity of France, Spain, and Italy, brought together by (1) their shared Catholicism, (2) their close language, and (3) and most importantly, a unity of civilization and what Kojève calls a Latin mentality. By preserving the political independence of the Latin Empire, a world in which "Latin" values exist is created: the cultivation of the art of leisure through the transformation of bourgeois well-being into aristocratic sweetness of living, and "delight" in pleasure. This would justify itself "to the world and to history."

> [To] the world, for if the two other imperial Unions will probably always be superior to the Latin Union in the domain of economic work and of political struggles, one is entitled to suppose that they will never know how to devote themselves to the perfection of their leisure as could, under favorable circumstances, the unified Latin West; and [to] History, for by supposing that national and social conflicts will definitely be eliminated someday (which is perhaps less distant than is thought), it must be admitted that it is precisely to the organization and the "humanization" of its free time that future humanity will have to devote its efforts. (Did Marx himself not say, in repeating, without realizing it, a saying of Aristotle's: that the ultimate motive

of progress, and thus of socialism, is the desire to ensure a maximum of leisure for man?)[36]

The "Latin" Empire is a model for posthistorical cosmopolitanism. The question, for Kojève, is what he calls here the "humanization of free time." The Latin Empire, the political home of the art of leisure and of contemplative man, stands distinct from both the Orthodox Empire of communism and the Protestant Empire of the worker man.[37] The end of history does not mean there is only one possibility. While the pseudo-cosmopolitanism of the Last Man is the general trend of history, "there is nothing to suggest that the 'liberalism' of great unregulated cartels and massive unemployment dear to the Anglo-Saxon bloc, and the leveling and sometimes 'barbaric' 'statism' of the Soviet Union, exhaust all possibilities of rational economic and social organization."[38]

Since history is over, it is no longer possible to live according to human values in a historical sense (that of fighting and work). Nonetheless, as "japanized man," we are capable of opposing ourselves to the object, as a snob, without seeking to transform it (as a human being) or consume it (as an animal). Similarly, the pursuit of aristocratic sweetness of living seeks to practice leisure without falling into immediate, brutish satisfaction, for no other reason than the (free) assertion that a (free) human is more than simply desire. In historical terms the human being sacrifices his immediate satisfaction in order to achieve a long-term goal. In the posthistorical world, a "human" sacrifices his immediate satisfaction for no other reason than to assert that he is "better" than an animal. This is why every posthistorical human is a snob, and the ethics of snobbery is the last remaining ethical position.

Kojève's vision of the Latin Empire envisions a cosmopolitan state not simply without the division between aristocrats and democrats or masters and slaves, but in which the division itself has been transcended, in the Hegelian sense of *aufhebung*. Kojève's project of the humanization of free time and the practice of the art of leisure and the aristocratic sweetness of life is an attempt to bring the positive aspects of mastery into the political world of the slaves. Bourgeois individualism gives the slave the brutish pleasure of mastery without the need to fight (honor). The bourgeois individual is a beast who neither works nor fights, but only consumes. The Hegelian *citoyen*, the human being fit to live in a cosmopolitan world, gives the slave the aristocratic cultivation of taste.

Notes

1. Immanuel Kant, "Perpetual Peace" and "Theory and Practice," in *Political Writings,* ed. H.S. Reiss (Cambridge: Cambridge Univ. Press, 1970), 86–87, quotation on 112.

2. On the relationship between Kant and Hegel, see William F. Bristow's *Hegel and the Transformation of Philosophical Critique* (New York: Oxford Univ. Press, 2007).

3. Kant, "Perpetual Peace" and "Theory and Practice," 145.

4. See G.W.F. Hegel, *The Philosophy of Right,* ed. Allen W. Wood, trans. H.B. Nisbet (Cambridge: Cambridge Univ. Press, 1991), par. 274 and remarks.

5. Alexandre Kojève, *Outline of a Phenomenology of Right,* ed. Bryan-Paul Frost, trans. Bryan-Paul Frost and Robert Howse (Lanham, MD: Rowman and Littlefield, 2000) (cited hereafter mostly by parenthetical page numbers). There is some difficulty with translating the French *droit* into English. Depending upon context, it can mean both "right" and "law." An additional confusion is that the English "right" has more ordinary connotations than either the French *droit* or the German *Recht.* In the context of Kojève's discussion, *Droit* means the principle of law as a category, but not merely in the sense of enactments or laws (*lois*). In the English translation of this work, the word *droit* is translated as "right" in the title but left untranslated elsewhere, in order to "allow readers the chance to judge for themselves the meaning Kojève attributes to this key concept." "A Note about the Translation" (xiii). I capitalize "Right" when I'm using *Droit* in the sense evoked by the French and the German; I use lowercase "right" in the particular sense of "having a right to something" or in terms of "rights," and "law" in the specific sense of actual laws.

6. Kojève's philosophical project is devoted to refuting relativism without turning to eternity for support. In this regard see his discussion of the philosophical impossibility of the temporality of knowledge. This is implied throughout his work but is made explicit in Alexandre Kojève, *Introduction to the Reading of Hegel,* ed. Allan Bloom, trans. James H. Nichols Jr. (Ithaca, NY: Cornell Univ. Press, 1969), 102 and 233n; in Kojève, *Outline of a Phenomenology of Right,* 31; and in a letter to Leo Strauss dated September 19, 1950, found in Leo Strauss, *On Tyranny,* rev. and expanded ed., ed. Victor Gourevitch and Michael S. Roth (Chicago: Univ. of Chicago Press, 1991), 256.

7. I borrow the term *a posteriori* to describe Kojève's thought from James H. Nichols Jr., *Alexandre Kojève: Wisdom at the End of History* (Lanham, MD: Rowman and Littlefield, 2007), 30. Kojève describes his position as "realist." As he says, "there is no 'deduction' in the *Phenomenology,* but rather the *Phenomenology* begins with objective reality, as it has happened, and then proceeds to deduce the, now finished, result." Or as he adds in the note, somewhat more pithily: "It is, in fact, absurd to want to 'deduce'—that is, to *demonstrate*—Realism. For if one could *deduce* the real from knowledge, Idealism would be right,

and there would be no reality *independent* of knowledge." *Introduction to the Reading of Hegel,* 153.

8. Michael Roth, *Knowing and History: Appropriations of Hegel in Twentieth Century France* (Ithaca, NY: Cornell Univ. Press, 1988), 142.

9. This is why there is no contract between citizen and the sovereign in Hobbes. The social contract is between human beings, presided over by the sovereign who remains unbound (that is, omnipotent) in relation to them. The problem of the *Leviathan* is that in the state of nature, everyone is his own judge, and hence there exists no one with the authority to judge. This allows an appeal to outside authority, which disrupts the civil peace and gives rise to war, ultimately, over the meaning of words. If the sovereign is a party to the contract (which is to say, plays the role of A or B), then either his authority is bound (he is genuinely B) and whatever binds him (acts as C) is the true sovereign, or he is unbound and there is no genuine contract (there is no C) and we are returned to the state of war. See, for instance, Thomas Hobbes, *Leviathan* (Indianapolis: Hackett, 1994), chaps. 18 and 29.

10. Kojève's account of justice is similar to Rawls's in some respects. The thought experiment of the original position is designed to determine what justice would be under the rule of "anyone at all." The problem with Rawls is that the "original position" and the "veil of ignorance" intentionally abstract from the actual conditions of life in the world in order to discover what our uncontaminated calculating self-interest would tell us is just. This is a problem on all fronts. First, contra Hegel, by abstracting from the real conditions of life, Rawls abstracts from the conditions that make justice valuable. Second, contra Kant, by basing it on an account of the human as a rational calculator, Rawls abstracts from the faculties of human beings that are most concerned with justice. If all we are is rational calculators, justice as fairness is merely a convenience used to facilitate the satisfaction of our desires.

11. This "end" is not foreordained. Rather, it is a product of the philosophy that understands history, that understands the history of Right and is able to successfully transform existing (positive) Right into universal Right by interpreting the history that has given rise to the final State in terms of a posteriori reason.

12. Kojève, *Introduction to the Reading of Hegel,* 170.

13. The bulk of the *Phenomenology of Right* consists of the comparison of his account of Right with historical interpretations of Right in order to show that they coincide.

14. Kojève's account of the dialectical structure of Being is found throughout his work. The most important extended treatments are "Interpretation of the Third Part of Chapter VIII of the *Phenomenology of Spirit*" and "The Dialectic of the Real and the Phenomenological Method in Hegel," both in *Introduction to the Reading of Hegel.* See also Barry Cooper, *The End of History: An Essay in Modern Hegelianism* (Toronto: Univ. of Toronto Press, 1984).

15. Thus, if institutional racism is the given A, and the civil rights movement is the negation non-A, affirmative action is one of the results. In historical reality the reaction against affirmative action, i.e., anti-anti-racism [- (-A)] is not a return to racism but rather a new thing, C.

16. See Kojève, *Introduction to the Reading of Hegel,* 233–34 and the note.

17. This must be desire for desire and not desire simply (as in animal desire), because animal desire is insufficient to explain self-consciousness. The positive content of desire, and thus the positive content of the "I" brought about by desire, is a function of the positive content of the negated "non-I." Animal desire is insufficient to give rise to the "I" because, directed toward the natural "non-I," the "I" that it reveals will itself be natural—that is, biological or animal. Which is to say that the "I" revealed by "animal" desire will be the Identity of Identity in nature (which changes in order to stay the same) and not the Identity of Identity and non-Identity that characterizes human existence.

18. From a Hegelian point of view, compromise is based upon mutual recognition and not mutual interest. If compromise is possible, it is not because the struggle for recognition is wrong; rather, the struggle for recognition explains whether and when compromise is possible. It is possible when, and only when, you are to the other what you are to yourself, and vice versa.

19. An excellent dramatization of the struggle for recognition is found in the film *Gattaca.* This movie portrays a future society in which genetic manipulation is the norm, and those with "faulty" genes are treated as second-class citizens. In the film there are two brothers, one with "perfect" biology and the other with a genetic predisposition to heart problems (Ethan Hawke). In one of their confrontations, Ethan Hawke recalls that when they were children they used to play a game of chicken by swimming out into the ocean. Whoever turned back first lost. Since they had to swim back to shore once the contest was over, each stroke out increased the danger of drowning. This is a precise description of the struggle for recognition. Each of the brothers is subjectively certain that he is superior. The contest confirms that subjective sense of self in the only way it can be confirmed. One brother chooses life and returns to the shore; the other chooses victory over life and continues swimming. As the faulty brother says, "You want to know how I did it? This is how I did it, Anton. I never saved anything for the swim back." For the spiritual master, the two choices are victory and death. The spiritual slave chooses life over victory.

20. As Kojève notes: "It is upon this principle that the relation between the lord and his serfs in the middle Ages is supposed to be based. And they tell us that this relation began to be considered unjust from the moment that the nobles no longer had the opportunity to fulfill their duty toward the serfs by defending them with weapons in hand" (258n).

21. Kojève is very much in agreement with Carl Schmitt's friend-enemy distinction. See Carl Schmitt, *The Concept of the Political,* expanded ed., trans.

George Schwab (Chicago: Univ. of Chicago Press, 1996). Their disagreement centers on whether the political can be transcended. See the "Kojève—Schmitt correspondence," trans. Erik de Vries, *Interpretation* 29, no. 1 (Fall 2001): 115–30.

22. This demonstrates the impossibility that the United Nations could act as a juridical third. The United Nations is composed of Nations who do not share domestic Right. However, if the United Nations, as presently constituted, is doomed to failure, that does not mean that a true international Right is impossible. It simply means that it must be founded upon a commonality of domestic conceptions of justice. The European Union demonstrates one such possibility.

23. In "Being, Time, and Politics: The Strauss-Kojève Debate," *History and Theory* (May 1993): 138–61, Robert Pippin makes the criticism that Kojève's characterization of the modern position is both excessively radical and underdeveloped. He suggests that the question of the free subjectivity of the modern individual, what Kojève calls the "free and historical human being that everyone thinks he is" (140), is not adequately addressed and that Kojève's "existentialist rhetoric" results in defending a revolutionary tyranny of "world spirit in limousines." Pippin's aim is to disentangle Kojève's "incomplete and vague" appropriation of Hegel from Hegel's more nuanced version of modernity. Hegel, instead of defending revolutionary zeal, "requires that some case be made that various concrete institutions in modernity (and not just the State) have achieved the legal, civil, and cultural conditions within which mutual recognition *is* possible, in which barriers to such recognition are not characteristics of the institutions themselves . . . [such that] as rational individuals (even if not wholly rational), there will be no *rational* basis for any dissatisfaction." The problem with Hegel's actual view, which according to Pippin does not come across in Kojève, is that even if we accept Hegel's critique of Kantian subjectivism and classical objectivism, we are still left with the problem that these supposed concrete, rational institutions may not exist. Pippin says that this problem does not arise in Kojève because "the only concrete *institutional* realizations of the Hegelian ideal which Kojève discusses are the revolutionary activities of contemporary, made tyrants." Pippin's reading here is incomplete. The purpose of the *Phenomenology of Right* is to demonstrate how our existing institutions are (1) already rational and (2) can be made more rational, (3) without reference to an eternal order and (4) without reference to a historical order requiring revolutionary action. His account is, on the whole, rather moderate and is explicitly designed to ward off revolutionary nihilism. Pippin's reading of Kojève, I suspect, arises not from Kojève's supposed revolutionary existentialism but rather from his aristocratic sensibilities and what Pippins calls "aristocratic" (mis)characterizations of "bourgeois" life. See Robert Pippin, "'Bourgeois Philosophy' and the Problem of the Subject," in *The Persistence of Subjectivity: On the Kantian Aftermath* (Cambridge: Cambridge Univ. Press, 2005), 3.

24. Kojève, *Introduction to the Reading of Hegel*, 160–61n.

25. Alexandre Kojève, "Colonialism in a European Perspective," trans. Erik de Vries, *Interpretation* 29, no. 1 (Fall 2001): 91–130. This lecture was arranged by Carl Schmitt.

26. Note that in advanced liberal democracies, the workers not only use their pay to buy the cars they make, but through pension plans, etc., they also become the owners of the modes of production.

27. Kojève to Strauss, September 19, 1950, in Strauss, *On Tyranny,* 256.

28. The auto industry is the perfect metaphor for the development of the North American economy. Postwar economic growth was driven by the development of the interstate highway system; the continental commercial system is based upon trucking; NAFTA is built upon the structure of the 1965 Auto Pact between Canada and the United States; the organization of cities in terms of inner cores and suburbs is predicated upon the automobile; and this is without discussing other exigencies such as the necessity for oil, or pollution.

29. That this is already happening can be demonstrated in a number of ways. For instance, the recent, and dramatic, rebound of the American automotive industry has been driven not by domestic demand, which remains lax, but by an increase of exports to China. Similarly, the sovereign debt crisis in Europe, far from supporting the claims of Euro-skeptics, is a moment in the consolidation of State power that follows economic integration. The dynamic of the Greek crisis is an increase of the economic standard of living within Greece, fueled by high levels of public debt, owned by Germany. This debt was used to buy German manufacturing products, which in turn drove German growth. In this way the expanded investment in the "developing" areas of Europe was rewarded with an expanded market for products. The 2010 bailout isn't simply of the Greek government but also of German banks and investors that own this debt. The subsidizing of Greek lifestyle has been a big part of German growth, while the sacrificing of sovereignty by Greece is simply the actualization of existing principles of Right (that for instance citizens must pay taxes) under the aegis of the consolidation of the sovereign authority of the European Union.

30. See Kojève, *Introduction to the Reading of Hegel,* 141–49.

31. Ibid., 159–60.

32. Ibid., 161–62, note to the second edition.

33. Ibid.

34. Alexandre Kojève, "Outline of a Doctrine of French Policy (August 27, 1945)," trans. Erik de Vries, *Policy Review* (August 2004), available at www.hoover.org/publications/policy-review/article/7750.

35. The meaning of the words "Latin" and "Catholic" need to be taken as loosely as possible here. Kojève is surely engaged in both political rhetoric and esoteric writing. Kojève, the neo-Marxist, is attempting to align the old idea of a "third way" of European Socialism, between Soviet Communism and American Capitalism, with interests that are hostile to Socialism. By naming the civilization Latin and Catholic, Kojève appeals to historical and religious values that

interested and necessary parties have in common, while neglecting those class interests that keep them apart. However, this move is not simply rhetorical. Kojève genuinely believes that class conflict between the left and the right is a by-product of nation-states and needs to be surpassed in a new form of political organization. In this respect the appeal to the Catholic Church is genuine. The Catholic Church, which aspires to spiritual universality, is the appropriate foundation for an Empire, which aspires to political universality.

36. Kojève, "Outline of a French Policy," 11. Hannah Arendt makes the same observation in *The Human Condition,* where she argues that Marx's goal is the *polis* without slaves. The problem is that the *polis* without slaves results in the consumer society. When the laborer is freed from his labor, the resulting spare time "is never spent in anything but consumption, and the more time left to him, the greedier and more craving his appetites. That these appetites become more sophisticated, so that consumption is no longer restricted to the necessities but, on the contrary, mainly concentrates on the superfluities of life, does not change the character of this society, but harbors the grave danger that eventually no object of the world will be safe from consumption and annihilation through consumption." *The Human Condition* (Chicago: Univ. of Chicago Press, 1958), 133.

37. Here Kojève makes a clear illusion to Weber's work on Protestantism and Capitalism. "On the one hand, it would be tempting to explain the prodigious flight of the Germanic and Anglo-Saxon countries in modern Times through the intimate interpenetration of Church and State in the Protestant World; and there is no doubt that the fundamentally 'capitalist' Anglo-Saxon or Germano-Anglo-Saxon Empire is, today, still distinctly inspired by Protestantism. (Certain sociologists even see in Protestantism the ultimate source of Capitalism.)" Kojève, "Outline of a French Policy," 11.

38. Ibid.

Lee Trepanier

The Postmodern Condition of Cosmopolitanism

The advent of globalization has prompted both democratic and cosmopolitan theorists to reconceptualize democracy, citizenship, and political community, as "the ideals of citizenship clash with the sovereign nation-state in which they were first developed."[1] No longer able to meet the pressures of globalization, notions like democracy must be transformed in order to continue to be relevant in this globalized age. Challenged by cosmopolitan thinkers, democratic theorists have been forced to reconceive what constitutes democracy and citizenship as the national community loses importance. However, cosmopolitan theorists also have a set of their own problems with globalization. They have yet to explain how democracy, citizenship, or political community could be accomplished at the global level and why such a feat would be desirable. In other words, they neglect the possibility that globalization can pose a problem to democratic theory itself.

With his philosophy of deconstruction, Derrida is such a theorist who addresses these concerns and provides us a path to navigate this debate between democratic and cosmopolitan theorists. For Derrida, democracy is a universal paradigm that transcends national community; and globalization has created a space for cosmopolitan values like hospitality to take the place of national ones. But Derrida also recognizes that any value, cosmopolitan or otherwise, inherently contains an aspect of violence and that globalization can actually make it easier for the worst rather than the least type of violence to occur. Globalization, with its implicit notions of cosmopolitan citizenship and values, therefore is neither a golden panacea nor an unsolvable problem for Derrida; rather, it presents new opportunities as well as dangers for us.

Critical to determining Derrida's views on globalization and cosmopolitanism is first to understand his philosophy of deconstructionism as a call for a certain existential mode of existence rather than as another philosophy that attempts to explain reality. Deconstruction is an appeal to be existentially open to the possibilities of existence rather than privileging one value over another, thereby marginalizing and doing violence to other people, values, or institutions ("the other").[2] This mode of existence Derrida names différance and messianic. Its contrary state is what I have called foundational. In a globalized world, the path of the least violence is one of deconstruction, and the path of the worst violence is foundational.

But before we explore these two divergent paths, an explanation of deconstructionism is required. After showing that deconstructionism is an existential mode of existence, I discuss some of deconstructionism's cosmopolitan values that, in spite of their positive benefits, will always possess an aspect of violence. The three sections that follow that discussion speak of how these values are realized in the political and globalized context of democracy, violence, and law. The essay concludes with a discussion of Derrida's place both in transcendental philosophy and in the debates between democratic and cosmopolitan theorists.

As a Mode of Existence

In his essay entitled "Et Cetera," Derrida presents the principles that define deconstruction:

> Each time that I say "deconstruction and X (regardless of the concept or the theme)," this is the prelude to a very singular division that turns this X into, or rather makes appear in this X, an impossibility that becomes its proper and sole possibility, with the result that between the X as possible and the "same" X as impossible, there is nothing but a relation of homonymy, a relation for which we have to provide an account. . . . For example, here referring myself to demonstrations I have already attempted . . . gift, hospitality, death itself (and therefore so many other things) can be possible only as impossible, as the impossible, that is, unconditionally.[3]

In other words, deconstructionism is a refusal to categorically define anything once and for all. It is a mode of existence that is never satisfied with conclusive definitions, aims, or ends, for such a task for Derrida is not only impossible but dangerous, because it would marginalize people, ideas, institutions—the "other"—keeping them from being acknowledged.

Deconstruction therefore rejects the foundational mode of existence that characterizes such philosophies as Platonic metaphysics, which assumes a transcendent reality that is transparent and structured in terms of oppositions, with one opposition more valued than another.[4] The marginalized other can be recovered by deconstructionism by first reversing the metaphysical hierarchies of power and then favoring the undervalued. In genealogically tracing the formation of the initial hierarchy to its first decision that privileged one value over another, the deconstructionist can reclaim and redefine the undervalued as the origin of the hierarchy itself. This favoring of the undervalued at the point of origin destabilizes the original hierarchy of power and thereby allows resources that were originally excluded from the metaphysical tradition to be now included.

An example of deconstructionism is Derrida's critique of Husserl's phenomenological project that emphasizes immediacy, transparency, and exhaustiveness of experience.[5] Husserl's phenomenology relies upon a transcendental ego, where the internal ego corresponds with the exteriority of the "now" moment: the experience of reality is immediate, transparent, and exhaustive. To Derrida, such a moment is impossible because every experience, even the foundational "now" moment, has some prior reference point and thereby is precluded from being self-contained and exhaustive. By making the "now" moment the referential experience for all of existence because purportedly it is exhaustive, the phenomenologist is merely privileging one particular moment over another, since the finality of meaning of any experience can always be deferred to either the past or the future. Thus, every time the phenomenologist pursues a metaphysical meaning for such an experience, the meaning "itself, if there is anything at all of it, slips away."[6]

It should be noted that the deconstructionist does not seek to replace one opposition value by another one, because doing so would only create a new hierarchy of power that would marginalize another set of "others." Rather than offering a positive philosophical program, the deconstructionist silently affirms the parasitic critiques of existing hierarchies in the hope of creating a state of tension or oscillation between an existing hierarchy and a potential one.[7] This existential mode of existence is known as différance, where neither the existing hierarchy nor the undervalued or potential one is privileged. The objective for the deconstructionist is not to replace one hierarchy with another but rather to oscillate between these two in order to create an existential openness to the realm of possibility for a person to "go there where you cannot go, to the impossible[;] it is indeed the only way of coming or going."[8]

The ethical underpinning of this mode of existence (différance), where the finality of meaning is continually deferred, is called messianic, meaning that we wait for ethical values like justice to arrive but do not expect them.[9] The state of tension does not exist for its own sake but for the hope of an ethical value to be realized. Structuring our existence as one of patience and openness to an indeterminate future, the messianic causes a certain skepticism toward such ideological movements as Marxism that purport to know a predetermined end to historical existence and consequently justify violence against others to achieve it. Opting for a mode of patience and openness rather than finality and certitude, the deconstructionist exists in a state of both tension and hope.

However, this existential mode of tension and patience should not be confused with passivity and abdication. For Derrida, when confronted with ethical demands, the deconstructionist should choose the path of responsibility rather than resignation, although in doing so, he would seem to adopt a foundational mode of existence and therefore be no longer open to an indeterminate future. The decision to accept responsibility is one that is beyond any type of rationality and does not emerge from any metaphysical or nonmetaphysical tradition. It is a decision that Derrida characterizes as madness, resembling a leap in faith that is beyond one's control and yet demands that he should act.[10] Borrowing from Kierkegaard, Derrida calls this decision of responsibility an "undecidable leap." It is beyond any and all preparation for such a decision and often places the participant in a zero-sum game, where one party will inevitably lose: "I cannot respond to the call, the request, the obligation, or even the love of another, without sacrificing the other other, the other others."[11]

Cosmopolitan Values

But when the deconstructionist chooses responsibility over resignation in his "undecidable leap," and recognizes that such a choice will prefer one party over another, how is it possible for him not to adopt a foundational mode of existence? Derrida addresses this problem in a paradox to show how ethical action is possible while also nonfoundational. For example, when one is asked to accept responsibility, he must submit to the conditions that make such ethical action possible while knowing that the same conditions also make such actions impossible. The conditions of possibility therefore are also the ones of impossibility. Derrida illustrates what he means by this when he examines certain ethical values such as giving, forgiveness, and hospitality, which are also for him cosmopolitan by nature. Thus, in order to understand Derrida's paradox, and by extension how ethical action is both possible and nonfoundational, we first need to know what Derrida means by cosmopolitan.

In his essay "On Cosmopolitanism," Derrida explores the relationships between the value of cosmopolitanism, especially in a world of banality and inhumanity, and the legitimate concerns of the police and the need for borders in controlling the immigration and the deportation of aliens.[12] The context of Derrida's essay is 1996, when France's Debret laws allowed police to extradite immigrations without right of residence. These laws provoked mass demonstrations of protest in Paris, with the International Parliament of Writers demanding that cities be established for immigrants. Addressing this audience, Derrida selects the concept of cosmopolitanism from the Western tradition to explore this specific and concrete issue. He ultimately proposes open or refuge cities for immigrants, where they will be protected from persecution, intimidation, or exile.

But this concept of the open city is an unfulfilled one. It is not new but emerged from a tradition that has been marginalized by the nation-state and consequently has never been conclusively defined. Derrida wants cosmopolitanism to resemble the ethic of hospitality, where one is more aware of one's past mistakes and the likelihood that one could commit similar mistakes in the future. This confessional cosmopolitanism is different from the triumph cosmopolitanism of Kant, whose paradigm of the unconditional (the common possession of the earth) and the conditional (habitat, culture, institutions) only politicizes all hospitality. For Derrida, Kant's paradigm has made all hospitality dependent upon the sovereignty of the state: "Hospitality signifies here the public nature of *public space*. . . . Hospitality, whether public or private, is dependent on and controlled by the law and the state police."[13] By contrast, Derrida wants hospitality to exist in a state of différance and in the messianic rather than in the triumphant or foundational mode of existence. On the one hand, unconditional hospitality should be offered to all immigrants; on the other hand, hospitality has to be conditional, for there has to be some limitation on the right of residence. Again, Derrida's identification of the contradictory logic at the heart of the concept of cosmopolitanism is not to paralyze political action but to enable it.

This contradictory logic of cosmopolitanism is also applied in his essay "On Hospitality," which also deals with other ethical values.[14] Genuine hospitality demands that the host relinquish control over who will receive such hospitality, but to relinquish control makes it impossible to host anyone. But not to relinquish control is to have power over one's guests, which is also contrary to hospitality. Likewise, a genuine gift can never be received, because the act of giving contains an implicit demand of taking.[15] The reception of a gift presumes that the giver is no longer indebted to the recipient, but such an acknowledgment actually draws both the giver and the recipient into a cycle of giving and taking. Wishing to escape this cycle, Derrida proposes that a genuine gift would require both the giver and the recipient to be entirely separated from each other, thereby nullifying any claims or obligations against each other. Of course, this is an impossible condition, for one cannot give without knowing it. The conditions of possible giving therefore are the same conditions of its impossibility.

Deconstructionism's contradictory logic compels us to negotiate between the impossible or unconditional and the possible or conditional: the irreconcilable yet indissociable demands of unconditional purity and the pragmatic and quotidian concerns of a specific context. For Derrida, responsible ethical and political action consists in navigating between these two poles: pragmatic action has to be linked with the unconditionality of infinite responsibility if it is not to be reduced to merely prudential demands of the moment, while, at the same time, the unconditionality cannot dictate incontestable ethical precepts to a specific context. This link provides the paradox of how conditions of possibility are also ones of impossibility and how ethical action is possible but nonfoundational.[16]

The Universalizable Paradigm

These ethical values of hospitality and the like are inextricably linked with Derrida's interest in global events, whether the International Criminal Court, the European Union's immigration laws, or the South African Truth and Reconciliation Commission. Derrida's concern is not only to expose the hierarchies of power that "hide[s] its[elf]; by its essence it tends to organize amnesia, something under the celebration and sublimation of the grand beginning"; but also to recover the marginalized other and thereby expand our horizons both historically and globally of what is possible for ethical action.[17] For example, the ethical value of forgiveness needs to be left undefined to create the possibility of more meanings and more ways to forgive; otherwise, humanity will not be able to learn from its past. A definitive way of forgiveness may result in temporary good effects, but it will exclude other forms that would have long-term negative consequences.

But before tackling global hierarchies of power, Derrida critiques the state. Throughout both essays in *On Cosmopolitanism and Forgiveness,* Derrida describes how legitimacy is created and sustained in the state: how the state is both a performance and a project in sustainable self-creation. What concerns Derrida is the state's attempt at closure in order to secure its legitimacy: to preclude other possibilities (legitimacies) for its existence. While we may expect this of authoritarian and totalitarian regimes, it is also a particular problem for democracies.

The legitimacy of democracy rests upon the political concept of sovereignty. But for Derrida, genuine sovereignty—ipseity—is prior to the political: "Before any sovereignty of the state, of the nation-state, of the monarch, or in democracy, of the people, ipseity names a principle of legitimate sovereignty, the accredited or recognized supremacy of a power or a force, a *kratos* or a *cracy*."[18] The concept of ipseity for Derrida is the power of the subject who is open to an encounter with the other; that is, he does not possess intentional consciousness that would privilege one set of values over another.[19] Ideally democracy should be a political form of a people's ipseity: "Democracy would be precisely this . . . a force in the form of a sovereign authority . . . the power and ipseity of the people."[20]

This openness to the other is coterminous with freedom understood as "the faculty to do as one pleases, to decide, to choose to determine oneself . . . and first of all to master oneself."[21] However, this freedom can be suspended and destroyed in a democracy—whether from the democratic rule of majority tyranny or the election of totalitarian parties into power—and thereby produces the paradoxical result of destroying one's own ipseity.[22] To preclude this outcome, Derrida proposes two subconcepts of a person's ipseity: autoimmunity and the untimely. The former is the protection of oneself by destroying one's own immune system; the latter is the affirmation of life that is rooted in ontology itself.[23] If either autoimmunity or the untimely were to exist by itself, then a person's ipseity would be compromised: both are necessary for a person's ipseity as well as for democracy to exist.[24]

These prior but weaker powers have the potential to become the basis of a genuine democracy. According to Cheah, democracy is "the only regime that is open to and welcomes the possibility of contestation and self-contestation. This openness stems from democracy's radically improper character and its lack of self identity";[25] or to quote Derrida: "What is lacking in democracy is proper meaning, the very meaning of the selfsame, the it-self, the selfsame, the properly selfsame or the it-self. Democracy is defined, as is the very ideal of democracy, by this lack of the proper and the selfsame. And so it is defined only by turns, by tropes and tropism."[26]

Democracy for Derrida therefore requires both autoimmunity and the untimely to exist for themselves and as the basis for a person's ipseity. Because it is structurally incomplete, democracy enables a questioning of its own idea and ideals. This right of public critique and radical self-critique reveals that democracy may be the only regime that can objectively express its autoimmune character. But public and radical self-critiques require a survival mechanism to sustain themselves, that is, the untimely; otherwise, they will collapse. The end result is that democracy becomes the structural condition of ipseity itself: an open-ended regime that allows self-critique while existing for the sake of a person's ipseity.

It should be clear that Derrida's suggestion of autoimmunity as the right to critique is distinct from Habermas's concept of *Öffentlichkeit:* the public use of reason to legitimate political sovereignty.[27] For Habermas, the power of universal human reason enables individuals to transcend particular interests for an idealized objective, where autoimmunity is merely a by-product of this process. For Derrida, autoimmunity comes not from universal human reason but rather from the historicity of our finite existence. There is no "unconditional promise" of democracy from the future, but only what exists in the here and now.[28] Whereas Habermas postulates a future endpoint that individuals eventually reach through the public use of reason, Derrida rejects any speculation of the future in favor of a present temporal framework where both autoimmunity (the right to critique) and the untimely (the affirmation of life) are essential and not merely by-products of a person's existence (ipseity).

Democracy is "the only paradigm that is universalizable" for Derrida not because it includes all rational human beings or best articulates universal human interests, but because democracy best embodies a person's ipseity: the person's autoimmunity (the right to critique) and the untimely (his affirmation of life).[29] Democracy is the deferral of any ultimate meaning (autoimmunity) as well as the creation of binary oppositions and hierarchy (the untimely). This tension between critique and affirmation within the regime enables democracy to avoid the errors of finality, ideology, or what Derrida calls "the worst."

The Globalization of the Worst

The "worst" is a concept that serves as a foil in Derrida's philosophy of deconstruction. The phrase means that in auto-affection there is always more than one person, with the result that one treats the other with the worst type of violence.[30] Distinct from Kant's notion of radical evil, the worst is when the other is completely appropriated by another and no other possibility exists. For Kant, radical evil is a phenomenon that is evil at its root, while for Derrida, radical evil consists of small, infinitesimal differences between one and another. These differences for Derrida are not absolute evil, because the other is still being acknowledged, while in the worst the other is completely absorbed by another.[31] The complete appropriation of the other results in the other's complete extermination: a violence that is of the worst sort.

Globalization has ushered in an era when the potency of the nation-state is now questioned, with transnational organizations and institutions, for example, the International Criminal Court, usurping nation-state sovereignty over human rights. Although some may see this development in a positive light, globalization also affects concepts like war, enemy, and terrorism negatively, where the traditional distinctions, such as civilians and military or friend and foe, lose their pertinence. With globalization there is no identifiable enemy in the form of the state, with whom one could wage something previously called war; instead, a "new violence is being prepared and in truth has been unleashed for some time now, in a way that is more visibly suicidal or auto-immune than ever. This violence no longer has to do with *world* war or even with *war*, even less with some right to wage war. And this is hardly re-assuring—indeed, quite the contrary."[32]

What Derrida means by more "visibly suicidal" is simply to kill oneself more, since the distinctions between states and therefore between friend and foe and civilian and military are no longer significant. For example, to immunize oneself against terrorists, one must discover and kill terrorists, whether domestic or abroad. But the more one destroys terrorists, the more one destroys oneself, in an era when borders are meaningless. By contrast, in the era of the cold war, the other was clearly delineated and therefore could be identified as an enemy to be killed. But in a globalized world, the enemy cannot be identified and consequently can never be killed. In fact, the number of enemies has multiplied to a point where they are unlimited. The result is one of global genocide, since the absolute threat no longer can be contained in the state. The threat of the worst is more possible in the era of globalization than in the period of the cold war.[33]

The purpose of deconstructionism in this globalized world is to push people away from the worst violence to the least one, for Derrida does not believe that violence itself can be eliminated: such elimination would be a rejection of the différance and messianic modes of existence for a foundational one.[34] For a globalized world, Derrida advocates a "return to the religious" as the path of least violence.[35] When examining the etymology of the Latin word for religion, Derrida discovers there are two sources of religion: *religio,* which implies restraint or remaining safe, and *re-legere,* which suggests a link with another through faith.[36] As in other concepts, Derrida teases out the oppositional values and the contradictory logic in these ideas. More importantly, he explores the link that defined religion before it became associated only with the bond between man and divinity. In other words, Derrida attempts to reconceive the link to be as open-ended as possible, such that the concept of religion can encounter the other without doing the worst violence to it.[37]

Violence will always occur when a person encounters the other, because an unconditional encounter is impossible for Derrida. There are always conditions when one encounters the other; therefore, the best one can do is determine which means are available for such an encounter and choose the one of least violence. Thus, such cosmopolitan values as hospitality will always contain a kernel of violence, for example, allowing some refugees in while refusing others. The impossibility of an unconditional hospitality means that any attempt to open the globe entirely to anyone is simply impossible; and attempts that mask themselves as unconditional hospitality could actually be a form of the worst type of violence. What we are left with is to practice a conditional and therefore violent hospitality; but this violence can be lessened when one approaches hospitality in a messianic rather than a foundational mode of existence. If the person is aware of his paradoxical situation and nevertheless still acts, then he will exist in a mode that is open to his encounter with the other as much as possible.

Decision and Justice

According to Derrida, globalization makes possible both democracy and the worst as genuine paths for us to follow. Democracy for Derrida can be all-inclusive of all human beings, and possibly even of all living things, if we are guided by the "link" of religion to the course of least violence, while the worst can lead us to a global suicide because such distinctions of the cold war as friend and enemy are no longer applicable. The question that now confronts Derrida is how one can distinguish between these two paths: "between the force of law of a legitimate power and the supposedly originary violence that must have established this authority and that could not itself have been authorized by any anterior legitimacy."[38] If violence is inescapable for political action, then how can we distinguish the dualisms of the worst and the least violence, illegitimate and legitimate power, and law and justice?

In his essay "Force of Law," Derrida addresses these issues directly. He distinguishes two types of violence: the genealogical (Greek, Christian, Enlightenment) and the expectant (Jewish and messianic).[39] With respect to the question of law and justice, Derrida argues that force is a necessary component of the law for its establishment and enforceability, but it is a threat to justice, for if justice were to partake in annihilation, it could not be justice. The most the deconstructionist could aspire to is the recovery of lesser forms of violence in the Western metaphysical tradition. For example, deconstructionism could show us that genealogical violence is heterogeneous rather than homogeneous and therefore capable of less violent forms than previously thought.[40]

One of these lesser forms of violence can be found in Derrida's comments about Walter Benjamin's "Critique of Violence." Benjamin's sanctioning of the workers' right to a general strike is a form of lesser violence when compared to the violence of the state.[41] However, Derrida distances himself from Benjamin's position by associating him with the conservatives of Weimar Germany such as Carl Schmitt. Although such an association initially appears incorrect—Benjamin's general strike may undermine the state without triggering the disorder of civil war, as Schmitt had argued—the two thinkers for Derrida are both representative of a messianic type of violence: Benjamin passively, Schmitt actively. Benjamin waits for someone, whether the state sovereign or the divine, to intervene, while Schmitt aggressively encourages some entity to intervene. Both are asking for the messianic to appear.

But for Derrida, the messiah will never arrive: justice will continually be delayed forever. Absent this arrival, we cannot abandon the first type (the genealogical) of violence about law; nor can we abandon the expectant, as was attempted in Nazism and the Holocaust.[42] Both types of violence are necessary, such that one exists in a state of oscillation between them.[43] When we do decide, this decision is part of the "undecidable" that can never be justified but nonetheless still must be made. Yet how does this decision differ from Schmitt's theory of decisionism, where the sovereign is able to decide the state of exception (*Ausnahmezustand*) and thereby becomes free from all legal constraints? How does Derrida's "undecidable" have an affinity with an ethics of responsibility rather than one of nihilism?[44]

For Derrida, deconstructionism's destabilization of oppositions always contains an element of risk: "Without the possibility of radical evil, of perjury, and of absolute crime, there is no responsibility, no freedom, no decision."[45] By embracing such a risk, Derrida is able to make us conscious of the origin of violence and therefore minimize our reliance upon it, in the hope of leading us toward a justice beyond law. Because justice can never be an object of cognition, we will never be able to identify the law with justice, although we try our best to conform law to a justice that will never come.[46] But when we recognize the contingency and origins of the law, we will make the law less arbitrary in its establishment and enforcement.

Decision in deconstructionism differs from Schmitt's decisionism in that Derrida forces a person to reconceptualize what constitutes law itself: "For a decision to be just and responsible, it must, in its proper moment if there is one, be both regulated and without regulation: it must conserve the law and also destroy or suspend it enough to have to reinvent it in each case, rejustify it, at least reinvent it in the reaffirmation and the new and free confirmation of its principle."[47] Decisions are simultaneously legal and extralegal, with the rules suspended not for license but for the possibility of responsibility. Derrida's theory of decision is associated with the expectation of justice; he is able to broaden the horizons of law, whereas Schmitt reduces it to power. Rather than restricting the realm of possibilities, deconstructionism seeks to expand it, and, in this manner, hopes to pave a path of responsibility for our decisions.

Conclusion

By being open to the realm of possibility, especially toward an indeterminate future where justice may (but never will) arrive, Derrida differentiates himself from transcendental philosophers like Kant and his heirs, whose philosophies are foundationalist: they subscribe to a universal and transparent rationality as a mode of operation, with a constructed endpoint in time that will be achieved by using this rationality.[48] Derrida thinks that unconditionality—whether justice, divinity, or any eschatological meaning—is beyond our cognitive faculties. Contrary to Kant, who argues that unconditionality enhances the power of finite reason, Derrida argues the opposite and instead liberates unconditionality from historicity: "not only from the Idea in the Kantian sense but from all teleology, all onto-theteleology."[49] The entrance of the unconditionality into the present would neutralize and annul any current action, because our anticipation would be destroyed. It must remain beyond the horizon for which we patiently wait.

This other world that we wait for is not the one of the current globalization, where present hierarchies of power are exacerbated, such as the economic inequalities between North and South; but rather a globalization where unconditionality like the cosmopolitan value of hospitality can be implemented transnationally.[50] What Derrida is calling for is a dynamic process of humanization across the world: "a particular space-time, a certain oriented history of human brotherhood, of what in a Pauline language . . . one calls *citizens of the world,* . . . brothers, fellow men, neighbors."[51] The present globalization deprives humanity of a genuine one, where international human rights, institutions, and law can be used to oppose the global political and economic institutions that exploit and dehumanize people.[52] For Derrida, a truly cosmopolitan citizen is not a product of the current age of globalization but one who exists between this world and the one that he waits for.

Derrida's deconstructionist philosophy therefore proposes a way out of the debates about globalization between democratic theorists, who contend that the national community must be the foundation for democracy, and cosmopolitan theorists, who advocate a cosmopolitan citizenship based on a global community.[53] Derrida rejects the democratic theorists' contention that the national community can be the only basis for democracy as well as the argument of cosmopolitan theorists, for example Habermas, that citizenship can be grounded in a universally accepted rationality. For Derrida, globalization presents the opportunity for democracy, justice, and other cosmopolitan values to be accepted if one accepts the deconstructionist mode of existence; but globalization can also lead to the danger of the worst forms of violence, with the ultimate result of global suicide. Thus, with the implicit claims of cosmopolitanism for citizenship, democracy, and political community, globalization is a source of both hope and despair for Derrida's deconstructionist philosophy.

Notes

1. Andrew Linklater, *The Transformation of the Political Community: Ethical Foundations of the Post-Westphalian Era* (Oxford: Polity, 1998), 182. For more about this debate, refer to Martha Nussbaum, *For Love of Country* (Boston: Beacon Press, 1996); David Held, "The Transformation of the Political Community: Rethinking Democracy in the Context of Globalization," in *Democracy's Edges*, ed. I. Shapiro and C. Hacker-Cordón (Cambridge: Cambridge Univ. Press, 1998); A. McGrew, ed., *The Transformation of Democracy? Democratic Politics in the New World Order* (Cambridge: Polity, 1997); Jürgen Habermas, "The European Nation-State: On the Past and Future Sovereignty and Citizenship," in *Inclusion of the Other: Studies in Political Theory*, ed. C. Cronon and P. DeGreiff (Cambridge, MA: MIT Press, 1998); B. Yack, "Popular Sovereignty and Nationalism," *Political Theory* 29, no. 4 (2001): 517–36; Catherine Lu, *The Political Theory of Global Citizenship* (New York: Routledge, 2001); Kok-Chor Tan, Russell Hardin, and Ian Shapiro, eds., *Justice without Borders: Cosmopolitanism, Nationalism, and Patriotism* (Cambridge: Cambridge Univ. Press, 2004); Seyla Benhabib and Roberet Post, eds., *Another Cosmopolitanism: Hospitality, Sovereignty, and Democratic Iterations* (Oxford: Oxford Univ. Press, 2006); Kwame Anthony Appiah, *Cosmopolitanism: Ethics in a World of Strangers* (New York: Norton, 2007); Stan van Hooft, *Cosmopolitanism: A Philosophy for Global Ethics* (Montreal: McGill-Queens Univ. Press, 2009).

2. For more about how Derrida's philosophy of deconstruction is a mode of existence and its place in modern Continental philosophy, refer to David Walsh, *The Modern Philosophical Revolution: The Luminosity of Existence* (Cambridge: Cambridge Univ. Press, 2008), 335–90.

3. Nicholas Royle, *Deconstructions: A User's Guide* (London: Palgrave, 2000), 300. For more about deconstructionism, refer to John Caputo, *Deconstruction in a Nutshell: A Conversation with Jacques Derrida* (New York: Fordham Univ. Press, 1996); John Caputo, *The Prayers and Tears of Jacques Derrida: Religion without Religion* (Bloomington: Indiana Univ. Press, 1997).

4. Jacques Derrida, *Positions*, trans. Alan Bass (Chicago: Univ. of Chicago Press, 1981), 41–42; also refer to Jacques Derrida, *Dissemination*, trans. Barbara Johnson (Chicago: Univ. of Chicago Press, 1981), 4–6.

5. Jacques Derrida, *Speech and Phenomena and Other Essays on Husserl's Theory of Signs,* trans. David B. Allison (Evanston, IL: Northwestern Univ. Press, 1973), 64–75.

6. Ibid., 104.

7. Jacques Derrida, *The Gift of Death,* trans. David Wills (Chicago: Univ. of Chicago Press, 1995), 65.

8. Jacques Derrida, *On the Name,* ed. Thomas Dutoit (Stanford, CA: Stanford Univ. Press, 1995), 75; also refer to Jacques Derrida, *Writing and Difference,* trans. Alan Bass (Chicago: Univ. of Chicago Press, 1978).

9. Jacques Derrida, "Psyche: Inventions of the Other," in *Reading De Man Reading,* ed. Lindsey Walters and Wlad Godzich (Minneapolis: Univ. of Minnesota Press, 1989), 60; also refer to Jacques Derrida, *Specters of Marx: The State of Debt, the Work of Mourning, and the New International,* trans. Peggy Kamuf (New York: Routledge, 1994).

10. Jacques Derrida, *Deconstruction and the Possibility of Justice*, ed. Drucilla Cornell, Michael Rosefeld, and David Gary Carlson (New York: Taylor and Francis, 1992), 26; also refer to Derrida, *The Gift of Death,* 65–80.

11. Derrida, *The Gift of Death,* 70.

12. Jacques Derrida, *On Cosmopolitanism and Forgiveness* (New York: Routledge, 2001), 6–8, 15.

13. Ibid., 22.

14. Jacques Derrida, *Of Hospitality: Anne Dufourmantelle Invites Jacques Derrida to Respond,* trans. Rachel Bowlby (Stanford, CA: Stanford Univ. Press, 2000), 151–55.

15. Derrida, *The Gift of Death,* 30; also refer to Jacques Derrida, *Memories for Paul de Man,* trans. Cecile Lindsay, Jonathan Culler, and Eduardo Cadava (New York: Columbia Univ. Press, 1989), 149. For similar logic with respect to other values, such as mourning, see *Memories for Paul de Man,* 6.

16. Perhaps the best formulation of this paradox is Derrida's comment about forgiveness as forgiving something that is unforgivable: "I must then and only then respond to this transaction between two contradictory and equally justified imperatives." Derrida, *On Cosmopolitanism and Forgiveness,* 54; also see 39–49.

17. Ibid., 57.

18. Jacques Derrida, *Rouges: Two Essays on Reason,* trans. Pascale-Anne Brault and Michael Nass (Stanford, CA: Stanford Univ. Press, 1998), 12.

19. Jacques Derrida, "Signature Event Context," in *Limited Inc.,* ed. Samuel Weber (Evanston, IL: Northwestern Univ. Press, 1988), 12, 18–19.

20. Derrida, *Rouges,* 13.

21. Ibid., 22–23.

22. Ibid., 24, 33–34.

23. Jacques Derrida, "Je suis en guerre contre-moi-même," *Le Monde,* August 18, 2004. The untimely is "the emergence of radically affirmative views of

surviving that . . . is derived neither from life nor death"; rather, the untimely is rooted in "survival [which] is an original concept that constitutes the very structure that we call existence, *Dasein,* if you will."

24. Derrida, *Rouges,* 45; also refer to Jacques Derrida, "Faith and Knowledge: The Two Sources of 'Religion' at the Limits of Reason Alone," in *Religion,* ed. Jacques Derrida and Gianni Vattimo, trans. Samuel Weber (Stanford, CA: Stanford Univ. Press, 1998), 73; and Jacques Derrida, "Autoimmunity: Real and Symbolic Suicides: A Dialogue with Jacques Derrida," in *Philosophy in a Time of Terror: Dialogues with Jürgen Habermas and Jacques Derrida,* ed. Giovanna Borradori (Chicago: Univ. of Chicago Press, 2003), 94.

25. Pheng Cheah, "The Untimely Secret of Democracy," in *Derrida and the Time of the Political,* ed. Pheng Cheah and Suzanne Guerlac (Durham, NC: Duke Univ. Press, 2009), 79–81.

26. Derrida, *Rouges,* 37.

27. Jürgen Habermas, *The Structural Transformation of the Public Sphere,* trans. Thomas Burger with Frederick Lawrence (Cambridge, MA: MIT Press, 1991); also refer to Jürgen Habermas, *Theory of Communicative Action,* vol. 1 (Cambridge: Polity, 1986); and vol. 2, trans. Thomas McCarthy (Cambridge: Polity, 1989).

28. John Caputo, "Without Sovereignty, without Being: Unconditionality, the Coming God, and Derrida's Democracy to Come," in *Religion and Violence in a Secular World,* ed. Clayton Crockett (Charlottesville: Univ. of Virginia Press, 2006), 137–56; also refer to Borradori, *Philosophy in a Time of Terror.*

29. Derrida, *Rouges,* 87.

30. Derrida, *Religion,* 65.

31. Jacques Derrida, *Of Grammatology,* trans., Gayatri Spivak (Baltimore: Johns Hopkins Univ. Press, 1974), 234; also refer to Borradori, *Philosophy in a Time of Terror,* 99.

32. Derrida, *Rouges,* 156.

33. Ibid., 105.

34. Derrida, *Writing and Difference,* 130.

35. Derrida, *Religion,* 42–43.

36. Ibid., 16.

37. Derrida even expands a person's link to animals. Jacques Derrida, *Points . . . Interviews, 1974–1994,* trans., Peggy Kamuf et al. (Stanford, CA: Stanford Univ. Press, 1995), 279.

38. Derrida, *Deconstruction and the Possibility of Justice,* 6.

39. Ibid., 21.

40. McCormick and Corson debate whether lesser violence could ever be transformed into nonviolence. Corson argues that this is not possible, a position with which I agree. Ben Corson, "Transcending Violence in Derrida: A Reply to John McCormick," *Political Theory* 29, no. 6 (2001): 866–75.

41. Derrida, *Deconstruction and the Possibility of Justice,* 34–35; also refer to Walter Benjamin, "Critique of Violence," in *Reflections,* ed. Peter Demetz (New York: Harcourt, Brace, Jovanovich, 1978), 277–300.

42. Derrida, *Deconstruction and the Possibility of Justice,* 60.

43. Corson speaks of a third form of violence. Regardless of how one counts the types of violence possible, my point is that Derrida would not privilege any type of violence. Corson, "Transcending Violence in Derrida," 870–71.

44. Lilla portrays Derrida's theory of decision as the same as Schmitt's. Mark Lilla, *The Reckless Mind: Intellectuals in Politics* (New York: New York Review of Books, 2001), 174, 184, 190.

45. Jacques Derrida, *The Politics of Friendship,* trans. George Collins (London: Verso, 1997), 219.

46. Derrida, *Deconstruction and the Possibility of Justice,* 44.

47. Ibid., 58.

48. An example of this view is Jürgen Habermas, *Between Facts and Norms: Contributions to a Discourse Theory of Law and Democracy,* trans. William Rehg (Cambridge, MA: MIT Press, 1998).

49. Derrida, *Rouges,* 87. Kant's "regulative idea" was that the opposition between finite reason and infinite generated a temporality that was inherently teleological. This opened the horizon for human capacity to develop and rationally progress toward an infinite goal in time: "That opens up the comforting prospect of the future . . . in which we are shown from afar how the human species eventually works its way upward to a situation in which all the germs implanted by nature can be developed fully, and in which man's destiny can be fulfilled here on earth." Immanuel Kant, "Idea of a Universal History with a Cosmopolitan Purpose," in *On History,* trans. Lewis White Beck (Indianapolis: Bobbs-Merrill, 1963).

50. Derrida refers to this first type as antiglobalization in Jacques Derrida, "Une Europe de l'espoir," *Le Monde diplomatique,* November 2004, 3, www.monde-diplmatique.fr., translated in Michael Naas, "A Last Call for 'Europe,'" *Theory and Events* 8, no. 1 (2005): 96–108; also refer to Jacques Derrida, "The University without Condition," in *Without Albibi,* trans. Peggy Kamuf and others (Stanford, CA: Stanford Univ. Press, 1995), 203–23, 225.

51. Jacques Derrida, "Globalization, Peace, and Cosmopolitanism," in *Negotiations: Interventions and Interviews, 1971–2001,* ed. and trans. Elizabeth Rottenberg (Stanford, CA: Stanford Univ. Press, 2002), 375.

52. Derrida, "Une Europe de l'espoir."

53. Derrida's unexplained dismissal of nationalism as a potential basis for a political community in the world yet to arrive has troubled some. Refer to Cheah, "The Untimely Secret of Democracy," 91–94.

Part 3

Cosmopolitanism in the United States

Luigi Bradizza

Madison and Republican Cosmopolitanism

Measured by diplomatic, cultural, military, economic, and political influence, America stands alone in the history of the world. Domestically, its people are generally wealthy and free. American nationality and sovereignty have helped Americans to define and defend an understanding of the common good that has contributed to these blessings. One might therefore imagine that there would be a consensus, at least among Americans, that American nationality and sovereignty are very good and desirable. But in fact, scholars question the extent to which Americans should see themselves as citizens of a sovereign nation. These scholars range from more moderate to more thoroughgoing proponents of cosmopolitanism. The more moderate Bryan Turner argues for an "ironic cosmopolitanism" in which a moderate patriotism allows for an understanding of and respect for foreign cultures, "assisted by an intellectual distance from one's own national or local culture."[1]

Martha Nussbaum and Kwame Anthony Appiah are typical of the more thoroughgoing approach. Both argue that transnational loyalties and attachments should precede national ones.[2] Aaron Keck has taken cosmopolitan proposals one step further. Rather than seeing cosmopolitanism as a departure from or in tension with the American Founding, he argues that the Founding permits it. Keck claims James Madison as an American proto-cosmopolitan, arguing that he "provide[s] . . . the means by which American identity *could* be understood in cosmopolitan terms, and an institutional framework by which a body of people linked only by their humanity could nevertheless unite under reliably republican political institutions."[3] Keck would place the authority of a figure central to the Founding behind current efforts at promoting the evolution of America toward a greater cosmopolitanism. We are therefore prompted to wonder how amenable Madison is to cosmopolitanism.[4] In fact, while Madison's political principles are universalistic, he supports a concept of the American nation that depends upon particular national attachments, one that is constrained by both politically significant geographic limits and his anti-utopianism.

The Social Compact: Members Only

Cosmopolitanism calls into question national loyalties, and in America, national loyalty is grounded on the free consent of individuals expressed through a social compact. No less than other Founders, Madison believes in social-compact theory. He holds that a government is properly established only by means of a compact: "The essential difference between a free Government and Governments not free, is that the former is founded in compact."[5] He explains: "The original compact is the one implied or presumed, but nowhere reduced to writing, by which a people agree to form one society. The next is a compact, here for the first time reduced to writing, by which the people in their social state agree to a Gov[ernment] over them. These two compacts may be considered as blended in the Constitution of the U.S."[6] One consequence of the social compact is that it separates America from other nations by defining it geographically, politically, and socially as that land over which and those people by whom the social compact was formed, in contrast to other lands and peoples. In short, the American nation and its sovereignty originate in the social compact.

To be sure, the social compact can be extended to foreigners. Madison allows and indeed hopes for immigration. But foreigners have no *right* to come to America. As Thomas G. West argues, Americans have a "*right to exclude* newcomers": "Once a people forms itself, no one has a right to join it without the consent of those being joined."[7] America's welcome to foreigners is not unbounded, and its restrictions on immigration can properly consider America's national interest. Madison's rationale for limiting immigration gives us some indication of the character he hoped to give the nation. In his view, immigrants must be prepared to be loyal to America, and not to any other nation; they must be attached to the Constitution and America's free political order; and they must be of good character. Recording his own contributions during the constitutional convention, Madison said that Congress "is to have the right of regulating naturalization, and can by virtue thereof fix different periods of residence or conditions of enjoying different privileges of Citizenship." It can "confer the full rank of Citizens on meritorious strangers." He hopes that "the most desirable class of people" will come to America, and he has in mind especially "great numbers of respectable Europeans; men who love liberty and wish to partake its blessings."[8] At the convention, Madison also said that he "wished to maintain the character of liberality which had been professed in all the Constitutions & publications of America. He wished to invite foreigners of merit & republican principles among us." He sought to prevent "men with foreign predilections," men "attached to their native Country," from gaining political office in America.[9]

Madison followed up on his statements at the convention. Gaillard Hunt observes that America's "second naturalization law, approved January 29, 1795, . . . introduced the five years' residence previous to naturalization and the declaration of intention three years before. It required also that good character and attachment to the Constitution be established, and that any title of nobility the applicant might bear must be renounced. This act was really the parent of our naturalization system, and its chief author was Madison."[10] Later in life, Madison indicated that immigrants could be restricted in number, the better to encourage their full integration: "The Cultivators of the soil are of a character and in so minute a proportion to our Agricultural population, that they give no foreign tint whatever to its complexion. When they come among us too, it is with such a deep feeling of its being for good & all, that their adopted Country soon takes the place [o]f a native home." But it is different with merchants, in consequence of their great proportion, wealth, and intelligence. Rather than integrating, they often have "pretensions, and even an influence among the native class. . . . They are also less permanently tied to their new Country by the nature of their property & pursuits than . . . other classes" of immigrants.[11] In his desire to wash out the "foreign tint" of immigrants, in his demands for their exclusive allegiance, Madison sits very far from the multiculturalists and cosmopolitans of our day. In Madison's view, America can and *should* shape its immigration policy so that it contributes to American liberty, the character of its free people, and its nationhood. On West's reading of the Founders, America has "a *duty* to exclude aliens whose excessive numbers or questionable character might endanger the citizens' liberty."[12]

Nonrational Attachments

In his thoughts on immigration, Madison lays out some of the basic requirements of American citizenship. In particular, immigrants and native-born Americans must be attached to the Constitution and the principles of liberty that undergird it. In practice, such attachments must be formed and sustained, and that effort requires nonrational (but not necessarily irrational) supports. Madison comes to this view because he is well aware that most men are not capable of living a fully rational life. He expresses himself on this point with some reserve in one letter: "The Americans are an enlightened and liberal people, compared with other nations, but they are not all philosophers."[13] Madison is more frank in *Federalist* no. 49, citing the weakness of human reason and cautioning us against expecting America to be a nation of philosophers.[14] Most Americans cannot subsist on a strict political diet of abstract truths. As Drew McCoy puts it, for Madison, "reason and principle were generally no match for expedience and interest, for faction and intrigue."[15] Nonrational supports are necessary for the fragile reason of the people if they are to sustain their belief in the very rational Constitution and political principles of the nation. These supports take two broad forms: an attachment to Founding heroes; and healthy "prejudices."[16] Madison places a substantial emphasis on both of these forms of attachments, and in the process he weakens the prospects for cosmopolitanism.

Heroes

Madison repeatedly calls upon Americans' historical memory of the Founders. Madison expressed this view in one resolution: "That [the] eminent virtues & services of our illustrious fellow Citizen G[eorge] W[ashington,] P[resident] of U.S. entitle him to [the] highest respect & last[ing] gratitude of his Country, whose peace lib[erty], & safety must ever remind it of his disting[uished] agency in promoting the same."[17] President Madison's proclamation to Americans at the outbreak of the War of 1812 appealed to them for support "as they value the precious heritage derived from the virtue and valor of their fathers."[18] In the course of that war, he called upon the people of Vermont by recalling their "valor" during the War of Independence and suggesting that heroic actions on their part in the current conflict would secure for them a place in history. The "proportionate exertions of her Citizens will add new lustre to their character."[19] By inviting them to be seen by future generations as part of the story of American heroism, Madison sought to expand the future possibilities for the political use of such heroism. Again during the War of 1812, President Madison appealed to the people, directing them "to an emulation of the glorious founders of their independence" and asking them to look "to the sacred obligation of transmitting entire, to future generations, that precious patrimony of national rights and independence."[20] After the invasion of Washington, D.C., he told Americans of "the glory acquired by their fathers in establishing the independence which is now to be maintained by their sons."[21]

We might expect any national leader to call upon the memory of heroes in times of war.[22] But Madison was consistently committed to connecting past heroism with American political ideas.[23] Upon being informed of James Monroe's death, he wrote: "We may cherish the consolation nevertheless, that his memory, like that of the other heroic worthies of the Revolution gone before him, will be embalmed in the grateful affections of a posterity enjoying the blessings which he contributed to procure for it."[24] Late in life, Madison cooperated with a project to write biographies of the Founders. He provided recollections of Franklin, Jefferson, Adams, and Hamilton. His reason for doing so was that "prevailing examples" of biographies of these men, "by omitting the private features of character, and anecdotes, which as condiments, always add flavor, and sometimes nutrition to the repast, have forfeited much of the due attraction."[25] It was precisely the nonrational attraction to particular historical details and character traits that could prove very useful in attaching Americans to the heroes responsible for securing their liberties.

In *Federalist* no. 43, Madison appeals more generally to "the remembrance of the endearing scenes which are past." Keck notes this passage's appeal to a "common historical memory" and notes a similar passage in *Federalist* no. 14, in which Madison refers to Americans' "many cords of affection," "kindred blood," and "mingled blood which they have shed in defense of their sacred rights."[26] Keck then writes that "Madison never again appeals to the American people as a 'nation' . . . joined emotionally by a common set of 'myths, memories, symbols and values' that set them apart from the rest of the world."[27] Yet this claim cannot withstand the evidence of Madison's rhetorical use of American heroes. McCoy is closer to the mark. He argues that Madison "sought . . . to anchor an evolving—perhaps drifting—republic to his own generation's heroic accomplishment. The Founding Fathers had been inspired by unborn generations in their quest for glory; they had viewed posterity as their audience, as well as their beneficiaries. Now posterity must not lose sight of them." Madison's aim was "a voluntary deference to the authority of ancestral intent."[28]

Colleen Sheehan goes further than McCoy. It is not only deference we owe the past but also repayment for debts incurred through predecessors' benevolent actions. In his reply to Jefferson's argument that "the Earth belongs to the living, not to the dead," Madison notes: "The *improvements* made by the dead form a debt against the living, who take the benefit of them. This debt cannot be otherwise discharged than by a proportionate obedience to the will of the Authors of the improvements."[29] Sheehan points out that Madison would not have Americans "forget what they owed to past generations who have sacrificed for their well-being."[30] But of course, Americans' debt to the Founders can be binding only if they understand what the Founders accomplished. Their "gratitude . . . is contingent on understanding the worth of the benefit conveyed." Honoring the Founders is not enough: "We must recognize and cherish the intrinsic good of the gift itself." And so we should seek to honor more their "principles of republicanism" than their persons.[31] Sheehan's analysis here is sound; Madison closely ties his desire to see the Founders honored with the substance of their achievements. We do not get the sense from Madison that we should honor the Founders simply for their courage and intelligence; we should instead honor them for their courage and intelligence in securing American liberty. All the same, it is important that we not read too much into this focus on the substance of the Founders' achievements. Madison gives no indication that we can dispense with honoring the Founders once we have grasped the value of their political achievements. Again, because we are not all philosophers, our appreciation of their achievements must be inextricably bound up with our appreciation of their character and their deeds.

Madison's reliance on Founding heroes places limits on the extension of American nationhood. Keck claims that there is no "indication that the extended republic he describes in *Federalist 10* is in any way incapable of extending beyond those who share a common historical memory."[32] Here too, the evidence suggests otherwise. Madison's reliance on historical memory in order to maintain liberty and promote military virtue indicates that the scope of American citizenship envisioned by him is limited to some extent by the capacity and willingness of people to adopt America's heroes as their own. For Madison, those beyond the reach of the memory of

George Washington and other Founders are in an important political sense beyond the reach of America.

If a people are to be part of the same nation, they must have more in common than abstract political principles. American historical memory cannot be ignored, and even though it could be said to encompass America's universalistic political principles, it cannot be reconciled with the historical memories of other peoples and nations. Even if America were to share the same universalistic political principles as another nation, the intermingling of those common principles with America's particular history would mean that the two countries' respective accounts of their founding would not adequately overlap. Of course, in the case of a nation that does not share America's ideals, America and that nation would have neither history nor political principles in common. In this case, the prospects for cosmopolitanism would clearly be even less promising. And so these persistent limitations of historical memory have the effect of separating America from most of the world and contributing to a distinct sense of American nationhood.

Healthy Prejudices

The second class of nonrational supports for American liberty consists of the healthy "prejudices" to which Madison refers in *Federalist* no. 49. We might also include habits and sentiments in this category.[33] In *Federalist* no. 49, Madison notes that frequent constitutional conventions aimed at enforcing the separation of powers "would carry an implication of some defect in the government" and so "would, in great measure, deprive the government of that veneration which time bestows on everything, and without which perhaps the wisest and freest governments would not possess the requisite stability." Since "all governments rest on opinion," that opinion, if it is sound, should not be disregarded. A reform of the government, however just in the abstract, must not threaten the attachment of the people to a basically sound political order. One danger of reform is that people may exhibit "passions most unfriendly to order and concord."[34] Sheehan notes that "for Madison, passion and interest are as much a part of man's nature as the capacity to reason, and they are all too often resilient to the power of conscience or evidence."[35] Madison makes a similar point in a letter to Jefferson, arguing that frequent changes to laws would diminish the "reverence" for them that is needed to combat a "licentiousness already too powerful."[36] A "veneration" for the past, however nonrational it might appear to a philosopher, can act in the less rational majority to suppress the greatest enemy of reason in politics: strong "public passions."[37]

The task of a statesman is not just to detect and respect healthy prejudices, but also to shape them. In the same time period during which he made his *Federalist Papers* contributions, Madison noticed trends indicating a drift away from a respect for private property. He proposed limitations on the franchise, designed to protect the right to private property. He hinted that a habit of respecting private property should be inculcated early on, so that it could withstand later backsliding: "The time to guard ag[ainst] this danger is at the first forming of the Constitution, and in the present state of population when the bulk of the people have a sufficient interest in possession or in prospect to be attached to the rights of property, without being insufficiently attached to the rights of persons."[38] Political and legal habits could supplement a cold reason weakened by passion and vice. Later in life, Madison expressed a similar view on another subject, arguing for a mode of constitutional interpretation involving "the uniform sanction of successive legislative bodies, through a period of years."[39] McCoy remarks: "Just as he generally relied on the authority of history as an essential source of constitutional stability, so too did Madison depend on the binding force of cumulative precedent."[40]

Since all of these supports are particular to the specific circumstances of America, since they are not strictly rational and universal, then, as in the case of Founding heroes, they too have the effect of contributing to a distinctive national character and separating America from other nations.

The "sphere of a mean extent" and National Limits

Madison's arguments for the necessity of nonrational attachments by no means mark him as cynical about the prospects for human rationality.[41] He hopes that America will become "one paramount Empire of reason, benevolence, and brotherly affection."[42] But Madison is attentive to the fragile conditions necessary for the advancement of the political understanding of most people. For this reason, and because he is cautious about the corrupting effects of unsupervised power, Madison believes that there are serious limits to the size of America, limits that must be respected if it is to remain a free nation. On this point, Keck picks up on only the second of these two reasons: a damaging separation between the citizenry and their government. Keck claims that "the 'practicable sphere' Madison describes in *Federalist 51*—the 'mean extent' beyond which republican government is unsustainable—is limited only by the degree to which a 'sympathy of sentiments,' national or otherwise, could be guaranteed between rulers and ruled."[43] We are told that there is much room for growth in this "sympathy of sentiments." In Keck's view, Madison believes that "because human beings . . . are inescapably diverse, *any* appeal to 'unity' is necessarily imaginary, a mere excuse for oppression and majority tyranny." Madison nonetheless sought a grounding for American nationhood. According to Keck, he found it on the most politically abstract of grounds. On Keck's reading of Madison, "the inescapable heterogeneity of human society meant that [his] sense of 'national' peoplehood ultimately had to rest on peoplehood itself—the only source of unity and 'sympathy,' Madison knew, that Americans (or any body of people) could take for granted."[44] And so, Madison stands revealed as a cosmopolitan; his America can expand to any people willing to be bound to any of their fellow human beings for no other reason than that they share a common humanity. The "'sympathy of sentiments' . . . between rulers and ruled" need only account for and rest on the "peoplehood" of the residents of the enlarged republic.

Keck can give us a cosmopolitan Madison because he cuts down to the bone Madison's requirements for national attachments and political community. But Keck's analysis suffers from two interrelated problems: he misses Madison's argument, described by Sheehan, for the advancement of the political understanding of ordinary Americans; and he therefore also misses the degree of political commonality possible to—indeed, necessary for—the American nation.

Sheehan demonstrates that Madison was concerned to restrain the size of the republic not only because he feared that distant politicians would be beyond the supervision of their constituents, but also because most constituents cannot receive a proper political education in a nation that is too large. That education is aimed at producing a refined and rational "public opinion" that is to be "the ruling authority in republican government."[45] In Madison's words, "public opinion sets bounds to every government, and is the real sovereign in every free one."[46] Sheehan is careful to note that "public opinion is not the sum of ephemeral passions and narrow interests; it is not an aggregate of uninformed minds and wills. Rather, Madison believed that public opinion results from a process that refines and transforms popular views, sentiments and interests. His goal . . . was to achieve political rule grounded in the 'reason of the . . . public' or 'reason of society.'"

Public opinion is shaped by "communication of the ideas of the literati to ordinary citizens throughout society."[47] A large territory and a diverse population contribute to this process of education by suppressing factions[48] while at the same time allowing for a "dynamic 'commerce of ideas' at the level of government and throughout 'the entire body of the people.'"[49] This "commerce of ideas," Madison tells us, depends crucially on "a free press, and . . . a *circulation of newspapers through the entire body of the people*."[50] Sheehan writes: "The literati are thus charged with the role of civic educators in Madison's republic." She continues: "The construction of public opinion involves a process of instructive dialogue and deliberation that permeates the whole society, from the influence of the literati, the statesmen, and the laws on the mores and views of the citizens, to the communication of ideas throughout the great body of the people, to the influence of the settled opinion of the community on the representatives in government. Accordingly, public opinion is both acted upon and is itself an active political agent upon which government depends for its direction."[51] Madison, Sheehan argues, did not believe that it was enough to arrange the American political order so that factions would be suppressed and thus prevented from acting against the common good. He also had in mind a more positive project: the creation of a more rational public opinion that would allow for public deliberation about the character of the common good.[52]

Madison's proposal for refining and elevating public opinion has limits. It cannot take place over too large a territory. As he puts it, "the larger a country, the less easy for its real opinion to be ascertained." To be sure, the apparent size of the nation can be reduced by internal improvements in transportation and communication.[53] Even so, these efforts can only go so far. A too-large territory, Sheehan writes, "lacks a vehicle for the political formation and expression of the society's will." The result is that "the public voice is effectually 'silenced.'" Madison therefore "considered the state (or 'local') governments essential to the collection and articulation of the public voice. Without a due degree of power at the state level of government, the extent of the territory would make it impossible for the people to communicate effectively and convey a united voice by which to control the government."[54]

But we should here notice that the mechanism of federalism cannot on its own be used to enlarge the nation indefinitely. Quite apart from the permanent risk of distant legislators slipping out of the control of their constituents, there is the difficulty of ensuring that newly added people are prepared to take up the significant burdens of active republican citizenship aimed at by Madison's project of geographically sensitive political education. Madison's thoughts on immigration make clear that newcomers must integrate and support liberty. The same requirement is surely present in the case of territorial expansion. But furthermore, the expanded political community must be just that: a political community, a people prepared to participate collectively in thinking, listening, learning, speaking, reading, writing, and voting. In short, they must have the character of a free people.[55] And there are still further limits on national expansion in consequence of the particular attachments to America's past and its Founding heroes needed, in Madison's view, to help form and sustain them as free people. And so, while federalism permits public opinion to be collected and expressed, it cannot overcome these important limits to the expansion of the nation. In particular, while Madison's America can grow to be quite large, it cannot spread to different peoples without threatening the character of its public life as a political community of free and active citizens. For Keck, with respect to the relationship between the government and the people, it is enough that the enlarged republic be able to hold its political leaders accountable. But on a Madisonian understanding of democratic accountability, the developed political community required for that accountability has national features that can't be reconciled with Keck's cosmopolitan intentions.

And these difficulties do not exhaust the political limitations on the enlargement of a republic. Madison cautions that "the more extensive a country, the more insignificant is each individual in his own eyes.—This may be unfavorable to liberty."[56] Madison here touches—but does not enlarge upon—a problem later identified by Tocqueville: that of a democratic despotism national in scope, and despotic precisely because of its national scope, that is, because of the authority mass opinion gains in consequence of the belief of the people in equality, and therefore in consequence of their inability to defy the individually equal but cumulatively overwhelming opinions of their many fellow citizens. Tocqueville puts the source of the problem this way: "As conditions are equalized in a people, individuals appear smaller and society seems greater, or rather, each citizen, having become like all the others, is lost in the crowd, and one no longer perceives [anything] but the vast and magnificent image of the people itself."[57]

Madison proposes dealing with the problem he identifies here by shrinking the apparent size of the nation—the same mechanism he would use to collect the rational "public opinion" of the nation. A smaller (but not too small) nation increases the possibility of a rational "public opinion" while it also limits the degree to which individuals feel overwhelmed by mass opinion. By contrast, on Madison's premises, we can expect a cosmopolitan arrangement to produce no rational "public opinion" on substantial issues, that is, on issues more concrete than the very abstract "peoplehood" of the citizenry. And we can further expect that any view that happens to achieve a cosmopolitan consensus would intimidate individuals, if for no other reason than that it is shared by so many people. Any benefit to liberty's flowing from the recognition of our common cosmopolitan "peoplehood" would have to be measured against the cost to liberty that comes from dwarfing the individual.

World Government?

Despite all of the intellectual and political support he provided for American nationhood, Madison was not wholly averse to cosmopolitan sentiments. He hoped for the widest possible acceptance of the principles of free government, and he wanted America to be an example for the world. He writes optimistically that "all Europe must by degrees be aroused to the recollection and assertion of the rights of human nature. . . . The light which is chasing darkness & despotism from the old World, is but an emanation from that which has procured and succeeded the establishment of liberty in the new."[58] At one point, he found himself thinking, "were it possible by human contrivance so to accelerate the intercourse between every part of the globe that all its inhabitants could be united under the superintending authority of an ecumenical Council, how great a portion of human evils would be avoided. Wars, famines, with pestilence the fruit of either, could not exist."[59] But he does not appear to have followed up on this thought. Quite the opposite; in his "Universal Peace" article, published in 1792,[60] Madison expresses skepticism at Rousseau's proposal for a confederation of European states designed to secure peace. Rousseau claims that peace is possible only through a "[conf]ederal government" that could "unite nations by bonds similar to those which already unite their individual members, and place the one no less than the other under the authority of the Law."[61] Madison criticizes Rousseau for being unaware "of the tendency of his plan to perpetuate arbitrary power wherever it existed; and, by extinguishing the hope of one day seeing an end of oppression, to cut off the only source of consolation remaining to the oppressed." Madison sees the project as almost hopelessly utopian: "A universal and perpetual peace, it is to be feared, is in the catalogue of events, which will never exist but in the imaginations of visionary philosophers, or in the breasts of benevolent enthusiasts." Madison has a pair of substantial objections. On the one hand, to the extent that wars are caused by governments and not the people, the appropriate reform is to bind governments to the will of their people. Yet Rousseau instead sets up a confederal government that does not alter undemocratic arrangements within the member states. On the other hand, to the extent that wars are caused by the people, Madison believes that wars "can only be controuled by subjecting the will of the society to the reason of the society; by establishing permanent and constitutional maxims of conduct, which may prevail over occasional impressions and inconsiderate pursuits." In particular, he recommends that each generation be required to bear the full financial cost of its wars. Unable to pass on the expense to subsequent generations, "avarice would be sure to calculate the expences of ambition; in the equipoise of these passions, reason would be free to decide for the public good." The hope that Madison holds out for world peace is based not on a confederal world government, but rather a bottom-up transformation of each nation's people into citizens dedicated to liberty. And effecting this transformation brings us back to the American nation's being an example for the world. Madison tells us that "had Rousseau lived to see the constitution of the United States and of France, his judgment might have escaped the censure to which his project has exposed it."[62] That would involve quite a reversal of opinion for Rousseau, who in elaborating his plan wonders "what . . . can possibly prevent the execution of a design which, after all, depends solely upon the will of those concerned?"[63] Following this rhetorical question is a list of a mere nineteen European powers—wills—whose consent would be sought in order to implement his plan. We should here repair to a relevant observation about Madison by Ralph Ketcham, that he "retained a skepticism about quick and easy solutions."[64]

Madison's discussion in "Universal Peace" cannot exhaust his objections; there are certainly more that he could have added. In light of the significant national differences among the nineteen European powers, Madison's elaborate arguments against confederal arrangements, both in general and in the particular case of the Articles of Confederation, apply at least as much to Rousseau's confederal plan as they do to the America of 1787.[65] Those same national differences would make a proposal for a *federal* arrangement in Europe untenable. Putting the problem of undemocratic states to one side, there is still the difficulty of forming, from among the various national groups, a united "public opinion" capable of speaking about and deciding upon substantial political questions.

Conclusion

Madison's political thought is resistant to cosmopolitan interpretations and extensions most fundamentally because it is rooted in the truth that humans are imperfect. As we have seen, Madison emphasizes the important influence of the conventions of language, culture, and geography. He holds the reason of most men to be weak, difficult to elicit, and in need of nonrational supports. And he is very sensitive to the corrupting effects and the danger to liberty of human passions. For Madison, human imperfection results in politically important human differences. Keck himself calls attention to a letter Madison wrote to Jefferson in 1787 in which he recounts some of the same reasons for human differences as in his more famous *Federalist* no. 10. In that letter, Madison argues that in a small, direct democracy, the majority will violate the rights of the minority because the people do not "have all precisely the same interests, and the same feelings in every respect."[66] And there is no prospect for change, since "no society ever did or can consist of so homogeneous a mass of Citizens." Besides differences originating in property and economic arrangements, there are "accidental differences in political, religious, or other opinions, or an attachment to the persons of leading individuals. However erroneous or ridiculous these grounds of dissention and faction may appear to the enlightened Statesman or the benevolent philosopher, the bulk of mankind who are neither Statesmen nor Philosophers, will continue to view them in a different light." These imperfections and differences mean that political systems must consider and incorporate nonrational attachments and should include only those people who can be integrated into the nation's political conversation and its politically significant particularities. So embedded are human imperfections in human nature that, for Madison, they are inescapable. As he famously wrote in *Federalist* no. 55: "In all very numerous assemblies, of whatever character composed, passion never fails to wrest the sceptre from reason. Had every Athenian citizen been a Socrates, every Athenian assembly would still have been a mob."[67] Madison's political thought indicates that cosmopolitan innovations put the cart before the horse, so to speak.

The prior step would be to produce nearly perfect philosopher-citizens in every country. But this is an outcome that his anti-utopianism forecloses.

Notes

1. Bryan S. Turner, "Cosmopolitan Virtue, Globalization, and Patriotism," *Theory, Culture, and Society* 19, nos. 1–2 (2002): 55, 57.

2. Martha C. Nussbaum, "Patriotism and Cosmopolitanism," in *For Love of Country?* by Martha C. Nussbaum et al., ed. Joshua Cohen (Boston: Beacon Press, 2002), 3–17. Kwame Anthony Appiah, *Cosmopolitanism: Ethics in a World of Strangers* (New York: Norton, 2006).

3. Aaron Michael Keck, "One Nation: Cosmopolitanism and the Making of American Identity from Madison to Lincoln" (Ph.D. diss., Rutgers Univ., 2008), 200, emphasis in original.

4. Besides Keck, Gary Wills and Gordon S. Wood also claim to have detected cosmopolitan elements in Madison. Wills writes that Madison "became very cosmopolitan in his reading and study." Gary Wills, *James Madison* (New York: Henry Holt, 2002), 11. Wood writes of the "contrast between localism and cosmopolitanism" after describing Madison's proposal for encouraging politicians to attend to the concerns of the "whole Society" rather than just a part. Gordon S. Wood, *The Creation of the American Republic, 1776–1787* (Chapel Hill: Univ. of North Carolina Press, 1969; reprint, New York: Norton, 1972), 511, and quoting Madison to Jefferson, October 17, 1787. But these references to Madison's supposed cosmopolitanism are more rhetorical flourishes than seriously pursued arguments.

5. Madison to N.P. Trist, December 23, 1832, in *The Writings of James Madison*, 9 vols., ed. Gaillard Hunt (New York: G. Putnam's, 1900–1910), 9:490. (Subsequent references are to *WJM*.) See also Madison to Alexander Rives, January 1833, in *WJM*, 9:497; and Madison, "Sovereignty," 1835, in *WJM*, 9:569.

6. Madison to N.P. Trist, February 5, 1830, in *WJM*, 9:355n. See also Edward J. Erler, "From Subjects to Citizens: The Social Compact Origins of American Citizenship," in *The American Founding and the Social Compact*, ed. Ronald J. Pestritto and Thomas G. West (Lanham, MD: Lexington Books, 2003), 163–97, quotation on 181.

7. Thomas G. West, *Vindicating the Founders: Race, Sex, Class, and Justice in the Origins of America* (Lanham, MD: Rowman and Littlefield, 1997), 157, emphasis in original.

8. Madison, "Journal of the Constitutional Convention," August 9, 1787, in *WJM*, 4:146–47. For an explanation of the Founders' expressed preference for Europeans, see West, *Vindicating the Founders*, 168–71.

9. Madison, "Journal of the Constitutional Convention," August 13, 1787, in *WJM*, 4:174.

10. Hunt, quoted in *WJM,* 6:231n1.

11. Madison to Richard Peters, February 22, 1819, in *WJM,* 8:424.

12. West, *Vindicating the Founders,* 160, emphasis in original.

13. Madison to Philip Mazzei, October 8, 1788, in *WJM,* 5:268.

14. Alexander Hamilton, James Madison, and John Jay, *The Federalist Papers,* ed. Clinton Rossiter, revised by Charles R. Kesler (1787–1788; New York: Signet, 2003), 311–12.

15. Drew R. McCoy, *The Last of the Fathers: James Madison and the Republican Legacy* (Cambridge: Cambridge Univ. Press, 1989), 82.

16. *Federalist* no. 49:312.

17. See Madison to Jefferson, September 2, 1793, in *WJM,* 6:192n1. See also Stuart Leibiger, *Founding Friendship: George Washington, James Madison, and the Creation of the American Republic* (Charlottesville: Univ. Press of Virginia, 1999), 176.

18. Madison, "Proclamation," June 19, 1812, in *WJM,* 8:201.

19. Madison to Jonas Galusha, November 30, 1812, in *WJM,* 8:232.

20. Madison, "Message to the Special Session of Congress," May 25, 1813, in *WJM,* 8:249–50.

21. Madison, "Proclamation," September 1, 1814, in *WJM,* 8:306.

22. The War of 1812 had the perhaps unintended effect of helping to shape and develop America's national identity. According to Albert Gallatin, "The war has renewed and reinstated the national feelings and character which the Revolution had given, and which were daily lessened. The people have now more general objects of attachment with which their pride and political opinions are connected. They are more Americans; they feel and act more as a nation." Gallatin to Matthew Lyon, May 7, 1816, in *The Writings of Albert Gallatin,* 3 vols., ed. Henry Adams (Philadelphia: Lippincott, 1879), 1:700. Robert Rutland recounts Gallatin's observation and concludes: "America was now a nation." Robert Allen Rutland, *James Madison: The Founding Father* (New York: Macmillan, 1987), 233. According to French envoy Louis Serurier, "The war has given the Americans what they so essentially lacked, a national character founded on a glory common to all." Quoted in Wills, *James Madison,* 157. Wills notes: "It makes little sense to ask whether Federalism or Republicanism won in 1815. Neither of them won. Nationalism did. The war eroded the purely ideological criterion for judging events." Ibid., 156.

23. See Ralph Ketcham, *James Madison: A Biography* (New York: Macmillan, 1971), 533.

24. Madison to Alexander Hamilton Jr., July 9, 1831, in *WJM,* 9:461n.

25. Madison to J.K. Paulding, April 1831, in *WJM,* 9:451.

26. Keck, "One Nation," 98–99.

27. Ibid., 194–95; cf. Lance Banning, *The Sacred Fire of Liberty: James Madison and the Founding of the Federal Republic* (Ithaca, NY: Cornell Univ. Press, 1995), 58, 304–5.

28. McCoy, *Last of the Fathers,* 82–83; see also 162.

29. Madison to Jefferson, February 4, 1790, in *WJM,* 5:438n1, emphasis in original.

30. Colleen A. Sheehan, *James Madison and the Spirit of Republican Self-Government* (Cambridge: Cambridge Univ. Press, 2009), 142.

31. Ibid., 3.

32. Keck, "One Nation," 195.

33. See Madison to John Adams, May 22, 1817, in *WJM,* 8:391; see also McCoy, *Last of the Fathers,* 65.

34. *Federalist* no. 49:311, 312.

35. Sheehan, *James Madison,* 151.

36. Madison to Jefferson, February 4, 1790, 5:440n.

37. *Federalist* no. 49:312; see also 314.

38. Madison, "Observations on the 'Draught of a Constitution for Virginia'" (1788), in *WJM,* 5:287.

39. Madison to Charles J. Ingersoll, June 25, 1831, quoted in McCoy, *Last of the Fathers,* 82.

40. McCoy, *Last of the Fathers,* 82.

41. The quotation in the preceding subheading is drawn from Madison to Jefferson, October 24, 1787, in *WJM,* 5:31.

42. Madison, "Consolidation," December 5, 1791, in *WJM,* 6:69.

43. Keck, "One Nation," 195.

44. Ibid., 65, emphasis in original; 197.

45. Sheehan, *James Madison,* 59.

46. Madison, "Public Opinion," December 19, 1791, in *WJM,* 6:70.

47. Sheehan, *James Madison,* 79–80.

48. See *Federalist* no. 10.

49. Sheehan, *James Madison,* 100.

50. Madison, "Public Opinion," 6:70, emphasis in original. See also Sheehan, *James Madison,* 103–4; and Banning, *Sacred Fire of Liberty,* 354–55.

51. Sheehan, *James Madison,* 104, 105.

52. See, e.g., ibid., 168–70.

53. Madison, "Public Opinion," 6:70.

54. Sheehan, *James Madison,* 99, 100, 132.

55. See Banning, *Sacred Fire of Liberty,* 371.

56. Madison, "Public Opinion," 6:70.

57. Alexis de Tocqueville, *Democracy in America,* trans. Harvey C. Mansfield and Delba Winthrop (Chicago: Univ. of Chicago Press, 2000), II.4.2, p. 641.

58. Madison to Edmund Pendleton, March 4, 1790, in *WJM,* 6:7.

59. Quoted in Ketcham, *James Madison,* 632.

60. See *WJM,* 6:88–91. Madison appears to have recorded his thoughts supporting world government in 1817, although he may have been looking back to "issues raised in the 1787 [constitutional] debates." Ketcham, *James Madison,*

725n21. If the earlier date corresponds to the origin of this idea, it would place it prior to his "Universal Peace" essay and thus provide some evidence that his more settled views on the matter are found in "Universal Peace."

61. Jean-Jacques Rousseau, *A Lasting Peace: Through the Federation of Europe; and The State of War,* trans. C.E. Vaughan (1756; London: Constable, 1917), 38–39. Vaughan mistakenly translates "confédérative" as "federal." See Rousseau, "Extrait du projet de paix perpétuelle de M. L'Abbé de Saint-Pierre," in *The Political Writings of Jean-Jacques Rousseau,* 2 vols., ed. C.E. Vaughan (Cambridge: Cambridge Univ. Press, 1915), 1:364–87, quotation on 365. See also Rousseau's five Articles (and especially the first and third) on pp. 61–64 of the translated work.

62. Madison, "Universal Peace," in *WJM,* 6:88–90.

63. Rousseau, *Lasting Peace,* 65.

64. Ketcham, *James Madison,* 632.

65. See, for example, *Federalist* nos. 18–20.

66. Madison to Jefferson, October 24, 1787, in *WJM,* 5:28–29.

67. *Federalist* no. 55:340.

Joseph R. Fornieri

Lincoln's Reflective Patriotism

An Alternative to Nationalism and Cosmopolitanism

> Intelligence, patriotism, Christianity, and a firm reliance on Him, who has never yet forsaken this favored land, are still competent to adjust, in the best way, all our present difficulty.
> —Abraham Lincoln, First Inaugural, March 4, 1861

Alexis de Tocqueville memorably described America's love of country in these unflattering terms: "One cannot imagine a more disagreeable and talkative patriotism. It fatigues even those who honor it."[1] While critical of an inflated and thoughtless national pride, the French foreign observer nonetheless appreciated the contribution of patriotism to democracy and human flourishing. Public-spiritedness may also constitute a bulwark against the inherent tendency of democratic individuals toward materialism and their like propensity to "withdraw into a narrow and unenlightened selfishness."[2] Love of country may elevate civic life by calling people to loftier aspirations beyond their own comfortable self-preservation. Counterpoised to the tendencies of democratic individualism, patriotism may inspire a sacrificial love that transcends the self. And sacrifice is necessary, even the ultimate sacrifice of one's life, to secure the blessings of republican liberty.

Unlike Tocqueville, who appreciated the problematic character of patriotism as a potentially ennobling or a degrading form of love, some of today's cosmopolitan and postmodern intellectuals denounce categorically love of country as a pure vice.[3] Patriotism, they contend, is practically indistinguishable from the sins of ethnocentrism, intolerance, chauvinism, nationalism, jingoism, fanaticism, and imperial dominion. It releases irrational passions that are diametrically opposed to critical reflection. Martha

Nussbaum, for example, maintains that "patriotic pride is both morally dangerous and, ultimately, subversive of some of the worthy goals patriotism sets out to serve."[4] Two recent works echo this opinion. In *Patriotism and Other Mistakes,* George Kateb describes love of country as "a mistake twice over: it is typically a grave moral error and its source is typically a state of mental confusion."[5] And in *The Truth about Patriotism,* Steven Johnston goes so far as to argue that "democracy's future depends on its emergence from patriotism's self-obsessive grip."[6]

Nussbaum prescribes cosmopolitan world citizenship as a remedy to the evils of patriotism. She contrasts the chauvinism and irrationality of patriotism with the universality and rationality of cosmopolitanism. World citizenship, she notes, is a "kind of exile—from the comfort of local truths, from the warm, nestling feeling of patriotism, from the absorbing drama of pride in oneself and one's own." In contrast to the solace of patriotism, "cosmopolitanism offers no such refuge; it offers only reason and the love of humanity, which may seem at times less colorful than other sources of belonging."[7] The cosmopolitan intellectual thus seeks to eradicate the prejudice of patriotism from the minds of students and to lead them to embrace the prospect of world citizenship, at least until the Parousia of world government abolishes all human particularity.[8] At stake, then, in the debate over cosmopolitanism and patriotism is the very nature and purpose of civic education.[9] Is civic education propaganda? Is patriotism indistinguishable from nationalism? Should civic education, whether patriotic or nationalist, be replaced with a cosmopolitan education that transcends national boundaries and teaches students that they are citizens of the world?

In response to the critics of patriotism and the apostles of cosmopolitanism, I seek to reveal how Lincoln's statesmanship manifests a love of country that is compatible with both reason and love of humanity. I use the term *reflective patriotism* (a term I borrow from Tocqueville) to characterize Lincoln's ordinate and just love of country. Contrary to both a nationalist chauvinism that abhors universal principles and a cosmopolitanism that abstracts from the love of one's own, Lincoln's reflective patriotism harmonizes allegiance to universal principles with the particular circumstances of the American regime.[10] Unlike other forms of reverence that demand a blind submission to the status quo, Lincoln's reflective patriotism invites national self-examination. Rather than merely sanctioning the status quo, it judges the present through a return to first principles and civic reflection upon their meaning.

While Lincoln's reflective patriotism involves dedication to the universal principles of the Declaration, it also embraces the particular places, people, politics, and occasions in American history that contributed to the advancement of ordered liberty at home and abroad. In his most recent work tracing the Puritan origins of American patriotism, George McKenna correctly emphasizes that patriotism in America is more than "deducing conclusions from the Declaration of Independence and other documents."[11] Citing Wilfred McClay, McKenna notes that "there is a danger in coming to regard America too exclusively as an idea, the carrier of an idea, or the custodian of a set of principles, rather than as a real nation that exists in a world of other nations, with all the features and limitations of a nation, including its particular history, institutions, and distinctive national character."[12] As will be shown, Lincoln's reflective patriotism encompasses more than an abstract idea. It invokes not only the timeless truths of the Declaration, but also "the mystic chords of memory."[13] In a word, it appeals to both the head and the heart.

Historically, Lincoln's reflective patriotism was articulated as a concrete response to rival forms of allegiance that he opposed as both unreasonable and unjust during the Civil War era—namely, the imperialism of Manifest Destiny, Northern and Southern sectionalism over slavery, the nativism of the Know-Nothings, and secession in defense of slavery. Lincoln maintained that each of these disordered forms of allegiance placed the self-interest of a faction above the common good of the whole. By violating the principles of the Declaration and the rule of law in the Constitution, these disordered forms of allegiance broke moral and fraternal bonds of liberty and union that Lincoln sought to perpetuate through an ordinate love of country guided by wisdom under God's providence.

Philosophically, Lincoln's reflective patriotism is constituted by his appeal to the natural law teaching in the Declaration, the republican legacy of the Founders, and biblical faith as mediated by the Puritan understanding of a city upon a hill (Matthew 5:14) under God's Providence.[14] In *Abraham Lincoln's Political Faith,* I contend that Lincoln's ultimate moral justification for American public life was constituted by three broad sources of political order: (1) reason, (2) revelation, and (3) republicanism.[15] I refer to these traditions as "the Three R's" of his political faith. Indeed, Lincoln's reflective patriotism similarly integrates these same sources to inspire devotion to the Union. This is vividly seen in his First Inaugural Address, of March 4, 1861, where he proclaimed: "Intelligence, patriotism, Christianity, and a firm reliance on Him, who has never yet forsaken this favored land, are still competent to adjust, in the best way, all our present difficulty."[16]

Much of the criticism of patriotism as chauvinistic and racist is misguided since it stems from critics' confusion of patriotism with romantic and/or ethnic nationalism.[17] In a seminal work on the topic, *For Love of Country,* Maurizio Viroli traces the republican roots of patriotism from antiquity to modernity. He distinguishes the republican love of ordered liberty both historically and theoretically from nationalist beliefs in racial purity, ethnic homogeneity, and imperial domination.[18] Throughout, he copiously cites ancient, medieval, and modern republican sources, from Cicero to Leonardi Bruni, a fifteenth-century medieval Florentine patriot, to Milton, Montesquieu, and Mazzini.[19]

Patriotism in the classical republican tradition may be defined as the love of liberty and the laws that sustain a free way of life. This love of country was understood primarily in political terms, involving gratitude, duty (*officiis*), care (*pietas*), and sacrifice for the common good.[20] The elements of classical republican patriotism are tersely expressed in Cicero's motto from *Tusculan Disputations* 4.43: "pro legibus, pro libertate, pro patria."[21] Unlike nineteenth-century nationalism, classical republican patriotism was inimical to despotism and tyranny. Ordered liberty was safeguarded by the rule of law. Cato of Utica epitomizes republican patriotism in his defense of the republic and resistance to Caesar.

Whereas republican patriotism had classical and medieval roots, nationalism was a nineteenth-century movement whose origins can be traced to the French Revolution and in response to Enlightenment universalism. Whereas republican patriotism was viewed in political terms as the basis of a common love of liberty, nationalism emphasizes racial, ethnic, and linguistic homogeneity as the basis of Union-Fatherland.[22] And whereas the proponents of republican patriotism saw it as rational virtue, nineteenth-century romantic nationalism emerged as a reaction against reason. Instead, it exalted feeling and passion as a more reliable source of achieving mystical communion with a tribe or ethnic group.[23]

Medieval Christians interpreted patriotism as a species of charity or love of neighbor. In a passage that has been attributed to Thomas Aquinas from *On Princely Government,* but was most likely written by Ptolemy of Luca, patriotism is described as being "founded in the root of charity [*Amor patriae in radice caritatis fundatur*] which puts not private things before those held in common, but the things held in common before the private as the Blessed Augustine says."[24]

The core elements of the classical and medieval tradition of patriotism—namely, its essence as a political virtue based on a shared love of liberty and the free institutions and laws that sustain the common good—would be transmitted to modern republican thinkers like Bolingbroke, Milton, Addison, and Montesquieu. These modern thinkers exercised a direct influence on the Founders, who, in turn, influenced Lincoln. Montesquieu, for example, identifies patriotism as the affective disposition to place the common good over private interest and ambition. "Love of the homeland," he states, "leads to goodness in mores, and goodness in mores leads to the love of the homeland. The less we can satisfy our particular passions, the more we give ourselves up to the passions for the general order."[25]

Though distinctive in its own right, the character of Lincoln's reflective patriotism may be further elucidated by means of comparison to the republican patriotism of Giuseppe Mazzini. While the love of country for both involved a devotion to universal principles, it also embraced particular places, peoples, and memories. Indeed, the patriotisms of Mazzini and Lincoln were both notable in combining "political ideas, culture, memories, and places. It was not just the political ideal of the republic, it was other things in addition to that; but culture, memories, and places—without the republic—are not sufficient to make the patriot feel at home."[26]

Contrary to nationalist chauvinism, Mazzini, like Lincoln, saw no necessary antipathy between the love of one's own liberty and that of others. Indeed, both recognize that love of liberty is not only inherent to man as a political animal, but that it may also be shared in solidarity with others. Mazzini famously states: "Without country you have neither name, token, voice, nor rights, no admission as brothers into the fellowship of the Peoples. You are the bastards of Humanity."[27]

Unlike the racism, chauvinism, and tribalism so characteristic of nationalism, Mazzini's love of country, like Lincoln's, strongly affirmed the unity of human nature and the equality of our common humanity while, at the same time, it appreciated the charm of diversity and the spirited "love of one's own" as a given part of human nature and human flourishing. In a word, Mazzini emphasizes that "love of country has to be enlarged and ennobled by allegiance to universal principles. Our nation deserves our love as long as it remains an instrument for 'the good and progress of all.'"[28]

Because Lincoln's reflective patriotism combines devotion to both the universal and the particular, it is imbued with a reverence and filial piety for the deeds and actions of the Founders, who sought to realize the principles of the Revolution through the concrete rule of law in the Constitution. As a young man, Lincoln read Parson Mason Locke Weems's *Life of Washington* as well as Pericles' funeral oration in *Plutarch's Lives.*[29] The patriotic themes of these works would have been unmistakable to him. Not surprisingly, Lincoln saw Washington, the *pater patriae,* as a patriotic role model. Notably, Washington's Farewell Address, which the youthful Lincoln had read and likely modeled his Lyceum Address after, contained two defining themes of his reflective patriotism: (1) maintaining the inseparable bonds of liberty and union, and (2) subordinating sectional interest to the common good of the country.[30] In terms that would greatly influence the young Lincoln, Washington reminded his countrymen that "your union ought to be considered as a main prop of your liberty, and that the love of the one ought to endear to you the preservation of the other. These considerations speak a persuasive language to every reflecting and virtuous mind, and exhibit the continuance of the Union as the primary object of patriotic desire." Washington further noted that "the name of American which belongs to you, in your national capacity, must always exalt the just pride of Patriotism, more than any appellation derived from local discriminations."[31]

While profoundly influenced by the themes in Washington's Farewell Address, the essence of Lincoln's reflective patriotism is articulated most cogently in his eulogy to Henry Clay: "He loved his country partly because it was his own country, but mostly because it was a free country."[32] Following both Washington and Clay's example, Lincoln likewise defined patriotism in terms of devotion to the country as whole against mere sectional interests or passions, whether Northern or Southern, that broke the inseparable bonds of liberty and an inclusive Union dedicated to the universal principles of the Declaration.

Indeed, Alexander Stephens went so far as to say that Lincoln's devotion to "the Union rose to the sublimity of religious mysticism." Though he meant this as a criticism, Stephens can at least be given credit for appreciating that love of country was a genuine motive of Lincoln's statesmanship. Lincoln's contemporaries well understood his patriotism, which is something we tend to overlook in our modern effort to uncover subconscious and hidden motives behind people's behavior. To be sure, much has been said about Lincoln's ambition, and even his melancholy, as a spur to his greatness.[33] In support of this view, many biographers and scholars cite William Herndon's oft-quoted remark that Lincoln's ambition was a "little engine that knew no rest." This is true enough. But these same scholars fail to recognize the extent to which love of country was an equally strong motive of Lincoln's statesmanship. I hope to remedy this deficiency in the Lincoln literature. As Michael Burlingame reveals in his latest biography, Lincoln also confided to Herndon his love of country as well as his ambition. "How hard—oh how more than hard," Lincoln said in 1851, "it is to die and leave one's Country no better for the life of him that lived and died her child."[34]

In the Lyceum Address of 1838, what many consider to be his first great speech, a young Lincoln forthrightly declared his patriotic aim to perpetuate the Founders' legacy of ordered liberty. Unfortunately, the overt patriotic motives of the speech have been overshadowed by psychoanalytic accounts of Lincoln's subconscious ambition. Some historians go so far as to claim that Lincoln actually projected himself into the figure of "the towering genius"[35] he warns against, an ambitious tyrant like Alexander, Caesar, and Napoleon who craves distinction at any cost, "whether at the expense of emancipating the slaves, or enslaving freemen."[36]

Lincoln's self-described task in the Lyceum Address springs from "gratitude to our fathers, justice to ourselves, duty to posterity and love for our species in general."[37] Indeed, this statement nicely encapsulates the key components of Lincoln's reflective patriotism.

Lincoln's love of republican liberty stirred him to oppose irrational impulses and passions implicit to democracy itself—namely, the passions of mob rule. In the Lyceum Address, Lincoln as a young Whig emphasizes that the preservation of ordered liberty in a democratic republic requires that it be exercised within lawful boundaries. Exhorting his fellow citizens to revere both the liberty promised by the Declaration and the particular rule of law established by the Constitution to safeguard it, Lincoln proclaims: "As the patriots of seventy-six did to the support of the Declaration of Independence, so to the support of the Constitution and Laws, let every American pledge his life, his property, and his sacred honor;—let every man remember that to violate the law, is to trample on the blood of his father, and to tear the character [charter?] of his own, and his children's liberty."[38]

In the same speech, it will also be recalled, Lincoln famously invoked "a political religion" based on "reverence for the laws" as a solution to the problem of mob rule.[39] If unbounded by the restraining force of law, passion will turn against itself and jeopardize the very liberty the patriots fought so hard to secure during the Revolution. Significantly, Lincoln demands that reverence be guided by reason, intelligence, and sound morality. "Passion has helped us," he states, "but can do so no more. It will in future be our enemy. Reason, cold, calculating, unimpassioned reason, must furnish all the materials for our future support and defence.—Let those [materials] be moulded into *general intelligence, [sound] morality,* and, in particular, *a reverence for the constitution and laws.*"[40] Thus, as early as the Lyceum Address of 1838, Lincoln distinguished between a blind allegiance based on passion and a thoughtful reverence based on reason and in accord with sound morality. Put another way, he called for a reflective patriotism.

Consonant with Mazzini's view of the potential harmony between love of one's own and the good of humanity, Lincoln's reflective patriotism envisioned America as an exemplar of free government to the world. Thus in the Lyceum Address Lincoln describes America as "the fondest hope, of the lovers of freedom, throughout the world." Lincoln would consistently articulate this view of America's mission to uphold the torch of democracy for the rest of the world throughout his public life.

In the decade that followed the Lyceum Address, 1840–1850, consistent with his earlier call for reverence based on reason, intelligence, and sound morality, whenever Lincoln mentioned patriotism, he did so in connection with wisdom. Moreover, he repeatedly qualified this type of patriotism as being thoughtful rather than impulsive. A close textual analysis shows that the words *intelligence* and *wisdom* consistently precede the word *patriotism* in Lincoln's speeches and writings. For example, on February 26, 1841, he states that the efforts of the Whig Party "required our utmost wisdom and patriotism."[41] And in his eulogy to Zachary Taylor on July 25, 1850, he declares, "I will not pretend to believe that all the wisdom, or all the patriotism of the country died with General Taylor. But we know that *wisdom* and *patriotism,* in a public office, under institutions like ours, are wholly inefficient and worthless, unless they are sustained by the confidence and devotion of the people."[42]

Indeed, the connection in Lincoln's mind between patriotism and wisdom and intelligence was no accident, but part of a pattern that can be traced from the Lyceum Address in the 1830s to his presidency. In each case, Lincoln, who carefully chose word order to convey meaning and emphasis in his speeches, deliberately places the words *wisdom* and *intelli-*

gence before *patriotism* in order to emphasize the extent to which the latter is to be governed and qualified by the former. As will be shown, Lincoln did not believe that all forms of patriotism are wise and intelligent. As a result, he opposed nativism and Manifest Destiny as disordered forms of love of country that were contrary to a more reflective patriotism based on wisdom and justice.

Contrary to a blind obedience, Lincoln's reflective patriotism demanded that he challenge his government when it betrayed itself. In speech and deed, his actions coincide with Edmund Burke's dictum that "to be loved a country must be lovely." Like the patriotic statesmanship of Burke, who believed that Great Britain had betrayed itself in flawed policies toward the American colonies, Ireland, and India, Lincoln's reflective patriotism demanded a critical engagement with his country when it pursued unjust and imprudent policies.[43]

This critical engagement is vividly seen in Lincoln's opposition to the Mexican War and in response to allegations about his own allegiance to the American regime. Such accusations were likely to have deepened his subsequent reflections on patriotism. As a first-term congressman from Illinois, Lincoln refused to support a resolution that called members of Congress to vindicate President James K. Polk's aggression during the Mexican War. In response, Lincoln accused Polk of initiating hostilities on Mexican soil, and, on December 22, 1847, he proposed his controversial "Spot Resolutions," demanding to know the exact spot where American blood was shed. Less than a month later, Lincoln made another speech in the House of Representatives condemning President Polk for abusing executive power, claiming that "the blood of this war, like the blood of Abel, is crying to Heaven against him [Polk]."[44]

William Herndon, Lincoln's law partner, warned him that he was committing political suicide. His opponents were already questioning his patriotism, derisively calling him "spotty Lincoln." Indeed, a decade later in 1858, during the Great Debates, Stephen A. Douglas would relentlessly attack Lincoln's patriotism for his stance during the Mexican War. For example, at Springfield on October 20, 1858, Douglas went so far as to accuse Lincoln of treason, alleging that he was a member of the "Mexican Party in the congress of the United States." "Lincoln's vote," according to Douglas, "did more to encourage the Mexicans and the Mexican army than all of the soldiers that were brought into the field; they induced the Mexicans to hold out the longer, and the guerrillas to keep up their warfare on the roadside, and to poison our men, and to take the lives of our soldiers wherever and whenever they could."[45]

Just as Lincoln opposed the nationalistic impulses of Manifest Destiny during the Mexican War, so he likewise opposed Douglas's imperial ambitions a decade later. In his 1859 Speech of Discoveries and Inventions, Lincoln satirized "Young America," the pro-Douglas, expansionist wing of the Democratic Party committed to Manifest Destiny.[46] More specifically, Lincoln opposed Douglas's efforts to annex Cuba under the principle of popular sovereignty. The Little Giant forthrightly proclaimed: "When we get Cuba we must take it as we find it, and leave the people of Cuba to decide the question of slavery for themselves without the interference of the federal government, or of any other State in the Union." As Harry V. Jaffa has aptly noted, Douglas saw slavery as a mere distraction that impeded the more important work of nationalist expansion and empire building. On the contrary, Lincoln opposed both slavery and imperialism as twin evils that were rooted in the same lust for power.[47]

In sum, Lincoln's criticism of American nationalist aggression and imperialism, whether it be the Mexican War or the annexation of Cuba ten years later, displays further the potential compatibility between his reflective patriotism and legitimate dissent. Whether or not his claim was true that Polk had initiated hostilities, the larger point is that Lincoln did not exploit patriotism as an excuse to shield leaders from public scrutiny or to quell debate. On the contrary, his love of liberty demanded that he speak out against his government when it betrayed its own principles and abused power in a way that was more consistent with monarchical despotism than republican freedom. Ironically, Lincoln's own actions as president in exercising broad power to crush the rebellion would test whether or not he would extend this same principle to political dissenters during the Civil War, especially in his letter to Erastus Corning, where he raises questions about the Democrats' loyalty in opposing the war effort.

Less than a decade after the Mexican War, in his 1852 Resolutions in Behalf of Hungarian Freedom, Lincoln further articulated a vision of reflective patriotism based on a common love of liberty and shared solidarity with other peoples. The resolutions were drafted in response to a freedom tour made by Louis Kossuth, the hero of the Hungarian independence movement, which had been recently crushed by the combined imperial forces of Austria and Russia. The Illinois Legislature was summoned to deliberate on whether or not the United States should intervene to aid the Hungarians.

Contrary to the belief that the American commitment to freedom necessarily leads to armed intervention, Lincoln began the resolutions by affirming the general principle of nonintervention. He then noted that the circumstance of Russian aggression could potentially justify foreign assistance. Such intervention, however, depended upon the prudential weighing and balancing of circumstances. Regardless of whether or not the United States ultimately intervened, Lincoln believed that as the exemplar of democracy to the world, at the very least, it was called upon to affirm, in principle, moral solidarity with the Hungarian people. "We, the American people," he declares, "cannot remain silent, without justifying an inference against our continued devotion to the principles of our free institutions."[48] One wonders how Lincoln would have reacted in 1956 to the Soviet invasion.

Lincoln's tribute to Kossuth shows that the love of liberty is not chauvinistic per se. Kossuth embodied the same principles that Americans hold dear. Lincoln thus praised him as "the most worthy and distinguished representative of the cause of civil and religious liberty on the continent of Europe. A cause for which he and his nation struggled until they were overwhelmed by the armed intervention of a foreign despot, in violation of the more sacred principles of the laws of nature and of nations—principles held dear by the friends of freedom everywhere, and more especially by the people of these United States."[49]

Lincoln often used the term "friends of freedom" to describe common love of liberty between different peoples and nations. Consistent with his devotion to the natural law principles of justice in the Declaration, this love of liberty must observe the "sacred principles of the laws of nature and nations." Such principles are "especially" "held dear" by the people of the United States, given our Puritan inheritance and self-understanding as "a city upon a hill," dedicated to the cause of civil and religious liberty.[50] The phrase "city upon a hill" is from Matthew 5:14, when Jesus tells his followers, "You are the light of the world. A city set on a hill cannot be hid" (RSV). The phrase entered into the American lexicon in John Winthrop's 1630 Sermon "A Model of Christian Charity," where he called for the new community in America to be a model of religious virtue, a "city upon a hill," for the rest of the world.[51] In sum, the Hungarian Resolutions show that a reflective patriotism involves flying the American flag alongside the flags of countries who share a common love of liberty.

Lincoln's Eulogy to Henry Clay of June 6, 1852 (the same year as the Hungarian Resolutions), is perhaps the most vivid and profound expression of his reflective patriotism. Lincoln admired Clay as his "beau ideal of a statesman, the man for whom I fought all my humble life."[52] While much attention has been given to the Lyceum Address as a window into Lincoln's soul, little attention has been given to his Eulogy to Henry Clay as a clearer window. In praising Clay, Lincoln affirms those qualities that he admires most in the man and his country. Not surprisingly, foremost among these qualities are: "wisdom, experience and patriotism." Lincoln extols Clay's patriotism in these powerful terms:

> Mr. Clay's predominant sentiment, from first to last, was a deep devotion to the cause of human liberty—a strong sympathy with the oppressed every where, and an ardent wish for their elevation. With him, this was a primary and all controlling passion. Subsidiary to this was the conduct of his whole life. He loved his country partly because it was his own country, but mostly because it was a free country; and he burned with a zeal for its advancement, prosperity and glory, because he saw in such, the advancement, prosperity and glory, of human liberty, human right and human nature. He desired the prosperity of his countrymen partly because they were his countrymen, but chiefly to show to the world that freemen could be prosperous.[53]

To be sure, in praising Clay, Lincoln was describing those virtues he sought to develop in himself as a young statesman.

Notably, in the eulogy Lincoln applauds Clay for envisioning national glory as something altogether different from military might and the projection of power throughout the globe. Rather, both Clay and Lincoln envision glory in terms of America's moral worth at home and moral influence abroad. The true glory of America is measured by the extent to which it advances the cause of liberty as a "city upon a hill." The republican critics of democracy said that it was prone to the extremes of tyranny and anarchy. In reply to these critics, Lincoln would subsequently characterize the Civil War as an ordeal that tested the viability of democracy. The success or failure of the American experiment would reverberate throughout the globe, providing hope or despair for the friends of freedom every where.

Because Clay's legacy belonged to the world as much as to America, Lincoln proclaims him as "freedom's champion." As we may recall, Clay's American System promised moral support for the fledgling democracies in Latin America who were struggling against Spain's colonial domination. Moreover, Lincoln followed Clay and the Whigs in opposing the Democratic policies of Manifest Destiny and imperial expansion.

Further consistent with what we have seen, Lincoln associates patriotism with the qualities of wisdom and intelligence. He admires Clay's "wisdom and patriotism." And he extols his undeniable legacy "amongst intelligent and Patriotic Americans,"[54] the implication being that those who place sectional interest above devotion to the Union, whether they are Northerners or Southerners, are both unreasonable and unpatriotic.

In particular, Clay's statesmanship was exemplary for Lincoln because it placed the common good of the Union above sectional interest. Praising Clay's patriotic devotion to the common good over factional interest, Lincoln explains: "As a politician or statesman, no one was so habitually careful to avoid all sectional ground. Whatever he did, he did for the whole country. In the construction of his measures he ever carefully surveyed every part of the field and duly weighed every conflicting interest. Feeling as he did, and as the truth is, that the world's best hope depended upon the continued Union of these States, he was ever jealous of and watchful for, whatever might have the slightest tendency to separate them."[55] Preserving the Union advanced a humanitarian end since the American experiment was the "world's best hope." It inspired freedom at home and abroad through one's right to resist tyranny.

Before proceeding further, it is worth pondering the contemporary philosophical and political implications of Lincoln's statement that Clay "loved his country partly because it was his own, but mostly because it was a free country." Today such a candid admission of the "love of one's own" would likely to be viewed with suspicion among intellectuals who aspire to transcend their particular allegiance to a nation-state in favor of a world government that will ensure an equal distribution of wealth and rights to all peoples of the world.

However, as Chantal Delsol and Pierre Manent have shown, the project to create a cosmopolitan world government is utopian, dangerous, and unpolitical.[56] It conceals an irrational fear of diversity. Homogenization is the price of globalization. Rousseau was prescient in seeing that global markets would not necessarily result in world citizenship, but in world consumers who think only of themselves when with others and only of others when with themselves.

If man is by nature a political animal, as Aristotle claimed, it follows that he will always be encumbered in a particular political culture. The natural and familiar boundaries of language, space, time, and culture limit human possibilities for cooperation. The meaningful fulfillment of duties can occur only within a particular context of family, friends, neighbors, community, and the nation. Politics necessarily involves a spirited defense of one's own and a distinction between one's own and the other. The love of one's own, which may be ennobled and is not necessarily unjust, is the natural starting point for developing habits that lead to the extension of compassion beyond one's own immediate group. Given the limits of a human life, the bonds of fraternity, however, are inevitably weakened through time and place. Despite the fact that the Internet has made the world a smaller place, a virtual community is no substitute for an actual community of family, friends, and citizens who are concretely intermeshed in our daily lives. We may live in solidarity with other lovers of liberty, but this is not identity. Harmony is not unity.

Though critics rail against the nation-state and wish to see it replaced by a world government, a European-style Union, the success of the sovereign nation-state in maintaining civilization, liberty, and democracy for its citizens should not be taken for granted. Can democracy, security, and liberty realistically be secured in a world government where decisions are made by bureaucratic elites who are removed from the particularities of one's own social and political circumstances? Is it not utopian to expect that these elites will be able to transcend completely their own cultural allegiances and backgrounds and to act for the world as whole? Lincoln and the Civil War prove how difficult it is to retain ordered liberty within the context of an extended republic, let alone an entire world! Tocqueville warned that such centralization would rob citizens of dignity and civic purpose, thereby converting them into timid herd animals dependent upon a shepherd, nanny state. In sum, Lincoln's thoughtful patriotism involves a defense of the sovereign nation-state as the best guardian of liberty and union.

The Whig devotion to the inseparability of liberty and union that Lincoln so admired in Henry Clay and that fueled his reflective patriotism would be challenged by threats of sectionalism over slavery, nativism, and secession in defense of slavery. Let us consider each in turn.

The essence of Lincoln's antislavery convictions, and the most vivid expression of political faith to date, are found in the Peoria Address of October 16, 1854. As Lew Lehrman has most recently shown, Peoria was a turning point for both Lincoln and the nation. Indeed, this pivotal speech deserves its proper place alongside the Gettysburg Address and the Second Inaugural as one of Lincoln's greatest. It was occasioned by the repeal of the Missouri Compromise, which opened up the new territories to slavery under the doctrine of popular sovereignty. Lincoln used the strong language of hate in exposing popular sovereignty as a smoke screen for the spread of slavery, which he condemns in equally visceral terms as a monstrous injustice: "This *declared* indifference, but as I must think, covert *real* zeal for the spread of slavery, I can not but hate. I hate it because of the monstrous injustice of slavery itself. I hate it because it deprives our republican example of its just influence in the world—enables the enemies of free institutions, with plausibility, to taunt us as hypocrites—[and] causes the real friends of freedom to doubt our sincerity."[57] Lincoln's righteous indignation at Peoria is the other side of his love for the Union. Slavery was a twin threat that violated both the moral and the territorial integrity of the Union. It undermined America's moral credibility abroad and its survival at home.

Because it preserved the Union on just terms that placed slavery on a path to ultimate extinction, the Missouri Compromise was rightfully praised as a "great patriotic measure."[58] Although Clay was its principal champion, Lincoln quotes approvingly the general view that "the honor was equally due to others as well as to him. . . . It had its origin in the hearts of all patriotic men, who desired to preserve and perpetuate the blessings of our glorious Union—an origin akin to that of the constitution of the United States, conceived in the same spirit of fraternal affection, and calculated to remove forever, the only danger, which seemed to threaten, at some distant day, to sever the social bond of union."[59]

Following the example of Clay, at Peoria, Lincoln denounced the extremes of both Southern and Northern sectionalism as threats to the inseparable bonds of liberty and union. "Stand with anybody that stands RIGHT," Lincoln intoned.

> Stand with him while he is right and PART with him when he goes wrong. Stand WITH the abolitionist in restoring the Missouri Compromise; and stand AGAINST him when he attempts to repeal the fugitive slave law. In the latter case you stand with the southern dis-

> unionist. What of that? you are still right. In both cases you are right. In both cases you oppose [expose?] the dangerous extremes. In both you stand on middle ground and hold the ship level and steady. In both you are national and nothing less than national. This is good old whig ground. To desert such ground, because of any company, is to be less than a whig—less than a man—less than an American.[60]

Significantly, the Peoria Address contrasts patriotism to sectionalism. Northern and Southern extremists are "less than . . . American" in placing factional interest above the common good.

Moreover, at Peoria, the Declaration comes to the fore as the inspirational source of Lincoln's leadership and his moral compass and centerpiece against slavery. Indeed, the principles of the Declaration constitute the very moral foundation of Lincoln's understanding of union. He exhorts patriots to join hands in striving to make the Union worthy of preserving. The Union, however, is worthy of preserving in light of the principles for which it stands—namely, the ideals of liberty, equality, and consent in the Declaration, what Lincoln described as the nation's "ancient faith" or "political faith." Lincoln's patriotism thus involves a critical reflection over the meaning of the first principles of natural law and right. It was part of his political genius to demonstrate so cogently how slavery, nativism, and imperialism violated the moral principles of America's "ancient faith."[61]

The poetry of Lincoln's reflective patriotism crescendos in the following passage, where he calls on his country to live up to its moral promise: "Let us re-adopt the Declaration of Independence, and with it, the practices, and policy, which harmonize with it. Let north and south—let all Americans—*let all lovers of liberty everywhere*—join in the great and good work. If we do this, we shall not only have saved the Union; but we shall have so saved it, as to make, and to keep it, forever worthy of the saving. We shall have so saved it, that the succeeding millions of free happy people, the world over, shall rise up, and call us blessed, to the latest generations."[62] In this last sentence, Lincoln applies the biblical symbolism of the Magnificat in Luke's Gospel to the American experiment. Just as Christ's birth holds significance for the entire world, gentile and Jew, the blessings of liberty promised by the American experiment hold a universal promise for all people who yearn to be free.

Based on such rhetoric, Walter Berns views Lincoln as America's greatest patriotic poet.[63] While Berns rightly notes that Lincoln's love of country was based on devotion to universal principles, his understanding of these principles as derived exclusively from modern secular rationalism is inconsistent with Lincoln's natural law understanding of the Declaration and the potential harmony between faith and reason. According to Berns, "the very idea of natural rights is incompatible with Christian doctrine and, by its formulators, was understood to be incompatible."[64] Bruce P. Frohnen offers a profound critique of Berns's conception of political religion and patriotism as "founded in total rejection of the western tradition of religion and morals."[65]

Compared to Berns's, Lincoln's understanding of the laws of nature that govern patriotic morality is more reminiscent of the view of James Wilson, a Founding Father and one of the foremost legal theorists of the Founding era, whose works Lincoln had read. "The law of nature," Wilson explains, "and the law of revelation are both divine: they flow, though in different channels, from the adorable source. The object of both is—to discover the will of God—and both are necessary for the accomplishment of that end. . . . The moral precepts delivered in the sacred oracles form a part of the law of nature, are of the same origin, and of the same obligation, operating universally and perpetually."[66] Moreover, as noted, the full range of Lincoln's patriotism embraces more than the love of an abstract idea or principle. It also embraces a love of the particular places, people, and institutions and the role of divine providence in preserving and perpetuating these ideals.

Lincoln's patriotic conception of the Union was elegantly conveyed in a letter to Alexander Stephens, future vice president of the Confederacy, during the secession winter of 1861. Seeking to preserve what is best about the American experiment in face of unreasonable efforts to reconcile liberty with slavery and secession, Lincoln used a biblical metaphor taken from Proverbs 25:11 ("apples of gold in pictures of silver" [KJV]) to elicit patriotic devotion to the Union, the Declaration, and the Constitution as complementary charters of republican freedom that sustain ordered liberty. Lincoln thus explained:

> There is something back of [the Constitution and the Union] entwining itself more closely about the human heart. That something, is the principle of "Liberty to all"—the principle that clears the *path* for all—gives *hope* to all—and, by consequence, *enterprize,* and *industry* to all. The *expression* of that principle, in our Declaration of Independence, was most happy, and fortunate. . . . The assertion of

> that *principle*, at *that time*, was *the* word, "*fitly spoken*" which has proved an "apple of gold" to us. The *Union*, and the *Constitution*, are the *picture* of *silver*, subsequently framed around it. The picture was made, not to *conceal*, or *destroy* the apple; but to *adorn*, and *preserve* it. The *picture* was made *for* the apple—*not* the apple for the picture. So let us act, that neither *picture*, or *apple* shall ever be blurred, or bruised or broken.[67]

Lincoln's metaphor makes clear that though the principles of the Declaration are morally prior to the Constitution, ordered liberty demands that they be realized within the rule of law and its concrete legal framework. Moreover, these principles are both apprehended by the head and entwined about the human heart.

A year after the Peoria Address, in 1855, in what would surely be considered blasphemous to an "unreflective patriot," Lincoln denounced the hypocrisy of Fourth of July celebrations in view of the newfound militancy of slavery extension. The failure of Henry Clay to achieve gradual emancipation in Kentucky, along with "a thousand other signs," convinced Lincoln that the nation was "off track." In a private letter, on the most patriotic occasion of the year, Lincoln indicted his country for its moral failures in characteristically republican terms: "On the question of liberty, as a principle, we are not what we have been. When we were the political slaves of King George, and wanted to be free, we called the maxim that 'all men are created equal' a self evident truth; but now when we have grown fat, and have lost all dread of being slaves ourselves, we have become so greedy to be *masters* that we call the same maxim 'a self-evident lie.' The fourth of July has not quite dwindled away; it is still a great day—*for burning fire-crackers!!!*"[68] Thus, like Frederick Douglass, Lincoln inveighed against the hollowness of America's pretensions to freedom in the face of slavery.[69] As with his dissent during the Mexican War, Lincoln's reflective patriotism calls for critical engagement and even denunciation when the nation betrays itself.

Nativism was yet another threat to the moral credibility of the Union and therefore a cause of concern to patriotic lovers of liberty like Lincoln. In a letter to Joshua Speed in 1855, Lincoln repudiated the nativist Know-Nothing Party, rhetorically claiming that if it ever took power, he would rather live in Russia, where the principle of "despotism can be taken pure . . . without the base alloy of hypocrisy":

> I am not a Know-Nothing. That is certain. How could I be? How can any one who abhors the oppression of negroes, be in favor of degrading classes of white people? Our progress in degeneracy appears to me to be pretty rapid. As a nation, we began by declaring that "*all men are created equal.*" We now practically read it "all men are created equal, *except negroes.*" When the Know-Nothings get control, it will read "all men are created equal, except negroes, *and foreigners, and catholics.*" When it comes to this I should prefer emigrating to some country where they make no pretence of loving liberty—to Russia, for instance, where despotism can be taken pure, and without the base alloy of hypocracy [*sic*].[70]

Lincoln's opposition to the chauvinism of nativism is illustrated by the following poignant story. A leader of the Know-Nothing American party, Richard H. Ballinger, stopped by Lincoln's office and asked him if he would consent to being on the nativist ticket for state assembly. Lincoln declined, saying that, "he was not in sentiment with this new party." He then pointed to the irony of the Know-Nothings' pretentions in claiming to be native by noting America's unjust treatment of indigenous peoples—the real Native Americans. "Do [the real native Americans]," he rhetorically asked, "not wear breech-clout and carry the tomahawk? We pushed them from their homes and now turn upon others not fortunate enough to come over as early as our forefathers. Gentlemen of the committee your party is wrong in principle." Lincoln ended his scolding by using humor to convey a moral message about national chauvinism: "When this Know-nothing party first came up, I had an Irishman, Patrick by name, hoeing in my garden. One morning I was there with him, and he said, 'Mr. Lincoln, what about the Know nothings?' I explained that they would possibly carry a few elections and disappear and I asked Pat why he was not born in this country. 'Faith, Mr. Lincoln,' he replied, 'I wanted to be, but my mother wouldn't let me.'"[71]

An appreciation of America's moral failures, however, did not blind Lincoln to its promise and progress. In a speech in Chicago in 1858, around the time of the Fourth of July, Lincoln provided a compelling vision of the unity that underlies American pluralism and its "melting pot." In this speech, he borrowed a biblical metaphor from Saint Paul to convey the potential harmony between national unity and diversity. Just as Paul in 1 Corinthians 12 spoke of church members with diverse spiritual gifts who are made one in spirit to serve the larger spiritual community through the mystical body of Christ, so in America diverse ethnic, racial, and religious groups are united by a common devotion to the principles of the Declaration and its moral promise. Though American immigrants cannot trace their ancestry back to the glory of the Revolution, they nonetheless can claim that equality is their birthright. This equality, Lincoln proclaims, is "the father of all moral principle in them, and . . . they have a right to claim it as though they were blood of the blood, and flesh of the flesh of the men who wrote that Declaration, and so they are. That is the electric cord in that Declaration that links the hearts of patriotic and liberty-loving men together, that will link those patriotic hearts as long as the love of freedom exists in the minds of men throughout the world."[72]

Unlike nationalism, which is exclusive, Lincoln's vision of the Union was inclusive.[73] Membership in the American Union was political. Regardless of race, creed, or color, Lincoln extended the principle of equality to include national citizenship for former slaves and immigrants.[74] The many in our national motto, *e pluribus unum,* are not abolished into a forced unison, but harmonized through their dedication to the shared political faith in the Declaration. This faith, as I have shown elsewhere, constitutes the minimal core convictions that make possible a shared public life in a pluralistic society.

As we have seen, the love of liberty is a recurrent theme of Lincoln's reflective patriotism. The maintenance of American liberty depends upon generously extending freedom to others. Lincoln thus asks, "What constitutes the bulwark of our own liberty and independence. . . . Our reliance is in the *love of liberty* which God has planted in our bosoms. Our defense is in the preservation of the spirit which prizes liberty as the heritage of all men, in all lands, every where. Destroy this spirit, and you have planted the seeds of despotism around your own doors."[75] In *Notes on the State of Virginia,* Jefferson famously warned not only of Divine Judgment over slavery, but also its corrosive effect on the slaves' "*amor patriae*" and the formation of habits that are inimical to liberty.[76] As with his eulogy to Clay, Lincoln's statement above reaffirms that national greatness is measured not in terms of the regime's military prowess, but in terms of its love of liberty and willingness to sacrifice for it.

Lincoln's reflective patriotism, defined as the ordered love of liberty, would be tested by the grave crisis of disunion. The preservation of the Union and its promise of liberty to all would depend upon his success in articulating a patriotic vision that could unite and mobilize preservation of the Union and its principles. Lincoln's Speech at Trenton on February 21, 1861, is exemplary in combining the various aspects of his reflective patriotism—devotion to abstract principles, reverence for the Founders, republican love of ordered liberty, and a belief in Providence under God.

At Trenton, Lincoln appealed to the principles of the Revolution as the moral foundation of the Union: "I am exceedingly anxious that the thing which they [Founders] struggled for; that something even more than National Independence; that something that held out a great promise to all the people of the world to all time to come: I am exceedingly anxious that this Union, the Constitution, and the liberties of the people shall be perpetuated in accordance for which that struggle was made."[77]

In addition, Lincoln appealed to the concrete places, people, and history who have struggled to sustain liberty for others. Accordingly, in the same speech, he invokes the common memories of George Washington and the Revolution as sources of fraternal affection that bind patriotic hearts. "May I be pardoned," he asks,

> if, upon this occasion, I mention that away back in my childhood, the earliest days of my being able to read, I got hold of a small book, such a one as few of the younger members have ever seen, "Weem's Life of Washington." I remember all the accounts there given of the battle fields and struggles for the liberties of the country, and none fixed themselves upon my imagination so deeply as the struggle here at Trenton, New-Jersey. The crossing of the river; the contest with the Hessians; the great hardships endured at that time, all fixed themselves on my memory more than any single revolutionary event; and you all know, for you have all been boys, how these early impressions last longer than any others. I recollect thinking then, boy even though I was, that there must have been something more than common that those men struggled for. I am exceedingly anxious [regarding] that thing which they struggled for; that something even more than National Independence; that something that held out a great promise to all the people of the world to all time to come.[78]

Consonant with the Three R's (reason, revelation, and republicanism) of his political faith, Lincoln's reflective patriotism is further informed by a biblical faith, the Puritan legacy of a divine calling under God's Providence. In the same speech, he regards himself as a "humble instrument" called to serve the purposes of the Almighty and the American people: "I shall be most happy indeed if I shall be an humble instrument in the hands of the Almighty, and of this, his almost chosen people, for perpetuating the object of that great struggle."[79] In referring to the Americans as an "almost chosen people," Lincoln acknowledges that his country must serve a higher moral obligation while, at the same time, consciously guarding against national pride that self-righteously equates the perfection of the heavenly city with any earthly city.

A day later at Independence Hall, Lincoln characteristically appealed to "the wisdom, the patriotism, the devotion to principle, from which sprang the institutions under which we live."[80] Once again, consistent with what we have seen, the word *wisdom* precedes *patriotism* in this speech. The Speech at Independence Hall also contains one of the most powerful articulations of the American Dream. Lincoln states: "I have often inquired of myself, what great principle or idea it was that kept this confederacy so long together. It was not the mere matter of the separation of the colonies from the mother land; but something in that Declaration giving liberty not alone to the people of this country, but hope to the world for all future time. It was that which gave promise that in due time the weights should be lifted from the shoulders of all men, and that *all* should have an equal chance."[81]

Not surprisingly, then, the reflective patriotism in Lincoln's First Inaugural on March 4, 1861, is further consistent with his earlier tendency to connect intelligence and patriotism. Thus, on the eve of the Civil War, Lincoln appealed to "Intelligence, patriotism and Christianity"[82] as the common social bonds and traditions that unite the country.

Lincoln regarded the South's inordinate sectional pride as unreasonable, unlawful, and unjust. Secession in defense of slavery broke the fraternal bonds of union, thereby jeopardizing the American experiment in ordered liberty. Indeed, Lincoln viewed secession as a kind of infidelity. He went so far as to describe it as the very essence of anarchy. In his Message to Congress in Special Session, on July 4, 1861, he once again invoked Washington's legacy by appealing to "the patriotic instinct of the plain people. They understand, without an argument, that destroying the government, which was made by Washington, means no good to them."[83] Though Lincoln articulated careful arguments against the sophistry of secession, once shots were fired, he also appealed to the plain patriotic instinct of the people, hoping that they would recognize that taking arms up against their government was wrong. Tragically, neither arguments nor an appeal to patriotic instinct persuaded the South to refrain from breaking the fraternal bonds of union. In the South, the combined forces of economic interest, tribal loyalties, and sectional pride turned a blind eye to Lincoln's reflective patriotism.

In the North, however, Lincoln would continue to appeal to a reflective patriotism to maintain the Union war coalition. Though an analysis of these later speeches is beyond the scope of this essay, I believe I have sufficiently demonstrated the meaning of Lincoln's reflective patriotism as an ordered love of liberty governed by wisdom and law, and enjoyed in solidarity with others.

While not incompatible with either reason or a broader concern for humanity, unlike cosmopolitanism, Lincoln's reflective patriotism appreciates our limits and duties as citizens who are encumbered within a particular time and place. It recognizes that the love of one's own is not only natural, but it may also be reasonable, honorable, and just. And that gratitude and care of our own inspires us to serve a greater good than our own self-interest. The abstract love of humanity implicit to cosmopolitan belief is a seductive yet illusory charm that disengages citizens from fulfilling their duties to fellow citizens and from loving concretely their neighbors. Cato may have loved humanity, but he sacrificed his life for Rome and died as a Roman.

This reflective patriotism combines the best elements of American conservatism and liberalism. It is conservative in looking back to preserve what is best in America, and it is liberal in looking forward to change what is wrong with it. Unlike President Obama, who invokes him as a role model, Lincoln never referred to himself as a "citizen of the world." Furthermore, our contemporary motto "think globally and act locally" omits the key object of his statesmanship: devotion to the Union, to our country. One of the defining features of our culture of narcissism is an utter lack of gratitude for the sacrifices and service of others.

In sum, Lincoln's reflective patriotism appreciates both the success and the failures of the American experiment. It invites national self-examination and critical reflection upon the first principles of our "ancient faith." It entails a sober, humble love of country that checks some of the triumphalist impulses of American exceptionalism. That is to say, it self-consciously guards against the temptation to regard "the city on the hill" as something that has already been realized in its moral purity here on earth rather than as a normative standard that is to be constantly approximated but never fully reached, given the limits of human nature. Thus Lincoln ironically referred to Americans as God's "almost chosen people," and contrary to the self-righteous assertion of the North's victory in the Civil War, he humbly observed in his Second Inaugural Address that the prayers of neither side could be answered fully.

At the same time, Lincoln's reflective patriotism may also be viewed as an antidote to self-loathing politically correct and deconstructionist accounts of American history that see only what is destructive and despicable in our past. It defends the rule of law as the best means to preserve the principles of the ancient faith and the legacy of those who sought to realize ordered liberty for others at home and abroad.

I conclude with a timeless appeal to patriotism from the end of Lincoln's First Inaugural Address, an appeal that every generation of Americans would do well to ponder in times of national strife: "I am loth to close. We are not enemies, but friends. We must not be enemies. Though passion may have strained, it must not break our bonds of affection. The mystic chords of memory, stretching from every battle-field, and patriot grave, to every living heart and hearthstone, all over this broad land, will yet swell the chorus of the Union, when again touched, as surely they will be, by the better angels of our nature."[84]

The song of those better angels will be forever heard by reflective patriots who must continue to strive to make our Union worth preserving.

Notes

Portions of this essay appeared in *Perspectives on Political Science* 39, no. 2 (April–June 2010): 108–17.

1. Alexis de Tocqueville, *Democracy in America,* ed. and trans. Harvey C. Mansfield and Delba Winthrop (Chicago: Univ. of Chicago Press, 2000), 585.

2. Tocqueville, 226, 2. Notably, in regard to the title of this essay, Tocqueville contrasted the "unreflective" and "instinctive patriotism of the monarchy" to the "reflective patriotism of the republic."

3. Patrick J. Deneen, "Patriotic Vision: At Home in a World Made Strange," *Intercollegiate Review* 37, no. 2 (Spring 2002): 33–40. Also see Alasdair MacIntyre, "Is Patriotism a Virtue?" in *Political Thought,* ed. Michael Rosen and Jonathan Wolff (Oxford: Oxford Univ. Press, 1999), 269–84.

4. Martha C. Nussbaum, *For Love of Country: Debating the Limits of Patriotism* (Boston: Beacon Press, 1996), 4.

5. George Kateb, *Patriotism and Other Mistakes* (New Haven, CT: Yale Univ. Press, 2006), 3.

6. Steven Johnston, *The Truth about Patriotism* (Durham, NC: Duke Univ. Press, 2007), 13.

7. Nussbaum, 15.

8. Eric Voegelin's diagnosis is noteworthy: "Of the profusion of Gnostic experiences and symbolic expressions, one feature may be singled out as the central element in the varied and extensive creation of meaning: the experience of the world as an alien place into which man has strayed and from which he must find his way back home to the other world of his origin." Eric Voegelin, *Science Politics and Gnosticism* (Washington, DC: Regnery, 1997), 7.

9. See Benjamin R. Barber's defense of civic education in his reply to Nussbaum in "Constitutional Faith," in *For Love of Country,* ed. Martha Nussbaum (Boston: Beacon Press, 1996), 30–37. Also see Barber's reply to Allan Bloom's *Closing of the American Mind* in *An Aristocracy for Everyone* (Oxford: Oxford Univ. Press, 1994).

10. Though I borrow the term *reflective patriotism* from Tocqueville, my use of the term is not identical with his. An exploration of the similarities and differences between Tocqueville's reflective patriotism in *Democracy and America* and my interpretation of Lincoln's reflective patriotism is beyond the scope of this essay, which focuses upon Abraham Lincoln, not Tocqueville.

11. George McKenna, *The Puritan Origins of American Patriotism* (New Haven, CT: Yale Univ. Press, 2007), 8.

12. Ibid. The original quote can be found in Wilfred M. McClay, "The Soul of a Nation," *Public Interest* 155 (Spring 2004): 5.

13. Abraham Lincoln, *The Collected Works of Abraham Lincoln,* ed. Roy P. Basler, 8 vols. (New Brunswick, NJ: Rutgers Univ. Press. 1953–1955) (hereinafter *CW*), 4:271.

14. See McKenna. Also see Mark A. Noll, *America's God: From Jonathan Edwards to Abraham Lincoln* (New York: Oxford Univ. Press, 2002), 32.

15. Joseph R. Fornieri, *Abraham Lincoln's Political Faith* (De Kalb: Northern Illinois Univ. Press, 2003).

16. *CW,* 4:271.

17. See Liah Greenfield, *Nationalism: Five Roads to Modernity* (Cambridge, MA: Harvard Univ. Press, 1992).

18. Maurizio Viroli, *For Love of Country: An Essay on Patriotism and Nationalism* (Oxford: Clarendon Press, 1995).

19. Viroli, 27.

20. Viroli, 19.

21. Viroli, 19–24.

22. Viroli states: "The language of patriotism has been used over the centuries to strengthen or invoke love of the political institutions and the way of life that sustain the common liberty of a people, that is love of the republic; the

language of nationalism was forged in late eighteenth-century Europe to defend or reinforce the cultural, linguistic, and ethnic oneness and homogeneity of a people. Whereas the enemies of republican patriotism are tyranny, despotism, oppression, and corruption, the enemies of nationalism are cultural contamination, heterogeneity, racial impurity, and social, political, and intellectual disunion." Viroli, 1–2.

23. Viroli, 24–25, 124. According to Viroli, the "love of *patria*—which is the basis of political virtue (*Politicam virtutem*) is a rational love because it is a love for a good (the free city) that is rational for each citizen to want to preserve" (124).

24. Quoted in Viroli, 21–22.

25. Charles de Secondat, baron de Montesquieu, *The Spirit of the Laws*, ed. and trans. Anne M. Cohler, Basia Carolyn Miller, and Harold Samuel Stone (Cambridge: Cambridge Univ. Press), 42–43.

26. Viroli, 154.

27. Giuseppe Mazzini, *The Duties of Man and Other Essays* (Stilwell, KS: Digireads.com, 2007), 53.

28. Viroli, 152; Mazzini, 41–50.

29. Garry Wills, *Lincoln at Gettysburg: The Words That Remade America* (New York: Simon and Schuster, 1992), 41–42, 46, 49, 52, 56, 57, 65; Mason Locke Weems, *The Life of Washington* (New York: M. E. Sharpe, 1996).

30. See Joseph R. Fornieri, "The Lyceum and Farewell Addresses: Parallel Covenants of Republicanism," in *White House Studies*, vol. 5, *Special Issue: The Great Presidential Triumvirate at Home and Abroad*, ed. William D. Pederson and Frank J. Williams (New York: Nova Science, 2006).

31. George Washington's Farewell Address, in *The Evolving Presidency*, 3rd ed., ed. Michael Nelson (Washington, DC: CQ Press, 2008), 42–46.

32. *CW*, 2:126.

33. Joshua Wolf Shenk, *Lincoln's Melancholy: How Depression Challenged a President and Fueled His Greatness* (Boston: Houghton Mifflin, 2005); David Herbert Donald, *Lincoln* (New York: Simon and Schuster, 1995); Edmund Wilson, *Patriotic Gore: Studies in the Literature of the American Civil War* (New York: Oxford Univ. Press, 1962), 108; George B. Forgie, "Lincoln's Tyrants," in *The Historian's Lincoln: Pseudohistory, Psychohistory, and History*, ed. Gabor S. Boritt and Norman Forness (Urbana: Univ. of Illinois Press, 1988), 296; Dwight G. Anderson, *Abraham Lincoln: The Quest for Immortality* (New York: Alfred A. Knopf, 1982).

34. Michael Burlingame, *Abraham Lincoln: A Life* (Baltimore: Johns Hopkins Univ. Press, 2008), 1:358.

35. *CW*, 1:114.

36. *CW*, 1:114.

37. *CW*, 1:108.

38. *CW*, 1:112.

39. *CW*, 1:112.
40. *CW*, 1:115.
41. *CW*, 1:246.
42. *CW*, 2:89.
43. Bruce P. Frohnen, "The Patriotism of a Conservative," *Modern Age* 48, no. 2 (Spring 2006): 105–18.
44. *CW*, 1:439.
45. Burlingame, 526–27.
46. For Douglas and Young America, see Stewart Winger, *Lincoln, Religion, and Romantic Cultural Politics* (De Kalb: Northern Illinois Univ. Press, 2003), 18–29, 43–44.
47. Harry V. Jaffa, *Crisis of the House Divided* (Chicago: Univ. of Chicago Press, 1984).
48. *CW*, 2:115.
49. *CW*, 2:116.
50. *CW*, 2:116, 115.
51. John Winthrop, *The Journal of John Winthrop, 1630–1649: Abridged Edition* (Cambridge, MA: Belknap Press of Harvard Univ. Press, 1997), 2.
52. *CW*, 3:29.
53. *CW*, 2:126.
54. *CW*, 2:127.
55. *CW*, 2:126.
56. Chantal Delsol, *Unjust Justice: Against the Tyranny of International Law* (Wilmington, DE: ISI Books, 2004); Pierre Manent, *Democracy without Nations? The Fate of Self-Government in Europe* (Wilmington, DE: ISI Books, 2007).
57. *CW*, 3:14.
58. *CW*, 2:251.
59. *CW*, 2:251–52.
60. *CW*, 2:273–74.
61. *CW*, 2:266.
62. *CW*, 2:276, emphasis added.
63. Walter Berns, *Making Patriots* (Chicago: Univ. of Chicago Press, 2001).
64. Walter Berns, "Comments," *This World* 6 (Fall 1983): 98. See the debate between Pangle and Jaffa in "Patriotism American Style," by Thomas L. Pangle, and "Our Ancient Faith: A Reply to Thomas Pangle," by Harry V. Jaffa, both in *National Review*, November 20, 1985, 30–36.
65. Frohnen, 112.
66. James Wilson, *Collected Works of James Wilson* (Indianapolis: Liberty Fund, 2007), 2:509, 521.
67. *CW*, 4:169.
68. *CW*, 2:318.
69. James Oakes, *The Radical and the Republican: Frederick Douglass,*

Abraham Lincoln, and the Triumph of Antislavery Politics (New York: Norton, 2007).

70. CW, 2:323.

71. Burlingame, 375.

72. CW, 2:499–500.

73. Rogan Kersh, *Dreams of a More Perfect Union* (New York: Cornell Univ. Press, 2001).

74. See Herman Belz, *A New Birth of Freedom: The Republican Party and Freedmen's Rights, 1861–1866* (New York: Fordham Univ. Press, 2000), 17–34; and Christian G. Samito, *Becoming American under Fire: Irish Americans, African Americans, and the Politics of Citizenship during the Civil War Era* (New York: Cornell Univ. Press, 2009).

75. CW, 3:95.

76. Thomas Jefferson, *The Life and Selected Writings of Thomas Jefferson,* ed. Adriene Koch and William Peden (New York: Random House, 1993), 257–58.

77. CW, 4:236.

78. CW, 4:235–36.

79. CW, 4:236.

80. CW, 4:240.

81. CW, 4:240.

82. CW, 4:271.

83. CW, 4:439.

84. CW, 4:271.

L. Joseph Hebert Jr.

Tocqueville, Cicero, Augustine, and the Limits of the Polis

The word *cosmopolitan* implies that the world itself can be regarded as a polis or political community and that it is possible for the human being to live as a citizen (*politēs*) of the world. For its proponents, this ideal of universal citizenship is associated with enlightenment and sophistication, the liberation of the heart and mind from parochial prejudice and attachments, which liberation is thought to clear the way for a politics of universal benevolence and the brotherhood of man. Yet this ideal is fraught with tension. If cosmopolitanism requires the transcendence of local ways or their rejection as comprehensive constraints on human life, does it not therefore entail the rejection of ordinary *politēs* as the equals, and therefore as the "brothers," of the world citizen? Must not the cosmopolitan consider himself superior to the place-bound masses? If so, and if this alleged superiority is to contribute to the progress of civilization, does it not become necessary to subordinate each particular political order (*politeia*) to one universal regime (*cosmopoliteia*) ruled by the cosmopolitan himself? Even if all men are potentially cosmopolitan, the realization of this human potential would still require a radical transformation of political orders, and of society as we know it. The horrors perpetrated in furtherance of cosmopolitan ideologies by Lenin, Stalin, and Mao, among others in recent memory, cannot permit us to dismiss this problem lightly.

The same tension is evident even closer to home, in the self-doubts increasingly plaguing the conscience of contemporary liberal democracy. Whether we look to the Declaration of Independence or to the Declaration of the Rights of Man and Citizen, we find that modern liberalism as a practical political project is rooted in the notion that political authority is subordinate to a set of principles that are self-evident and universally binding because they derive from the very nature of humankind. From their earliest stages, the American and French revolutions understood themselves and were regarded by others to be experiments in liberty applicable to all the world. So far were they from being the affairs of isolated political communities, they were in fact nothing less than harbingers of a *novus ordo seclorum*. Little surprise, then, that many whose way of life is threatened by this new order—from the heirs of feudal monarchy to the Islamic extremists of today—have exhibited a mortal hatred of this "experiment" in self-government. While early modern liberals were willing to take on their opponents at all costs, however, latter-day liberals are far less comfortable with the hegemonic implications of their cosmopolitan heritage.[1] Repugnance at the injustices of Western imperialism has fueled the desire not only to tolerate but even to embrace the "other," hostile as that other may be to the principles of liberalism itself.

Moral relativism and multiculturalism would seem to have rendered a confident universalism impossible in the postmodern West. Yet liberalism cannot deny its cosmopolitan origins or destiny. The very discomfort of contemporary liberals with the struggle for empire reflects a belief that all peoples of the world can and must coexist in harmony. Whatever its proximate application may demand, acceptance of the other is intended to promote this mutual accord and must therefore assume that the "other" already accepts, or will one day be brought to accept, the fundamental—cosmopolitan—principles of liberalism. Liberalism is and cannot help being hegemonic, and yet it has become all too painfully aware of the question of how such hegemony could be justified. Rather than hypocritically denying the necessity of imperial ambitions, or thoughtlessly embracing this imperialism as an unmitigated good, contemporary liberalism can best respond to its dilemma by seeking to reflect more profoundly on the reasons underlying its claim to universality as well as on the methods appropriate for advancing this claim and the measure of its prospects for realizing the world order it envisions.

Where must such reflection begin? Although several options present themselves, this essay will focus on what we can learn from the political thought of Alexis de Tocqueville, especially in his master work *Democracy in America*. This point of departure is auspicious for several reasons. Foremost among them is Tocqueville's concern with and consistent attention to the problem of justifying democracy. Although he ultimately accepted the cosmopolitan revolutionary force of modern liberal democracy as both inevitable and in many respects just, and although he even supported instances of liberal imperialism,[2] Tocqueville admits to regarding the advance of democracy with a "religious terror" born of the consciousness that its fundamental tenet—human equality—can be destructive as well as constructive, tyrannical as well as liberating.[3] Tocqueville is keenly aware of the evils democracy threatens to impose as well as the benefits it promises to provide, and he frequently reminds us of the goods being lost as well as the injustices being remedied in the transition to an enlightened liberal democratic order. In the final analysis, Tocqueville is a friend to modern democracy and to that species of cosmopolitanism upon which it is founded, but he is never their flatterer (400).

Another of Tocqueville's virtues—less noted by commentators and less trumpeted by Tocqueville himself—is his profound engagement with the history of political thought. We know of the classical education Tocqueville received and of the stack of great texts he consulted while composing *Democracy*.[4] This essay attempts to contribute to the awareness of just how subtly and crucially Tocqueville addressed the ideas of major political philosophers in his writing—alluding to, building upon, criticizing, and modifying these ideas in the development of his own analysis of modern democracy.[5] Beginning with Tocqueville's misgivings about the cosmopolitan trajectory of modernity, I shall turn to Tocqueville's theory of natural right and the means for its realization in politics. I shall then examine the insights Tocqueville drew from the classical and Christian accounts of cosmopolitanism—represented by Cicero and Saint Augustine, respectively—in light of which he sought to correct, however gently, the modern cosmopolitanism whose dominion he accepted. My study will demonstrate that, in Tocqueville's qualifiedly classical-Christian view, the very thing that justifies cosmopolitanism—human nature, whose universal claims cosmopolitanism seeks to further—also places significant limits on the scope and manner of its influence over human affairs.

Tocqueville and the Limits of Modern Cosmopolitanism

The common basis of classical, Christian, and early modern cosmopolitanism is the concept of human nature, a set of faculties and ends proper to all human beings regardless of temporal and spatial variations in customs, habits, and laws. For Tocqueville, understanding human nature—both in itself and in relation to the variables of political life—is the core task of political science, its actual application to particular circumstances being the job of political art. Although Tocqueville is adamant that the political scientist as such must not deviate from his theoretical mission and become mixed up in partisan political disputes, he also insists that political science can and must set the stage for genuinely artful politics. If practice is to be informed by theory, the gap between universal needs and particular deeds must be bridged, on the part of political science, by clarifying not only the universal demands of human nature, but also the ways in which the peculiar situations of particular political communities promote or impede the realization of those universal claims.[6] It is in this sense that Tocqueville declares, in the introduction to *Democracy in America,* that "a new political science is needed for a world altogether new." The "mother thought" holding together the parts of this master work is therefore nothing less than the defense of humanity and its universal claims—of what we can accurately call "natural right"[7]—in the context of modern democracy (7, 13–14).[8]

At first glance it may seem that Tocqueville regards the circumstances of democracy—by which he means a condition of social equality and not a form of government—as favoring, at long last, the vindication of human nature. Tocqueville's introduction proclaims what his subsequent analysis confirms: the "providential" force with which equality is sweeping over all of Christendom is due to its basis in nature (6 ff). This is not to say that natural inequalities do not exist among men or that they are insignificant. Tocqueville believes that human greatness is possible but rare and that the good of political society requires the leadership of the "natural aristocracy" in its midst, and hence a certain degree of hierarchical order (50). Yet natural aristocracy is not the same as conventional aristocracy, and the political inequalities of old did not consistently reflect natural inequalities, which "Heaven distribute[s] haphazardly" (5). Nothing could be more unnatural, Tocqueville observes, than the rigidity with which feudal Europe sought to separate human beings into classes of perpetual rulers and perpetually ruled (328). Growing recognition of this discrepancy between nature and convention is what rendered the democratic revolution far more than a passing or localized phenomenon and made it instead a permanent and global transformation of political and social life.

In contrast to conventionally aristocratic societies, which falsely treat different classes of men as if they were members of different species, democratic society seems to be founded on a genuine insight into the natural similarity of human beings. This apparent enlightenment makes modern democracy a promising candidate for the realization of the cosmopolitan dream. Tocqueville explores this promise in a chapter of *Democracy* concerning "honor in . . . democratic societies" (589ff.). Honor, in Tocqueville's usage, is "the sum of rules with the aid of which one obtains" the esteem of one's fellows; honor exercises a powerful influence over the will of man even when it conflicts with his beliefs about right and wrong. The basis of honor, in Tocqueville's analysis, is the perception by a social group of its fundamental needs or interests. In "aristocratic times," when men are divided into distinct and seemingly dissimilar communities and classes, the peculiar interests of these insular groups easily overshadow those common interests of humankind that Tocqueville regards as the basis of genuine morality. By contrast, the confusion of classes and leveling of conditions in democratic societies renders the formation of clear and distinct codes of honor next to impossible. In the short term, "the particular needs of the nation" replace caste-based codes of honor in developing democracies; but as nations democratize and draw closer to nature, they too lose much of their distinctness, raising the possibility that "all the peoples of the world should come to the point of having the same interests and the same needs." Were this to happen, "one would cease entirely to attribute conventional value to human actions," and "the general needs of humanity that conscience reveals to each man would be the common measure" (599). The final replacement of political right by natural right would correspond to the achievement of a cosmopolitan social order.

It is important to note that this scenario is hypothetical. Does Tocqueville in fact regard such an achievement as possible or good? Closer attention to the details of the chapter in question raises doubts about both points. The Americans, partly due to their democratic social state, are "unceasingly impelled toward commerce and industry" and have developed a code of honor no less "arbitrary" and "condemnable in the eyes of general reason and the universal conscience of the human race" than were the former honor codes (594). If, per impossible, all the world were to become America, peoples would still be united under conventions far friendlier to avarice than the "moral laws adopted by common humanity" would allow (596). Honor, like dogma (407), seems to be a permanent and necessary feature of human society. Nonetheless, Tocqueville clearly believes that the decline of particular authorities in democratic times will lead to the loss or weakening of detailed and rigid honor codes (598). Since honor is defined by factionalism—placing the needs of a part above the needs of the whole community—this weakening would appear to be unabashedly good, freeing democratic man to act in greater accordance with "the natural order of conscience" (591). Yet this conclusion falsely assumes that the decline of one motivating factor will be met by the rise of another, healthier one. From the beginning of his discussion of democratic mores, however, Tocqueville makes clear that the replacement of political (or conventional) right with natural right as the proximate standard for human action leads to a weakening and distortion of the notion of right in itself (535–45).

Democratic man, regarding all his fellows as similar to himself, easily sympathizes with their sufferings and comes to their aid in small matters. Yet the feudal lord and vassal, regarding one another as members of almost separate species, were far more likely to risk life and limb in fulfilling their mutual duties. Democratic man, by contrast, is less inclined to make great sacrifices for any reason (8, 675, 545). Instead, he is in danger of losing all sense of ambition, becoming wrapped up in his individual affairs, narrowly defined, and sinking into apathy concerning all matters of public or universal concern. This danger—which he simply calls "individualism"—is the central threat against which Tocqueville marshals the forces of his new political science (599–604, 606–17, 643–73). In order to understand this threat, we must consider the complex political psychology informing Tocqueville's analysis of democracy.

Tocqueville's reference to the possible realization of cosmopolitan morality comes in the section of *Democracy* devoted to "mores properly so-called," or "habits of the heart." Far earlier in the work, Tocqueville had expressed the centrality to his thinking of mores (*moeurs*) taken in a broader and more ancient sense, including the habits of the mind as well as of the heart (275). Volume 2 of *Democracy* contains separate parts devoted to the intellectual, sentimental, and moral life of democracies, yet Tocqueville does not believe that these distinct elements of life can or ought to be separated completely. Rather, Tocqueville is at pains in *Democracy* to see and explain the inevitable causal intertwining of thought and passion in human life, as well as to identify the most beneficial ordering of the three: idea, sentiment, and action (compare 10–11). The failure of democratic society, or any other society for that matter, to achieve this ideal ordering—good mores in the broadest and truest sense—explains both the need to treat these elements separately and the impossibility of a simply cosmopolitan (or natural) moral order.

What is the ideal ordering of thoughts, passions, and actions, according to Tocqueville? It is no accident that, in speaking of universal or natural morality, Tocqueville always refers to its basis in reason as well as in humanity. Justice, for Tocqueville, is a "general law" "made or at least adopted" by the "universal society" of the "human race" (240). Since the human race cannot meet to legislate, justice cannot be positive law. Rather, it must be akin to the classical notion of natural law: rooted in the natural good of man and apprehended by practical reason.

Tocqueville accepts the premise of classical natural right that man is fundamentally rational in a particular sense and that human society is essentially "a union of rational and intelligent beings" (227). His articulation of natural right subtly but forcefully defies the modern variant according to which reason is instrumental in the pursuit of material self-interest.

In an empirical sense, Tocqueville considers man rational in that almost all of his actions—and at least some of his strongest sentiments—flow from the "general idea" he forms of the order of the universe (417). This order, to which man is drawn by his intellect, is both informative and prescriptive; it consists in the general idea of God, His relations with the human race, the nature of the human soul, and the duties consequent upon these facts. Human behavior is influenced by beliefs about these subjects, whether those beliefs are true or false, and whether or not particular men are always true to their beliefs (589).

In a normative sense, man is rational for two reasons. First, his soul is degraded by actions that conflict with his beliefs about the moral order (8). Although certain sentiments may tempt a man to act against his conscience, the inner discord he feels upon giving in to such sentiments reveals his own perception of the superiority of intellect to passion in the healthy human soul (520). Second, man is rational in that he longs not only to act in accordance with an opinion about moral order, but actually to grasp the truth about such order. For Tocqueville, the greatness of human sentiments (and hence of their expression in word or deed) is measured by the greatness of the objects to which they correspond—not merely by the perceived greatness of those objects (456). In fact, the greatest of all sentiments is nothing but the sublime desire for truth (435). Virtue, or the natural greatness of man, is characterized by a liberality or independence of mind rooted in the love of truth, not in the dictates of passion or will (247). In sum, Tocqueville holds that human sentiments and actions ought to be ruled by reason and that reason ought to seek out and apply to action the "admirable order of all things" (273, 505).

The influence of moral order on human behavior demonstrates the deep confluence between the "is" and the "ought" in human affairs. Yet the actual condition of political societies reveals a morally distressing gap between the two. Two primary factors intervene to prevent most human beings from achieving virtue as Tocqueville describes it. First comes egoism or the passion for narrow self-interest that so frequently colors not only the actions, but even the opinions, of men (273). Next, and perhaps more fatally, comes the disinclination or inability of most human beings to engage in the philosophic pursuit of the truth about the order of things. Tocqueville stresses the weakness of human reason and the difficulty in formulating general notions about the most important things—"God and human nature"—that do not distort their objects. Through the "slow, detailed, conscientious work of the intelligence," significant knowledge on such subjects is attainable, and Tocqueville's confidence in the tenets of his own political science attests to his own efforts in this direction. Yet humanity as a whole is unwilling to make or incapable of making such efforts, leaving human societies vulnerable to "very superficial and very uncertain notions" about these indispensible matters (411–15, 417–19).

From the perspective of the moralist or the virtue-seeking political scientist, a paradox emerges. Considered in themselves, reason is good and is the ground of human excellence, while irrational passions and prejudices are degrading to humanity. Practically speaking, however, man's rational nature is commonly expressed in gross simplifications about the nature of things. In "aristocratic times," the ubiquity of hierarchy and distinction habituate the mind to discover inequality and dissimilarity even where equality and similarity exist; in "democratic times," the mind is tempted to regard even natural and beneficial inequalities as offenses against justice and to demand equality even where it is ruinous to the greatness and happiness of humankind (420–28, 469–72). The statesman or practitioner of the genuine political art must recognize these errors for what they are and attempt to steer particular political communities closer to those virtues defined by the true nature of humanity (518). Yet, given the aversion of citizens to the rigorous philosophic examination of nature, naked appeals to reason are unlikely to succeed at correcting society's course (613). In fact, the false identification of reason with faulty general ideas may render some appeals to reason counterproductive. The art of the legislator therefore requires leaders to guide citizens closer to the demands of reason by appealing to other, nonrational and even otherwise irrational motives and experiences, to the extent that such means are capable of moderating the intellectual errors besetting a given society (502–3). In other words, political science reveals that natural right must be pursued by means of political (or conventional) right, however imperfectly suited it may be to the task.[9]

This paradox of politics helps to explain both the problem of individualism as Tocqueville defines it in *Democracy* and the solutions he proposes to it. Left to itself, the democratic idea of and passion for equality will exacerbate the natural egoism of man by convincing citizens that no one has either the ability or the right to surpass the crowd in knowledge, influence, or any other characteristic of virtue. The opinions, feelings, and habits of men will conspire to make them turn in on themselves and become absorbed in private life, abandoning all concern with philosophy, religion, and politics to mass opinion and its manipulative representatives, especially the state. Although each citizen will retain and even guard with jealousy a preference for his own professional knowledge and private needs and tastes, none will dare to assert or even to entertain ideas or feelings in matters of universal concern that are truly their own; to do so would be against the general idea of equality, and hence intolerable. The final result of such "reasoning" will be the erection of a vast administrative order subjecting men to its mild and benevolent but enervating rules rather than fitting these rules to men—an order designed to suppress the natural greatness of man in the name of a superficial and degraded notion of "natural" right (479–84, 599–617, 640–73).

What can prevent such a despotism from forming? Although Tocqueville believes this nightmarish outcome to be contrary to nature well understood, he regards it nonetheless as the natural result of democracy's natural inability to grasp the whole truth about nature. His conclusion is explicit: in democratic times, as in all others, nature must be defended by artifice (645). More specifically, those who see natural right well must counteract the general misapprehension of nature by promoting those habits, opinions, and points of honor that cut against the errors of the age, whether or not they are per se reasonable (518).

Although there are countless examples of such statesmanship in *Democracy*, two features of Tocqueville's strategy for regulating democracy stand out: local government and the Christian religion. Both are features of the New England township, whose blending of the spirit of liberty and the spirit of religion Tocqueville calls the key to his own work (27–44). Both are elaborated at length and celebrated throughout his book. Succinctly put, participation in local government counteracts individualism by providing citizens with concrete experiences of the necessity and goodness of public-spiritedness and social cooperation (415–16, 485–500); and Christianity checks administrative despotism by connecting citizens, through their regular worship, with an order of things neither wholly egalitarian nor tolerant of a state that would seek to remake man in its own image (275–82, 517–21). Whatever may be true of the philosopher or the statesman, Tocqueville maintains that the average citizen will come far closer to virtue through the experience of self-government and the doctrines of faith than through the power of abstract reason alone.

Tocqueville is well aware of the dangers of local prejudice and religious intolerance, but he disappoints the simplistic hopes of modern cosmopolitanism by insisting that true enlightenment recognizes the permanent need for political and religious institutions that foster the natural potential of humanity even while they divide humanity into distinct communities.

Cicero and the Limits of Classical Cosmopolitanism

Some have faulted Tocqueville for defending liberal democracy American-style while ignoring the Declaration of Independence and indeed the entire doctrine of natural rights.[10] Others have regarded Tocqueville's frequent appeals to the quasi-classical notion of virtue as incomplete without an accompanying discussion of the best regime.[11] Both points suggest something important about Tocqueville's thought, but neither observation is sufficient without a careful exploration of Tocqueville's reasons for proceeding as he does.

Tocqueville's ambivalence toward the language of natural rights is explicable on the basis of our previous inquiries. In democratic times, appeals to nature will be taken for appeals to equality. Although there is a species of equality consistent with human greatness, there is also a depraved form of equality that would level all natural differences among men—and it is toward this latter equality that democratic man is naturally inclined (52, 479–82, 640). Tocqueville is therefore careful to separate the language of rights from that of equality or nature and to stress instead the connection of rights to virtue and the practical experiences of political life (227–29).

In lieu of the Declaration's appeal to "life, liberty, and the pursuit of happiness," Tocqueville quotes John Winthrop's "beautiful definition of [genuine] liberty" as the "holy liberty" "to do without fear," and in union with proper authority, "all that is just and good" (42).

The grounds of Tocqueville's reticence toward classical political thought become most evident in a close reading of the second chapter of *Democracy,* the one Tocqueville calls the key to his work and the one dealing with the allegedly Puritan foundations of American political order (27–44). Tocqueville's second chapter concerns the "point of departure" for American democracy—and, it turns out, for his book as well. It opens with the argument that virtue and vice develop in the human being from the youngest age. Both Tocqueville's focus on virtue and his substantive claim about its "point of departure" are in line with the teachings of classical thinkers.[12] Yet Tocqueville has introduced individual virtue or its lack as an analogy for the character of nations. His closing remark, then, must be applied to America: "The man"—or the nation—"is so to speak whole in the swaddling clothes of his [or its] cradle" (28). Here the allusion to classical political philosophy is explicit, and it connects Tocqueville with that major theme of classical thought he apparently ignores: the best regime.

In Cicero's *De Re Publica,* the philosophic statesman Scipio is asked to give his opinion on the best regime. On the premise that Rome embodies this notion, he gives an account of its foundation by the legendary Romulus, concluding with the remark that, "by the wisdom of a single man, a new people was not simply brought into being and then left like an infant crying in its cradle, but was left already full-grown and almost in the maturity of manhood." Scipio's interlocutor, the philosophic statesman Laelius, responds by noting that Scipio has adopted a new mode of discourse, one not employed by the Greeks. Whereas Socrates discussed a best regime existing only in speech, and his successors discussed the types and principles of political society without extensive examples, Scipio presents his own ideas about politics while giving credit for them to others. Through Scipio, Cicero himself refers principally to what those like Romulus did by chance or necessity and confines himself to the discussion of one regime: republican Rome. He thereby imports the Greek philosophic tradition in a rhetorical guise best designed to assure its acceptance in and applicability to the Roman world.[13]

Later in *Democracy,* Tocqueville argues that the careful study of Greek and Roman literature is essential to the formation of virtuous democratic leaders. Ancient texts are a "salutary diet" sorely needed to correct the errors of the modern age, and yet their virtues are inapplicable to modern times without the prudent translation of those who have mastered them (450–52). By alluding to Cicero so early in his book,[14] Tocqueville presents those who are already careful readers of classical texts, and who are also willing to be careful readers of his, with a lesson in how to apply classical concepts to modern democracy. Just as Cicero embraced the Greek notion of the best regime while adapting it to the context of republican Rome, Tocqueville is adapting a classical teaching to changing circumstances. And just as Cicero felt obliged to communicate his principles through the words and examples of others, Tocqueville uses America—and especially the words and deeds of its early New England men—as a vehicle for his political teaching. A complete account of Tocqueville's thought must therefore examine not only the coherent philosophy informing his analysis of modern democracy but also the way in which it carries forward and adapts the political thought of his predecessors.

Tocqueville's debt to classical political thought is signaled by his elevation of virtue over rights (227),[15] his allusion to Cicero's *De Re Publica,* and his celebration of the New England township for exhibiting "a real, active, altogether democratic and republican political life" "as in [ancient] Athens" (40).[16] Aside from the comments mentioned above, however, Tocqueville never explicitly stresses the importance of classical thought. In part this is explained by the width of the gulf between the ancient and the modern political states: what the ancients called democracy, Tocqueville points out, would more aptly be called a large aristocracy by modern standards (450ff.). Yet Tocqueville takes his ambivalence toward the ancients much further, at least in one passage. In his only explicit reference to Cicero, Tocqueville denounces the classical philosopher and orator for feeling keen sorrow over the fate of a Roman citizen crucified, while remaining indifferent to the lot of those over whom the Romans triumphed. "It is evident," Tocqueville claims, "that in his eyes a foreigner is not of the same human species as a Roman" (539). This failure of the heart seems rooted in a failure of the intellect: earlier, Tocqueville had accused "the most profound geniuses of Rome and Greece" of failing to grasp the general but simple idea "of the similarity of men and of the equal right to liberty that each bears from birth"—an idea self-evident to Tocqueville's modern audience (413).

As with his allusion to *De Re Publica,* Tocqueville's accusation of Cicero and his ancient ilk proves far more meaningful to those who have studied the latter. One cannot help noticing that Cicero, in his political-philosophic writings, articulates a doctrine of natural law according to which all human beings share equally in a universal community of rational beings.[17] Neither the similarity of human beings as such, nor the moral duties consequent to it, can be said to have escaped the ancients in general or Cicero in particular—as Tocqueville was certainly aware. Furthermore, the evidence Tocqueville cites against Cicero—that he felt more for Roman than for foreign sufferings—is taken from the latter's forensic oratory.[18] As a lawyer and an accomplished student of classical rhetoric, Tocqueville knew that the orator must adapt his speech to the inclinations of his audience. In a Roman court, for instance, one must appeal both to the legal concept of citizenship and to the sentiments fellow citizens are likely to have for one another. In fact, Tocqueville might be accused in these passages of appealing to the prejudice of moderns—who believe themselves, without reflection, to be wiser than ancients—to denigrate the intellectual status of classical authors, who had at least an equal grasp of the point in question: the universality of human nature and the consequent moral dignity of man.

Tocqueville's point would be better taken had it less to do with what the ancients were capable of *knowing* and more to do with what they were capable of *applying* in practice. This reading is confirmed by Tocqueville's own elaboration on the way moderns have come to recognize the truth of human equality: "it was necessary," he claims, "that Jesus Christ come to earth to *make it understood* that all members of the human species are naturally alike and equal" (413, emphasis added). Although both classical and modern philosophy knew and argued for a morality based on universal human nature, Tocqueville credits neither with making this doctrine accepted by the bulk of humankind. It was not the philosophic self-examination of humanity, nor even the propaganda of enlightenment *philosophes*, but rather the Christian dogma of the adoption of humanity by an incarnate God, that led to the enlightenment of man on this point. Reflection on this fact will shed light on Tocqueville's reasons for keeping his rhetorical distance from, while utilizing the insights of, classical political thought, and placing more stress upon the need to retain explicitly Christian elements of cosmopolitanism.

Tocqueville's position is best understood in light of the internal development of political thought as its various proponents encountered the problem of applying its universalist or cosmopolitan insights to the realm of particular politics. The classical doctrine to which Tocqueville alludes through Cicero began with Plato's Socrates. In Plato's *Republic* (*Politeia*), Socrates explores the connection between human nature, human excellence, and political order. He argues that reason is the sovereign part of man and that the life devoted to reason—the philosophic life—constitutes the perfection of man's nature. Although Socrates uses an imaginary regime of perfect justice to aid in the understanding of individual virtue, it turns out that the city, even in theory, is incapable of achieving the unified devotion to truth characteristic of philosophic excellence. Hence, in an ironic twist, the philosopher has to be compelled to rule a city that has to be compelled to obey him.[19] One is left with the impression that the virtue available to man by nature is to be pursued by extraordinary individuals, whose ability to elevate the life of the communities of which they form a part will be limited at best.[20]

Based on a similar understanding of nature, Plato's student Aristotle attempts to fashion a political science capable of further enriching political practice. In his *Ethics,* Aristotle demonstrates that the sovereignty of reason—and hence genuine human excellence—can find expression in the practice of those moral and intellectual virtues demanded by social and political activity. In his *Politics,* he goes so far as to define man as a political animal, one who naturally finds his fulfillment through active partnership in a community defined by rational deliberation about just and unjust actions. Other than the rare philosopher, who achieves a divine happiness through almost self-sufficient contemplation, human beings as such ought to seek fulfillment in a political life suffused with opportunities to perfect their rational nature.[21]

The extent to which men can be persuaded to seek perfection in this manner, however, is another question. In both of his political works, Aristotle makes clear that universal human nature is the standard of virtue and justice. Yet in both works he also notes the implacable tendency of actual political regimes to distort the notions of justice and human worth in order to accommodate their own partial perspectives and partisan agendas. The obvious response would be to assert natural law against conventional error, and Aristotle admits the inherent legitimacy of this move (1129b).[22] Yet he quickly retreats from it, protesting that nature itself is changeable (1134b) and gearing his political science mostly toward mitigating the errors of dominant political factions, rather than constructing a regime devoted to genuine virtue (1279b–1288a).

It seems that natural right can never truly become natural law because law, consisting as it does in generalities, cannot do without authorities capable of applying it to particular circumstances (1137b, 1286a–1288a). The general truths available to our reason by nature will never find expression absent a concrete political-social authority, and yet no actual authority is willing or able to enforce nature with accuracy and constancy. The Aristotelian statesman will certainly seek to improve his society by the light of natural right, and Aristotle does call for a new educational system and hence for a potentially promising intellectual revolution among political society's leaders (1337a–1342b). Yet it remains unclear at best how explicit and forceful his project to mitigate the factionalism and elevate the universal goods of political life can ever become.

As a professed admirer of both Plato and Aristotle, Cicero inherits this problem of the weakness of reason.[23] As a Roman statesman, he inherits a particular form of this problem. For Aristotle, political particularity contained both a threat and a promise. If the ways of the polis cut citizens off from the rest of humanity, the concrete experiences of self-government nonetheless provided opportunities for the cultivation of humane virtues, under the guidance of wise statesmen.[24] By Cicero's day, the classical polis had been swallowed up by its own outward success: Rome, the greatest city, held sway over the civilized world. Empire had brought the city, in its particularity, face to face with the existence of the universal human community. The question under these circumstances was not whether the polis could be brought to consider such universality, but what notions it would draw upon in doing so.

The task of the philosophic statesman, for Cicero as for his predecessors, is twofold: to seek the truth about human nature dialectically and to convey this truth to particular political communities through a suitable rhetoric. Such rhetoric is necessary because philosophy appeals only to human reason, to which most men are deafened by the enticements of pleasure and the bonds of local community. In addition to rhetoric, philosophy requires the support of law or political authority in order to improve the tone of human life. Political authority is necessary, in part, because it reinforces persuasion with force. Yet the exercise of force and the glory it brings can easily corrupt those who wield it and make them less receptive to the dictates of reason. This was Cicero's particular fear about Rome: in conquering the world, even with the aid of genuine virtue, the Romans were tempted to cast virtue aside and seek dominion for its own sake. Obsession with military power, coupled with a willingness to ignore justice in dealings with other peoples, was setting the stage for a collapse of moral restraint at home and the erection of domestic dictatorship.[25]

In light of this threat, Cicero deemed it necessary to invigorate the rhetoric by which philosophy seeks to influence political practice. In the passage of *De Re Publica* to which Tocqueville alludes in connection with his own rhetorical strategy, Cicero signals his intention to bring the insights of political philosophy fully to bear on Rome, the first universal polis. Such attention is of course flattering, and Cicero does not hesitate to ingratiate himself to his audience by asserting that Rome, in the course of its historical development, came to exemplify the best regime. Yet, as Laelius's comments attest, Cicero is quite open about the irony of his praise, and he also accompanies it with a highly elevated set of expectations.

By virtue of their rational nature, Cicero argues, all men are members of a cosmic polis ruled by the gods. All human beings, regardless of citizenship or ethnicity, are equal in their potential for virtue; all possess the dignity of membership within this divine order. This cosmic order does not do away with the necessity for particular political communities. Man is naturally attached to his own as well as to what is good in itself. His duties must begin with his family and place of birth and extend from thence to his actual polis. Yet particular political orders are themselves members of a moral order that is itself political in the sense that its dictates—the precepts of practical reason—are law: the law of nature, promulgated by God in humanity itself and enforced by the misery consequent to its violation.[26] Only if the polis (Rome) is willing to know and abide by this cosmopolitan law, will its achievement of universality (empire) redound to the betterment of civilization rather than to its degradation.

Even as he composed the works meant to convey this philosophic rhetoric to the Roman republic, Cicero was undergoing a persecution that culminated in the triumph of that which he so vehemently opposed: the empire of the Caesars. On its own terms, Cicero's philosophic statesmanship seemed to fail. Yet the lessons Cicero sought to impart were not lost on all ears. In modified form, they came to define a school of political thought much despised in modern times but indispensible to an understanding of modernity's development: the classical-Christian tradition of natural law.[27] In order to grasp Tocqueville's assessment of the prospects for realizing the potentialities of human nature in the political realm, we must examine the thought of that school and the influence it had on Tocqueville.

Augustine's Christian Cosmopolitanism

Along with Cicero's *De Officiis,* Saint Augustine's *The City of God* became foundational for the medieval understanding of political order. As the Roman empire began to crumble, Christians were accused of undermining the polis through their rejection of its pagan gods and civic virtues. In a charge that resurfaced in the Enlightenment period, Christians were faulted for withdrawing their loyalties from the earthly city and despising its concerns in favor of an imaginary, heavenly homeland.[28] In answering this accusation, Augustine paid tribute to the teaching of the great pagan philosophers, who had already established the necessity of a kind of dual citizenship or division of loyalties between particular and universal authority—the first necessary but flawed, the second virtuous but often ineffectual. Plato, Cicero, and others had sought to improve the character of political life by subjecting it to the universal standards of reason and natural virtue. Had they succeeded, Augustine implies, Rome might not have faced the problems it did in his day. The collapse of Rome was not due to any slackening of its particularistic energies, but rather to the intrinsic dangers of its peculiar obsession (glory) and to the failure of the philosophic project to counterbalance Roman citizenship with membership in a higher moral order. Christianity, by embracing and advancing that philosophic project, actually had the potential to cure the ills of late antiquity, if it was not too late for such a cure.[29]

To illustrate his point, Augustine references the status of poetry and religion in the classical world. By the light of natural reason, the corrupting tendencies of both were perfectly evident. Thus Plato's Socrates expelled Homer from the educational curriculum of his polis in speech. In practice, however, reason was impotent to reform this crucial component of ancient life. Roman law, for instance, placed only the most minimal restrictions on the theater and was unable to prevent the vilest excesses from taking place in the worship of the gods. Although Cicero appealed to God as the giver of the natural law of right reason and virtue, neither he nor any philosopher was able to counteract the social disorder wrought by pagan belief. Religion is too powerful among men for reason to displace it, and classical religion was set against reason in a battle the latter could not possibly win.[30]

The advent of Christianity, according to Augustine, made possible a limited but substantial progress in addressing this political-philosophic problem. By proclaiming the sovereignty of one God alone—the God who is *Logos* or divine reason—Christianity expelled the demons who had run rampant in the classical polis. Contrary to its accusers, Christianity preaches essentially the same virtues as the pagan philosophers, rooted in the same reason and the same universal nature of man, but it reinforces nature, reason, and virtue with an appeal to a purified and unified divine authority. Since the influence of faith in society is far more extensive than that of reason alone, Christianity transforms the political environment, rendering it much more receptive, or at least much less hostile, to the counsels of reason.[31] The classical philosophers had seen this possibility and had tried to appeal to myth as well as reason in advancing the claims of the latter; but their appeals had been weak and unconvincing in themselves.[32] Christianity, by transforming the hearts of citizens, offers the only realistic basis of a truly just political order—one balancing the need for local attachments and dogmatic beliefs with the sovereignty of a rational, transpolitical, and cosmopolitan moral order.[33]

The power of Christian cosmopolitanism can be seen in the way it captured the late Roman empire and became the foundation of European society for at least a millennium. From the beginning, however, its power had acknowledged limits. Augustine was quick to admit that the capacity of faith to transform hearts is qualified by free will and an ingrained proclivity for vice. The City of God, though present on earth in the hearts of believers, is always confronted by the city of sinful man, also present in many hearts, and often in the very same ones. If all men were completely converted by the Gospel, earthly republics would flourish, but such perfection is not to be expected in this life. Instead, Christians must be prepared to endure the worst of republics here, in hopes of entering the heavenly republic hereafter. Yet this very hope is effectual in the here and now, making a foreshadowing of heavenly bliss attainable in this life and therefore inspiring the practice of virtue in the city of man. Precisely because the Christian does not expect absolute perfection from the earthly polis, he is willing to persevere in otherwise discouraging situations and is able to contribute more to the polis's relative perfection.[34]

This attitude of detached benignity toward the polis, which also characterized the classical philosopher-statesman, is made accessible to any citizen by the Christian faith. Without seeking to replace or displace institutions of local membership and rule, Christianity subjects the souls of believers to a universal law enforced temporally as well as eternally and reinforced by the frequent and tangible practices of worship as well as by belief in things unseen. Eventually, this overarching authority fostered the growth of an elaborate doctrine of natural law, formulated most powerfully by Saint Thomas Aquinas, echoed in documents such as the Declaration of Independence and in the speeches of Abraham Lincoln and Martin Luther King Jr., and constituting the basis of the Catholic Church's moral, social, and political teachings to this day. Its influence on Tocqueville's qualified cosmopolitanism remains for us to consider.

Tocqueville's Classical-Christian Cosmopolitanism

Tocqueville, in his own way, adopts a version of this Christian cosmopolitanism. Though not a believer himself,[35] Tocqueville appreciated the strength of Augustine's defense of Christianity in light of the goals of classical political philosophy. Tocqueville recognized that it had taken Jesus Christ, in addition to Socrates, to make the bulk of humankind understand their common humanity. By the same token, he did not believe modern philosophy could succeed at founding a healthy cosmopolitan order on doctrines of human nature divorced from religious belief.[36] While he was a friend to modern democracy and a proponent of democratic liberalism, Tocqueville rejected and sought to separate liberalism from the anticlassical and anti-Christian principles of modern philosophers and statesmen (11–12, 278–88, 417–25, 504–6, 517–21). A brief examination of those principles and his reasons for eschewing them will complete our sketch of Tocqueville's unique blending of elements from classical, modern, and Christian cosmopolitanism.

The roots of Enlightenment thought can be discerned in the infamous yet immeasurably seminal writings of Niccolò Machiavelli and Thomas Hobbes. At its foundation is a reprise of the ancient Roman critique of Christianity: by dividing men's hearts and diminishing their concern for earthly things, religion undermines political authority and effectually fosters civic disorder and earthly impotence. The Augustinian defense of Christianity as the effecter of classical virtue is met with a transformation of the very concept of virtue in repudiation of its classical form. No longer is virtue sought for its own sake, for the perfection of human nature and the achievement of happiness. The very notion of moral perfection is cast aside as fanciful and dangerous, as nothing but a mask for selfish ambition.

The peace and unity of humankind, grounded in the rational apprehension of human nature, remains the Enlightenment ideal. Yet modern political thought holds that this ideal cannot be achieved on the basis of an appeal to an imaginary and divisive higher order. Rather, religion and classical virtue must be replaced by the liberation of material desire and the construction of a political-social order focused on collective selfishness, or the relief of man's estate through the drastic reorientation of both natural and political science. Only on the basis of this "low but common ground" can the common interests of mankind be advanced and the backwardness of particular authorities be left behind.[37]

Modern cosmopolitanism elevates what is low in man by making it the key to the universal flourishing of mankind. Tocqueville is keenly aware of this characteristic of modern political thought, and he makes it a central task of his political science to combat it (11–12, 643). As a prudent statesman, however, Tocqueville's mode of attack is subtle and corrective, rather than destructive. He acknowledges that self-interest exerts a powerful influence on the men of all ages and that its acceptance as a legitimate motive for human action is the inevitable fruit of modern democracy (500–503). Yet he consistently exposes the errors of modern rationalism, points to the dangers of its unmitigated acceptance, and suggests various means of guiding its adherents back toward a more classical form of virtue. Since classical virtue itself was limited in its appeal to human societies, however, Tocqueville seeks to promote it in large part by appealing to that form of religious belief most successful in bringing classical ethics to life: Christianity.

Both the power and the limits of anti-Christian cosmopolitanism are evident in the phenomenon of the French Revolution. Like the Reformation, the Revolution drew to its side men from all families and nations. The transpolitical appeal of both revolutions stemmed from their respective groundings in cosmopolitan thought. Catholicism and Protestantism offered conflicting views of the universal brotherhood of man, and the Enlightenment offered yet another. In this respect, Christianity and modernity are competing religions. In principle, each is capable of uniting all human beings in a common bond of moral obligation; in practice, however, Enlightenment thought had proved no better at procuring universal harmony than had Christianity, and it had even proved far more dangerous than its predecessor in certain respects.[38]

In attempting to replace the City of God with the religion of earthly progress, the French Revolution precipitated an extended culture war that continued to divide the France and the Europe of Tocqueville's day. Nor was this division an accident of history, to be forgotten when the republic of reason finally prevailed over the kingdom of darkness. "Man did not give himself the taste for the infinite and the love of what is immortal," Tocqueville contends. "These sublime instincts . . . have their immovable foundation in his nature. . . . He can hinder and deform them, but not destroy them" (510). The attempt to eradicate these instincts will lead to perpetual conflict as long as humanity is able to resist the unnatural attempt "to materialize man" (11). Should the forces of "enlightenment" prevail and compel submission, however, they will have succeeded only in denaturing and degrading citizens, at enslaving them to their own worst tendencies, and not at liberating humankind in any genuine sense (508–14, 517–21, 661–73). This is why Tocqueville, although he accepted the fact of modernity and attempted to reconcile its warring factions, himself declares war on the materialist underpinnings of modern thought.

Tocqueville's new political science seeks to moderate material acquisitiveness and channel human energies as much as possible toward the development of moral and intellectual virtues. The key to Tocqueville's strategy is found, as he indicates, in his chapter treating the Puritans as the founders of American political society (27–44). It is not the Puritans' bizarre and tyrannical proclivities, but rather their blending of the spirits of liberty and religion that interests Tocqueville. More precisely, it is their peculiar blend of local liberty and universal religion that he finds instructive. As in ancient times, the Puritan focus on active self-government provides opportunities for philosophic statesmen to inculcate virtues in otherwise unphilosophic citizens (46, 191). Unlike the classical polis, however, the early New England township was neither fully self-contained nor under the influence of pagan superstitions. It belonged not only to the British empire, however loosely this bond was felt, but also to Christendom. As zealous Christians, New Englanders could not help regarding the most local of their political acts in light of the laws of God and the universal brotherhood of man. Consumed as they sometimes were by the spirit of the sect (39), that spirit nonetheless aimed at the betterment of the world through the shining example of liberty virtuously employed (32). Through his account of the Puritans, Tocqueville expresses his hope that a civic virtue reminiscent of the classical polis can be blended with the cosmopolitan morality of Christianity and the fact of democratic modernity to preserve societies from the debilitating effects of a purely modern conception of reason, nature, and rights.

Tocqueville did not advocate a return to classical Rome, medieval Christendom, or seventeenth-century New England. He was well aware of the threats of local majority tyranny and religious oppression. Yet he was also aware of the waning power of both civic and religious ties in modern times (228, 482–84). A far greater threat to humanity, in his view, came from the nearly invisible despotism of a materialistic individualism that would lull citizens into surrendering the use of their most sublime and essential human faculties (519, 665). Part of his strategy for averting this disaster involved reaching out to modern souls with the doctrine of self-interest well understood, while counseling that true self-interest demanded the preservation and cultivation of civic life and religious belief (500–506), both of which contain a vision of human flourishing that is "aristocratic" in its aspiration toward virtue (481, 517) but democratic in that all men can participate meaningfully in the economies of self-government and religious practice.

Tocqueville did not consider the *doctrine* of self-interest, however well understood, sufficient for the cultivation of virtue. Of far greater importance was the *experience* by citizens of the sublime satisfactions made possible only by the *practice* of virtue (228, 415–16, 485–500). When enough citizens have a sufficient glimpse of the splendor of human excellence—a thing generally made possible only by an active life of politics and religious worship—then it is possible to sustain a popular love of liberty, and hence an environment conducive to the pursuit of those goods constituting the greatness and happiness of the human species. Although such a model does not promise to liberate citizens entirely from the sway of all authorities save human reason itself, and hence departs from the modern Enlightenment blueprint for the construction of a global order of justice, this model does in Tocqueville's considered view better accord with the limits of the human nature on which all cosmopolitanism is based. If Tocqueville is correct, accepting these limits, and thus moderating the modern cosmopolitan dream, may represent the best hope of realizing it to the extent that nature allows.

Notes

I am deeply grateful to Devin Schadt, Khalil Habib, Carl Eaton, Matthew Holbreich, and two anonymous readers, for their thoughtful comments on earlier versions of this essay. All remaining flaws are of my own provenance.

1. Jennifer Pitts documents the opposition of *early* liberals to European imperialism and denies on this basis that liberalism entails empire. Yet if liberalism provokes violent resistance by promoting radical change in all or most societies,

it is difficult to imagine the success of a liberalism never willing to use force in the advancement of these imperial ambitions. The question then becomes when, not whether, force is justified. "Empire and Democracy: Tocqueville and the Algeria Question," *Journal of Political Philosophy* 8, no. 3 (2000).

2. Tocqueville was critical of injustices committed by Europeans against native peoples, but he tended to regard the "empire or influence" of Europeans throughout the world as both inevitable and beneficial to humanity. He saw the potential in colonization both for the improvement of "half-civilized" populations and for the reinvigoration of public spirit in an increasingly individualistic Europe. For critical accounts, see Jennifer Pitts, "Empire and Democracy"; and Melvin Richter, "Tocqueville on Algeria," *Review of Politics* 25 (1963); for a qualified defense, see Bruce Frohnen, *Virtue and the Promise of Conservatism: The Legacy of Burke and Tocqueville* (Lawrence: Univ. Press of Kansas, 1993), 119–22. Although space does not permit an adequate discussion of the issue here, it must be noted that Tocqueville's political philosophy attempts to realize universal natural right through the artful use of particular institutions and customs. The centrality of mores (see below) to Tocqueville's political science both limits the possibilities of universalist reform, in that mores are difficult to change, and accentuates the need for such reform, insofar as bad mores are capable of powerfully frustrating the fulfillment of human nature.

3. Alexis de Tocqueville, *Democracy in America,* trans. and ed. Harvey C. Mansfield and Delba Winthrop (Chicago: Univ. of Chicago Press, 2000), 6ff. Unless otherwise noted, parenthetical references are to this work. I have occasionally made slight alterations to the translation.

4. See André Jardin, *Tocqueville: A Biography,* trans. Lydia Davis with Robert Hemenway (Baltimore: Johns Hopkins Univ. Press, 1998), 59–60; Alexis de Tocqueville, "Letter to Beaumont, April 22, 1838," in Tocqueville, *Selected Letters on Politics and Society,* ed. Roger Boesche, trans. James Toupin and Roger Boesche (Berkeley: Univ. of California Press, 1985), 131.

5. The literature tends to emphasize Tocqueville's debts to Rousseau, Montesquieu, and Pascal; see Harvey Mansfield and Delba Winthrop, "Editor's Introduction," in Tocqueville, *Democracy,* xxx–xxxix. Though genuine, these debts should not overshadow the influence of other authors and traditions on Tocqueville's thought or the critical distance he maintains from all his sources.

6. See Alexis de Tocqueville, "Speech to the Academy of Moral and Political Sciences," *Oeuvres I,* ed. A. Jardin, Edition Pléade (Paris: Gallimard, 1991), 1215–26. An English translation can be found in *Tocqueville and the Art of Democratic Statesmanship,* ed. Brian Danoff and L. Joseph Hebert (Lanham, MD: Lexington Books, forthcoming), chap. 1.

7. Natural right refers to "a standard of right and wrong independent of positive right" and "discernable to human reason." Leo Strauss, *Natural Right and History* (Chicago: Univ. of Chicago Press, 1953), 4, 9.

8. For a more detailed version of this argument, see L. Joseph Hebert, *More*

Than Kings and Less Than Men: Tocqueville on the Promise and Perils of Democratic Individualism (Lanham, MD: Lexington Books, 2010), 29–35, 46–54.

9. In this, Tocqueville closely follows Montesquieu, although the version of natural right Tocqueville promotes is more classical, and Montesquieu's is more modern. See Charles de Montesquieu, *The Spirit of the Laws,* ed. Anne M. Cohler, Basia C. Miller, and Harold S. Stone (Cambridge: Cambridge Univ. Press, 1989); Paul Carrese, *The Cloaking of Power: Montesquieu, Blackstone, and the Rise of Judicial Power* (Chicago: Univ. of Chicago Press, 2003); Tocqueville, *Democracy,* 89, 567.

10. See Thomas West, "Misunderstanding the American Founding," in *Interpreting Tocqueville's Democracy in America,* ed. Ken Masugi (Lanham, MD: Rowman and Littlefield, 1991).

11. See Mansfield and Winthrop, "Editor's Introduction," xxx.

12. See Plato *Laws* 765d–e; Aristotle *Nicomachean Ethics* 1.4, 2.3, 10.9; and Cicero *De Officiis* 1.32.

13. Cicero *De Re Publica* 2.11 and context.

14. This reading does not exclude the possibility that other allusions were couched in the same phrase, e.g., allusion to the "swaddling clothes" of Jesus Christ.

15. For Tocqueville, virtue is the free choice of what is good, and virtue is what renders men great. Virtue demands liberty, but liberty is good only when used virtuously. Tocqueville likewise subordinates equality to liberty and greatness. See Alexis de Tocqueville, *Journey to England and Ireland,* trans. Lawrence Mayer (London: Faber and Faber, 1957), 117; Tocqueville, *Democracy,* 42, 52, 227.

16. Tocqueville's defense of township government clearly borrows from Rousseau's defense of city-based government. See Jean-Jacques Rousseau, *On the Social Contract: With Geneva Manuscript and Political Economy,* ed. Roger D. Masters, trans. Judith R. Masters (New York: St. Martin's Press, 1978). Yet Tocqueville rejects Rousseau's reliance on the general will, his view of politics as denaturing, his contention that Christianity is incompatible with sound politics, and his preference for wholly independent city-states. See Tocqueville, *Democracy,* 56–65, 89–90, 275–88, 410, 583.

17. Cicero *De Re Publica* 1.13, 3.22; Cicero *De Legibus* 1.4–12, 1.22–24, 2.4–5.

18. See Cicero *Verrine Orations* 5.26, 66.

19. Plato, *The Republic of Plato,* trans. Allan Bloom (New York: Basic Books, 1968), esp. 500d, 519d, and Bloom's essay. My reading of *The Republic* is deeply indebted to my teachers Michael Palmer, Clifford Orwin, and Thomas Pangle.

20. As Mark Kremer points out, Plato's very project of Socratic apologetics implies that he believes political society can be elevated, however imperfectly, by a poetic rendering of philosophic virtue. "Interpretive Essay," in *Plato's Cleito-*

phon: On Socrates and the Modern Mind (Lanham, MD: Lexington Books, 2004), 27–34.

21. Aristotle *Ethics* 1.7, 10.7–8; Aristotle *Politics* 1.2.

22. In this and the next paragraph, parenthetical references are to Aristotle's *Ethics* and *Politics*.

23. From a cosmic perspective, Scipio observes, Rome and its empire seem as nothing; yet in actual human experience, the loss of a city seems like the loss of a world. Cicero *De Re Publica* 6.16, 3.23. Although reason draws us toward universal truth, it is difficult if not impossible for human beings to find truth except as embodied in particular institutions. In his vision of heaven, Scipio cannot help gazing back toward the earth (6.19).

24. Aristotle *Politics* 2.2ff., 3.4–5, 7.4.

25. Cicero *De Legibus* 1.10–11, 22–24; 2.6; Cicero *De Officiis* 1.11–12, 19, 25; 2.7–8; 3.11, 17–22. See also James Fetter and Walter Nicgorski, "Magnanimity and Statesmanship: The Ciceronian Difference," in *Magnanimity and Statesmanship,* ed. Carson Holloway (Lanham, MD: Lexington Books, 2008).

26. Cicero *De Re Publica* 2; 3.22; 4.1; 6.4; 20; Cicero *De Legibus* 1.1, 4–12, 22–24; 2.1–4, 10; 3.1; Cicero *De Officiis* 1.14–18, 28, 41, 45; 3.5–6, 10–11.

27. Cicero, *De Officiis,* trans. Walter Miller (Cambridge, MA: Harvard Univ. Press, 1913), introduction.

28. Note Tocqueville's care to defend the Puritans on this very point. *Democracy,* 32, 35.

29. St. Augustine, *Political Writings,* ed. Ernest L. Fortin and Douglas Kries, trans. Douglas Kries and Michael W. Tkacz (Indianapolis: Hackett, 1994); Augustine *De Civitas Dei* 2–8; compare Plato *Republic* 592a–b; and Cicero *De Legibus* 2.2.

30. Augustine, *Political Writings,* secs. 2, 4, 6–7; Plato *Republic* 376e–398b; Cicero *De Legibus* 2.4, 8–17.

31. Augustine, *Political Writings,* sec. 2.

32. Plato *Republic* 614a–621d; Cicero *De Re Publica* 6.3–26.

33. For Tocqueville's tribute to the *moral effectiveness* of Christianity in Jacksonian America, see Tocqueville, *Democracy,* 245, 278–79, 517–21.

34. Augustine, *Political Writings,* secs. 1–2, 5, 14, 19–20.

35. Tocqueville flatly admitted his lack of belief in private correspondence; refer to Sanford Kessler, *Tocqueville's Civil Religion* (New York: State Univ. of New York Press, 1994), 193nn1–3. This unbelief is evident in Tocqueville's lack of interest in the workings of divine grace (*Democracy,* 284, 419) and in his insistence that the free mind take nothing on faith (273, 410, 417–18). See Hebert, *More than Kings,* 136.

36. It was conceivable to Tocqueville that a new religion might yield the same benefits as Christianity, yet he considered this practically impossible in modern, skeptical times. *Democracy,* 408, 519. Instead, he feared the growth of enervating forms of spirituality, such as pantheism (425). Tocqueville's stan-

dard for measuring religion is based on the need to direct liberty toward virtue, and not all religions accomplish this equally, in his view (419–20). Tocqueville also acknowledged the importance of orthodoxy in the maintenance of religious belief (406), rendering blanket toleration and syncretism a threat to virtue. See Tocqueville, "Letter to Kergorlay, 1831," in *Selected Letters,* 46–53.

37. See Machiavelli, *The Prince,* trans. Harvey C. Mansfield (Chicago: Univ. of Chicago Press, 1998); Hobbes, *Leviathan,* ed. Edwin Curley (Indianapolis: Hackett, 1994); Leo Strauss, *What Is Political Philosophy? And Other Studies* (Chicago: Univ. of Chicago Press, 1959). For Tocqueville's response to this line of thought, as embodied in René Descartes, see L. Joseph Hebert Jr., "Individualism and Intellectual Liberty in Tocqueville and Descartes," *Journal of Politics* 69 (2007).

38. Tocqueville, *The Old Regime and the Revolution,* ed. François Furet and Françoise Mélonio, trans. Alan S. Kahan (Chicago: Univ. of Chicago Press, 1998), 1:2–3.

Part 4

Practical Cosmopolitanism

Paul Seaton

European Dreamin'

Democratic Astigmatism and Its Sources

It is a truism to note that there are multiple cosmopolitanisms. In my view, cosmopolitanism is a genus containing species of rather different sorts. Cosmopolitanism has marked moral attitudes, political life, philosophical thinking, and religious aspiration for millennia. Perhaps each epoch, though, hosts its distinctive versions. This essay takes aim at a widespread contemporary type, one characteristic of advanced democracy. It looks at this cosmopolitanism's European incarnation, but America harbors this form of dreamy antipolitical thinking as well. It may be easier to assess critically when looked at from afar.

While present today, this cosmopolitanism is not simply a contemporary phenomenon without antecedents and roots. But recent events gave it opportunity and impetus; they put wind in its sails. The collapse of Communism in 1989–1991 was decisive in this regard. With the end of the bipolar, superpower-structured world, a type of democratic humanitarianism saw its opportunity in Europe. It came more and more visibly to the fore, making its bid for ascendancy and hegemony. One could see it at work in the heavy-handed ratification of the Maastricht Treaty, as well as in the show trial of Slobodan Milošević a decade later (in which, however, he refused to play his assigned role).

I first saw it on the European scene with the assistance of French thinkers. In the post-9/11 period, I translated two books that dealt centrally with the phenomenon. One was by the political philosopher Pierre Manent, the other by the philosopher Chantal Delsol.[1] Earlier works by them had talked about the mind-set in question, so I was already more than a little aware of the form of ideological thinking they descried and dissected.

Other Americans observed much the same thing. What follows is something of a *compte rendu* of the descriptions and diagnoses of the troubling mentality by three well-known American thinkers, Robert Kagan, James W. Ceaser, and Mark Lilla, who are situated at different points on our political spectrum. It ends, however, with Manent's deeply critical engagement with what he calls a "post-political illusion" prevalent in Europe today. His philosophical analysis is at once more penetrating and more damning than the Americans'. Because of its French provenance, the thought that it is only Americans who find European humanitarian utopianism troubling can be laid to rest.

In bringing together these authors, I hope to present a specimen, or at least elements, of what a productive transatlantic intellectual alliance might look like today, as both democratic continents seek to orient themselves reasonably and effectively in the world. That orientation, I believe, must always be some form of the political perspective (the phrase is Manent's). The political perspective is a way of looking at the human world that, as Tocqueville said, does not ignore the views of partisans but tries to see farther than they and hence to refine them. It recognizes the harsh, sometimes intractable, realities that all too often circumscribe human hopes and action, while also being cognizant of the opportunities for, and higher motives of, individual and collective action. Aristotle and Thucydides gave classical expression to this point of view.

We democratic Westerners, despite all our differences from the ancient Greeks, continue to be specimens of Aristotle's *zoon politikon.* As he famously said, we are political animals because, and when, we seriously employ our faculty of *logos,* of reason-giving discourse, to talk about life and the good life (*Politics* 1.2, 1252b29f.), when we seriously "put speeches and actions together" (*Nichomachean Ethics* 6.1126b10ff.) to form *koinōnia,* community. I bring these four thinkers together to form a transatlantic dialogic community of sorts, one revolving around the necessity and nature of the political dimensions of human life.

This is not to imply that they see eye to eye on everything.[2] Manent disagrees with Kagan's liberal internationalism, for example. And Manent and Ceaser are stouter proponents of the nation-state than the other two. These differences, however, make the commonalities of their critiques even more striking.

And if the reader should observe that what follows is very much a one-sided dialogue, a sustained critique of an absent interlocutor, in my defense

I would invoke another Greek thinker, Socrates. For he has taught us that an essential part of political philosophy consists in bringing to light and dissecting the worldview and characteristic motivations of representative individuals, *especially those that bid fair to rule.* In our advanced democratic times, this means attending to hyperdemocratic views and aggressively progressive souls.

Here, therefore, are four analyses dissecting contemporary democratic humanitarianism in Europe. They all are at the service of political thinking, that is, serious human thinking about what we in fact have in common, as well as what we can and should put together to form humanly viable orders. As Aristotle indicated at the end of the *Politics,* this begins with territory and population, then ascends to military instruments and organization. One might call these "the material and martial aspects" of political life. The contemporary European Union of twenty-seven nations is woefully undecided in the former areas and dangerously ill-equipped in the latter. All our thinkers point out the real-world consequences of failing to provide oneself with shield and sword, as well as of failing to think seriously about when and how to employ them.

Political life, again according to Aristotle, goes beyond these necessary ingredients and centrally involves shared *but debatable* notions of justice and nobility. In critiquing contemporary European humanitarianism, none of the propolitical thinkers aim to foreclose real debate or to deny legitimate differences of opinion concerning the right and the estimable, as well as concerning war and peace. Far from it. But they do agree that it is necessary today to escape from paralyzing illusions about what already is achieved in the world, or what can be achieved by human beings and communities. Having escaped the totalitarian illusion, democratic peoples need to be liberated today from another tempting illusion, the humanitarian. Insofar as it is antipolitical, it is deeply antihuman. One might therefore call this humanitarianism "humanism, falsely understood." In view of the martial deficits alluded to above, one might also call it "cosmopolitanism, dangerously misunderstood."

Euphoric Breezes and Dark Clouds

I begin by briefly recalling for the reader the events that circumscribed, and the conflicting moods that characterized, the post-1989 situation. This sets the stage for the analyses that follow.

The period 1989–1991 witnessed the collapse of the Soviet empire and the release of central European countries from communist rule. As a great symbol, first the Berlin Wall came down and then Germany itself was reunited. These marvelous events happened in a breathtaking manner that seemed to be compelled by the spirit of the times. In these ways and others, the developing post-cold-war European reality often had a surreal character to it, and euphoria coursed through multitudes' feelings and leaders' discourses alike. Realist political analysts and practitioners were often confounded. Adding to the remarkable mix, the 1991 expulsion of Saddam Hussein from Kuwait by an American-gathered and -led coalition seemed to inaugurate a New World Order of multilateralism and of American servant-leadership.

But there were clouds on the horizon even then, and such euphoric hopes were disturbed early and late. The 1990s opened and closed with what many deemed atavistic ethnopolitical troubles in the Balkans, troubles to which European leaders for the most part responded dilatorily. Having learned from the first inadequate response, America under Bill Clinton once again, at the end of the decade, exercised hegemonic leadership through the instrumentality of NATO (and not the United Nations) to address the messy problem on Europe's southeastern flank. The Dayton Accords—what could be more American than Dayton!—seemed to confirm Madeleine Albright's characterization of America as the indispensable nation. Even Hubert Védrine's double-edged term *hyperpuissance,* which was coined to characterize America's unique status, recognized some such role.

Then came 9/11. After immediate expressions of solidarity, important Western European leaders and the Bush administration found themselves failing to see eye to eye on the nature of threats, as well as strategic objectives and appropriate manners of response. Donald Rumsfeld infamously referred to Old Europe. President George W. Bush more tactfully referred to a coalition of the willing, which did not include France or Germany. The state of things was dramatically symbolized and enacted in the back-to-back presentations of Colin Powell and Dominique de Villepin at the UN Security Council.

Power and Weakness

Robert Kagan earned the honor of making more than journalistic sense of the situation by providing an analysis that went beyond particular administrations and personalities, whether in America or France or Germany. His June 2002 *Policy Review* article "Power and Weakness" impacted discussion on both continents with remarkable force.[3] Its vivid formulations immediately became current: Americans are from Mars, Europeans from Venus. Europeans live in a Kantian paradise of peace; Americans are compelled to live and operate in an Hobbesian international state of nature. And so on.

Broader analysis underlay these striking statements. Kagan sketched the peripities of European and American strategic and diplomatic *history*, as Europe and America shifted places and perspectives on international order. One partner—America since 1917—had acquired great power status, and the other, Europe since World War II, had lost it. Each, Kagan suggested, might learn something about the other's current point of view from its own past.

Even more provocatively, he provided a contemporary structural analysis of Europe and America in material, ideological, and "interested" terms. By material he meant the possession of military means and the ability, as well as the will, to project them. Hard power was a currency still possessed by the United States, while Europeans had transferred the post-cold-war peace dividend into social welfare programs and made a virtue out of necessity by preferring to exercise soft power. As Kagan perhaps exercised diplomatic tact himself, the European military weakness of the title was more directly called impotence in the body of the argument. While Kagan spent some time dissecting the "psychology of the weak," which played an important role in European risk-assessment, he also paid Europeans the tribute of attending to their minds and expounding their ideology concerning international order and the legitimate role of force therein.

By ideology Kagan meant the ideals, principles, and normative perspective on international order and the use of force therein informing the different actors.[4] And by interest he meant the distinctive world orders that powerful nation-states preferred versus the type that weaker nations naturally would hope for or, in Europe's case, hope for and demand. Lilliputians prefer a world in which Gulliver either doesn't exist or operates at their command. Gulliver, in contrast—even a Gulliver like America, undeniably committed to values and norms of liberal civilization—has and perceives an interest in an international order that allows him to exercise his independence and to maximize his strategic advantages. Weakness dreams of one sort of world, one in which international law and norms govern, in which multilateralism is the primary mode of foreign affairs, and in which carrots rather than sticks induce rogues and recalcitrants to better behavior. Power, in contrast, can live in and, truth be told, embraces, another sort of world, one that recognizes and rewards its liberty of action.

What is remarkable, according to Kagan, is that the dream of the weak has become Europeans' post-cold-war reality. They have achieved a world historical "miracle" of genuine regional security based upon mutual transparency and habits of pacific settling of differences. Military conflict and war between European states is simply inconceivable. For various reasons, including the guilt-ridden desire to expiate their colonial and imperial pasts, many now want Europe to be the model of peace and security for the rest of the world.

Unfortunately, however, America stands in the way because of its ongoing commitment to state-agency and national sovereignty, not to mention its ability and demonstrated willingness to exercise force at the service of independently judged national interests. Thus emerged another of Kagan's striking phrases: Europe's new *mission civilisatrice* finds in its erstwhile cold-war ally the greatest obstacle to the worldwide expansion of its vision of international order. Not Saddam Hussein (or Islamist terrorists) but the United States is the real obstacle to an international order of law, security, and peace *à l'européen*. So believe many Europeans.

Having laid out these sharp structural and ideological contrasts, Kagan concluded with a rather vapid appeal for mutual understanding. America should be more humble in dealing with Europe, more sensitive to Europe's reduced status on the world stage, and more appreciative of the important contribution a pacified Europe makes to world security and peace. Few would disagree with these counsels, but even fewer would think they change the basic structural situation laid out by him. Europe, on the other hand, should . . . well, Kagan didn't really say what Europe should do in acknowledging and accommodating America's different status and its commitment to older notions of sovereignty and political agency. The hard edges of his analysis thus remained.

As one can well imagine, Kagan's article immediately became a major point of reference for domestic, as well as international, discussions about transatlantic relations. Many other analyses followed Kagan's effort. A few, we could appreciate in retrospect, had anticipated it.

Relegating the Nation-State to History's Dustbin

The political scientist James W. Ceaser was one of the prescient predecessors. A month before Kagan's bombshell, Ceaser published a short but penetrating analysis of American-European relations entitled "America's Ascendancy, Europe's Despondency: Why We Horrify Them, and They Exasperate Us." It appeared in the politically center-right periodical *The Weekly Standard.*[5]

It opened practically: "*A gulf is opening between our two continents,* and the responses are not just temporary or political. *Deep-seated trends in Europe,* quite apart from President Bush's particular policies, all *point to a growing ambivalence about America and its position in the world*" (italics added). Like Kagan, Ceaser affirmed that it is necessary to understand the reasons for European ambivalence, so that one can respond intelligently. He offered two sorts of reasons. The first is correlated with American ascendancy itself and involves the fact that Europeans have to look up to America. They too often find themselves dependent upon, or bypassed by, America: In Ceaser's words, "It sometimes seems that the only thing Europeans fear more than American failure is American success. American setbacks may endanger Europe's security and economic well-being, but American victories injure Europeans' pride, forcing the painful acknowledgement that the great issues of world politics pass through Washington, not Paris, Berlin, or Brussels."

With this tart synthetic comment, Ceaser began to supply what Kagan's analysis presupposed but did not explicate, a concept of politics as such. Ceaser has his own understanding of men's political nature and the nature of politics. Pride is a component of both, as well as security and economic well-being. Politics' alpha is security and their omega, he says later, is meaningful political life, with meaningfulness sometimes attaining great heights. (Economic well-being, one might infer, has an important middle-range niche.) Not all political issues are created equal; some are greater than others; some even impact world politics.

Within this framework, Europeans' ambivalence vis-à-vis America is understandable and even indicates something of a political attitude on their part. Being jealous of a hegemon is a political sentiment. This chastened pride, however, is not all that is at work in European ambivalence, according to Ceaser. Other factors are present in Europe that bear upon Europeans' thinking and judgment. There are deeper causes than their pride. These include certain "postnational, postmodern ideas" that advanced Europeans use to judge the contemporary scene and which they are at work implementing at home and abroad. These move in a different, decidedly antipolitical, direction.

To see this requires historical perspective and some philosophical learning. While Ceaser himself is a learned scholar, at this juncture he invokes the work of Pierre Manent. Manent's magisterial work of political philosophy, *Cours familier de philosophie politique,* had appeared the year before and amply provided what was required.[6] Chief among the philosophical notions he supplied was the idea of political form, different ways of organizing peoples' political lives. These run a gamut from tribes, cities, and nations to empires. Europeans are leaving one political form, the nation-state, but what they want to put in its place leaves much—much that is political—to be desired and determined.

Europeans and Americans currently have "different views of the source of 'agency' in world politics." History puts this in perspective: "For centuries it was recognized that the primary actor in international affairs was the nation-state, aided at the fringes by semi-permanent alliances and international organizations." Today, though, this view is no longer dominant in Europe. Quite to the contrary; for some time now European elites have been engaged in dismantling the sovereign nation-state and denationalizing European life. To be sure, this demoting of state and nation takes place within the context of an apparently even greater political endeavor, the construction of Europe. Appearances are deceiving, however, and the process needs to be scrutinized.

The construction is based upon certain presuppositions. First among them is a certain ideational deconstruction: "Before the European Union can be 'constructed' (whatever it may ultimately prove to be), not only existing nation-states, but also *the idea of the nation-state itself,* must be called into question" (italics added).

Now, if the nation-state is subordinated in Europe and its very legitimacy called into question, what is its status in the international arena? Can it be delegitimated at home and recognized as legitimate abroad? Hardly. It follows that Europeans would tend to look askance at America, the nation-state par excellence.

We are back with Kagan's analysis. Ceaser, too, deems it necessary to delve more deeply into the European ideas about politics and international order that seek to replace older ones. Together, they possess a certain coherence. Whether they can stand the predictable tests of reality, especially the harsher realities of world politics, is a separate question.

One idea consists in a distinctive representation or interpretation of history, especially European history since the nineteenth century. Another involves a certain reconceptualization of war and war-waging. In brief, history is seen as progressive, as a necessary or inevitable movement toward a benign *telos:* "European theorists and their American followers speak of the death of the nation-state and *the movement to some new form of international organization* as if it were *a sure thing*" (italics added). An essential component of this progressive view of history is the belief that major war is a thing of the past.

History's movement can be, perhaps needs to be, helped along. Europeans, accordingly, "have been the partisans of globalization in the realm of security, where they have sought to combine the protection offered by international alliances with low defense spending for themselves." Whether the guiding projection of history is inevitable or assisted, central to it is the notion of the disappearance of major war. For this to occur requires the eradication of the enabling conditions and causes of major war, including most importantly the sovereign nation-state. "In the judgment of advanced Europeans today, the nation-state system has proven an abject failure." As a culpable cause, the nation-state must be dethroned, if not dismantled, and its fueling sentiment nationalism exorcized.

As for the limited security threats that remain, such as outbreaks of recrudescent nationalism or tribal warfare, they can be handled by international peacekeeping operations under the United Nations or other international organizations. And to complete the scheme of necessary means and definitive ends: "This internationalization of security would be supplemented by various international courts, all situated in Europe, which would resolve conflicts using evolving norms of international law."

The complete ideational package is clear enough: The nation-state may continue to be a unit of human existence and even collective agency but it is to be strictly subordinate to international norms, institutions, and interests. "Above all, mobilization for war must not rest on any national principle." All this is history's will and agenda. As nineteenth-century European nation-states considered themselves to be the peak and vanguard of human history, their chastened and wizened twenty-first-century descendants ride its crest in a totally different direction. They have become lawful, moral, and pacific, and the world should—and will—follow the same path. This, Ceaser calls "the new internationalist paradigm." The parallels with Kagan's analysis are again striking.

At the end of his analysis, however, Ceaser sketched a critique of this internationalist outlook. In brief, it is that while this conception of affairs applies to the European theater, the rest of the world is different. Powerful states and even superpowers exist and will continue to exist—not all of the American sort. State rivalries and conflicts will, too. "It [is] clear that rivalries among states—including superstates such as China—would continue to pose the traditional problems of international politics." How would internationalist Europe handle a provocative China? Would it repair to the UN Security Council, on which China sits? Has it indicted China before an international court for its deeds in Tibet?

The recent historical record had not been reassuring in this regard. When the United Nations proved "inadequate or unavailable" in the Balkan crisis, a new security regime operating under NATO was brought in, purportedly "keeping American force under alliance control." This, however, amounted to "a shell game" whose purpose was to conceal the principal actor, the United States. When utopian dreams confronted harsher political reality, hypocrisy resulted. Ceaser thus goes beyond Kagan's sympathetic understanding of the European *différence* to point out the systematic distortions that inhere in the utopian vision and the political posturing it systematically engenders. Manent will lay out even more.

Fantasies and Their Causes

Ceaser's basic criticisms were echoed a year later by another American political theorist, Mark Lilla. Lilla wrote of "The End of Politics" in Europe in the center-left journal *The New Republic*.[7] Not mincing words, he spoke of European fantasies. For example, "It is simply a fantasy to think that the perennial problems of politics can be dissolved through progressive juridification or humanitarian aid, which is what some very serious European thinkers, notably Jürgen Habermas, clearly have in mind." Rivalry, conflict, and war are inevitable; they are among the perennial problems of politics. It is a sign of dangerously deranged thinking to believe otherwise. Older moral-political wisdom better counseled: *si vis pacem, para bellum*.

Like Kagan and Ceaser, Lilla saw the need to delve into the character of this remarkable mind-set, and he provided important additional elements via an analysis of how this state of mind came to be. Like Ceaser and Manent, he made the nation-state, understood as a distinctive sort of political form, central to his analysis. "It is the idea of the nation-state, and the related concepts of sovereignty and the use of force" that are "in crisis in Europe today."

Lilla's main method is that of contrast. Most fundamentally, he contrasts serious political thought with political pathologies, intellectual collapse, and fantasy. His norm is "serious political thought, understood as disciplined and impartial reflection about distinctively political experience." In the light of this norm, he considers two periods of intellectual life on the Continent. During the cold war, Marxism and structuralism dominated; they "absorb[ed] [almost] all thinking about political experience into amorphous discussions of larger historical, economic, or linguistic forces."[8] The distinctively political could not come into focus.[9]

Ten years on after the collapse of Communism, in Lilla's judgment things had not significantly improved. Europeans have generally ceased to think responsibly about matters of war and peace, law, morality, and politics. To understand the current intellectual myopia, however, another factor beyond intellectual fashions needed to be recognized: the eclipse of European sovereignty during the cold war. During this long period, European countries were either under Soviet rule or dependent upon the United States. In either case, their sovereignty—their capacity for independent judgment and action in matters of war and peace—was severely compromised. It would have taken a mighty effort of imagination and foresight to continue to think about national sovereignty in those circumstances. By and large, this was lacking.

And since nature abhors a vacuum, it occasioned a number of unhealthy intellectual consequences, which lasted even into the postcommunist period when European countries regained independence. Among these today is "an extremely uncritical embrace of the 'idea of Europe' among Western European intellectuals generally, and its invocation as a kind of charm against the most difficult political questions facing the Continent today."[10] In its turn, "the blissfully undefined notion of 'Europe' inspires pacific, post-political hopes." We are now in the realm of European dreaming.

Postpolitical is the key term in the foregoing. Like Ceaser, Lilla has a normative notion of the political. Generally, one can say that for him politics, on one hand, respond to certain human needs, while, on the other, they generate certain conundrums to which the political association must respond. Human beings need political life as the site and focus of communal attachment, legitimate authority, and effective action in the world, as well as to engage in serious reflection on the human scene. While being a necessary and elevating response to these human needs, politics also generate problems of their own. This ambiguity must be acknowledged and embraced, for these problems will always exist in some form or another. Accordingly, the eternal travail of political life must be taken up by each generation. Many in Europe, though, wish otherwise.

In the light of his concept of politics, Lilla maintains that "the nation-state has been the best modern means discovered so far [of addressing these human needs and conundrums], opening a political space for both reasonable reflection and effective action." On the other hand, one of the lessons that Europeans have drawn from their twentieth-century history is that national allegiance is always a danger, that it can infect and eventually destroy liberal democracy. There is truth to this. Many, however, make it the whole truth and, as it were, throw the baby out with the bathwater, finding no distinctions among nationalism, national identity, and patriotism. All vital allegiance to the particular, to *la patrie,* is threatening; hence the call and efforts to construct a cosmopolitan Europe.

But "what Europe means *as a distinctly political entity* remains a mystery to all involved" (italics added). In particular, serious reflection about the nature of European sovereignty and its relation to national sovereignty has been rare since the formation of the European Union (a few academic specialists excepted). Thus, while there may be a democratic deficit in the current configuration of the European Union, more fundamentally and ominously, there is a political deficit, a grave lack of political thinking and of appropriate political instrumentalities, including military means, on the European/EU scene. Lilla's hesitant judgment was that while "it may be that the European Union will turn out to be something new, and beneficent, on the European political landscape . . . I am skeptical."

Among his reasons for skepticism were (as with Ceaser) the debacle of the Balkans in the late 1990s and Western Europe's painfully slow response to the threats of political collapse and even genocide there. Why the tardiness? "Europeans no longer think of the nation-state as the sole place where foreign policy should be determined and military means chosen, but they are not yet able to treat the European Union as that place." Europeans are politically and conceptually betwixt and between.

The lack of serious political thought is found again, in a significantly aggravated manner, in a complementary view found among intellectuals. "It was said by some intellectuals that Europeans, given their recent history, have discovered the need to regulate such matters through international law and organizations." Lilla detects the same sort of juridical internationalism as do Ceaser and Kagan. He, however, can barely contain himself in responding to this view, containing as it does an apparently infinite amount of folly or presumption. "But this simply removes the problem to a higher, and far less stable, plane. If the sovereignty and the political legitimacy of the European Union is a complicated business, the moral and political authority of the United Nations or a World Criminal Court or non-governmental organizations is infinitely so." The cognitive status of this view is so low that it requires a designation—fantasy—reserved often for the delusional. It is the antithesis of serious political thinking. Gesturing toward an intriguing but undeveloped notion of the perennial problems of politics, Lilla brusquely retorts: "It is simply a fantasy to think that the perennial problems of politics can be dissolved through progressive juridification or humanitarian aid." Here, dismissive scorn took the upper hand from analysis.

Remarkably, the political philosopher whom Ceaser invoked, Pierre Manent, had earlier employed a similar term in describing a proposed international regime of law. He referred to a widespread "illusion" that informs the minds and stirs the passions of many of his fellow Europeans. He, however, gave the democratic-humanitarian illusion a good deal of analysis. He thereby wins the palm for the earliest as well as philosophically deepest study of these features of the contemporary European scene. To him and his thought we now turn, that is, to political philosophy.

The Empire of Law

At the beginning of the penultimate chapter of *A World beyond Politics?* Manent summarizes the guiding thread and main thesis of his book-long investigation into the contemporary European democratic world: "Since the beginning of this book, I have underlined what seems to me the major trait of the present world, to wit: a tension between, on one hand, what some will call 'the old order,' others 'the natural order,' of politics and, on the other, the project and hope for a new order, one that is metapolitical or post-political, a new order of a unified humanity." Manent is much closer to the former view, but this does not exempt him from dispassionately analyzing the latter view. To begin with: "There are two principal ways of conceiving a metapolitical Humanity, a Humanity having overcome or surpassed its political condition. This can be a humanity organized according to law[;] this can be a humanity living in accordance with morality. A humanity living according to morality is a humanity living in respect for human dignity."

One chapter is devoted to "The Empire of Law" and another to "The Empire of Morality." We will be able to consider only the first sort of empire, according to which laws protecting human rights would reign supreme over both domestic and international affairs. It is with real regret that I pretermit his discussion of contemporary democratic morality.[11] His discussion of imperial law, however, bears upon the fundamental issues of European depoliticization and of war and peace that our previous analysts engaged and found Europeans intellectually and militarily unequipped to handle. Manent's philosophical dissection considerably advances these themes.

First, however, there is a matter of terminology and translation. The French word in the title of the chapter is "droit." The word *droit* is somewhat difficult to translate into English. Marc LePain renders it "law," which is quite standard. A closer reading of the chapter, however, reveals that it is primarily a certain kind or understanding of law that Manent has in mind. It is law (*droit*) insofar as it is based upon rights (*droits*) and is at the service of rights—natural rights, the rights of man, human rights. It is a distinctly democratic conception. Therefore, at the risk of awkwardness, I will render it "law-and-rights" in order to keep the two connected concepts together. A number of contemporary judges certainly do, those who claim to rule directly in the name of this fundamental stratum of democratic justice and morality. To law-and-rights we now turn. Manent begins phenomenologically.

From Phenomena to Situations, Minds, and Hearts

That is, certain legal or judicial phenomena in Europe catch Manent's eye and attract his philosophical attention. Operation Clean Hands in Italy, the Spanish judge Baltasar Garzón, and certain recent *arrêts* from the French *Conseil constitutionnel* figure on Manent's list, while one easily could add others from the European Court of Justice, the International Criminal

Court, and elsewhere. Looking at *Mani pulite* from Paris, Manent observes that "Italian judges changed the political map of their country without the Italian people being consulted at any point." They thereby "effected a political revolution." Such a revolution assuredly commands the attention of the political philosopher. Among other things, it indicates despotic potentials in judicial hands, perhaps even a new ruling jurisprudence.

Judicially attempted revolution appeared elsewhere as well. While installed in Spain according to its democratic constitutional system, in 1998 Baltasar Garzón attempted to exercise a truly international jurisdiction, one that refused to honor a political decision of Chilean democracy and which called upon British judicial brethren to help effect. This is remarkable on many fronts. What does it indicate? Where might it lead?

As for his native France and its (imperfect) equivalent of the U.S. Supreme Court, the Constitutional Council, he sees "profound changes . . . these past years." In this period the Council had "acquired powers," effectively "breaking with the French constitutional tradition, in fact with both [France's] rather antithetical, constitutional traditions—the republican, revolutionary, 'pro-legislature' tradition and the consular, 'revisionist,' or Gaullist tradition which reinforces the executive." What is going on here and abroad? Do these judicial revolutions happen in a vacuum? Or are they rooted in something deeper?

While there doubtless are many particular causes, upon reflection all this points toward a broader contemporary phenomenon, that of "law-and-rights (*le droit*) claiming to be the *sole* regulator of society" (italics added). Of course, to put matters this way is to personify law. The real referent is elsewhere, in the French people, their increasingly antipolitical thinking, and their increasingly depoliticized situation.

The French case responds to the new political and moral situation of the democracies. They more and more "reject political authority as such—and thus the two powers which politics principally make use of, the legislative and the executive." As for the French themselves, they "more and more envisage social life in a juridical perspective taken in a broad sense, i.e., as having to be more and more exclusively organized according to the rules of law-and-rights, administered or guaranteed by judges or quasi-judges."

While this attitude and endeavor has several contributing factors, one is immediately noteworthy. It comes from a "*moral demand* which is as strident as it is vague" (italics added). It is the demand that human rights and dignity be universally recognized, immediately applied, and unconditionally enforced. This, it is held, is the judge's supreme duty, more than even his or her sworn constitutional duty. Both Manent and the adherents of this morality note that it—or moral legalism—in principle requires "the destatification and the depoliticization of the rules of social life." Basic rights are not to be captive to the vicissitudes of legislatures or the discretion of executives; their protection must not be restricted to national borders. "We envisage a world in which law-and-rights would be guaranteed without the means of the nation-state."

As a political philosopher who takes the adjective *political* with normative seriousness, what does Manent think of this? "Among the illusions that tempt our laziness, none is more present today than that law-and-rights ought to be, and more and more will be, the sole regulator of social life. It is urgent to bring to light the vacuousness of this illusion." Illusion, sloth, vacuity—these are pejoratives of a high order. Analysis and political counsel, not simple dismissal, however, characterize Manent's response. On one hand, he instructs his French and European readers as to where their ideas come from; on the other, how they conflict with political reality understood in terms of its necessities and challenges, as well as its opportunities and possible nobility. To help him, he enlists Tocqueville and the original articulators of liberal constitutionalism, Locke and Montesquieu.

First of all, according to Manent, what is an illusion? "In the broadest sense, and it is thus that I understand the term, an illusion is a representation tied to a desire." It has ideational content and emotional motivation. We enter into the realm of what one might call democratic social psychology. There are antecedents to this sort of investigation in Plato and Tocqueville, among others. As we saw above, current European democratic psychology specifically includes "not only the *desire that law-and-rights* reign, but that they *reign alone*" (italics added). As we also saw, this is a major component of a yet broader democratic conception, that of a virtually unified humanity. So the illusion's positive components at this stage are the view and project of a unified humanity living subject to a legal order jealously protective of human rights and dignity.

Now, this image and this desire did not spring from contemporary democrats, as Athena did from Zeus; they have antecedents and roots of various sorts. To begin with, modern democracy itself is "inseparable from the perception, as if self-evident, that there is something like Humanity." Tocqueville in particular noted this central facet of democratic society and psychology. We should pause here a moment, because here we encounter a central element of Manent's analysis: the dynamically developing nature of democracy.

Tocqueville's Prescience

In 1982 Manent published *Tocqueville and the Nature of Democracy.*[12] Tocqueville taught him that a new form of democracy, what we call liberal democracy, cannot adequately be comprehended by traditional liberal categories (the individual, civil society, and the state). Beyond them, enveloping them, it is a dynamic social-spiritual order possessing a distinctive nature. That nature contains certain essential elements, structures, and active tendencies. These include such distinctive social-spiritual phenomena as individualism, materialism, and civic apathy. This is well-known Tocquevillian teaching.

Less well known is that Tocqueville counseled the practice of a political or statesmanly art to counteract these natural democratic tendencies. The ones we listed above, for example, all sap democratic citizens' civic self-awareness and self-governing capacities. Tocqueville accordingly extolled the American framers' wisdom expressed in the *Federalist Papers* and at work in American federalism. They had wisely combined centralization with decentralization, and their institutionalization of aristocratic elements was a great boon to the fledgling republic. (He also went beyond them and theorized the essential contribution to American liberty of the township as well as the master science of democratic liberty, the art of association.) Manent's appeal to his fellow democratic Europeans, that they recall their own political natures and make provisions for the political conditions of human existence, echoes Tocqueville's. Like Tocqueville as well, he does not merely exhort but also analyzes, so as to instruct democrats about the precise nature and sources of their intellectual blind spots and untoward sentimental impulses.

Tocqueville saw such efforts as necessarily Sisyphean, though, as they go against democracy's powerful tendencies. Harvey C. Mansfield Jr. and Delba Winthrop summarized the thought with the lapidary phrase "democracy democratizes."[13] By this they meant that, unattended and uncurbed, democracy will absorb and recast after its own image and likeness more and more of human life, with humanly ambiguous and politically deleterious results. In his earlier Tocqueville work, Manent faithfully followed Tocqueville's lead and extrapolated the spiritual evisceration and civic enervation to which democracy's built-in (and hence ineradicable) tendencies lead. This *terminus ad quem* provided him with a template through which to view actual democracy's progress in reshaping itself and its members. Over the years, he has tracked the unfolding of democracy's nature in various countries and through historical time. "The Empire of Law" continues this longtime effort.

Thus, at the beginning of the chapter, Manent puts today in a wider democratic context and affirms that "in sum, it is *natural* that societies born under the sign of the rights of man should end by explicitly placing law-and-rights at the center of their action as well as their consciousness, that they end by wanting to be societies wholly governed by law-and-rights" (italics added).[14] Democracy democratizes.

More Kantian than Kant

In addition to Tocquevillian insights into democracy's nature, one could further note that much of nineteenth-century European thought developed, in one way or another, a related humanitarian thought, that the human race itself is increasingly connected and interconnected; humanity is increasingly living a common history. European colonialism and imperialism, as well as the development of international commerce and the export of European universalist ideas, contributed to this notion. This complex has been called the dawn of universal history. On the plane of theory, one can mention the names of Kant, Hegel, and Marx, but Comte and Nietzsche also come to mind. Kant, for example, wrote about "the idea of a universal history from a cosmopolitan point of view."

It is not surprising, then, that Manent speaks of "our Kantian consciousness" in this connection. In important respects Europeans are Kant's progeny, as well as democracy's. Kant is the philosophical originator of the idea of humanity living under sovereign law, respecting the rights of all human beings. For example, "in a vivid formulation, Kant already wrote in 1795: 'Nature wills in an irresistible way that the supreme authority would finally revert to law-and-rights.'" It was he who "sought with the greatest tenacity the means of overcoming the political and human order that presupposes and includes war, in order to arrive at 'perpetual peace.'" *Qui vult pacem vult regnum aut imperium legis cosmopolitae.*[15]

There are differences as well as similarities between Kant and contemporary Europeans. In telling ways, Europeans are more Kantian than Kant. Kant eventually opted for a federation of free or republican states that would form a model for other countries to imitate and serve as an initial core of peace-loving states others could join. Political sovereignty or independence, however, both within the federation and without, were expressly recognized by Kant. This was demanded by morality itself, that is, out of respect for the capacity for self-government of human beings *and collectivities*. Sovereignty of this sort, however, is denied by the newest legal internationalism.[16]

The Religion of Humanity

Nor is this the only telling difference between Kant and contemporary Europeans. Here we broach the important, if controversial, issue of the theological significance of democratic humanitarianism (what some have called atheistic humanism).[17] Kant himself had recourse to the concept of Providence in explaining the course and meaning of the human adventure, in articulating the *telos* of humanity.[18] Areligious Europeans do not and cannot. Nor is this the only distancing of contemporary Europeans from the founding faith of Europe.

In chapter 1 of *A World beyond Politics?* Manent argues that *insofar as they adopt* modern science as the highest form of reason and a specifically modern notion of liberty as the proper understanding of human freedom, contemporary European democrats are effectively atheistic.[19] A subsequent chapter, "The Religion of Humanity," then discusses the full-blown expression or concept of the self-deification of mankind. Manent points out that the father of positivism, Auguste Comte, was the self-proclaimed first high priest of this humanitarian religion. According to Comte, the theological and metaphysical epochs of Western mankind were to give way to the final positivistic period. Manent sees this thought, shorn of its Comtean trappings, present on the contemporary scene. As such, democratic humanitarianism has deeply theological, or antitheological, resonance. Other former lodestars of Western humanity have been dimmed by it as well, starting with any normative notion of nature.

Unlike Kant, we, Manent reports, "would hesitate to say that 'Nature wills' this or that"—especially the final triumph of law, the cosmopolitan regulation of humanity—since nature has become more than problematic as any sort of a moral-political guide for mankind. The scientific distinction between facts and values, for instance, presupposes that nature, in Joseph Cropsey's phrase, is "a moral blank."[20]

On the other hand, Manent states, "There is no doubt that we will (*voulons*) that 'the supreme authority would finally revert to law-and-rights.'"

Will now joins with desire: the volitional side of democratic psychology expands even as its subjects, democratic human beings, continue to reduce their stock of normative authorities.

One should again credit Tocqueville with foreseeing this repudiation, by individuals and peoples subject to democracy's dynamism, of any authority above mankind. He explicitly argued that democratic human beings would be hard pressed to locate intellectual authority in anything but public opinion and, tendentially, in humanity itself.[21] Nothing above humanity, and no human authority claiming to speak in its name, is congenial to the *thoroughly democratic* mentality. Binding tradition becomes mere information, while authoritative institutions such as the Catholic Church will become increasingly isolated in democratic society. On the other hand, Tocqueville's discussion of democratic historians, intellectuals who credit the historical process as the greatest Whole or Agency known to democratic mankind, indicates that he was aware of yet another authoritative possibility in democratic times.[22] In Manent's judgment, a number of his contemporaries have sworn allegiance to it. "Many among us are convinced that history's movement leads us *irresistibly* in this direction."

What emerges from this democratic-theological excursus is a certain complex of ideas revolving around Humanity and History (as well as attendant volitional components). Humanity is understood as significantly self-contained and on the verge of being harmoniously unified under law. History in turn is understood as irresistible, yet most benign. The two are brought together in the thought of imminent (and immanent) reconciliation and culmination. In other words, there is an eschatological horizon within which many contemporary democrats think and act. As we will see soon enough, it particularly is at work in contemporary thinking about war and peace and the thoroughgoing "legalization" of both.

The Ought and the Is

Already, though, we can better appreciate the subtle Kantian categories in Manent's initial formulation of this view. As you recall, it holds that "law-and-rights must be (*devoir être*), and more and more will be (*sera de plus en plus*), the sole regulator of social life." The ought and the is (or will be) are combined in this view. Moral imperative joins with historical necessity. It will be convenient to employ this distinction in the next sections of our exposition. It is not that between domestic and international, although Manent employs this distinction as well. Judges both domestic and international claim to base their extraconstitutional actions on solid democratic bases, upon the moral basis of all democratic constitutions: human rights and dignity. They thus claim to directly obey and enforce the ought at work in democratic consciousness.

It is in the area of the use of force, of military means, that History comes to the fore. To be sure, it is a History in which morality plays an essential role, including the role of being historically realized. Not just any morality will do, though. The requisite morality is emphatically egalitarian, humanitarian, and pacific. It is a democratic morality that maintains that in principle there are no truly serious human differences, differences that in fact could, or arguably should, lead to conflict and war. Furthermore, it is a democratic morality that sees political authorities and military instruments as principally at its service, while it is at the service of human dignity and human rights, of human unity and world peace. All this requires an essential reworking of political authority and politics themselves. It also requires a thoroughgoing moral transformation of humanity. The latter is so extensive, however, that even Manent's contemporaries have their "hesitations and perplexities" about it.

Human-Rights Despotism

With these distinctions in mind, let us turn to Manent's discussion of moral judges, then of thoroughly moralized and law-abiding peacemakers. The former are firmly in the grip of the democratic passion for immediacy. Justice must be done now, constitutional forms and legislative hesitancies and compromises, that is, outmoded limits to the realization of justice, be damned.

For many today, "the power of judges is ultimately based not only on the laws of the particular nation, not even on its Constitution, but on what is the principle of the laws and the Constitution, to wit: the 'rights of man' and the idea of 'humanity.'" "Brushing aside local laws, received customs and international conventions and treaties, they increasingly claim to speak *immediately* in the name of humanity and its rights." Theirs is an unconditional jurisdiction—no circumscribing or qualifying features—because it appeals to the true basis, human rights and dignity, and to the widest subject of law and judging, humanity wherever it may be found.

Such judges, however, have forgotten Locke's sobriety, not to mention his political and constitutional wisdom. He was devoted to the protection of individuals' rights. But he knew that protection was a complex matter and that men and societies were about much more than the legal and judicial protection of individual rights. Political authority or government needs to reflect and address these complexities. Hence he developed a complicated constitutional and political scheme.

A number of judges and legal theorists today have simplified the rights-protection problem, however, and tend to make it the sole or chief political task. But their simplification itself has many attendant serious difficulties. Manent sketches three, falling under the rubrics of arbitrariness, despotism, and war. Against their own intentions, contemporary proponents of the "government of judges" reintroduce elements into the social and human world that they hope to eliminate. Bringing these untoward consequences to their attention is one important way that the political philosopher can bring them up short and, perhaps, move them to reflect upon the inadequacies of their views.

First of all, rights, while "doubtlessly more noble," are much vaguer than national laws and constitutions. The oft-observed judicial expansion (or creation) of rights and sharp, unresolved debates over them in legal and other circles indicate as much. In the new optic, it is up to the individual judge or court to determine whether X is a right and whether Y's right to X has been violated or not. Evolving standards are really no standard. Nor does cross-jurisdictional consultation and (purported) consensus really address the subjectivism involved. Apart from constitutional forms and legal traditions, apart from democratic legislatures' specifications, judicially determined rights are infected with an increasingly palpable arbitrariness.[23] This, however, is "precisely what [modern] regimes wanted to prevent against by instituting the control of constitutionality." While the first, this is not the only contemporary judicial sin against liberal constitutionalism.

Arbitrariness paves the way for despotism, because "a power that discovers that it can act arbitrarily, does not delay in using and abusing this latitude." The infamous phrase "our robed masters" comes to mind. But Manent is particularly keen to bring to the attention of his readers a third difficulty that risks coming to the fore in the foreseeable future. It is, as it were, his own discovery; at least people haven't yet sufficiently reflected upon it. It is the return of the state of nature. That condition, we recall, consists in the absence of an acknowledged legitimate arbiter of human disagreements. Absent such, each individual has the right to judge and punish violations of rights, transgressions of the law of nature. The social contract in liberal theory was intended to establish just such an umpire (along with sovereign legislative and executive powers).[24]

Certain contemporary judges, however, in their zeal for justice contravene this wider conceptual and governmental scheme. They claim to be the final, that is, sovereign, declarers and protectors of human rights and dignity. They can authoritatively pronounce upon human rights even without express constitutional authority, even against expressed democratic will. But one might ask, why should they be the only ones engaged in the enterprise?

That is, if judges' primary justification for such immediate and unconditional jurisdiction is human rights and their defense, what *in principle* is to exclude anyone else from claiming the same? Nothing, really, except for the nonnormative circumstances of individuals' wills and means.

Judicial power in the older understanding came from, and came with, a more complex framework of nature and convention, which included the sovereignty of a particular people, a democratic delegation of powers, and intricately separated powers, each making its essential contribution to the protection of individuals and their rights and of society as a whole. If judges sever themselves from this understanding (which continues to empower them today), what is to bar anyone else, whether at home or abroad, from doing the same? In other words, "the [new understanding of] the power of judges risks leading us back to the state of nature" in which everyone is a judge of rights and their violation. As Manent reminds the reader, "this is another name for the state of war."

Disinterested Respect?

We thus are led to our final topic. As before, Manent began by listening carefully to the distinctive discourse of the times surrounding war and peace, war-waging and peacemaking. President George Herbert Walker Bush spoke of a New World Order in connection with Operation Desert Storm, while the State Department regularly posted its list of rogue states, malefactors and troublers of the peace such as Libya, Iran, Iraq, and North Korea. They did not fit into this new order. And in a remarkable instance of the dog that did not bark, the NATO military intervention in the conflict between Serbia and Kosovar Albanians at the end of the 1990s was not declared to be a war; many termed it a humanitarian intervention, a morally dictated response to ethnic cleansing and other crimes against humanity.

This newspeak bespoke new ideas and attitudes about legitimate violence and peace, about international law and military action. Manent set about studying the implications of the change of paradigm. And once again the application of Kant's thought shed important light on contemporary attitudes.

He began his analysis with the phrase with which many wish to replace the term *war* in the lexicon of legitimate interstate violence: *international police action.* What does it entail, lexically or conceptually, to replace *soldiers* with *police forces, war* with *policing*? A simple reflection is quite revealing: "To put it in a word: today people suppose, without always being conscious of it, that states can be motivated to act, in particular to act militarily, out of a pure respect for law, a respect detached from their particular state interest. If military action is an action of international police, those who conduct it have no more particular interest in this action than, within states, the police who arrest a murderer or bank-robber. . . . They are perfectly disinterested."

It is again in terms of Kantian thought that Manent draws out contemporary implications, invoking the famous Kantian dichotomy between morality understood as disinterested respect for law and interests as human goals characterized (and tainted) by selfish particular motivations. From individuals it is extended to collective individuals, to states. Their military action is to be moralized in this distinctive sense.

At this early juncture, Manent contented himself with posing an apparently rhetorical question: "Can one imagine that states will be more and more likely to conduct themselves on these principles, foreswearing therefore this motive, interest—the national interest—which until now has been generally admitted to be legitimate?" Now, as it happens one can imagine this state of affairs, since it is an ingredient in the image of a metapolitical or postpolitical Humanity that informs many Europeans' discourses and initiatives. However, the transformation required for such a thoroughly disinterested condition cannot but boggle the mind.

Peace's Presuppositions

So much so, that even Manent's contemporaries are daunted by such a requirement; they hesitate, perplexed before it. But then they press on, in large part because of specific assumptions they make about the world and the times. He lays them out: "We have never been closer than we are today to peace[;] it *must be there* (*devait être là*); peace is the natural order of mankind[;] no national interest or political difference justifies taking to arms." These presuppositions especially come to light when they run up against recalcitrant reality, when actions that have been a priori delegitimated occur, as they do.

Language is again telling. The agents that ought not to be are called "rogue states," or "troublers of the peace"; when they violate the law of peace, they are termed "criminals." Against the background of definitive peace, they stand out as aberrations and anomalies. They therefore need to be "brought to justice" (the phrase is telling); once that is done, the inherently pacific order of mankind will blossom. "Now, this presupposition is tautological," observes Manent (while others might call it a *petitio principii,* a begging of the question). In either case, "if we suppress in thought all the troublemakers, what in fact remains if not peace and tranquility?" However, in so presupposing, then excising as need be, we "simply forget to think about the next troublemakers who will not fail to arise." Something is wrong with a position that generates a systematic failure to account for that which will inevitably arise.

This tautological treatment of inconvenient facts does indicate that this mind-set is somehow aware of perforations in its pacific viewpoint; it recognizes the need for some sort of effort at overcoming such anomalous recalcitrants. But it steadfastly continues to see this need, and to place these anomalies, in the horizon of *a definitive peace that imminently will be.* In other words, it thinks eschatologically. In this recourse to quasi-religious categories, the desperate straits to which the insistent expectation of peace can lead become visible. Both logic and faith are traduced.

Christian hopes for final peace, for a new heaven and a new earth, are based upon belief in the Word of God. Democratic humanitarians cannot avail themselves of these theological grounds. Nonetheless, they retain some of what pleases them in the Christian worldview, but they discard the rest. This, as we said, is both unreasonable and unfaithful. However, the pressure to do so is considerable. In the reworked democratic optic, what is at stake in disposing of each successive disturber of the peace is enormous. At stake is what we might call (with apologies to Pascal) the "grandeur of humanity without God." Their defeat would usher in the advent of the true, that is, this-worldly, reality of heaven on earth.

In borrowed religious language, "we suppose that the 'end times' have arrived and that after a 'final battle' we will enjoy the golden fruits of peace." The human adventure is near an end, at least in this decisive sense:

the definitive achievement of peace. We today have the privilege and task of bringing the *eschaton* to pass. Manent continues, "We therefore anticipate these 'last times,' we anticipate the peace to come, and we act *as if* it already existed." It admittedly is difficult to keep one's balance in such pregnant, expectant times. However, with the imaginary peace-cart in this way put before the imaginary final battle-horse, the real horses and riders (the actual belligerents, the real stakes and character of the conflict, etc.) are systematically misunderstood and miscast. A recent episode was available to illustrate this predictable distortion of reality.

A Paradigmatic Case

Manent draws on Charles Péguy's idea of a *cas éminent,* a paradigmatic case, a particular instance that reveals more than simply itself. The sixty-nine consecutive days of bombarding of Serbia by NATO airplanes gave him ample opportunity to reflect upon one such event. NATO's action, in his judgment, was the first significant military operation conceived as a humanitarian intervention. As such, it was especially revealing of the new way of conceiving military action.[25]

War itself was not declared, a fact to which we will return. But much high-minded moralistic and dire catastrophic talk was uttered before the fighting. "Western councils were obsessed with the pure idea of 'humanity,' on one hand, and the pure idea of 'crime against humanity,' on the other. Our leaders seemed incapable of thinking or saying anything without the assistance of this contrast." Nor was the discourse simply about the Serbian and Albanian protagonists, with the former cast as demonic, the latter often as angelic.

"We placed ourselves at the pinnacle of all the virtues," observed Manent, as neither "executioners nor victims"[26] but as those who were simply engaged in "the pure fight for justice." Europeans were disinterestedly humanitarian, their brothers' keepers. Now, not just the skeptic but a person with only a passing knowledge of the complexity of human motives might object that this humanitarian discourse was but a fig leaf to cover a multitude of unavowed motives. Manent does not simply disagree: "All sorts of different interests certainly boiled in the cauldron of our deliberations." These interests were the *aspects of political reality* that continued to impinge upon otherwise humanitarian consciousness. They would include understandable worries about regional instability, refugee populations, and untoward examples given to other leaders and countries; longtime historical, cultural, and diplomatic ties; a desire to show European countries' ability to handle their own affairs; and so forth. Genuine political thinking would have acknowledged them and tried to knit them together into a coherent whole of objectives and means.

Such, however, was not to be. Humanitarian ideology and a deep decline in the capacity for genuinely political thinking conspired to cast Milošević as incarnate evil, as a potential latter-day Hitler, and the KLA (the Kosovo Liberation Army) as unimpeachable freedom fighters. Onto the stage of this morality play we entered. Here Manent's analysis becomes, if possible, even more sharply pointed. I count at least six items on his litany of at-the-time shameful perverse effects.[27] His thesis statement sets the tone: "This action allowed one to observe all the ambiguities, of which some run the risk of being truly catastrophic, of humanitarian action." It is urgent, therefore, to dissect the abuse of humanitarianism as a substitute for political action. "It cannot but have perverse effects and end up serving particular agendas."

First of all, the United Nations was bypassed. Why is this perverse? The United Nations in principle represents humanity in its ensemble; it therefore is the natural organization to authorize such action. But because of the makeup of the Security Council, alternative ways had to be taken. Elementary rules of international law were disregarded.

The massive bombardment of a country, week after week, was not declared war. But if these are not acts of war against a sovereign state, what are? The failure to declare war was a moral-political lie of great amplitude: Manent asserts, "We lied, and we lied to ourselves about what we were doing." The straightforward and honorable position would have been to say we were waging war for reasons at once moral and political. Instead, a simply "moral" posture was adopted. Even the enemy, Milošević himself, was degraded by these evasions, as were the undeclared belligerents themselves. "I find it morally odious, even when the enemy conducts himself in an inhuman manner, to refuse him this minimum of recognition which consists in calling him an 'enemy' and declaring war on him. In the name of humanitarianism, we sunk into inhumanity."

Having introduced the category of the morally odious, Manent turns to an aspect "yet more odious" of the bombing campaign. "War, which is a terrible thing, in a certain way 'repairs' its own immorality by a form of morality, by the fact that all those who take part in it risk their lives." This, however, was not the case with the American-led NATO forces. They bombarded from the skies and did not fight on the ground, and in fact they were ordered to avoid coalition casualties above all else. In this way, the moral architecture of the enterprise collapsed. Manent's conclusion is deeply sardonic: "The NATO action marked a progress in, and brought a refinement to, moral posturing."

This, however, is inherent in the motive of the action, pity for others' suffering. Compassion is a sentiment that is very ambiguous. It supposes that we perceive the other suffering but on the condition that we also feel that we ourselves escape the suffering. "We experience 'the pleasure of not suffering.'" Hence, a world that exalts compassion at the same time exalts the sentiment and the desire not to suffer. When an action has a strictly humanitarian motive, it renders sacrifice very difficult. One wants one's succouring of others to occur at little or no cost to oneself. Happily, another component of modern democratic psychology, a reliance upon technology, was available to help resolve this constitutive conundrum of compassion. Our enormous superiority in military means allowed us to inflict harm on the oppressors without endangering our own pilots and crews.

The high-altitude bombing of Serbian infrastructures, with its significant collateral civilian damage, thus became the very emblem of humanitarian war, which is "war without any human communication with the enemy from whom we remain separated by our compassion and our technical means." Perhaps wishing to interject something of a positive note in the course of his analysis and critique, Manent did venture the thought that perhaps European publics were in the process of discovering that the "dialectics of humanitarianism" produce, at least in certain circumstances, the contrary of what is intended. At the very least, one could note that the bombing, which initially was widely approved by European governments and populations, eventually gave rise to many hesitations, regrets, and even reproaches among those who had approved it. Humanitarian enthusiasms were forced to confront what they had wrought and thus to experience other sentiments. Reflected upon, they might point the way to more sober moral-political thought.

Some of these regrets occurred "during the fact"; some came after the fact when people and leaders had to ask, What now? In Manent's judgment, the gravest political consequence of this refusal to recognize that one was engaging in war was the extreme difficulty in securing the peace. Peoples who did not want to live together were told they had to. This was because we had not considered what was politically feasible for human beings who, after all, "have the right not to be angels." The moralistic optic through which things were viewed ruled out the compromises and deals in terms of borders and partitioning and new forms of authority that diplomatic savvy or common sense might suggest.

Almost a decade later, Kosovo Albanians took things into their own very human hands and declared their independence. Humanitarian-inspired peacekeeping, UN resolution 1244, and years of unsuccessful negotiations finally engendered, and had to confront, the return of the political.[28] Tellingly, the former coalition allies expressed various reactions—politically motivated reactions—to this emphatically political decision. Some accepted it, some hailed it, and some decried it. All had their complex, understandable reasons. Next to none were based upon humanitarian considerations or impulses.

This recent turn of events is yet more evidence to support Manent's thesis in *A World beyond Politics?* that, because of a hyperdemocratic worldview and attendant utopian hopes, contemporary Europeans find themselves living a debilitating tension between an older order of politics and the project of a postpolitical world. Moreover, it supports his judgment that political circumstances, including the form of government, remain decisive for men and societies. The capacity to think and act politically therefore remains an imperative for the European political animal.

Conclusion

I would be the first to acknowledge that primarily critical analyses, while sometimes necessary, are frequently unsatisfying. Are they fair to the target? Do they hide weaknesses in the critical criteria? What is the positive alternative? These questions are legitimate. At another time I would be happy to engage them.

This essay, however, has had a more restricted set of purposes: to bring together the strikingly convergent analyses of well-known thinkers and through them to bring to light for critical inspection the worldview and presuppositions of a distinctive sort of democratic mentality. As we went through the critiques, I tried to indicate topics and categories that any serious reflection upon the contemporary European scene should consider. These include such basic topics as one's understanding of politics, the relationships between law, morality, war, and peace, and the trajectory of the democratic adventure within human history. Central to the issues raised was the relationship between democracy, politics (including war and peace), and legitimate and illegitimate hopes concerning both. I believe—and certainly hope—that any reader would profit from considering such topics through the lenses provided.

To be sure, I am more than a little sympathetic to the critiques. I believe they hit a real target. As the critics have tried to argue, much is at stake in the debate. The truth about man's political nature and the reality of the erosion of civic life in Europe, the nature and proper exercise of reason itself, especially in connection with politics and history, and even the purity of the Christian faith—all these important matters are implicated and, if the critics are to be believed, at risk in Europe. Given their importance, we American democrats would do well to look at them in the European mirror. At a distance, and through the revealing medium of others, we might gain some insights into democracy and politics, reason and faith, that could translate into American self-knowledge.

Notes

1. Pierre Manent, *Democracy without Nations? The Fate of Self-Government in Europe,* trans. and with an introduction by Paul Seaton (Wilmington, DE: ISI Books, 2007); Chantal Delsol, *Unjust Justice: The Tyranny of International Law,* trans. and with an introduction by Paul Seaton (Wilmington, DE: ISI Books, 2008).

2. The greatest range of differences obtains between Manent and Kagan. In terms of particular judgments, (1) Manent, as we will see, opposed the NATO bombings of Serbia in the late 1990s, whereas Kagan was a proponent; (2) Manent was opposed to the invasion of Iraq (not Afghanistan) after 9/11 on prudential grounds, whereas Kagan approved. In terms of general propositions, (3) Kagan has made his peace with the transnational-internationalist European Union; Manent is an opponent of the post-Maastricht trajectory of the EU. (4) Manent is a critic of two opposite forms of hegemonic "democratic universalism," while Kagan's liberal internationalism tends to involve Western democracies in the democratization project.

3. Rather quickly the article was inflated into a somewhat expanded book: Robert Kagan, *Of Paradise and Power: America and Europe in the New World Order* (New York: Knopf, 2003), 112 pages.

4. In fact, Kagan spent considerably more time analyzing the dominant European perspective than an American one.

5. James W. Ceaser, "America's Ascendancy, Europe's Despondency," *Weekly Standard* 7, no. 35 (May 20, 2002), available at www.weeklystandard.com/Content/Public/Articles/000/000/001/235nzhek.asp. Subsequent quotations in this section are from the same source.

6. Pierre Manent, *Cours familier de philosophie politique* (Paris: Fayard, 2001). The book was translated into English and appeared as *A World beyond Politics? A Defense of the Nation-State,* trans. Marc LePain (Princeton, NJ: Princeton Univ. Press, 2006). For my review, see *Review of Politics* 69, no. 4 (Summer 2007): 1–6. Five years after *Cours familier,* Manent updated his analysis of contemporary Europe in *La raison des nations: Réflexions sur la démocratie en Europe* (Paris: Fayard, 2006). It was translated and appeared in English as *Democracy without Nations? The Fate of Self-Government in Europe.* In between the two, an important article, "The Autumn of Nations," was published in *Azure* 16 (Winter 2004): 32–49. For Manent's most recent thinking about political forms and the *Sonderweg* of Europe, see *Les métamorphoses de la cité* (Paris: Flammarion, 2010). His fascinating account of his intellectual itinerary appeared at the same time: *Le regard politique* (Paris: Flammarion, 2010).

7. Mark Lilla, "The End of Politics," *New Republic,* June 23, 2003, available at www.tnr.com/article/the-end-politics. Subsequent quotations in this section are from the same source. In the article, Lilla refers to Robert Kagan's "powerful little book *Of Paradise and Power.*"

8. I add "[almost]" because Lilla explicitly excepts a handful of thinkers, Raymond Aron and Norberto Bobbio among them, from the generalization.

9. In connection with Lilla's broader point, the reader should consult James W. Ceaser, *Reconstructing America: The Symbol of America in Modern Thought* (New Haven, CT: Yale Univ. Press, 1997). In this tour de force of intellectual history, Ceaser incisively critiques various Continental modes of thought that purport to comprehend the political realm of reality in nonpolitical categories, whether from below (economics, race, even geography) or above (culture, History, "metaphysics"). Deftly employing Publius, Tocqueville, and Leo Strauss, Ceaser provides illuminating alternatives—what he calls traditional political science and political philosophy—to these apolitical and antipolitical modes of thought.

10. Cf. Manent's presentation of such an "Idea of Europe" in *Democracy without Nations?* 7, 34.

11. This morality is a *mélange* of rights divorced from any notion of normative nature, dignity understood as radical autonomy (but without any of Kant's original rigor), and subjective values or identities, the softened, democratically filtered residues of Nietzsche's and Max Weber's more pointed and "pathetic" characterizations of human beings.

12. Pierre Manent, *Tocqueville et la nature de la démocratie* (Paris: Juilliard, 1982; Fayard, 1993); English translation: *Tocqueville and the Nature of Democracy,* trans. John Waggoner (Lanham, MD: Rowman and Littlefield, 1996).

13. Harvey C. Mansfield Jr. and Delba Winthrop, introduction to *Alexis de Tocqueville's Democracy in America* (Chicago: Univ. of Chicago Press, 2000), xviii.

14. The French word *conscience* contains the intriguing combination of consciousness, that is, mental self-awareness, with moral standards and judgment: conscience. Both are implied in the passage.

15. While the sentence is mine, the thought is Kant's. It apes (and gently mocks) Kant, who had a fondness for Latin aphorisms.

16. For a similar analysis of the differences between Kant's thought and contemporary thinking, see Delsol, *Unjust Justice.*

17. The classic study is Henri de Lubac's *The Drama of Atheistic Humanism,* published in 1944.

18. See "Perpetual Peace (First Supplement: On the Guarantee of Perpetual Peace)," in Immanuel Kant, *Perpetual Peace and Other Essays,* trans. Ted Humphrey (Indianapolis: Hackett, 1983), 120–22.

19. Manent writes of "the effectual and dynamic truth of modern liberty, to wit, that *man is the sovereign author, in fact and by right, of the human world.* He is and ought to be [sovereign]. The world, in any case the human world, 'society,' does not have for its author God, or the gods, nor nature, but man himself. This fundamental truth of our condition, which in former societies was hidden and as it were buried, becomes visible in democratic societies. Democracy *puts on stage and to work* this human sovereignty." Manent, *A World beyond Politics?* 3. Manent adopts the final formulation from Claude Lefort.

In considering Manent's presentation of the atheistic presuppositions of what he calls modern liberty and modern democracy, American readers will think of the American Declaration of Independence with its fourfold invocation of God and note our different theological-liberal democratic conjugation.

20. Joseph Cropsey, "Liberalism, Nature, and Convention," *Independent Journal of Philosophy* 4, no. 1 (1983): 21.

21. See Alexis de Tocqueville, *Democracy in America,* vol. 2, part 1, chap. 2, "Of the Principal Source of Beliefs among Democratic Peoples."

22. Ibid., chap. 20, "Of Some Tendencies Particular to Historians in Democratic Centuries."

23. For comparable analyses, see Delsol, *Unjust Justice;* and John Bolton, "Courting Danger: What's Wrong with the International Criminal Court," *National Interest* (Winter 1998–1999), available at http://nationalinterest.org/article/courting-danger-633.

24. For Manent's treatment of Locke's constitutionalism, see "Locke, Labor, and Property," in Pierre Manent, *An Intellectual History of Liberalism,* trans. Rebecca Berlinski (Princeton, NJ: Princeton Univ. Press, 1995), esp. 47–52.

25. "In fact it [the intervention in Kosovo] was the first great example of the type of action that claims to transcend politics in order to act solely in function of humanitarianism." Pierre Manent, "La tentation humanitaire," *Géopolitique* 68 (January 2000): 9.

26. The well-known phrase is from Albert Camus.

27. At this point I turn to Manent's analysis in "La tentation humanitaire."

28. For details and analysis, see Christopher J. Borgen, "Kosovo's Declaration of Independence: Self-Determination, Succession, and Recognition," *ASIL Insights* (American Society of International Law) 12, no. 2 (February 29, 2008) (available online). Cf. Borgen's statement "Kosovo presents a quintessential 'tough case,' demonstrating the ways in which the political interests of states affect how the international law is given effect."

Brian Domitrovic

Cosmopolitanism for Thee but Not for Me

Big and Small Countries in the Modern Era of Monetary Nationalism

At a monetary conference in 1973 at the Siena, Italy, villa of Robert Mundell, who went on to win the Nobel Prize in economics in 1999, the host welcomed his guests with these words:

> In the Palazzo Publico [of Siena] there are two murals, commissioned . . . in the year 1337, . . . portraying good government (*il buon govierno*) and bad government (*il cattivo govierno*). . . .
>
> They were described very eloquently 100 years later by San Bernardino of Siena. He said: "When I turn to the picture of peace I see merchants buying and selling, I see dancing, the houses being repaired, the workers busy in the vineyards or sewing in the fields, while on horseback others ride down to swim in the rivers; maidens I see going to a wedding, and great flocks of sheep and other peaceful sights. And for the sake of these things men live in peace and harmony with one another. But if I turn my eyes I see no commerce, no dancing, only men destroying men; the houses are not repaired but demolished and gutted by fire; no fields are plowed, no harvests sown, no riders go down to bathe in the river, nor is the fullness of life in any wise enjoyed. Justice lies in the dust. . . . And wherever man goes, he goes in fear and trembling."
>
> I wish the International Monetary Fund (IMF) would likewise commission a painter to make two paintings: one of world trade as it works under an ideal monetary system; another of world trade as it is when the international monetary system is working badly. In one picture we would see trade expanding, full employment, and happy

> faces of central bankers; in the other we would see trade declining, rising unemployment, and unhappy faces. We would call the first "*un sistemo buono*" and the other "*un sistemo cattivo.*"[1]

When Mundell spoke these words in 1973, he had just seen, over the past several years, the breakdown of an international consensus on how the world monetary system should run. This was the consensus first hammered out at the insistence of the United States in 1944, at the Bretton Woods resort in New Hampshire, and largely sustained in practice for the following twenty-five years, whereby each country involved refrained from managing its currency for national purposes. Nations managed their currencies for the purpose of the international consensus.[2]

The specifics were as follows. Each country ensured that its currency would never trade in private markets above or below its official exchange rate to the dollar. The policy rule of central banks conducting monetary policy was to incur this result, with the IMF available to correct any mistakes. The United States, for its part, guaranteed the stability of the dollar, the "key currency" as it was called, by means of making sure no one in the private markets would think to buy or sell gold above or beyond the official price, thirty-five dollars per ounce. Again, this was to be achieved through U.S. monetary policy's targeting this result.

What Mundell thought of the Bretton Woods arrangement—which for all its fits and starts supervised the most substantial period of economic growth the industrialized world has ever seen—can be in no doubt. As Mundell said in 1965, in testimony to Congress: "Who would complain if the world economy were as prosperous in the next fifteen years as it was in the last fifteen?" And as he later reflected, in 1981: "The quarter century of this regime [of Bretton Woods] was exemplary in its stability, growth, and economic development, perhaps unmatched at any time outside an imperium, such as the Roman Empire."[3]

There can also be no mistake that as Mundell welcomed his guests to Siena in 1973, he lamented the demise of Bretton Woods, of fixed exchange rates and a U.S. commitment to stable gold, which demise had begun several years before. As Mundell said ten years afterward, "We have got more experience with international monetary [policy] in the past 12 years than we have ever had in the history of man"—and he did not mean this as a compliment.[4]

Those twelve years—the long 1970s—saw economic growth at levels far below those of the halcyon years of "postwar prosperity" supervised by

Bretton Woods. And as for international monetary cooperation, under the system of "flexible" or "floating" exchange rates that emerged in the early 1970s, currency issuers, which is to say nations, found themselves free not to make commitments about the value of their currencies with either their home populations or their neighbors abroad.

This new beast was not quite the *sistemo cattivo* Mundell thought he saw on the horizon in Siena. To be sure, the breakdown of the *sistemo buono* (in Mundell's eyes) of Bretton Woods had given way to something more ad hoc and disorderly, but the warfare and depredations seen on the Sienese mural had not yet in the 1970s materialized in contemporary world affairs, at least in any extreme sense. But there was reason to worry. The real value of a currency is implicitly a contract. If that real value changes markedly—particularly if it goes down—at some point somebody is going to be affronted and turn to the use of force. Restoring an international monetary system whereby currencies generally hold value "would certainly make a contribution to world harmony," as Mundell said as he accepted the Nobel Prize in 1999.[5]

It is useful in the context of a discussion of cosmopolitanism to bring up these historical monetary affairs. Cosmopolitanism, at a basic level, is being curious about and indulgent, in a prudent fashion, in the ways of the world, particularly as practiced by foreigners. In the matter of the world economy, surely it is cosmopolitan for nations to issue a currency that a foreign holder will find retains its value. After all, if the foreign holder finds otherwise, the foreigner will drop the currency and be skeptical about acquiring it in the future. This in turn foretells a decline in cross-border trade, and thus of intercultural acquaintances. Perhaps it even foretells wars of predation, in that economies that do not trade must be successful in being self-sufficient, and the historical record of successful autarkic countries is not large. Can cosmopolitanism exist in a world where currencies do not keep their value? Even if there is to emerge some supernational "single-world currency" managed by an international bureaucracy, if this currency loses real value, it stands to be shunned, at the price of economic transactions.

Mundell, in particular in the work that won him the Nobel Prize, has informed us about the stakes involved in these matters perhaps better than any other economist. In this work, dating from the early 1960s, Mundell showed that most attempts at monetary nationalism are self-defeating. Indeed, the conclusion he inevitably pointed to was that, in monetary affairs, countries should submit to the judgment of the world—a rather extreme form of economic cosmopolitanism indeed. Doing otherwise, Mundell indicated, would lead to a persistent "disequilibrium system" that would incur unpleasant things like inflation and unemployment, if not the kind of horrific—and anticosmopolitan—things painted on the wrong side of that mural in Siena.[6]

"A Theory of Optimum Currency Areas"

The first article referred to in the Nobel citation of Robert A. Mundell is "A Theory of Optimum Currency Areas" (1961), by all accounts one of the most famous and most referenced articles in economics since Keynes. Mundell's article makes fairly plain that it takes its inspiration from J.S. Mill—one of the most determined advocates of cosmopolitanism in the entire Western tradition.

The basic purpose of "A Theory of Optimum Currency Areas" was, some fifteen years into the Bretton Woods era, to caution countries against the idea of bolting from the system. There are always charms to flexible exchange rates, not least the "flexibility" they give currency masters to flood their economies with money so as to address an unemployment problem or to encourage exports. "A system of flexible exchange rates is usually presented, by its proponents," Mundell wrote, "as a device whereby depreciation can take the place of unemployment. . . . But the question then arises whether all national currencies should be flexible. Should the Ghanian pound be freed to fluctuate against all currencies?"[7]

Of course, Mundell implied, the Ghanian pound, or any such currency of a new and untried nation, should not be flexible. Who would hold it in lieu of a proven currency such as the dollar? Nobody, proving the old concept of "seignorial privilege," whereby currency issuers with long and solid reputations get a free pass on monetary creation. By the processes of seignorial privilege, people will let a dominant country like the United States commit a list of policy mistakes before they forsake denominating their retirement accounts in its currency. In contrast, the Ghanian pound may be well managed indeed, but unless it is by express commitment at a fixed rate of exchange relative to a major reputable currency, it will be shunned. The Chinese policy from 1994 to 2010 to fix the renminbi to the dollar is expressive of this reality.

Mundell did more, however, than argue that flexible currencies are unadvisable on seignorage grounds. He also indicated that flexible currencies, especially in any proliferation, decrease economic efficiencies. Mundell asked, "What is the appropriate domain of a currency area?" Certainly it is not some little land mass such as those that were coming into existence in great numbers in the thick of decolonization in 1961. The appropriate domain was larger. It was essential to "elucidate [that] the national currency area does not coincide with the optimum currency area."[8]

The central idea of Mundell's article is that the optimum currency area corresponds to that geographical space, that region, in which there is *factor mobility.* "The argument for flexible exchange rates based on national currencies is only as valid as the Ricardian assumption about factor mobility. If factor mobility is high internally and low internationally a system of flexible exchange rates based on national currencies might work effectively enough. But if regions cut across national boundaries or if countries are multiregional then the argument for flexible exchange rates is only valid if countries are reorganized on a regional basis."[9]

The factors Mundell was referring to were labor and capital. If people can easily switch jobs or make investments across a region, having one currency in that region will be vastly superior to having multiple currencies. In such a region, superior employment opportunities attract workers from less productive and remunerative jobs, and investments in low-return projects are quickly moved into high-return ones. Such a region is characterized by quick shifts in how the elements of its productive processes are allocated and is unlikely to be exactly coextensive with a sovereign nation. Mundell pointed out that if a region is beset with multiple currencies that fluctuate in value, the real opportunities seen by labor and capital, real opportunities that would ordinarily result in salutary transfers of labor and capital, will be undermined.

The stylized example Mundell gave in the article was of Eastern and Western North America (the United States and Canada), where the special industries are cars and timber. The example was actually rather true to life. Detroit and London, Ontario, have all sorts of people who are skilled at working or making investments in the automotive industry, just as Washington state and British Columbia have the same with respect to timber. If a worker in London realizes he could provide more value at a Detroit plant, he will go for the opportunity—absent the possibility that his standard of living would take a hit if the United States devalues its dollar. Similarly, an investor who knows the timber industry in Washington may take advantage of his special expertise about a promising forest opportunity in British

Columbia—provided the returns on that investment are not threatened by some devaluation of the Canadian dollar. A single currency in these respective regions would remove an obstacle to taking advantage of opportunities. Multiple currencies, if not at a permanently fixed rate of exchange, will interpose a barrier to this efficient process.

From the point of view of cosmopolitanism, the very fact that people are active across borders in economic affairs indicates that they are considerably familiar with and interested in each other's activities, indeed even to the extent that they would like to take part in these activities if the opportunity presented itself. This bespeaks a developed degree of social and cultural curiosity and acceptance if not integration. And it would be severely reduced, if not lost, if fluctuating currencies divided the region.

Mundell permitted that fixed exchange rates were not absolutely necessary among optimum currency areas. If there is little trade and there are few capital transfers between two regions, after all, it does not much matter whether their currencies' rates of exchange stay consistent. But in a world (such as that of Bretton Woods) in which factor mobility is on the rise globally, the legitimate space for flexible exchange rates becomes correspondingly more attenuated. Mundell approvingly quoted Mill's fixed exchange-rate if not one-currency view: "So much of the barbarism, however, still remains in the transactions of most civilized nations, that almost all independent countries choose to assert their nationality by having, to their own inconvenience and that of their neighbors, a peculiar currency of their own." "Money is a convenience," Mundell added, "and this restricts the optimum number of currencies. In terms of this argument alone the optimum currency is the world, regardless of the number of regions of which it is composed."[10]

Perhaps it could be countered that acquiescence to the peculiar aspects of another's currency—including, say, the prospect of its devaluation—is itself part of the open-mindedness required of cosmopolitanism. National moneys also typically look interesting and exotic, even to domestic holders—is it not cosmopolitan to be excited about this? In other writings, Mundell has marveled at the phenomenon across history:

> To sell their coins and create the mystique, a full panoply of devices was called upon [by currency issuers]. Religious symbols helped to reinforce the mystique. Whether the symbol was called Marduk, Baal, Osiris, Zeus, Athena or Apollo, or Jupiter or Juno, or St. John the

> Baptist, its purpose was the same; the latter symbol made the florin the most famous coin of the Middle Ages. The gods changed but the principles stayed the same! Just look at the Masonic hocus-pocus that still remains on our dollar bills! "In God We Trust" [was] introduced on our dollar bills in 1862 when their gold backing was dropped.[11]

Since currencies are a means of exchange, any enhancement in their own oddity entails that there will be reduced access via cosmopolitan commerce to all the other uniquenesses of a place. The odder a currency is, the less it is universal money. The cost of having a currency at a fixed rate of exchange is that the currency lacks particular identity; the benefit is that this itself dramatically expands the opportunity for persons to indulge in everything else in the commercial realm that has particular identity, namely the goods and services of other places.

The Policy Mix

The second article referred to in the Mundell Nobel citation is "Capital Mobility and Stabilization Policy under Fixed and Flexible Exchange Rates" (1963). Here Mundell discussed a common case in which countries have to submit to the judgment of the world in a certain realm of economic transactions. This is where countries, typically lightly populous ones, as currency issuers enjoy very little seignorial privilege rights if any at all. "I assume," Mundell wrote in introducing the article, "the extreme degree of [capital] mobility that prevails when a country cannot maintain an interest rate different from the general level prevailing abroad."[12]

Countries that find themselves in this situation pose a curious problem: they are de facto not in control of their economic affairs. Major large countries can do things like depreciate the currency and impose onerous taxation without incurring a complete departure from their currencies. This is because these countries are too big, important, historic, and productive not to do business with. But the smaller countries that are the subject of Mundell's article will find their currencies immediately vacated as soon as their efforts at economic management stray from the correct course. Currency holders by nature grant leeway to large and important countries and do not to smaller and less significant ones.

All this hinges, again, on the degree of factor mobility, in particular that of capital. If money is free to enter or leave a small, unimportant country, that country will have to see to it that investments within it are at least as profitable as the prevailing rate of return in the world. In itself, this is a sort of default cosmopolitanism, where countries submit entirely to prevailing prices (such as the rate of interest). These countries see what price prevails in foreign lands and then adopt that price at home. In the productive process, costs must then be aligned so that they do not exceed prices. Prices are *given* by the world and *taken* by the small countries, with labor and capital in the small country coordinated to be profitable in view of what must be taken from the world, the price.

To escape this rigor, the country in question could close itself, through capital controls, trade barriers, immigration restriction, and whatnot. But by definition the country in this state of affairs would not be particularly productive, since it is small. The autarkic course of action makes the alternative of submission to world price levels not only attractive, but probably necessary.

In the article, Mundell explored the possibilities that small countries face as they seek to "stabilize" their economies (which is to say reduce unemployment and inflation) by means of macroeconomic policy. He determined that in a system of fixed exchange rates, it is useless, indeed counterproductive, to attempt to stabilize (or stimulate) by means of monetary looseness. All this does is make the exchange rate untenable, which is a violation of the system. Under fixed exchange rates, stabilization policy falls to the fiscal side.

In contrast, under flexible exchange rates, Mundell found that monetary policy can prove an apt tool in stabilization policy, although fiscal policy cannot. Monetary looseness addressing an unemployment problem causes the exchange rate to deteriorate and thus the price of exports to go down, in turn causing an increase in domestic employment and income.

And yet in view of "A Theory of Optimum Currency Areas," Mundell had already strongly suggested that this sort of stabilization cannot last very long. For to the degree to which there is factor mobility between two countries (as opposed to simply trade in goods and services), economic production will go down in the face of flexible exchange rates that indeed flex. For the potential output implied by factor mobility cannot be reached if there are intraregional currency differentiations that slow down the natural course of factor mobility. In other words, a small country can get away with devaluations so long as its economic relationship with the rest of the world is almost solely one of trade. As soon as that relationship involves movements of workers and investments in any degree, the optimum currency area quickly expands beyond national size, and a fixed rate of exchange within that area becomes necessary.

Buono to *Cattivo* to *Buono*?

Today, Mundell's articles serve to indicate that economic sovereignty does not logically or practically extend to control of major macroeconomic variables such as the value of the currency, the terms of trade, the employment level, or interest rates. Indeed, the articles strongly suggest that only to the degree that nations strive to defer to the outside world on matters of macroeconomic management is there any hope for sustained national prosperity. Nations are price takers in many if not all aspects of economic management. Any failure on the part of nations to realize this fact will result in a "disequilibrium" situation that lessens prosperity.

The implications for cosmopolitanism are serious. Mundell's prize-winning theory heavily implies that acquiescence to the tastes and desires of the world, of the "the other," is the only route to *domestic* prosperity. Here, effectively, cosmopolitanism is raised to the level of *raison d'état*. Indeed, in Mundell's work, to any extent that governments strive to manage their economies, they make their nations uncosmopolitan. By not forthwith taking what the world is offering in the economic sphere, whether by means of manipulating the value of the currency, trade barriers, or other strategies, governments create an insularity that inevitably leads to a decline in their own prosperity. On the other hand, to the extent that governments submit to the world's independent valuation of their currency and their goods and services—that is to say, when countries submit to the judgment of the world—countries maximize their own benefits, let alone those of the world. The one complication in Mundell's view is that these lessons are painfully obvious to small countries but obscure to large ones. Small countries immediately recognize that such moves as currency devaluations prompt a global shunning of their means of exchange. Large countries, in contrast, are for a time given more leeway by the world as they chase after the wind of national economic management. Therefore, small countries must acclimate themselves immediately to economic cosmopolitanism, if they are to have any hope of prosperity. But large nations can linger in the delusion that they can control their own economic outcomes for the good by shutting out the normal operations of international economic transactions. The irony unfolds: small and large countries alike must be cosmopolitan for the sake of everyone's prosperity. But large countries can stave off the realization of this fact. And to the extent they do, they undercut the cosmopolitanism of smaller nations.

It is a startling truth that for a great part of the twentieth century and beyond, including the three and a half decades that have passed since Mundell's monetary conference in Siena, there has been no express international monetary system. Indeed, for about half the century, including the 1930s as well as the post-1971 period, nations have not sought to guarantee the value of their money on the international markets, much less to the domestic users at home.

To two researchers from the Council on Foreign Relations, Benn Steil and Manuel Hinds, authors of *Money, Markets, and Sovereignty* (2009), this is one of the most unusual, indeed bizarre developments in the history of the world. Money has come now to be issued by *nations,* who in turn expressly back it by *nothing* (not even in an agreement for it to hold value, let alone in a reserve asset such as gold). For historically, money has typically been created by the most efficient issuer, of whatever political standing; and it has been backed by an international unit of value, such as gold, if not coextensive with that unit in the first place. "It is only the most recent three decades that monies flowing around the globe have been claims on . . . nothing. . . . All of these monies are conjured by governments as pure manifestations of sovereignty," write Steil and Hinds. "Monetary sovereignty is [a] mythology . . . [and is] of considerably more political and economic consequence today than it was in earlier times."[13]

National money—that is, money created by a nation's sovereign government and representing to a great extent the currency of that nation's economy—has profound implications for a nation's cosmopolitanism, more than we know, and perhaps more in actual practice than in theory. If there is one calling in life that over the centuries has produced more opportunities for cultivating cosmopolitanism than commerce, it can only be evangelical religion. For commerce is precisely the thing that brings persons of different circumstances who have a guarded curiosity about each other together. In embarking on a commercial deal, one is of necessity curious about the possibility of doing business with another; and in knowing all along that a price will clear when a transaction is done, there are also of necessity standards that apply when commerce occurs. Perhaps this is not the same thing as enlightened curiosity—the high bar of cosmopolitanism; but in its essence, commerce is consistent with cosmopolitanism, indeed a simulacrum of it.

It is needless to say that the thought of commerce has prompted many to set sail and otherwise pack off from their own places to encounter new places and faces. Commerce, indeed, has been the sinews of cosmopolitanism throughout world history. This is not at all to hold that commerce cannot foster a sort of cosmopolitanism manqué, whereby cross-spatial connections intensify the world's antihumanity. One need not read too deeply into Michael McCormick's archaeological and economic history of the Dark Ages, *Origins of the European Economy* (2001), to realize that commerce intensified the hunt for slaves in the first millennium. And there are, of course, the Marxists of yore, who argued that international commerce bred exploitation in every corner of the globe. But let us also recall (1) that the rise of the European financial instrument enabled European traders in time to clear transactions with money rather than human chattel and (2) that even the Marxists conceded that capitalism was necessary to provide all the material stuff that the utopian Communist stage of history had to have as an inheritance.[14]

The twentieth century saw a recrudescence of anticosmopolitanism, in the form of its great political tyrannies, unlike anything that could have been imagined before, Heinrich Heine and Fyodor Dostoevsky to the contrary notwithstanding. And nearly all of the great tyrannies strove to be autarkic—economically self-sufficient, not only so that the vagaries of foreign trade and currency devaluations would not threaten domestic prosperity, but so that the cosmopolitanism yielded by international commerce would not diminish the nationalistic ardor back home. This was manifestly obvious in the case of Mao's China, a closed society on a grand scale if there ever was one, as well as of Pol Pot's Cambodia, and it was the ambition of Hitler's Germany, nationalist Japan, and a Soviet Union consigned to the Russian space after the Warsaw battle of 1920.

Autarky, indeed, was the great trend of the 1930s, whereby even the previous big dogs of world trade, such as the United States, preferred to sit behind protectionist walls and take advantage of their own munificent resources. In the American case, these were the "amber waves of grain" covering the vast space between "California and the New York island," to quote the song "This Land Is Your Land," which not at all coincidentally became an ersatz national anthem in New Deal years. Smaller countries, realizing that autarky would mean poverty, bolted for it anyway, as in the case of Franco's Spain. Those countries that longed to continue with the old order of prosperity through trade and solid currencies were left to sit on inert gold stocks. In time, as in the case of Argentina, politicians got itchy fingers to spend the gold anyway and created mass machines of domestic political patronage and hence historic inflations.

Autarky is a sort of antithesis to cosmopolitanism. We therefore should not be surprised that whatever the Marxists have told us about the insidiousness of international commerce, the cessation of it in the past century coincided with monstrous results. For one can be cosmopolitan in an autarkic context only to the degree that there is diversity within one's own country. More likely is that appeals to anticosmopolitan things like *Blut und Boden* will take root in countries completing bids for economic self-sufficiency.

After World War II, two decisive decisions were made by the international community, at the behest of the leading nation, the United States, to forestall the autarky trend of previous years. These were to reestablish currency convertibility across the globe and to commit to lessening trade barriers. Both of these decisions were formalized at the Bretton Woods conference. Over the two and a half decades that followed, the precondition for cosmopolitanism through commerce reemerged. And yet this consensus had foundered by the time Mundell made his remarks in Siena in 1973.

Flexible exchange rates have been with us since that time. In the 1970s, the world economy went through one of its rougher patches across all the centuries since the industrial revolution, and in geopolitics, the "first world" began to give way to the second. In the 1980s and 1990s, flexible rates became tested less as the Bretton Woods order saw an informal and patchy reprise, enough to polish off Communism. The price of gold stayed roughly consistent against the dollar for twenty years; some countries even fixed to the dollar again, given its new stability; and an optimum currency area in Europe became formally organized as such.

Yet now once again gold serves not as a guarantee of the dollar's stability but as a storehouse of value in lieu of the dollar's maintenance of that capacity. Countries that fixed to the dollar (such as China) now see precisely the development they thought a fix would prevent: a rapid devaluation. Europe, what with its demographic distribution, had thought it was doddering off to retirement. For a moment, in the wake of 2008, Europe had to wonder if the task of asserting a benign hegemony in world monetary affairs was falling to it, before the Greek crisis made it clear that that was not a possibility.

When Robert Mundell accepted his Nobel Prize in 1999, he made these remarks: "The experiment with flexible exchange rates in the 1970s started off as a disaster from the standpoint of economic stability, but nevertheless it set in motion a learning mechanism that would not have taken place in its absence. The lesson was that inflation, budget deficits, big debts, and big government are all detrimental to public well-being and that the cost of correcting them is so high that no democratic government wants to repeat the experience."[15] Also not wanting to repeat the experience are those with a cosmopolitan outlook hankering to do business outside of their own little world.

Notes

1. R.A. Mundell, "The Santa Columba Conclusions," *Economic Notes* 2, no. 2 (May–August 1973): 15.

2. The notable exception was the United States, which strove, in the 1960s, to manage its currency for national purposes, an effort that resulted in the breakdown of the international system. This matter is taken up by the present author in Brian Domitrovic, *Econoclasts: The Rebels Who Sparked the Supply-Side Revolution and Restored American Prosperity* (Wilmington, DE.: ISI Books, 2009), chap. 4.

3. Robert A. Mundell to the Joint Economic Committee, July 28, 1965, 89th Cong., 1st sess.; Mundell, "Gold Would Serve into the 21st Century," *Wall Street Journal,* September 30, 1981.

4. Robert A. Mundell, "A 'Pre-Williamsburg' International Monetary Conference," May 17, 1983, p. 19, W304, F "The Republican Study Committee, binder with the proceedings of 'A Pre-Williamsburg,'" Jack Kemp Congressional Papers, University at Buffalo (now in Manuscript Division, Papers ca. 1964–2009, Library of Congress).

5. Robert A. Mundell, "A Reconsideration of the Twentieth Century," in *Nobel Lectures, Economics, 1996–2000,* ed. Torsten Persson (Singapore: World Scientific, 2003), 242.

6. Robert A. Mundell, "The International Disequilibrium System," *Kyklos* 14, no. 2 (May 1961): 153–72.

7. Robert A. Mundell, "A Theory of Optimum Currency Areas," *American Economic Review* 51, no. 4 (September 1961): 657–65, quotation on 657.

8. Ibid., 657.

9. Ibid., 661.

10. Ibid., 662.

11. Robert A. Mundell, "The International Monetary System in the Twentieth Century: Could Gold Make a Comeback?" Lecture at St. Vincent College, Latrobe, PA, March 12, 1997, www.robertmundell.net, 2.

12. Robert A. Mundell, "Capital Mobility and Stabilization Policy under

Fixed and Flexible Exchange Rates," *Canadian Journal of Economics and Political Science* 29, no. 4 (November 1963): 475.

13. Benn Steil and Manuel Hinds, *Money, Markets, and Sovereignty* (New Haven, CT: Yale Univ. Press, 2009), 244.

14. Michael McCormick, *Origins of the European Economy, A.D. 300–900* (New York: Cambridge Univ. Press, 2001).

15. Mundell, "Reconsideration of the Twentieth Century," 240.

Contributors

Luigi Bradizza is assistant professor of political science at Salve Regina University.

Brian Domitrovic is assistant professor of history at Sam Houston State University. He is the author of *Econoclasts* (ISI Books, 2009).

Joseph R. Fornieri is professor of political science at the Rochester Institute of Technology. He is the author of *Abraham Lincoln's Political Faith* (Northern Illinois Univ. Press, 2003).

Khalil M. Habib is associate professor of philosophy and director of the Pell Honors Program at Salve Regina University. He specializes in classical, Islamic, and early modern political philosophy and ethics.

L. Joseph Hebert Jr. is associate professor and chair of political science and leadership studies and director of prelaw studies at St. Ambrose University. He is the author of *More Than Kings and Less Than Men: Tocqueville on the Promise and Perils of Democratic Individualism* (Lexington Books, 2010) and a coeditor of *Alexis de Tocqueville and the Art of Democratic Statesmanship* (Lexington Books, 2011).

John von Heyking is associate professor of political science at the University of Lethbridge. He is the author of *Augustine and Politics as Longing in the World* (Univ. of Missouri Press, 2001) and a coeditor of *Friendship and Politics: Essays in Political Thought* (Univ. of Notre Dame Press,

2008), *Civil Religion in Political Thought: Its Perennial Questions and Enduring Relevance in North America* (Catholic Univ. of America Press, 2010), and two volumes of the *Collected Works of Eric Voegelin.*

Gaelan Murphy is assistant professor of political science at Grant MacEwan University.

Mary P. Nichols is professor of political science at Baylor University. Her fields of interest include the history of political philosophy, especially Greek political thought, and politics, literature, and film. She has published numerous articles in *Political Theory,* the *Journal of Politics, Polity,* the *Review of Politics,* and *Perspectives on Political Science.* Among her books in classical thought are *Citizens and Statesmen: A Commentary on Aristotle's* Politics (Rowman and Littlefield, 1992) and *Socrates on Friendship and Community: Reflections on Plato's Symposium, Phaedrus, and Lysis* (Cambridge Univ. Press, 2008).

Michael Palmer is the Abraham Lincoln Professor of Political Philosophy, professor of political science, and professor in the Honors College at the University of Maine, where he has taught since 1983. His books include *Love of Glory and the Common Good: Aspects of the Political Thought of Thucydides* (Rowman and Littlefield, 1992); *Political Philosophy and the Human Soul: Essays in Honor of Allan Bloom* (coedited with Thomas L. Pangle, Rowman and Littlefield, 1995); and *Masters and Slaves: Revisioned Essays in Political Philosophy* (Lexington Books, 2001).

Thomas L. Pangle is the Joe R. Long Chair in Democratic Studies in the Government Department and the codirector of the Thomas Jefferson Center for the Study of Core Texts and Ideas at the University of Texas at Austin.

Paul Seaton is associate professor of philosophy at St. Mary's Seminary and University. He specializes primarily in French political thought and has written on and translated several contemporary French thinkers, including Pierre Manent, Chantal Delsol, and Philippe Beneton.

Lee Trepanier is associate professor of political science at Saginaw Valley State University. He is the author of *Political Symbols in Russian History* (Lexington Books, 2007), the coauthor with Lynita Newswander of *LDS* *in the USA: Mormonism and the Making of American Culture* (Baylor Univ. Press, 2012), and the editor of several volumes, the most recent being *Eric Voegelin and the Continental Tradition* (coedited with Steven F. McGuire, Univ. of Missouri Press, 2011).

Richard Velkley is Celia Scott Weatherhead Professor of Philosophy at Tulane University. His publications include three books: *Freedom and the End of Reason: On the Moral Foundation of Kant's Critical Philosophy* (Univ. of Chicago Press, 1989), *Being after Rousseau: Philosophy and Culture in Question* (Univ. of Chicago Press, 2002), and *Heidegger, Strauss, and the Premises of Philosophy: On Original Forgetting* (Univ. of Chicago Press, 2011).

Index

www.ingramcontent.com/pod-product-compliance
Lightning Source LLC
LaVergne TN
LVHW090803070826
844660LV00022B/1063

9780813134703